BILLY RUFFIAN

BY THE SAME AUTHOR

Marine Painting in England

Nicholas Pocock, Marine Artist

Life Among the Pirates:
the Romance and the Reality

Pirates: an Illustrated History

Ships and Seascapes:
an Introduction to Maritime Prints, Drawings and Watercolours

Heroines and Harlots:
Women at Sea in the Great Age of Sail

BILLY RUFFIAN

THE BELLEROPHON AND THE DOWNFALL OF NAPOLEON

The Biography of a Ship of the Line, 1782–1836

DAVID CORDINGLY

BLOOMSBURY

Published by Bloomsbury, New York and London
Distributed to the trade by Holtzbrinck Publishers

All papers used by Bloomsbury are natural, recyclable products made from
wood grown in sustainable, well-managed forests. The manufacturing
processes conform to the environmental regulations of the country of origin.

Library of Congress Cataloging-in-Publication Data has been applied for.

ISBN 1-58234-193-1

First U.S. Edition 2003

1 3 5 7 9 10 8 6 4 2

Typeset by Palimpsest Book Production Limited,
Polmont, Stirlingshire, Scotland
Printed in Great Britain by Clays Ltd, St Ives plc

This book is dedicated to my literary agents
Suzanne Gluck and Gill Coleridge

No I don't care a rap
For any Frenchy chap,
When they come they'll get the dressing they deserve;
I've the best four in the fleet,
That the French well could meet,
With the Fightin' Billy Ruff'n in reserve.
                              Billy Blue −
Here's to you, Billy Blue, here's to you!

As she broke the line with Howe,
So she's game to do it now,
And repeat her 'First o' June' here in these seas;
With their name for dauntless pluck,
and the Billy Ruff'n's luck,
I will fight as many Frenchmen as you please!
                              Billy Blue −
Here's to you, Billy Blue, here's to you!

Verses 6 and 7 of 'The Ballad of Billy Blue' which commemorated the action
known as Cornwallis's Retreat. This took place off Brest on 17 June 1795.
'Billy Blue' was the sailors' nickname for Admiral William Cornwallis.

CONTENTS

ACKNOWLEDGEMENTS

This book is based on the marvellous collection of Admiralty documents held by the Public Record Office at Kew, in particular the ships' logs, captains' letters, minutes of Navy Board meetings, progress books, court martial reports and documents relating to the dockyards. It is also heavily dependent on the books of other writers and maritime historians past and present and I would particularly like to acknowledge my debt to the works of Brian Lavery, Tom Pocock, N.A.M. Rodger, Oliver Warner and the many fine books produced and edited by Robert Gardiner.

I am most grateful to Colin White and Brian Lavery for answering numerous questions and for generously drawing my attention to material I would otherwise have overlooked. Pieter van der Merwe has, as always, proved a mine of information and was particularly helpful in the matter of the last days of the *Bellerophon*. I would like to thank Pascal Cariss for his ideas and input, and Nicholas Blake for checking the dates, ships, figures and nautical terminology for errors and maritime howlers but would stress that I am responsible for any errors that remain. I owe a special debt of gratitude to Derek Barnard, the author of *Merrily to Frindsbury*, who has shared his local knowledge and with whom I spent an enjoyable day trying to find the exact spot where the *Bellerophon* was built. I would also like to thank Sir Malcolm and Lady Pasley, and Alan Maitland for their hospitality and for the information which they provided about their illustrious ancestors. My thanks also to all those people who have kindly supplied me with information and answered my queries, especially Bob Todd, Stephen Humphrey, Rev. Hilary W. Jackson, Alston Kennerley, Peter Langford, John Munday, Michael Nash, Richard Noyce, Graham and Jill Robin, Norman Swales, Brian Thynne, Barbara Tomlinson, Lisa Verity, and Jenny Wraight, as well as the staff of the British Library, the British Museum Print Room, the Hydrographic Office, the London Library, the Medway Archives and Local Study Centre, the National Maritime Museum, the Newspaper Library at Colindale, the Public Record Office, the Royal Naval Museum at Portsmouth, and the Southwark Local History Library.

Finally I would like to thank my publishers for the support which they have given me throughout this project: in particular Bill Swainson for taking it on board and for his advice and his guiding hand from the outset, but also the valuable input of Edward Faulkner, Kelly Davis, and Lisa Birdwood. As always my family have been supportive, and my thanks especially to my son Matthew for his enthusiasm and suggestions, and my wife Shirley for her constant help and encouragement.

D.C.
Brighton, Sussex. May 2003

LIST OF ILLUSTRATIONS WITH CREDITS

Illustrations in the text

A view of Frindsbury from Rochester Bridge, by Samuel Scott. *Private collection.*

The plans of the *Bellerophon* based on surviving plans of similar ships designed by Sir Thomas Slade. *Norman Swales.*

Detail of a chart of the River Medway in 1840. *National Maritime Museum, London.*

Woodmen, by W.H.Payne. *The British Library, London.*

A timber wagon, by W.H.Payne. *The British Library, London.*

The *Bellerophon* ready for launching at Frindsbury. *The British Museum, London.*

The board room of the Admiralty office in Whitehall. *Royal Naval Museum, Portsmouth.*

Early drawing of Napoleon from life, 1785. *Malmaison.*

The captain's cabin at the stern of a ship. *National Maritime Museum, London.*

A sheer hulk by E.W. Cooke. *National Maritime Museum, London.*

Four aerial views of the Battle of the First of June by Nicholas Pocock. *National Maritime Museum, London*

The *Queen Charlotte* and the *Bellerophon* in action on 29 May 1794, by Nicholas Pocock. *National Maritime Museum, London.*

Captured French ships at Portsmouth. *National Maritime Museum, London.*

Cornwallis's Retreat with the *Bellerophon* in the foreground. *National Maritime Museum, London.*

A plan of the royal dockyard at Portsmouth. *National Maritime Museum, London.*

Chart of the port of Brest in 1800. *National Maritime Museum, London.*

A chart of Cadiz in 1762. *National Maritime Museum, London.*

A map of the Mediterranean showing the track taken by Nelson's fleet in 1798. *The British Library, London.*

A plan of the Battle of the Nile from *The Life of Admiral Lord Nelson* by Clarke and MacArthur. *The British Library, London.*

A Martello tower on the coast near Hastings. *The British Library, London.*

British troops guarding the coast, by Rowlandson. *Private collection.*

The telegraph station on Southsea Common, 1805. *National Maritime Museum, London.*

A plan showing the position of the fleets at Trafalgar, from *The Life of Admiral Lord Nelson* by Clarke and MacArthur. *The British Library, London.*

The *Bellerophon* under fire from four enemy ships at Trafalgar. *National Maritime Museum, London.*

Charts of Basque Roads in July 1815. *The British Library, London.*

Napoleon being rowed out to the *Bellerophon* on 15 July 1815. *National Maritime Museum, London.*

Napoleon being transferred from the *Bellerophon* to the *Northumberland*. *National Maritime Museum, London.*

A prison ship in Portsmouth harbour, by E.W.Cooke. *National Maritime Museum, London.*

The chapel and a prison ward on a convict hulk. *Private collection.*

A British warship off St Helena, by William Innes Pocock. *National Maritime Museum, London.*

The sails of a square-rigged ship, by J.T. Serres. *National Maritime Museum, London.*

Illustrations for black-and-white insert

View of Rochester from Frindsbury. *Private collection.*

Portrait of Sir Thomas Slade. *National Maritime Museum, London.*

Portrait of Rear-Admiral Sir Thomas Pasley. *National Maritime Museum, London.*

Napoleon at Arcole in 1796, by Antoine-Jean Gros. *Giraudon/Bridgeman Art Library.*

Captain William Johnstone Hope. *National Maritime Museum, London.*

The Battle of the Glorious First of June, by P.J. de Loutherbourg. *National Maritime Museum, London.*

Portrait of Admiral Lord Howe. *National Maritime Museum, London.*

Portrait of Nicholas Pocock, by Isaac Pocock. *Private collection.*

Sketch by Pocock of the aftermath of the battle. *National Maritime Museum, London.*

Captain Henry D'Esterre Darby. *National Maritime Museum, London.*

Captain Edward Rotheram. *National Maritime Museum, London.*

Shipping in Portsmouth harbour. *Royal Naval Musuem, Portsmouth.*

Napoleon at the Battle of Wagram in 1809, by Horace Vernet. *Lauros/Giraudon/Bridgeman Art Library.*

British ships off the island of Martinique, 1794. *National Maritime Museum, London.*

Portrait of Captain John Cooke. *National Maritime Museum, London.*

The capture of the *Resistance* and *Constance*. *National Maritime Museum, London.*

Portrait of Lieutenant William Pryce Cumby. *Private collection.*

Portrait of Captain Frederick Maitland. *Private collection.*

Miniature portrait of Lady Maitland. *The British Library, London.*

Captain Maitland's ship *La Loire* in the action at Muros, 1805. *National Maritime Museum, London.*

Portrait of Napoleon on the *Bellerophon*, by Sir Charles Eastlake. *National Maritime Museum, London.*

List of illustrations for colour inserts

Bow view of a model of the 74–gun ship *Bellona*. *National Maritime Museum, London.*

Stern view of a model of the *Bellona*. *National Maritime Museum, London.*

Traditional tools used by shipwrights. *Private collection.*

Chatham dockyard in 1777, by Robert Wilkins. *Private collection, photography courtesy of Richard Green Gallery, London.*

The *Defence* at the Battle of the Glorious First of June. *National Maritime Museum, London.*

A book of flag signals used at the Battle of the Glorious First of June. *National Maritime Museum, London.*

The old Commodore, by Thomas Rowlandson. *National Maritime Museum, London.*

The Advanced Squadron off Cadiz, by Thomas Buttersworth. *National Maritime Museum, London.*

The midshipmen's quarters in a British warship, by Augustus Earle. *National Maritime Museum, London.*

The Battle of the Nile with *L'Orient* on fire, by Thomas Whitcombe. *National Maritime Museum, London.*

Portrait of Nelson in 1800, by John Hoppner. *Royal Naval Museum, Portsmouth.*

Napoleon at Boulogne in July 1804, by Jean-Francis Hue. *Giraudon/Bridgeman Art Library.*

View of the town and harbour of Halifax, Nova Scotia. *National Maritime Museum, London.*

Shipping off the coast of Jamaica in 1793, George Tobin. *State Library of New South Wales, Sydney.*

The Battle of Trafalgar, by Clarkson Stanfield. *Tate Gallery, London.*

Photography of the middle gun deck of the *Victory*. *Royal Naval Museum, Portsmouth.*

The Full of Nelson at Trafalgar, by Denis Dighton. *National Maritime Museum, London.*

The *Victory* towed into Gibraltar after Trafalgar, by Clarkson Stanfield. *Guildhall Art Gallery, London.*

The wooden figure of a lieutenant used as a shop sign outside the London shop of William Heather. *National Maritime Museum, London.*

The accommodation ladder, by Thomas Rowlandson. *Royal Naval Museum, Portsmouth.*

Portsmouth seen from the anchorage at Spithead, by J.M.W. Turner. *National Museums, Liverpool (Lady Lever Art Gallery).*

Napoleon on the *Bellerophon*, by Sir William Quiller Orchardson. *Tate Gallery, London.*

The *Bellerophon* in Torbay, by Thomas Luny. *Private collection.*

The *Bellerophon* in Plymouth Sound, by John James Chalon. *National Maritime Museum, London.*

Sheerness as seen from the Nore, by J.M.W. Turner. *Richard Green Gallery, London.*

The *Fighting Temeraire* tugged to her last berth, 1838, by J.M.W. Turner. *National Gallery, London.*

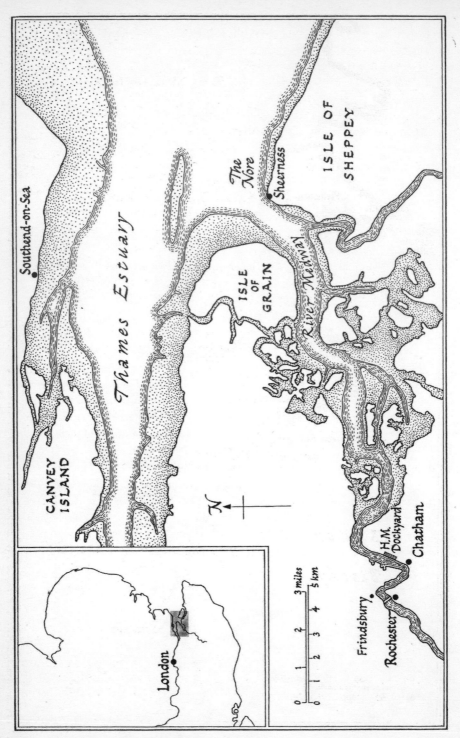

Map of the River Medway from Rochester to Sheerness and the Nore.

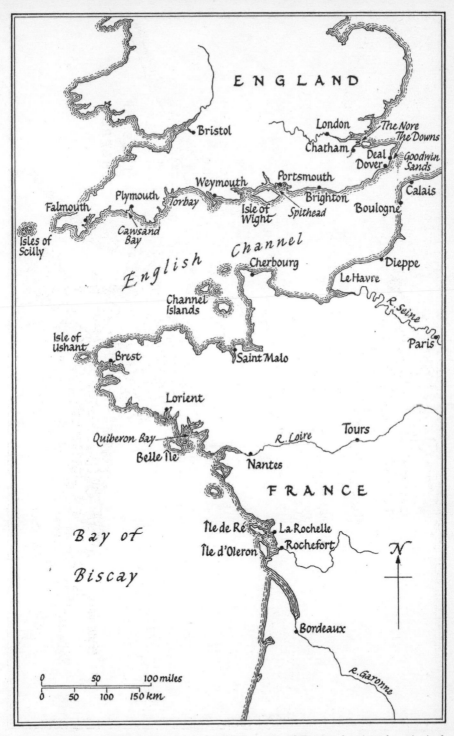

Map of the English Channel and Atlantic coast of France showing the principal ports, naval bases and anchorages.

Map of the Mediterranean in 1798.

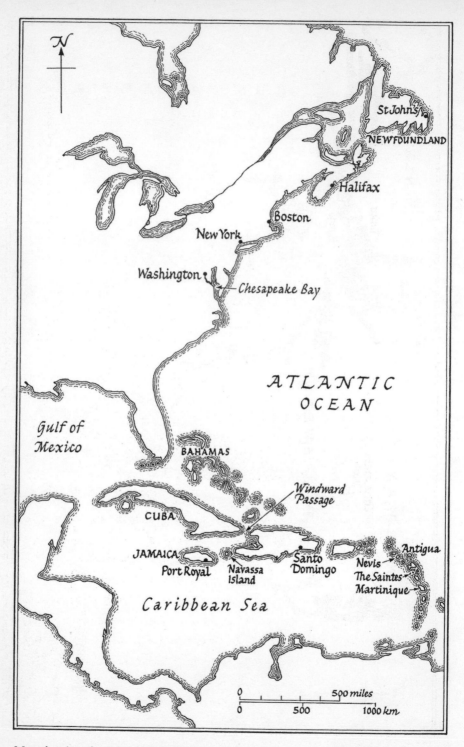

Map showing the West Indies, the coast of North America and Nova Scotia.

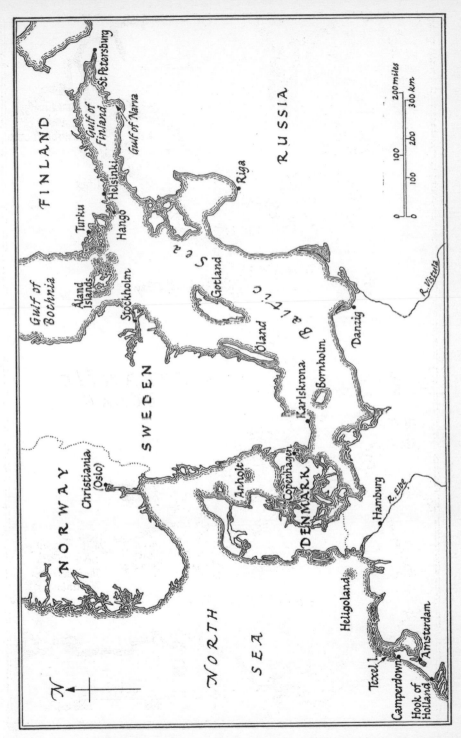

Map showing the Baltic Sea and the coast of Holland and Denmark.

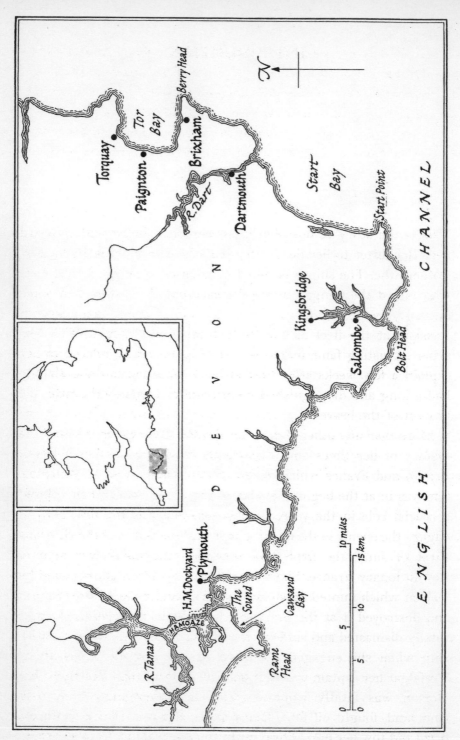

Map of the coast of Devon showing Torbay, Brixham, and Plymouth Sound.

INTRODUCTION

This is the story of one ship, from her birth in a small shipyard near Rochester to her death fifty years later in a breaker's yard at Rotherhithe. The ship was called *Bellerophon*, after the Greek hero who tamed the winged horse Pegasus, but the sailors had some difficulty in pronouncing her name and so she became known throughout the fleet as the 'Billy Ruffian' or 'Billy Ruff'n'. She achieved lasting fame in 1815 when Napoleon surrendered to her captain a few weeks after the battle of Waterloo but she already had a long and distinguished record and had earned the title 'the bravest of the brave'.

More than any other ship of her day the *Bellerophon* reflected the history of her times and in particular the long conflict between Britain and France which began in 1793 and ended at Waterloo. She was in at the beginning, she was in at the end, and she played a crucial role in the years in between. She was the first ship to engage the enemy in the opening moves of the Battle of the Glorious First of June, the first fleet action of the naval war against Revolutionary France. She was with the squadron commanded by Nelson which hunted down the French fleet in the Mediterranean and destroyed it at the Battle of the Nile: in that action she was totally dismasted and suffered the highest casualties of any British ship when she engaged the huge French flagship *L'Orient*. At Trafalgar her captain was shot dead by a musket ball shortly before Nelson was fatally wounded. Her first lieutenant took over command, fought off four enemy ships, and went on to capture a prize and tow her into Gibraltar. In the intervening years she spent months baking in the tropical sun as part of the squadron on the

Jamaica station charged with defending the West Indian colonies. She spent many more months being battered by winter storms off Ushant and in the Bay of Biscay as part of the fleet blockading the French coast. She escorted convoys across the Atlantic and kept watch on the Spanish fleet at Cadiz. She was a crucial link in the Wooden Walls of England, that extended line of British ships which finally put an end to Napoleon's ambitious plans to invade England and march on London.

The later life of the ship reflected a less glorious side of British history. For twenty years the *Bellerophon* was a convict hulk, first on the River Medway at Sheerness and then near the dockyard at Plymouth. Her masts were cut down, her gunports replaced with iron bars and four hundred prisoners were crammed into cages built on her lower decks. There is an alarming scene in the first chapter of *Great Expectations* when Pip meets an escaped convict in a church-yard beside a great marsh. The convict has an iron on his leg and has escaped from a prison ship anchored out in the estuary. Charles Dickens described it as a 'black hulk lying out a little way from the mud of the shore, like a wicked Noah's ark, cribbed and barred and moored by massive rusty chains . . .' Such a ship was the *Bellerophon* at this period in her life. The convicts ranged from murderers to minor thieves and pickpockets. Some were as young as ten. Indeed for several years the ship was exclusively reserved for young offenders below the age of fourteen. They were expected to be productive during daylight hours and according to one report they managed to produce in the course of one year no fewer than 6,000 pairs of shoes, 15,500 garments and various articles of bedding. At night the boys were locked into cells. A chaplain who was allotted to the ship to teach them scripture and improve their morals complained that 'some are destitute of the abilities to learn, and others are so depraved that they will not apply themselves.'[1]

But the most famous episode in the life of this extraordinary ship took place in the summer of 1815. When Napoleon escaped from Elba and resumed command of the French army, the British Admiralty despatched a squadron under the command of Admiral Hotham to keep watch on the French coast. The *Bellerophon* was ordered to guard the approaches to the port of Rochefort. On 28 June her Scottish commander, Captain Maitland, captured a local vessel and learnt that Napoleon had been defeated by Wellington at Waterloo. Two days later he received a mysterious message from a spy. Written on thin paper and concealed in a quill, it warned that Napoleon was heading for Bordeaux with the intention of fleeing the country. This was followed by orders from Admiral Hotham which directed Maitland to use his best endeavours to prevent Napoleon from escaping to America on one of the French frigates anchored off Rochefort. Maitland spent an anxious week patrolling the approaches to the port, searching every outgoing vessel, and making plans to intercept the French frigates if they should attempt to fight their way out to sea. After listening to the conflicting advice of his followers Napoleon decided to surrender to Captain Maitland and throw himself on the mercy of the British nation, 'the greatest, the most constant and the most generous of my enemies'.

Early on the morning of 15 July Maitland wrote in his log-book, 'At 7 received on board Napoleon Bonaparte late Emperor of France and his suite.' The suite included three generals, two French counts and countesses and their four children, ten army officers, a doctor, two cooks, twenty-six servants, the imperial dinner service and silver plate, and several boatloads of luggage. They sailed back to England and anchored first at Torbay and then, a few days later, in Plymouth Sound. For two weeks the ship was the centre of intense interest while negotiations took place regarding Napoleon's future. When news spread that the most famous man in the western world was on board a warship at Plymouth the *Bellerophon* was besieged by small boats laden with sightseers. Admiral Keith, who commanded the Channel Fleet, told his daughter, 'I am miserable with all the idle people in England coming to see this man,' and Lieutenant Bowerbank calculated that on one day they were surrounded by ten thousand people in yachts, fishing boats and rowing boats. The crew kept the onlookers informed by holding up boards with chalked messages, 'At breakfast', 'Going to dinner', 'In the cabin with Captain Maitland', and every evening around 6 pm Napoleon appeared on deck to show himself to the spectators.

It has been possible to build up an extremely detailed picture of life on board the *Bellerophon* during the three weeks that Napoleon was on the ship because everyone present was aware that they were watching history in the making, and many people kept notes and journals. 'I think myself very lucky to belong to the old Bellerophon at this important time,' wrote a junior officer in a letter to his mother, providing her with a vivid pen picture of Napoleon's appearance, his clothes, what he ate and how he spent his days.[2] Several of Napoleon's followers, notably his valet Louis-Joseph Marchand and Count Las Cases, later published their memoirs and included their observations of their time on the British warship. By far the most detailed account was that produced by Captain Maitland himself. He had been asked by friends and family to put together all his notes and when Sir Walter Scott was shown the resulting text he strongly recommended that it be published. 'The whole narrative is as fine, manly, and explicit an account as ever was given of so interesting a transaction,' he wrote, and provided his own notes and additions to what he considered a document of national interest.[3]

A great deal of material also exists for the three battles in which the *Bellerophon* took part. There are the log-books of all the ships, and the letters, memoirs and journals of many of the officers who were present. For the Battle of Trafalgar in particular there is the graphic account which William Pryce Cumby, the heroic first lieutenant of the ship, wrote for his son Anthony, describing his experience of the action. For the Nile there are the scribbled, hand-written notes which were sent to Captain Darby by George Bellamy, the ship's surgeon, in which he listed the dead and wounded with details of the horrific wounds suffered during the battle. And there are the numerous paintings, prints and drawings that were made to record these famous British victories. Those of the marine artist Nicholas Pocock are of particular value because he was an experienced seaman, was an eye witness at the Battle of the Glorious First of June, and always went to immense pains to gather first-hand information from officers who had taken part in the many actions which he illustrated.

The log-books of the *Bellerophon*, in common with those of other British warships, are held by the Public Record Office in Kew and they provide a continuous record of the ship's movements from the day she was commissioned at Chatham in 1790 until the day that Captain Maitland hauled down her commissioning pennant at Sheerness in 1815. They are written in a brisk, seamanlike style and a form of nautical shorthand which allows no room for human emotions. They are a wonderful source for the weather: they describe the wind force and direction, the visibility, and the sea state every day. They make it possible to follow the movements of the ship from port to port: they describe the course steered, the speed, sail changes, and other ships sighted; they also describe the loading of stores, and the punishments meted out to the crew.

Although the log-books are short on human detail the existence of a crew list compiled by one of the ship's captains allows us an unusual insight into the appearance and background of the *Bellerophon*'s crew.[4] Every naval ship had to complete a muster roll at regular intervals but this was mainly for pay purposes and was restricted to basic details such as the name, age and rank of every member of the crew. Captain Rotheram, who took over command of the *Bellerophon* after Trafalgar, conducted a remarkably detailed survey of all the seamen in the crew, listing their height, the colour of their hair and eyes, the shape of their faces, the type of complexion (sallow, pale, fresh, dark, swarthy, negro), their dialect, and any special distinguishing marks such as tattoos, scars and injuries.

He recorded where each man was born, where his wife or parents lived, and whether they were married or single. He also listed their occupations before going to sea and this provides a vivid picture of the skills present in a man-of-war at any one time: the crew of the *Bellerophon* included barbers, basketmakers, brushmakers, black-smiths, buttonmakers, cabinet makers, carters, farmers, glaziers, grooms, hatters, millers, plumbers, poulterers, shoemakers, snuff-makers, tallow chandlers, watchmakers, weavers and wheelwrights.

Although this is primarily the story of one particular ship of the line it is also, to a lesser extent, the story of Napoleon. For fifteen years (until Wellington eventually demonstrated in the Peninsular Campaign that the French armies could be defeated) the British Navy was the only effective defence against the territorial ambitions of

France and in particular Napoleon's plans to invade and conquer
Britain. The movements of the *Bellerophon* and Britain's other
warships were very often the direct result of the Admiralty's response
to the threat posed by Napoleon and his armies. Although there were
many reasons for Napoleon's downfall, notably his disastrous attempt
to invade and conquer Russia, it is not too far-fetched to suggest
that the *Bellerophon* played a significant role in thwarting his ambitions. As one of the ships which spent years blockading the French
ports and naval bases she played her part in crippling France's trade
and preventing her fleets putting to sea and supporting an invasion
of Britain. At the Battle of the Nile she attacked the flagship which
had taken Napoleon to Egypt. The subsequent destruction of the
French fleet left Napoleon's armies stranded and he was forced to
abandon his ambitious plans to conquer the East. As he later told
Captain Maitland, 'If it had not been for you English, I should have
been Emperor of the East; but wherever there is water to float a
ship, we are sure to find you in our way.'[5] Although Napoleon had
decided to postpone his plans to invade Britain several weeks before
the Battle of Trafalgar, the wholesale destruction of the Combined
Fleet of France and Spain in that famous action, in which the
Bellerophon played such a distinguished role, effectively put an end
to any future plans of invasion. And finally, by blocking his path to
the open sea off Rochefort in 1815, the *Bellerophon* prevented him
from escaping to America as he had planned and ensured that he
never again disrupted the peace of Europe.

ONE

Born of Oak

1782–6

The *Bellerophon* was born on the north bank of the River Medway at Frindsbury, near Rochester. Today the village of Frindsbury has merged into the sprawling collection of housing estates and shopping centres, factories, office blocks and car parks which compose the Medway towns. Only the church remains untouched, standing in a green oasis of chestnut trees and venerable gravestones on the high ground above the river. Down on the waterfront is an untidy jumble of warehouses, shipyards and the remnants of a once thriving cement industry. Hidden among the corrugated iron sheds is a concrete slipway. It was here, or very close to this spot, that the *Bellerophon* was built at the shipyard of Mr Edward Greaves.

In the 1780s the Frindsbury peninsula was an almost empty expanse of fields and low-lying marshland. There were a few houses in the vicinity of the church, and there was a windmill in the field above the shipyard but little else except for a few grazing cattle. Across the river from the shipyard the ancient city of Rochester huddled beneath the Norman castle and cathedral, the grey stone towers and spires providing distinctive landmarks for ships heading upstream from the Thames Estuary. A mile downstream, around the bend in the river, the redbrick buildings of Chatham dockyard hugged the waterfront, surrounded by windswept pastures and isolated farms. And to the east, beyond the royal dockyard, the river meandered

A view from Rochester Bridge showing the river bank near the place where the *Bellerophon* was built, with Frindsbury church in the distance. An engraving after the pen and wash drawing by Samuel Scott.

through desolate marshes frequented only by seagulls, wading birds and the occasional fisherman.

The design of the *Bellerophon* was based on plans drawn up by Sir Thomas Slade, a remarkable man who was generally considered the finest ship designer of his day. One of his successors as Surveyor of the Navy described him as 'truly a great man in the line he trod, such an one I believe never went before him, and if I am not too partial, I may venture to say will hardly follow him.'[1] A portrait of Slade shows a burly-faced man with a stolid expression; the face of a man who could be relied on to do a workmanlike job. In fact he had a genius for ship design and it seems likely that Anson, the celebrated circumnavigator and later First Lord of the Admiralty, had spotted his talent and had supported his appointment as Surveyor.

Slade had worked his way to the top the hard way. He was born in 1703 or 1704 and came from a shipbuilding family.[2] In the 1740s he was overseeing the building of several naval ships in the private shipyard of John Barnard at Harwich. This was a job usually carried

out by a dockyard foreman and gave no hint of the influence he was
later to have on ship design. In 1747, during one of his many visits
to the east coast, he married Hannah Moore. She came from the
village of Nacton, near Ipswich, and was the daughter of a local sea
captain. Nothing is known of their family life beyond the words which
appear on Slade's gravestone in the churchyard of St Clement's,
Ipswich. These note that 'In the most endearing scenes of private
life, he was an affectionate husband, an indulgent Father, a steady
Friend, and an honest man.'[3]

By 1750 Slade was assistant master shipwright at Woolwich dockyard, the first step on the ladder which would take him to the top
of his profession. In that year he moved to Plymouth dockyard as
master shipwright and this was followed by a series of rapid promo-
tions as he moved from one royal dockyard to the next. In 1752 he
was back at Woolwich as master shipwright and a year later moved
to Chatham. By 1755 he was master shipwright at Deptford, a key
post from which Surveyors of the Navy had been drawn in the past.
In August of that year the then Surveyor, Sir Joseph Allin, fell ill.
Within a few days the Admiralty ordered that Allin should be
pensioned off, on the grounds that he was 'disordered in his senses
and incapable of performing the duty of his office'.[4] In his place they
appointed Thomas Slade and William Bately as Joint Surveyors.
Bately had been Assistant Surveyor of the Navy for six years and
was to design some fine ships, but it was Slade who was to put his
stamp on an era of British shipbuilding.

During the 1730s and 1740s the design of warships in Britain had
gone through a bad patch. Captains complained that the ships of the
1745 establishment did not 'steer easy, nor sail so well, as was
expected.'[5] More seriously it was pointed out that the ships heeled
over so much in blowing weather that they were not able to open
their lee gunports. The Admiralty and serving naval officers were
acutely aware that many Spanish and French ships were superior to
their British counterparts. Sir Joseph Allin had attempted to rectify
the faults of the earlier British designs but he had no fresh ideas and
the period of his tenure as Surveyor was one of stagnation as far as
British ship design was concerned.

All this changed with the appointment of Slade and Bately. Within three weeks of taking up his new post Thomas Slade had produced a design for a ship called the *Dublin* which was to become the first of an astonishingly successful series of 74-gun ships. Unlike Fredrik af Chapman, the great Swedish naval architect of this period who brought an intellectual rigour to the beautiful ship designs in his famous treatise *Architectura Navalis Mercatoria*, Thomas Slade relied on the practical experience he had gained in the shipyards. His approach was both pragmatic and instinctive. He took the best from the French designs of his day and made them better. And he constantly searched for improvement. He produced no fewer than nine versions of the 74-gun ship, each building on the experience of the previous designs so that during his sixteen years as Surveyor of the Navy the 74-gun ship was brought to perfection and came to be regarded as the ideal warship. As one experienced observer noted, 'She will not shrink from an encounter with a First Rate ship on account of superior weight, nor abandon the chase of a frigate on account of swiftness. The union of these qualities has therefore, with justice, made the 74-gun ship the principle [sic] object of maritime attention, and given her so distinguished a pre-eminence in our line of battle.'[6]

In 1761 the *Bellona*, one of Slade's earlier designs for a 74, engaged in a single-ship action with the French 74-gun ship *Courageux*. There was a fierce gun battle but within thirty minutes the French ship was forced to surrender, although she was larger by 100 tons and had 150 more men than the *Bellona*. Slade's designs were to prove equally successful in the great fleet actions of the wars against France, notably in the three battles in which the *Bellerophon* took part. There were ten of Slade's ships at the battle of the Glorious First of June in 1794. No fewer than eight of the twelve British 74-gun ships which annihilated the French fleet at the Battle of the Nile were Slade designs. And at the Battle of Trafalgar, which took place more than thirty years after his death, seven of the ships were Slade designs, including the *Victory* of 100 guns, generally regarded as his masterpiece and arguably the most famous warship of all time. Of course it was often the morale and fighting qualities of the British officers and seamen which were responsible for the spectacular victories of the age of Nelson, rather than the design of the ships, but the fact was that Slade's ships were severely tested in a variety of conditions. They were the subject of comprehensive sailing reports sent in by captains, and again and again they proved their superiority. This explains why so many ships were built to Slade's designs and why it became recognised that a British ship could invariably beat a French ship in single-ship actions even though the French ship might be up to 50 per cent more powerful in terms of her guns.

It would make for a better story if we could say that on a certain day Sir Thomas Slade sat down at his drawing board and started work on his designs for the *Bellerophon*. He had his office in Crutched Friars, near the Tower of London, and we could picture him there, surrounded by ship models, with plans and sketch designs pinned up on the walls around him. But Slade had been dead for ten years when the Navy Board ordered the building of the *Bellerophon*. He had died in 1771 at the age of sixty-eight, leaving an impressive legacy of ship designs and a reputation for honesty and hard work. To quote from his gravestone again, 'He had constantly in view the improvement of the King's Yards, and the English Navy; which great end he steadily pursued with an unwearied application and spotless integrity.'[7]

The *Bellerophon* was one of fourteen ships built to the design of the *Arrogant* which had been designed by Slade in 1758. Other ships in the same class included several which would play distinguished parts in forthcoming conflicts, notably the *Goliath* which led the British fleet into action at the Battle of the Nile, and the *Elephant*, Nelson's flagship at Copenhagen. Although the plans for the *Bellerophon* and the *Arrogant* have not survived there are a number of other plans of 74-gun ships bearing Slade's signature in the National Maritime Museum in London. Like all plans for naval ships of the period these are drawn to a 1:48 scale and show the four key aspects of the ship which the shipbuilders needed in order to fashion the oak and elm timbers into the shapes required. The first aspect was the side elevation or profile; the second was the plan view of one half of the ship, which was usually drawn underneath the profile view; the third and fourth aspects were drawn

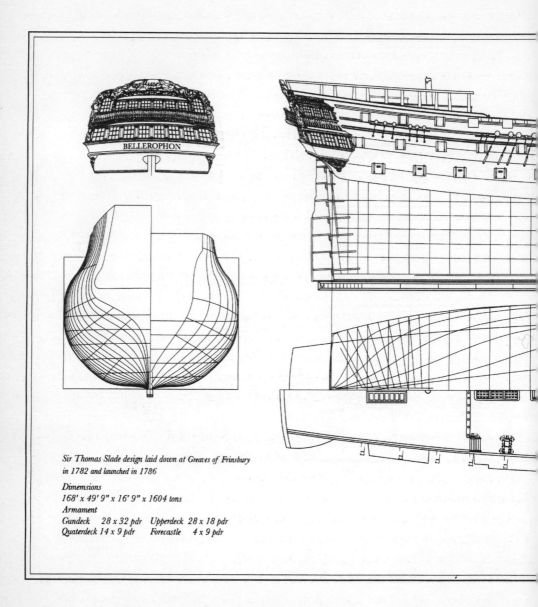

*Sir Thomas Slade design laid down at Greaves of Frinsbury
in 1782 and launched in 1786*

Dimemsions
168' x 49' 9" x 16' 9" x 1604 tons
Armament
Gundeck   28 x 32 pdr   Upperdeck 28 x 18 pdr
Quaterdeck 14 x 9 pdr   Forecastle   4 x 9 pdr

The lines of the *Bellerophon* drawn by Norman Swales and based
on the surviving plans of the *Edgar*, a 74–gun ship of the
Arrogant Class designed by Sir Thomas Slade

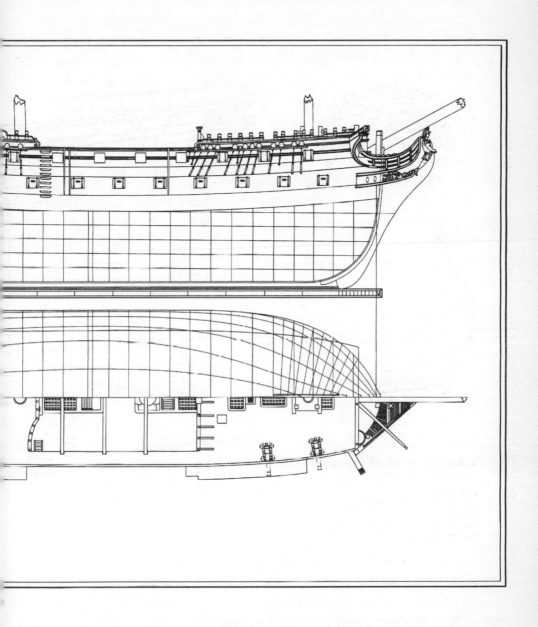

together as a composite plan, one half showing the cross-section of the ship viewed from the bow and the other showing the ship viewed from the stern.

It would have been the job of a draughtsman in the Surveyor's office to make an exact copy of the plans of the *Arrogant* by pricking through the master plan onto a sheet of paper below and then re-drawing it as accurately as possible. Sir John Henslow, the Surveyor who succeeded Slade and who so much admired him, would have checked the new plan, signed it, and then arranged for it to be placed in a specially designed box and delivered to Chatham dockyard. The senior officers at Chatham were responsible for supervising the building of any navy ships built at private yards on the River Medway. From Chatham the plans would have been passed on to Mr Edward Greaves at Frindsbury.

While Thomas Slade can be regarded as the father of the *Bellerophon*, the role of the mother, or at least the midwife, must belong to Edward Greaves because it was he who was responsible for bringing the ship into the world. Unfortunately we know very little about him apart from his correspondence with the Navy Board and the occasional mention of ships built by him which appear in various Admiralty documents. We do know that he was a shipbuilder of considerable experience because he already had a flourishing shipyard on the Thames at Limehouse where he had built several ships for the navy.[8] These were mostly small ships and he was evidently keen to build a ship of the line. It must have been with this in mind that he took on the lease of the shipyard at Frindsbury.

A contemporary picture of the shipyard gives the impression that it was no more than a few wooden sheds crouching uncertainly at the water's edge. However the yard was put up for auction in 1790, four years after the launch of the *Bellerophon*, and the advertisement which appeared in the *Kentish Gazette* suggests that it was unusually well set up for a private yard. We learn that the property was 'delightfully situated in the parish of Frindsbury', and 'In the shipbuilders yard there has lately been built ships of war of 74 guns, and other vessels and is as commodious as any private yard in the kingdom either for builders or timber merchants, with a good rope walk and

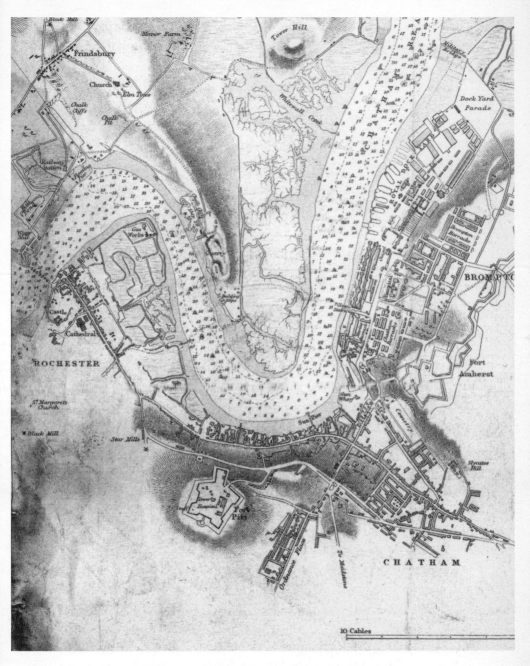

Detail of a chart of the River Medway in 1840 showing
Rochester and Frindsbury. The royal dockyard at Chatham
is on the right of the picture

every suitable convenience.'[9] During the 1770s the yard had been owned by Henniker and Nicholson, and at least three naval warships had been built there. Sir John Henniker was a local grandee (he is commemorated by a lavish monument in Rochester Cathedral) and, although it was presumably Mr Nicholson who managed the yard, Sir John may well have ensured that it was provided with everything necessary for the construction of ships of all sizes.

In December 1781 Edward Greaves approached the Navy Board with a proposal to build a 64-gun ship at his yard on the Thames, and a 74-gun ship and a frigate at Frindsbury.[10] He was turned down on all counts. The minutes of the Navy Board for 14 December are curt and to the point: 'Acquaint him we do not approve of building a ship of 64 guns at his Dock in the River nor of building a 74 gun ship and Frigate at Sir Jn. Hinnikers Yard opposite Rochester.'[11]

The Navy Board had arranged for his building slipway at Limehouse to be surveyed and decided that nothing larger than a 44-gun ship could be built there; and they were concerned that the shipyard at Frindsbury was too close to the royal dockyard at Chatham. Merchant yards usually offered higher wages than those in the royal dockyards and they did not want Greaves poaching skilled workmen from Chatham. Greaves overcame the Navy Board's objections to Frindsbury by entering into an agreement 'not to employ any Artificers from the Kings Yard'.[12] On 8 January 1782 the Navy Board agreed that 'Sir Jn Hinnikins Yard at Frinsbury is a proper place for building a 74 gun and 32 gun ship' and informed Greaves of their decision. For some reason Greaves did not reply immediately because on 16 January the Navy Board were pressing him to let them know whether he was prepared to go ahead with the building of the 74-gun ship at Rochester. He wrote back at once. His letter is hidden among dozens of dusty letters with names beginning with the letter G which are crammed into a cardboard box in the Public Record Office. It is a key document in the life story of the *Bellerophon*:

Hon.d Sirs

I return you thanks for the offer you are pleas'd to make of a 74 Gun Ship to Build near Rochester & am willing to undertake to Build Her on

the same Terms as the River Thames for Ships of a similar contract as
that you mean to favour me with. Also a 32 Gun Frigate to Launch in
two Years if it meets your approbation. I remains Sirs

                              Your much obliged &

Jan. 18. 1782   Obedient honble Servant

                              Edwd Greaves

PS. Please to favour me with the Payments on the 36 Gun Frigate I have
taken the same manner as 44 Gun Ships.[13]

A month later, on 19 February 1782, Greaves put his signature to
the formal contract for the building of the ship. The original contract
still exists and is an impressive document. It consists of twenty-four
pages of closely printed text with measurements and particular
details added in pen and ink. It covers every single aspect of the
construction of the ship's hull and internal fittings from the stem to
the sternpost. In addition to specifying the exact size of the keel,
main frames, decks, gunports and so on, it also instructs the shipbuilder to provide removable cabins for the officers with bed places
and lockers, cabins and stores for the boatswain and carpenter; fish
and bread rooms, and a store for spirituous liquor. Ladders, gratings,
pump cisterns, a fire hearth and hammock racks are specified, as are
the decorative details at the stern of the ship. Outside the captain's
great cabin at the stern, for instance, there is to be 'a handsome walk
or balcony, with ballisters as shall be directed by the Officer or
Overseer inspecting the said works; and the whole stern finished
agreeable to ships of her class built in His Majesty's Yards.'[14]

In April 1782 we learn from the minutes of the Surveyor's Office
that the ship is to be called 'Bellerophone'.[15] Who chose the name,
and why were so many ships named after Greek and Roman gods
and heroes? It is said that Lord Sandwich, the First Lord of the
Admiralty, had a copy of Lemprière's classical dictionary on his desk
and simply picked a name from this. The dictionary gives a lengthy
account of the story of Bellerophon, who was the handsome son of
the King of Ephyre. He was wrongly accused of making love to the
wife of King Argos and was sent to kill the three-headed monster
Chimaera in the expectation that he would die in the attempt.

However, with the help of the goddess Minerva and the winged horse Pegasus, he killed the monster, conquered the Amazons, and returned to marry the daughter of the King of Lycia. The problem with naming a ship after this particular hero was that, while naval officers educated in the Classics might have no difficulty in pronouncing Bellerophon correctly, the ordinary sailors were totally baffled by it and came up with various alternative names. 'Billy Ruffian' or 'Billy Ruff'n' seem to have been the most commonly used names, but a Rowlandson cartoon of 1810 refers to the ship as 'Belly Rough One', and Captain Marryat, who was serving in the navy while the *Bellerophon* was in commission, has a passage in his novel *Poor Jack* in which an old seaman calls the ship 'the Bellyruffron'.[16]

On 26 April Mr Greaves wrote to the Navy Board to tell them that he had got in a large quantity of timber at Frindsbury for building the *Bellerophon* and the 32-gun frigate and he wanted it inspected so that he could obtain his first payments for building the two ships. The Navy Board ordered the officers at Chatham to inspect the timber and two months later Greaves was given a certificate for his first bill.[17]

Apart from the keel, the hull of the *Bellerophon* was almost entirely built of oak, as were all British ships of the line at this period. Indeed oak was the preferred building material for the warships of all the maritime countries of the western world. This was because oak was hard and tough and far more resistant to rot than other woods. The presence of tannic acid contributed to its durability, although in the long term this did not prevent the ravages of the teredo worm, particularly in ships which spent time in tropical waters. Of the many varieties of oak, the tree most favoured by British shipbuilders was the English oak, or *quercus robur*, a species which had been established in Britain for thousands of years. It was the dominant tree in the woodlands and hedgerows of southern England and acquired a special significance through its long association with the ships of the Royal Navy. The patriotic song 'Heart of oak are our ships, Jolly tars are our men' was only one of many which linked the tree with the fortunes of the country.

Warships required vast numbers of oak trees for their contruction. It was usual to measure the quantities of wood used for shipbuilding in terms of 'loads'. A load consisted of 50 cubic feet of wood, roughly the equivalent of a single large tree, which was as much as could be loaded onto a cart. A 74-gun ship used between 3,000 and 3,700 loads for the building of her hull, which means that more than 3,000 oak trees were felled for the creation of the *Bellerophon*.[18] Apart from the sheer quantity involved there were further considerations. Oaks for shipbuilding must be between 80 and 120 years old. Trees younger than this would not be large enough for the great pieces of timber required for the construction of a ship of the line. Older trees were subject to decay. It was also essential that the trees be within easy reach of a waterway because it was difficult, if not impossible, to transport a heavy and unwieldy tree trunk for any distance on an eighteenth-century road in the days before tarmac was introduced. In England it was reckoned that any tree more than 40 miles from water transport was of no use for the navy. In France this was such an important consideration that no one was allowed to fell an oak tree within 15 leagues of the sea or 6 leagues of any navigable river without first giving six months notice to the Council of State or the Grand Master of Forests and Waterways.

So how did Mr Greaves get the trees he needed to build the *Bellerophon*? Long before he secured the contract from the Navy Board, the trees would have been selected by government officials. We can imagine these men riding on horseback across the fields and along the lanes of Kent, Sussex and Hampshire, scouring the countryside for suitable oaks. They would have had the weatherbeaten faces of farmers and gardeners, and they were expert at assessing the age and condition of the trees which they inspected. They visited the great estates of noble landlords, they rode across farmland, and they searched the woods and the few remaining forests of southern England. Forest and woodland oaks tended to grow tall and straight as they reached upwards to the light and these provided the straight timbers required for sternposts and planking. But what the government men were particularly looking for were the isolated trees growing in fields and hedgerows. These were a very different shape from forest trees. They had room to spread their branches sideways and, buffeted by wind and weather, they developed the curves which yielded the valuable 'compass timber' needed for the frames or ribs of a ship, and for the knees which supported and reinforced deck beams.

Having selected a suitable tree, the men stamped a broad arrow on the tree trunk to indicate that it was now government property. The trees were felled at the end of autumn or in early winter when the leaves had dropped and the sap was no longer rising, and before the heavy frosts came along. Timber merchants who had secured contracts from the Navy Board sent out tree-fellers with teams of horses to cut down and haul away the selected trees. It was heavy and demanding work. The axes swung by the tree-fellers needed constant sharpening because the oak was so dense and hard, and the tree must be felled without breaking the valuable curved and forked branches. When the tree had crashed down, the smaller branches were lopped off and the great trunk was either slung between wheels or hauled onto a sturdy timber cart. Several pairs of cart-horses then dragged the load to the nearest water. The River Medway was navigable as far as Tonbridge, and timber felled in the surrounding area was floated downstream on the river or one of its tributaries for the first part of the journey. At Prentice's Wharf in Maidstone the trunks were loaded onto massive wooden barges with the aid of a primitive crane. The barges were flat-bottomed, with slab sides, and could

Woodmen cutting branches off oak trees,
from W. H. Pyne's *Microcosm* of 1803

carry four or five trees. They could be towed or rowed downstream with the current, or sailed with a single large square sail. From Maidstone the timber barges followed the swinging curves of the Medway through the Kentish fields to Rochester. There they passed under the arches of the medieval stone bridge and out into the wide expanse of river beyond where they anchored off Mr Greaves's shipyard until high tide when they were brought alongside the wharf and unloaded.

Meanwhile the yard's shipwrights had been busy working on Sir Thomas Slade's plans on the floor of the mould loft. Since the plans were drawn to the scale of 1:48 it was necessary to enlarge the frames shown on the drawing to full size. The mould loft was in a large barn-like building and had a smooth floor on which the shapes of the timbers to be used in the ship's construction were drawn in chalk. From these chalked patterns the men made up templates or moulds of thin wood battens which enabled them to transfer Slade's designs to the oak timbers which were now piling up in the yard outside.

The mould loft was the womb in which the form of the ship was created but the birthplace was the slipway down by the water's edge. There were two slipways, or slips as they were called, at Greaves's yard. The *Bellerophon* was built on one of these and on the other was built the *Meleager*, the 32-gun frigate which had been ordered at the same time as the *Bellerophon*. The slip was a ramp which sloped down

Woodmen loading a timber wagon,
from W. H. Pyne's *Microcosm* of 1803

to the river at a gentle angle of about 4 degrees. By long experience this was reckoned to be steep enough to allow the finished hull of the ship to slide slowly into the water when the time came for her launch. A line of wooden blocks was laid along the centre of the slip and on these rested the massive elm timbers which formed the keel of the ship. Elm was preferred over oak for keels because it was more readily available in long, straight lengths, and because elm, provided it was kept submerged, was even more resistant to rot than oak. A line of scaffold poles was erected on each side of the slip; as the ship grew upwards the poles provided supports for working platforms for the shipwrights. At each end of the slip were sheerlegs which acted as cranes to raise into place the timbers for the stem and sternposts, and the frames which formed the ribs of the ship.

With two ships on the go, the yard was a bustle of activity from dawn to dusk. Building a ship was highly skilled work but it was also labour intensive and physically strenuous. Apart from the teams of horses used to drag timber to and fro, every job in the yard was carried out by hand, just as it would be later when the ship put to sea. As on a sailing ship the only mechanical aids were the various forms of block and tackle, and the windlass or capstan. Shipwrights' tools were few and simple and had scarcely changed for centuries. The principal tools were the axe, the adze, the auger for drilling holes, and the saw. The larger timbers were sawn into shape by men working in sawpits, one man working the saw from above and the other heaving it down again from the bottom of the pit. Once the rough shapes had been sawn out, skilled shipwrights got to work with adzes, cutting and smoothing each piece of oak to its final shape. The sweet smell of sawn wood, sawdust and fresh oak chippings filled every corner of the yard, mingling with the coarser smells of horse manure and tar and the smoke from the blacksmiths' workshops. The families living in the neighbourhood, and the men working on the boats out on the river, became accustomed to the constant banging and thudding of iron tools, and the shouts and curses of the men and the boy apprentices as they slowly converted the raw oak branches and tree trunks into finely curved frames, futtocks, knees, stemposts, sternposts and neat piles of planks.

By the end of the first year the keel was in place and a line of curved frames marked the shape which the ship was to take. From a distance she rose into the air like the skeleton of a huge animal stranded on her back. And then, as the planks were laid, first on the inside of the frames and then along the outside, the skeleton became a ship. Every plank had to be fastened in place with trenails (literally 'tree-nails' but pronounced 'trunnels'). These were wooden pegs like dowel rods. They were made of oak and were hammered into the holes drilled with the auger. They were better than iron nails because they did not rust, swelled when wet to a watertight fit and would not damage the shipwright's tools when the final smoothing and shaping of the planks took place.

No documents have survived to indicate how many men were employed by Edward Greaves, but the surviving records of the royal dockyards suggest that there must have been two or three hundred men at work in the shipyard during the building of the *Bellerophon* and the *Meleager*. When the 58-gun ship *Sunderland* was in the early stages of construction at Portsmouth dockyard in the 1740s no fewer than 186 shipwrights and twenty joiners were working on the ship during the course of one week.[19] At a later stage the shipwrights would have been joined by caulkers whose job it was to make the outer planks and the decks watertight. This was done by caulking the seams or spaces between the planks with unravelled strands of old rope called oakum. The oakum was hammered into the seams and then sealed with hot pitch to prevent it from rotting. Alongside the men working in wood were the blacksmiths who had to convert crude pieces of iron into dozens of specialised fittings ranging from stern lanterns, stanchions and rails to the hinges for gunports and cabin doors.

According to Edward Greaves' agreement with the Navy Board, the hull of the *Bellerophon* should have been completed in twenty-four months from the signing of the contract, which meant that she should have been ready to launch in April 1784. She was not ready that summer, nor the following summer, and was still on the slip in October 1786, four and a half years after her keel had been laid down. Since it was certainly possible to build a 74-gun ship in two years (indeed some were built in eighteen months) there must have been a good reason for the delay. We can find the explanation hidden in the contract for the ship. Towards the end of the document, before the penalty clauses and the details of the stage payments, there is a hand-written note concerning the time of launching which says that 'in case the said Commissioners think proper that the said ship should stand to season it is agreed that whatever time she shall so stand to season should be allowed the Contractor . . .'

For years the navy had experienced problems with ships built of unseasoned timber. Such ships were likely to succumb to rot much more rapidly than ships built of timber which had been allowed to weather and dry out in the yard for two or three years. In the royal dockyards large quantities of oak were therefore stored out in the open or under cover in special seasoning sheds and regulations were introduced which laid down that ships under construction must be allowed to season in frame: that is to say, the partially completed hull would stand on the slip for two or three years before being launched.[20] A private shipyard could not always afford to buy in large quantities of expensive timber and then allow it to remain unused for two or three years while it was seasoning. It is clear that the officers from Chatham dockyard who were responsible for checking on the progress of the *Bellerophon* ordered Greaves to delay the launch for two years to give the ship's timbers time to dry out. The Admiralty would have had no problem with this because there was no longer such an urgent need for warships. In February 1783 the Peace of Paris had been signed, bringing to an end the war with Britain's former colonies in America.

The war had begun with the revolt of some of the colonists in Massachusetts in 1775 and had developed into the bitter and hard-fought struggle which the British call the American War of Independence and which is usually referred to as the American Revolution on the other side of the Atlantic. France and Spain saw the war as a golden opportunity to revenge themselves for the setbacks of the Seven Years War of 1756–1763 during which France had lost all Canada, as well as several West Indian islands, to Britain. In 1778 France joined on the side of the Americans and declared war on Britain. Spain followed in 1779 and laid siege to Gibraltar. The result was that Britain's navy was stretched to the limit: ships were needed on the east coast of America to provide support for the British troops fighting General Washington's forces; ships were needed in the West Indies to combat French attacks on St Lucia, Grenada and St Kitts; a fleet was sent to relieve Gibraltar; and a fleet was needed in the English Channel to guard against a threatened invasion.

A series of military disasters in America culminated in the surrender at Yorktown of a British army commanded by General Cornwallis. Britain abandoned her rule over the American colonies and in November 1782 she signed a peace treaty with a new nation, the United States of America. Three months later the Peace of Paris was signed at Versailles which brought an end to the war with France and Spain. For the next ten years the countries of western Europe remained in a state of uneasy truce. *The Gentleman's Magazine* summed up the situation in October 1786: 'Peace and war are suspended in equal balance, and it is not possible at present to determine on which side the scale will turn. The continental powers are busied in arranging their armies to be in readiness for war; and the maritime powers in increasing their marine.'[21]

It was during this temporary suspension of hostilities between Britain and France that the *Bellerophon* was finally launched.

TWO

A Stormy Launch

1786

As with so many events in British history, the weather played a significant part in the launch of the *Bellerophon*. She should have been completed and in the water several weeks before the autumnal gales of 1786. In June of that year the *Kentish Gazette* announced that the ship would be launched in August. In September the newspaper contained a letter from Rochester dated 13 September which noted that, 'The Bellerophon, a beautiful ship of 74 guns, now building at Frinsbury for the use of the government, will be launched the 23rd of this month.' For some reason she was not launched on the 23rd and it was arranged that she should be launched two weeks later, early in the afternoon of Saturday 7 October. High water that day at Chatham was at 12.05.

Commissioner Proby was invited to launch the new warship. He was a former naval captain and had been the Resident Commissioner of Chatham dockyard for the past fifteen years. Also invited to the launching ceremony were the Bishop of Rochester, the mayors of the three Medway towns and representatives of the Admiralty and Navy Board. An elaborate dinner was ordered from the landlord of the Crown Inn which was situated across the river from the shipyard and had rooms overlooking Rochester Bridge.

The weather had been blustery during September but in the first week of October southern England was hit by violent storms.

On 5 October the wind blew hard from the north-west, uprooting trees and taking slates off rooftops. The next day the wind veered round to the south-west and on 7 October gale-force winds swept up the English Channel. At Shoreham a Danish timber ship was driven onto the beach and dashed into pieces in the surf with the loss of all her crew. A small house alongside the fish market at Brighton was washed into the sea by breaking waves, and the piers at Newhaven were so badly damaged that ships had difficulty getting in and out of the harbour. Sweeping across Kent and the Medway valley, the wind brought down fruit trees and hop poles, and nearly blew away a field of recently cut radishes. Several houses in eastern Kent lost their roofs and the top of the church spire of Minster in the Isle of Thanet was blown to the ground.

The *Bellerophon* was in a vulnerable position on the low-lying land of the Frindsbury peninsula. From the north she was partly sheltered by the chalk escarpment on which the church stood, but her massive hull was fully exposed to winds from the south and west. She was safe enough during her building because she was firmly supported by timber shores around her hull and her elm keel rested solidly on the wooden blocks of the slip. But during the summer of 1786 a launching cradle had been constructed to hold her upright as she moved towards the water; the slipway itself had been heavily greased with tallow, and many of the supporting shores had been removed. A drawing of the ship which was made shortly before her launch shows her towering over the surrounding buildings and sheds of the shipyard. She is depicted with huge flags flying from temporary flag staffs above her newly completed hull: the red ensign flies at her stern, a small union flag at her bows; the Admiralty flag, the royal standard, and a large union flag fly from poles erected where her masts will be stepped after her launch. It was customary for these flags to be flown whenever a warship was launched in Britain to signify that the vessel was one of the King's ships and was under the immediate control of the Lords Commissioners of the Admiralty. The flags had been made in the flag loft at Chatham and brought across from the dockyard.

As the wind howled down the Medway valley the flags strained at

An anonymous watercolour showing the *Bellerophon* ready for launching at Frindsbury. The buildings of Chatham dockyard can be seen in the distance beyond the low-lying land of the Frindsbury peninsula.

the poles, tugging like sails and causing the hull to shiver on her cradle. The wind continued to increase during the morning of Saturday 7 October and the *Bellerophon* began to rock dangerously as if anxious to be on her way. Some of the shores supporting her hull started to shift and then to collapse. After hurried consultations with his shipwrights Mr Nicholson decided that he had no alternative but to launch her prematurely. There was no time for speeches or ceremonial. He grabbed the bottle of port which Commissioner Proby was to have broken across the ship's bows, and hurled it at the ship. Whether he shouted above the wind 'Success to his Majesty's ship the *Bellerophon*' we do not know. There were only the shipyard workers there to hear him and they were more concerned about seeing the result of their labours safely in the water than about recording the event.

In those days ship launches, like fairs and public executions, always attracted large crowds. The families and friends of all the men and boys concerned in the building of the ship came along. So did the local gentry and their servants. Contemporary paintings of ship launches on the Thames show the riverbanks lined with spectators, and dozens of yachts, barges, rowing boats and skiffs out on the river where their passengers and crews could get a grandstand view of the proceedings. A band would be hired for the occasion to play patriotic and martial tunes, and as the ship hit the water everyone cheered and waved and threw their hats in the air. But when Commissioner Proby, the Bishop of Rochester, the mayors and the sightseers from Rochester and the surrounding villages arrived that afternoon they found the *Bellerophon* already afloat. She was pulling at her anchor cables as the outgoing tide swept past her hull, the surface of the water whipped into short, steep waves by the fierce winds. She was little more than a bare hull with no masts and no rigging and she floated too high in the water because she had yet to be weighed down with guns, barrels of water, casks of provisions and some 300 tons of iron and shingle ballast. But although the weather had disrupted the proceedings the launch was considered a success. Commissioner Proby despatched a letter to the Admiralty to inform their lordships that 'His Majesty's Ship Bellerophon was safely launched from Mr Graves's Yard at Friendsbury this day,'[1] and the following day the Rochester correspondent sent a report to the *Kentish Gazette*:

> Yesterday about four minutes after twelve o'clock, the Bellerophon, of 74 guns, was launched from Messrs Graves and Nicholson's Yard at Frinsbury, near this city. The launch was very fine, but very few people were present on account of its being sooner than expected. Messrs Graves and Nicholson on that day gave an elegant dinner to many of the principal gentlemen of the Three Towns, &c, at the Crown Inn, in this city. The band of musick, belonging to the Chatham Marines, were engaged on the occasion.[2]

In London the gales had blown down a house in Castle Street, damaged the roofs and chimneys of waterfront houses in Westminster, and sunk several small craft on the Thames but otherwise life went on much as usual. King George III and Queen Adelaide went to see the celebrated actress Sarah Siddons performing in James Thomson's play *The Tragedy of Tancred and Sigismunda* at the Theatre Royal, Drury Lane. They were accompanied by the Princess Royal, Princess Augusta and by Fanny Burney, the young writer whose first novel *Evelina* had been highly praised and who had recently been appointed a lady-in-waiting to the Queen. Mrs Siddons performed to a brilliant and crowded house and, according to *The Times*, 'added laurels to her fame . . . every step she takes, every word she speaks, and every cast of countenance is chaste and interesting to the auditor.'[3]

From *The Times* we also learn that Sir Joshua Reynolds was putting the finishing touches to a portrait of Lady Cadogan. John Singleton Copley was working on a vast painting of the siege of Gibraltar: to help him visualise the scene he had a model made of the fortress at Gibraltar and all the gunboats and ships' gear that were used in the action. Another fashionable artist, George Romney, had just completed a fine portrait of Mrs Warren which it was believed would greatly enhance his reputation. The previous year he had devoted much of his time to painting the ravishingly beautiful Emma Hart, soon to be better known as Lady Hamilton. Emma was now twenty-one and had recently arrived in Naples where she was staying in the elegant home of Sir William Hamilton, the British ambassador. Her previous lover, Charles Greville, had wished to marry an heiress and had sold her to his uncle, Sir William, for the price of the payment of his debts. Emma thought she had come to Naples with her mother for a holiday and was outraged when she learned of the arrangement. However she felt she had no option but to go along with the situation. She learnt Italian, took music lessons and singing lessons, and soon became a celebrated figure in Naples society, famous for her beauty and her theatrical performances. A few years later she married Sir William.

Meanwhile the man who would become Emma Hamilton's most famous lover was in the West Indies. Nelson was a 28-year-old captain in October 1786. He was living alone in the senior officer's house at English Harbour in Antigua while his ship HMS. *Boreas* was being refitted in the dockyard. He complained of the mosquitoes which ate him alive during the day and kept him awake at night. A few months earlier he had met Frances Nisbet on the West Indian island of Nevis and fallen in love with her. Frances, or Fanny as she was always called, was the daughter of the senior judge on the island and her uncle was the President of the Council. In 1779 she had married Josiah Nisbet, a doctor, and moved to England where they had a son. In 1781 Nisbet died and Fanny had returned to Nevis with her son and become her uncle's hostess. When Nelson met her she was an attractive and accomplished 27-year-old woman. Nelson's naval duties kept them apart for months at a time so he resorted to writing her passionate letters filled with lively descriptions of his life and his feelings. 'Separated from my dearest what pleasure can I feel? None! Be assured my happiness is centred with thee and where thou art not, there I am not happy.' And of English Harbour he wrote, 'My good Fanny, Most sincerely do I regret that I am not safe moored by thee instead of being in this vile place.'[4]

On another island a young artillery officer had recently returned home on leave. Napoleon Bonaparte had spent a year attending the military academy in Paris. He had completed the course in a year (most of his fellow cadets took two or three years) and received his commission as a second lieutenant at the age of sixteen. In January 1786 he joined his regiment which was stationed in the south of

France at Valence on the River Rhône. There his days were spent on army exercises, gun drill and lectures on ballistics, trajectories and fire power. His evenings were spent reading. He devoured a variety of books, ranging from Plato's *Republic* and Buffon's *Natural History* to historical novels and a book entitled *The Art of Judging Character from Men's Faces.* He recorded his observations on his reading at this time in a notebook. From this we learn that the book which interested him most was a French translation of *A New and Impartial History of England, from the Invasion of Julius Caesar to the Signing of Preliminaries of Peace, 1762,* by John Barrow. The British nation, which was later to prove his most steadfast enemy, already held a peculiar fascination for him.

The earliest known drawing of Napoleon
taken from life, 1785.

In September 1786 Napoleon left his regiment and went home to the island of Corsica where he had been born and brought up. The family home was situated in a narrow street in Ajaccio, the capital of the island. It was a big house, as befitted his parents who were both from ancient and noble families. His father, Carlo Bonaparte, had been a lawyer and administrator but had died in 1785, leaving his wife Letizia with eight young children to look after. Napoleon, now aged seventeen, was the only one of them with a profession and a salary. A profile drawing made of him around this time shows a thoughtful youth with long, straight hair, a strong aquiline nose and firm mouth and chin. Although short in stature he was generally considered handsome and had a confidence and an unflinching gaze which made a lasting impression on those who met him. A lady who met him in Paris a few years later described him as 'Very poor and as proud as a Scot . . . You would never have guessed him to be a soldier; there was nothing dashing about him, no swagger, no bluster, nothing rough.'[5] When Fanny Burney saw him in 1802 she was impressed by the plainness of his dress and thought he had 'far more the air of a student than a warrior'.[6]

It would be ten years before Nelson and Napoleon played any part in the life of the *Bellerophon*. Meanwhile there were two government departments back in London which were instrumental in determining the movements of the ship from the moment the order was placed for her building until the day that she was decommissioned. These departments were the Board of Admiralty and the Navy Board which were responsible for the organisation and management of the navy.[7] Every year Parliament voted sums of money for the maintenance of the ships and dockyards, for the building of new ships, and for the wages of seamen. The government of the day, and in particular the prime minister and the Cabinet, decided naval strategy and policy but it was up to the Admiralty to carry out the decisions and to allocate the money voted by Parliament.

The Admiralty office was an inconspicuous building in Whitehall beside the Horse Guards. It was set around a small, gloomy courtyard and shielded from the clamour of Whitehall by an elegant screen wall designed by Robert Adam. In the high-ceilinged board room, with its Grinling Gibbons carvings, its rolled-up maps on the walls, and its wind indicator linked to a weather vane on the roof, their lordships decided on the movements of fleets, and the appointment and promotion of naval officers. Although the Admiralty Board managed an operation involving hundreds of ships, thousands of men, and naval bases around the world, it was a surprisingly small department. Sitting on the board were six or seven Lords Commissioners of the Admiralty, three or four of whom were usually senior naval officers. They were assisted by the Secretary, a civil servant who occupied a key position in the department. He read all the incoming correspondence, decided which letters should be referred to their lordships, and answered the correspondence on their behalf. From 1763 to 1795 the Secretary was Philip Stephens and it was to him, or to his successor Sir Evan Nepean, that the captains of the *Bellerophon* addressed their letters when reporting the arrival of their ship in port, putting in a request for leave, or recommending an

A view by Rowlandson and Pugin of a meeting in the board room of
the Admiralty office in Whitehall around 1800.

officer for promotion. Behind the scenes in the Admiralty office were some thirty staff which included administrators, clerks, messengers, porters and "1 necessary woman".

The board was headed by the First Lord of the Admiralty who was a member of the Cabinet and was sometimes a senior admiral and sometimes a civilian politician. The most astute and effective civilian First Lord in recent times had been Lord Sandwich, a large, shambling man of great charm who had supported Captain Cook's voyages of exploration, reorganised the dockyards and ensured that the navy recovered from the disasters of the war with America. He had retired in 1782 and had been succeeded briefly by Admiral Keppel and then by Admiral Howe. Howe was a formidable and much-respected admiral but he was more at home on the quarterdeck of a warship than in the corridors of power in Westminster. He had less influence with William Pitt, the Prime Minister, than Charles Middleton who was the Controller of the Navy and the man in charge of the Navy Board.

The Navy Board was answerable to the Board of Admiralty but was responsible for most of the day-to-day business of running the navy, including the maintenance of the ships and buildings, the administration of the dockyards, and the appointment of warrant officers (masters, surgeons, pursers, boatswains, carpenters and cooks). It also supervised the Victualling Board, and the Sick and Hurt Board, and it made agreements with civil contractors for the building of ships. It was the Navy Board which carried on all the correspondence with Edward Greaves, drew up the contract for the building of the *Bellerophon*, and decided on the amount and manner of the payments for the ship, and the date by which the construction must be completed.

When the *Bellerophon* was launched in 1786 the Navy Board was still situated in Seething Lane behind the Tower of London but in 1789 the whole department moved to Somerset House in the Strand. There, in the magnificent new building designed by Sir William Chambers, the Navy Board operated for the next fifty years. The offices overlooked the Thames and were conveniently close to the Admiralty office in Whitehall. Much of the credit for the strength of the British Navy at this time must go to Middleton, who was Controller of the Navy from 1778 to 1792.[8] He had been appointed by Lord Sandwich and proved to be an outstanding administrator. He was priggish and narrow-minded with an arrogant belief in his own abilities and a contempt for the abilities of those around him, including the various First Lords he served under. He was, however, a master of detail and capable of getting through a mountain of work each day. As one of his clerks observed, 'The Comptroller is the most indefatigable and able of any in my time. The load of business he gets through, at the Treasury, at the Admiralty and at his own house is astonishing . . .'[9]

Next in importance to Middleton on the Navy Board were the two Surveyors of the Navy, who were responsible for ship design and building. (Sir Thomas Slade would have attended the meetings of the board in the 1760s.) Other members included the commissioners of the royal dockyards, and the Clerk of the Acts who acted as secretary to the board. The minutes of the meetings of the board and the letters addressed to the commissioners can be seen today in the Public Record Office and they make awesome reading. Middleton himself described the correspondence as 'very voluminous, and the business, from its variety, inexpressibly intricate.'[10] Day after day, with scarcely a pause for Christmas, the board made decisions on every naval matter imaginable: on a given date this might include the building of a 98-gun ship at Woolwich, the construction of a storehouse in the dockyard at Antigua, the despatch of 2,000 hammocks from Deptford to Plymouth, the appointment of a ship's cook to a frigate, and sending a rat-catcher to destroy the rats infesting the ships at Chatham.

In an age when every letter and every order had to be handwritten and then delivered by a messenger on foot, on horseback, or by a sailing vessel for an overseas destination, communications were inevitably slow and unreliable. Moreover the sheer volume of work which faced the members of the Admiralty Board and the Navy Board meant that hasty decisions were often made, and important matters were sometimes overlooked or passed on the nod. And not all Board members were as able or as conscientious as Middleton, who observed that, 'Some members were overloaded with business, while others came and went as best suited their conveniency; and it fell of course to my share to bring things to some conclusion out of this undigested heap, before the day ended, be it right or wrong.'[11] And yet in spite of the difficulty of communications, the ignorance, incompetence and lax attitudes of some Board members, and the inevitable instances of bribery, corruption and nepotism, the system worked remarkably well. It would be tested to its limit during the next thirty years and would prove more than equal to the challenge.

THREE

His Majesty's Dockyard at Chatham

1787–90

For six months after her launch the *Bellerophon* remained out in midstream, moored bow and stern to buoys which were anchored deep in the river bed. On calm days she lay quiet, the wintry sunshine warming her newly laid decks, but when the wind got up she tugged impatiently at her mooring lines as the wind and rain lashed her hull. She was one of a long line of moored vessels which stretched for nearly 5 miles from Rochester Bridge, around the Frindsbury peninsula, past Chatham dockyard and Upnor Castle to Gillingham. It was a formidable sight and a French spy surveying the scene from the tower of Frindsbury church would have gained a great deal of information about the strength of Britain's navy at this time. He would have counted no fewer than sixty-three warships moored out in the river. These included two massive first-rate ships of 100 guns, four second-rate ships of 90 guns, and no fewer than thirty-one third-rates, mostly 74-gun ships like the *Bellerophon*. There were also twenty-one frigates, three fireships, and two armed sloops. All these ships were lying in ordinary; that is to say they were lying in reserve with their upper masts or all their masts and rigging removed until such time as the Navy Board decided to put them back into commission. If the spy had visited the other naval anchorages he would have discovered that out of the total fleet of 308 ships and vessels, Britain had 215 ships lying in ordinary at this time. The 93 ships in commission were either acting as guardships to protect key anchorages or were on patrol around Britain's coasts, or were stationed in Nova Scotia, Newfoundland or the West Indies. Soon all this would change and the ships in ordinary would be hastily fitted out, armed, provisioned and made ready for action.[1]

Meanwhile the scene on the Medway was relatively peaceful. Hay barges, merchant brigs and local fishing boats with worn and patched sails made their way up and down. There was also a regular movement of small boats to and from the warships because every ship in ordinary had a few men on board to keep the bilges pumped out, make running repairs, and ensure that the ship was not vandalised or burgled by local thieves. From the moment of her launch the *Bellerophon* had become a floating home and workplace for half a dozen men, and by the beginning of November she had thirteen men on her books. Some of them camped on board, living in their cramped quarters under the foredeck; some of them lived in lodgings in Chatham or Rochester and came and went each day. These men were the warrant officers and their servants or assistants. Warrant officers were intended to be permanently assigned to the ship (unlike commissioned officers who moved from ship to ship in response to orders from the Admiralty or a senior officer). In normal circumstances they would remain with her whether she was out at sea or laid up in harbour. They included Thomas Watkins the ship's carpenter, Robert Roberts the boatswain, John Hindmarsh the gunner, Aaron Graham the purser, and Michael Hogan the ship's cook. Watkins the carpenter was the highest paid, earning £52 per annum. His servant was Benjamin Watkins, and the presence of another Thomas Watkins, rated as an able seaman, and John Watkins, deputy purser, suggests that the carpenter had managed to secure positions on board for other members of his family.[2]

For five months the *Bellerophon* lay out on the river. Then on 7 March 1787 she was towed downstream and floated into one of the dry docks at Chatham dockyard to have her bottom sheathed with copper. After many experiments with primitive forms of anti-fouling, such as whale oil and resin or a mixture of tar, pitch and sulphur, none of which were very effective, the navy had recently discovered that thin copper plates nailed onto the bottom of a ship discouraged the growth of weed and were extremely effective against the teredo worm which ate into the underwater timbers of ships in tropical waters. This was a major discovery: it meant that ships could stay at sea for longer because they did not have to keep returning to port to have their bottoms cleaned and repaired; it also lessened the pressure on the navy's dry docks which were free to undertake urgent repairs on ships damaged in action or suffering from storm damage. Equally significant was the fact that ships with copper bottoms sailed much faster that those without. So impressive were the results that in 1778 the Admiralty ordered the entire fleet to be coppered and within three years eighty-two ships of the line, and 231 smaller warships, were copper-bottomed. This gave British ships a valuable edge over those of her enemies for several years and it contributed directly to the success of several actions in the West Indies, notably Rodney's victory at the Battle of the Saints in 1782.[3]

The *Bellerophon* was thirteen days in dry dock and during that time some 2,700 rectangular copper sheets were nailed over her underwater planking with copper nails.[4] This was the first of a series of operations carried out at Chatham to prepare the ship for sea and, since the dockyard played a key role in *Bellerophon*'s early life, it is time we had a closer look at this impressive organisation. Chatham dockyard was one of the six royal dockyards in Britain which built, repaired and serviced the ships of the Royal Navy. The others were at Deptford, Woolwich, Sheerness, Portsmouth and Plymouth. Between them these yards built all the navy's first- and second-rate ships, and until the 1750s they also built most of the third- and fourth-rate ships. But then the demands of the Seven Years War and the American War put the royal dockyards under such strain that it became increasingly necessary to contract out the building of new ships to private or merchant yards.[5]

Until the industrial revolution got into its stride, and the factories of the cotton, wool and steel industries were established in the Midlands, the royal dockyards were the biggest and most complex industrial centres in the country. Chatham dockyard covered an area of nearly 70 acres and employed around 1,700 people. It was surrounded by a high brick wall and entered by a formidable gatehouse surmounted by a finely carved and gilded royal coat of arms. The wall was a precaution against sabotage and theft but could not prevent the flagrant thieving by dockyard employees. The local newspaper regularly reported such thefts, and in the week that the *Bellerophon* was launched two men from the yard were publicly whipped in Chatham marketplace for having 'attempted to embezzle his Majesty's stores, and carry them off in a boat'.[6]

Viewed from the wooded hills which rose up behind the dockyard, the whole place had a remarkably orderly appearance. The predominantly redbrick buildings were set out in long lines separated by open spaces like parade grounds on which lay stacks of timber arranged in neat piles. The storehouses, the smithery, the rigging house, the mould loft, the mast house, the ropery, and even the timber seasoning sheds and carpenters' workshops combined Georgian proportions with a strictly functional and workmanlike appearance. The long terrace of officers' houses was as elegantly designed as any terrace in Bloomsbury or Bath. Along the waterfront were four dry docks, and three slips with ships in various stages of construction.

The small army of men and boys who worked within the dockyard walls from 6 in the morning till 6 in the evening included an astonishing variety of trades. There were shipwrights, caulkers, sawyers, sailmakers, riggers, ropemakers, blacksmiths, blockmakers, quarter boys, oakum boys, wheelwrights, house carpenters, masons, joiners, locksmiths, bricklayers and plumbers, as well as clerks, gatekeepers and several hundred unskilled labourers. The man in overall charge of this workforce was Charles Proby, the dockyard Commissioner. If anyone is to be regarded as the godfather of the *Bellerophon* it must surely be Commissioner Proby. Although the autumn gales had caused him to miss her launch, he should have officiated on that occasion, and he was nominally responsible for her when she came into the world. It was Proby and his officers who had recommended to the Navy Board that Edward Greaves should build her at Frindsbury. Throughout the building of the ship, an overseer from Chatham dockyard made regular inspections to ensure that materials and workmanship were up to standard.[7] And it was Proby who was ultimately responsible for the men who fitted out the ship after her launch.

Like most dockyard commissioners, Charles Proby was a former naval captain. When the *Bellerophon* was launched in 1786 he had been the Commissioner at Chatham for fifteen years. Now aged sixty-one, and recently widowed, he divided his time between running the dock-yard and worrying about his six children, particularly his four teenage daughters.[8] His duties as Commissioner were not unduly demanding. The day-to-day running of the dockyard was in the hands of his senior officers. The most important of these was Nicholas Phillips, the capable and experienced Master Shipwright who was in charge of shipbuilding and ship repairs. The finance and much of the administration of the dockyard was handled by the Clerk of the Cheque, the Clerk of the Survey and the Storekeeper. In addition there was the Master Attendant who was responsible for all the ships laid up in ordinary as well as for navigation, moorings and pilotage on the river. Proby headed up this team and reported to the Navy Board in London, sometimes attending the board's meetings but mostly keeping in touch by corre-spondence. For this he was paid an annual salary of £500 (plus £12 for paper and firewood). This was modest compared with the £1,866 earned by a full admiral but was considerably more than the £364 earned by the captain of a first-rate or the £200 per annum earned by the master shipwright and other senior officers in the dockyard. It was a fortune compared with the £80 earned by the yard's boatswain or the £12.7s. which was the annual pay of an ordinary seaman.

Apart from having the use of the *Chatham* yacht and a longboat with a crew of oarsmen to take him up and down the river, the biggest perk of the job was undoubtedly the house. This was a handsome Queen Anne building with an impressive staircase and entrance hall dominated by a spectacular painted ceiling. From the front of the house the grey waters of the Medway could be glimpsed between the towering hulls of ships under construction. The back of the house looked out onto a charming walled garden with terraces, a kitchen garden and an orchard. It was an ideal house in which to bring up a large family. Proby had married Sarah Pownoll in 1758 when she was a pretty seventeen-year-old and he was a 33-year-old captain. During the space of ten years Sarah and Charles Proby had seven children. When Sarah died after a short illness in 1785 Commissioner Proby was devastated. He asked the Admiralty to grant him six weeks leave of absence because 'The recent loss I have sustained by the death of Mrs Proby has had such an effect upon my mind, as to make it impractical for me to give the necessary attention to the public business at this port.'9

Proby's four daughters were aged between nine and sixteen when their mother died. Unlike the boys, who were sent away to boarding school, the girls were educated by private tutors but Proby does not seem to have stinted on this and was determined they should have the best teachers available. He was, however, extremely strict about their attending dances. Their visits to the assembly rooms in Rochester were limited to three visits before Christmas and two after. 'The going more frequently and all times during the season would have been, in my opinion, not only totally unnecessary but also calculated to have introduced them into the mania of Dissipation, so destructive of all Domestic Cares and Duties, Virtue in all its species.'

While Commissioner Proby worried about his daughters' upbringing, events were taking place across the English Channel which would shake the foundations of social order in Europe. The French Revolution began with a few local riots but gathered pace with alarming speed. The winter of 1788–9 had been unusually hard: the Seine and many other French rivers had frozen, trade had been disrupted, and cattle and sheep had died in large numbers. The price of bread and meat rose sharply and led to violent protests in a number of towns and villages. The sharp difference between the wealth of the aristocracy and the abject poverty of the working classes fuelled the mood of unrest. But it was the imposition of new taxes which started the chain reaction leading to the summer of revolution. The French intervention in the American Revolutionary war had been successful in political terms but extremely costly in financial terms and it became necessary to impose additional taxes to replenish the depleted French Treasury. In May 1789 the Estates General was summoned for the first time for 150 years in order to obtain nationwide support for the taxes. The bourgeois Third Estate used the opportunity to establish a National Assembly that was more representative of the people. This move towards a more democratic government seemed admirable to many observers in Britain until violence on an unprecedented scale broke out in Paris.

On the morning of Monday 14 July 1789 the soldiers encamped on the Champ de Mars were persuaded to join a large group of Parisians who were intent on protest. Together they marched on the Hôtel des Invalides, seized the guns and ammunition and then stormed the Bastille and released all the political prisoners. The governor of the Bastille and the commandant of the garrison were led through the streets to the place of public executions where they were beheaded. Their heads were stuck on tent-poles and paraded in triumph to the Palais Royal. The mob then attacked the Hôtel de Ville, stabbed and beheaded the mayor of Paris, and hanged the lieutenant of police from a lamp post. During the next few days the revolution spread across the city and into the countryside. Several prominent noblemen were imprisoned and their houses looted. Government grain stores were plundered, and the roads became unsafe because travellers were attacked by thieves and deserters who had been freed from the public prisons.

English observers were divided in their opinions on the gathering revolution. Charles James Fox, a former Foreign Secretary, and an outspoken champion of liberal causes, considered the storming of the Bastille to be the greatest and best event in the history of the world. Edmund Burke, a politician noted for his oratory and his uncompromising views, warned of the terrible consequences. Speaking in the House of Commons, he said that the French people 'had erected a bloody democracy in the room of order, tranquillity and peace', and in 1790 he published his *Reflections on the French Revolution*, an eloquent treatise in which he argued that the events in Paris would lead to war, tyranny and the destruction of human rights. For many months his was a minority opinion. The immediate reaction of many British people was actually one of relief because they believed that the turmoil in France must reduce the ever-present threat which France posed to Britain. In 1790 France had a population of more than 25 million and the largest army in Christendom, while Britain had a population of barely 8 million and a relatively small army. Only the English Channel separated the two old enemies and on a fine day the cliffs of Dover were clearly visible from Calais.

The navy was Britain's only effective defence against invasion and this largely determined British naval strategy in the eighteenth century.[10] It was to guard against invasion that the bulk of Britain's fleet was kept in home waters, and the Channel Squadron was established to patrol the western approaches of the English Channel. Neither France nor Spain had a naval base in the Channel. The principal French naval ports were at Brest, Rochefort and Toulon, and the Spanish fleet was divided between the bases at Cadiz, Ferrol and Cartagena. So even if an invasion force was assembled in the Netherlands, or in one of the French ports in Normandy, the fleet of warships to protect the crossing must sail up the Channel from the west, just as the Spanish Armada had done in 1588. Since most of Britain's trade also came up the Channel, the patrolling warships of the Channel Squadron could also protect the incoming and outgoing convoys of merchant ships.

In peacetime most of the fleet was kept in reserve in anchorages at Plymouth, Portsmouth and the Medway, ready to be mobilised if the need should arise. In 1790 a minor incident on the other side of the world led to just such a mobilisation. This meant that when the French Revolution spawned the war which Edmund Burke had foretold, Britain was in an unusual state of readiness. The minor incident was the Nootka Sound crisis. It scarcely appears in the history books but it was directly responsible for the *Bellerophon* being fitted out and sent to sea. In 1788 the British East India Company had established a trading post in Nootka Sound, a sheltered anchorage on the western coast of Vancouver Island. Captain Cook had charted this stretch of the Canadian coast ten years years before during the third of his great voyages of exploration and had repaired his ships in Nootka Sound, making use of the pine trees along the shore for much-needed masts and spars. When Spain got news of the British trading settlement she invoked the 1494 Treaty of Tordesillas under which the Spanish Crown laid claim to the entire Pacific coast of the American continent. She backed this up by sending two warships from Mexico. They seized the crews of the three British merchant ships anchored in the Sound and sent the men to Mexico as prisoners in irons.

News of this reached England on 4 May 1790 and caused outrage. Members of Parliament were united in their condemnation of an act which was considered an attack on Britain's commercial rights and an insult to the British flag. The Admiralty moved with astonishing speed to mobilise the navy. Press warrants were issued and within two days press gangs were at work around the coast. On 6 May every merchant ship on the Thames from London to Gravesend was stripped of her crew, an operation which secured some 2,000 experienced seamen in the space of four hours. There was also what was described as 'a very hot press' in Portsmouth, Gosport, Southampton and the other south coast ports which rounded up several hundred more seamen. The Navy Board ordered the dockyards to put ships back in commission and to work overtime to achieve this. A powerful naval squadron under the command of Admiral Lord Howe was ordered to assemble at Spithead with the aim of enforcing the right of free trade in the Pacific Northwest.

On 11 May a messenger arrived at Chatham with orders for Commissioner Proby to fit for sea the 98-gun *London*, and the 74-gun ships *Vengeance*, *Marlborough* and *Monarch*. To this end he was instructed to employ the workers in the dockyard 'all the extra they can perform by daylight, morning and evening'. In the weeks that followed, further orders were received in Chatham. As the shipwrights and riggers went about their work, the ships moored in the Medway were transformed from empty hulks to fully rigged and armed warships. By the middle of June the harbours at Portsmouth and Plymouth, and the anchorages in the Downs and the Nore, were filling up with ships of the line and frigates under sailing orders.

The *Bellerophon* had to wait her turn. The weeks went by and other ships had their masts stepped, their rigging set up and their guns lifted aboard, before departing to join the fleet assembling downstream at the Nore. Then on Monday 19 July the first of the fourteen men who would command the *Bellerophon* during the course of her life was rowed out to the ship. His name was Thomas Pasley and he was aged fifty-two (considerably older than any of the other captains who would succeed him). For the past three years he had been commander-in-chief of the ships in the Medway with the title of commodore. And, until his appointment to the *Bellerophon*, he had been in command of the 60-gun *Scipio*, the guardship on the Medway.

Thomas Pasley was a Scotsman and a veteran seaman who had served on ships in the West Indies, on the Guinea coast of Africa, and on the Newfoundland station. He had been present at several minor engagements during the Seven Years War but had yet to take part in a major fleet action.[11] In 1774 he had married Mary Heywood, daughter of the Chief Justice of the Isle of Man. He later described her as 'my beloved Mary, my wife, friend, and companion'. They had two daughters to whom he was devoted. For several years he kept a personal journal recording his daily experiences as a captain in command of frigates, and his writings reveal a man of intelligence and sensibility. He was strict but fair with his crew, and seems to have inspired their loyalty and trust. Contemporary observations on his character stress his warmth and his 'unbounded benevolence' and this is borne out in the portrait by Sir William Beechey which shows a man with a strong but kindly face.

When he stepped onto the newly laid planks of the *Bellerophon*'s deck he noted that the ship was far from ready for sea. Shipwrights and carpenters from Chatham dockyard were still working below deck. The masts were in place but a gang of riggers was at work, some of them high up the masts and others on deck, heaving the hemp rope into place and constructing the elaborate network of standing rigging which would take the strain of the wind in the sails when the ship left her anchorage.

An anonymous watercolour showing the captain's
cabin at the stern of a ship.

After inspecting the ship from stem to stern, the captain made his way to the great cabin. Like everywhere else on the ship it had a low ceiling but the generously proportioned stern windows filled the room with sunlight, and additional light was reflected off the shimmering surface of the river onto the fresh white paint of the ceiling. The captain seated himself at the mahogany table which had been brought over from the *Scipio* and opened the neatly ruled pages of the ship's log-book. As was customary he made a note of the weather, which was moderate and clear with a wind from the west, and he also noted that Mr Malcolm, the third lieutenant, had come on board. He then settled down to write a series of letters to Philip Stephens, Secretary to the Admiralty, asking him to persuade their lordships to transfer various key members of his former ship to the *Bellerophon*. The letters were short and to the point:

Sir,

Understanding that the proper carpenter of His Majesty's ship Bellerophon under my command is appointed carpenter of the Canada; I beg you will be pleased to move their Lordships to appoint Mr Brooks the present carpenter of the Scipio to the Bellerophon in his place.

I have the honour to be your obedient servant,

Thomas Pasley.

Two weeks later the riggers and shipwrights had finished their work, seven massive anchor cables had been hoisted aboard, the boatswain's and carpenter's stores had been stowed in their proper places, and the lower deck guns and gun carriages had been lifted from a barge alongside, brought on board through the gun ports and made fast. Meanwhile provisions were coming on board in ever-increasing quantities. On one day William Lloyd, the ship's master, recorded the delivery of ten bags of bread, ten hogsheads of beer, one barrel of salted beef and one of pork, 134 pounds of fresh beef, one hogshead of peas and another of oatmeal, one firkin of butter, one barrel of cheese and twenty-seven barrels of water.

By mid-August four of the ship's five lieutenants had reported for duty. The carpenter, the boatswain and twenty seamen from the *Scipio* had joined the crew, as well as seven boys from the Marine Society. But the captain needed at least fifty more men before he could take the ship to sea, and many more than that before he could take her into action. The official complement of the *Bellerophon* was 550 which meant that Captain Pasley had to spend much of his time trying to persuade the Admiralty to give him sailors from other ships in the Medway. He managed to get hold of sixty-seven men from HMS. *Sandwich* and then he resorted to the press gang.

Press gangs have acquired a notorious reputation and have become as closely identified with the darker side of the eighteenth-century navy as flogging, sodomy and hangings from the yard-arm. Unlike hangings which were rare, and sodomy which was no more common in the navy than it was among the civilian population, the press gangs which forcibly recruited men to serve on warships were only too active around the coasts of Britain, particularly during the war against Revolutionary France. The system had been in operation since Tudor times and took several different forms. The first was a land-based operation which was run by the Impress Service. By 1795 the service had eighty-five gangs which were based in seaports around the coasts of Britain. There were thirty-two regulating captains, each in charge of a district; and under them they had lieutenants who led the gangs as they searched the ports and surrounding areas for suitable recruits. Popular ballads and prints highlighted the fate of young men from farms and country villages who were dragged away from their wives and sweethearts by the press gangs but, although such incidents did occur, the primary aim of the Impress Service was to find experienced seamen. In each district a rendezvous was established (usually a tavern frequented by sailors) where volunteers could be enlisted and where pressed men were confined until they could be despatched under armed guard to the fleet. In London there was a rendezvous on Tower Hill and another at St Katharine's by the Tower, both of them conveniently placed for recruiting seamen from the hundreds of ships in the Pool of London.

The second method of recruiting was to intercept incoming merchant ships. Sometimes this was carried out by a warship coming alongside a merchant ship as she approached a port. On other occasions a naval party would be sent out by a captain in one of the ship's boats. Sometimes the navy hired tenders for the purpose: these were usually brigs or sloops manned by a naval officer and a crew of armed seamen. The legal basis of a system which was universally hated and involved the kidnapping and forcible abduction of hundreds of merchant seamen and fishermen had occasionally been challenged in the courts. The conclusion of the judges was that 'the power of pressing is founded on immemorial usage, allowed for ages,' and that 'His Majesty . . . has a right to demand the service of these people whenever the public safety calls for it.'[12] So in times of war every captain was issued with press warrants. These were printed forms, signed by the Lords of the Admiralty, which began: 'We do hereby Impower and Direct you to impress or cause to be impressed so many Seamen, Seafaring Men and Persons whose Occupations and Callings are to work in Vessels and Boats upon Rivers, as shall be necessary either to Man His Majesty's Ship under your Command or any other of His Majesty's Ships, giving unto each Man so impressed One Shilling for Prest Money.'[13]

Few naval officers were in favour of impressment and it was generally reckoned that one volunteer was worth three men who had been pressed into the navy. Nevertheless most captains had to resort to the press gangs to make up the necessary numbers and the system undoubtedly produced results. Captain Pasley managed to get hold of fifty-two men from the rendezvous at Tower Hill. Two dozen merchant seamen were impressed from West Indiamen in the Thames Estuary, and a party of seamen sent ashore at Sheerness rounded up another dozen unwilling recruits. By the middle of August the *Bellerophon* was ready to sail.

High tide on 16 August was early in the morning. As the tide began to turn, Captain Pasley gave the order to get under way. A slip-rope which led from the ship to the ring of the mooring buoy was let go and the foretopmen, perched perilously high up on the yards of the foremast, let loose the topsail. The fresh easterly breeze filled the sail and the *Bellerophon* slowly began to gather way. The bellowed orders of the ship's officers carried across the water to the dockyard but her departure was scarcely noticed among the constant activity out on the river. The comings and goings of warships were as familiar a sight to the workers in the dockyard then as the comings and goings of buses would be nowadays to workers on a building site in central London. However, Commissioner Proby was informed of the ship's departure and later that day he sent a letter to the Admiralty informing their lordships that His Majesty's ship *Bellerophon* had this day sailed to join the fleet at the Nore.

FOUR

Preparations for War

1790–4

On 31 August 1790 the *Bellerophon* sailed out of the Thames Estuary, rounded the North Foreland, sailed past Ramsgate and the chalk cliffs lining the great sweep of Pegwell Bay and Sandwich Bay, and headed for the Downs. There, in the sheltered waters off Deal, she rounded up into the wind, dropped anchor and fired a 13-gun salute to the admiral of the fleet of warships gathered in the anchorage. For three years she had been part of a fleet in mothballs, a hulk without masts and guns: one ship in a line of thirty or forty similar hulks, rising and falling with the tide on the River Medway. Now for the first time she joined the fleet as an armed and operational ship of the line. For the next month she was part of the extraordinary activity which took place whenever a fleet was gathered in the Downs.

It is hard for us to picture the scene which would have greeted an onlooker on the beach at Deal in those days. When the steamships came along in the nineteenth century the Downs lost the key role which it had played for centuries in the lives of seamen sailing up and down the English Channel. Today the once famous anchorage has no significance for the crews of the container ships and bulk carriers passing through the Dover Straits, or for the thousands of passengers on the cross-Channel ferries from Dover and Ramsgate. And yet in the eighteenth century and the first half of the nineteenth century it was not unusual for several hundred ships to be gathered in the Downs, waiting for favourable winds to take them down the English Channel or up around the North Foreland and into the Thames Estuary. A first glance at a chart of the area suggests that it is an unlikely place to choose as an anchorage. The shore is bleak and exposed with no coves to provide sheltered landing places for boats. The shingle beach shelves steeply into deep water and boats have to be launched and landed through the surf. And 4 miles offshore lie the Goodwin Sands, notorious as one of the greatest hazards to shipping in the world. But although the Goodwin Sands were, and are, a graveyard of ships they also provided shelter from easterly and south-easterly winds for ships anchored in the Downs; while the white cliffs of the South Foreland and the angle of the coast at this point provided shelter from the full blast of south-westerly gales. So for weeks at a time the water-front at Deal, and the anchorage beyond, were as busy as the Pool of London. Ships of all sizes and many nationalities waited there for fair winds. Anchored among the fishing boats and the merchantmen were the warships, easily distinguished by their flags and pennants streaming in the wind, and the constant booming of their guns. During the three weeks that the *Bellerophon* was anchored in the Downs she fired a 19-gun salute for the anniversary of the King's accession, she fired her guns to salute the comings and goings of admirals, she fired guns to draw attention to various signals, and she devoted one whole morning to gunnery practice, 'exercising the great guns'.

In addition to the forest of vessels anchored offshore there was a constant coming and going of small craft: bumboats filled to the gunwales with baskets of bread, fish, fruit and vegetables for the warships and Indiamen; naval longboats weighed down with barrels of water, rum and beef; gigs ferrying naval officers from ship to shore; local boats taking pilots out to the ships; and fishing boats being hauled up the beach with the aid of capstans. The *Bellerophon* spent a busy three weeks anchored amidst this bustle of activity. She took in water and provisions, had her sides painted, sent a press gang to take hands off some West Indiamen, and on 25 September set sail down the Channel to Portsmouth. Two days later she dropped anchor at Spithead, the fleet anchorage in the Solent, opposite the entrance to Portsmouth harbour. There were warships everywhere, their commanders awaiting orders to put to sea. For the next two months the crew of the *Bellerophon* passed the time blacking and tarring the rigging, painting the gun carriages, stowing ballast, and getting drunk. Pasley punished several seamen with two dozen lashes for drunkenness, neglect of duty and theft. And early one morning William Knight, an able seaman, fell into the harbour from the jib boom and was drowned.

By the end of October 1790 it was clear that the threatened conflict with Spain was not going to happen. Britain's warlike preparations had made a considerable impression on the Spanish. An agreement was reached in which Spain abandoned her claims to exclusive trading rights to the north-western coast of America and she also agreed to pay reparations for the damage inflicted on the British ships. On 21 November the *Bellerophon*, in company with five other ships of the line, was sent back to Sheerness. A year later she was back on her moorings in Chatham. Her crew were paid off, her masts were taken out, her guns removed, and she resumed her place in the long line of decommissioned ships on the Medway, waiting for the next call to arms.

Meanwhile events in France were leading up to a war which would involve most of the countries of western Europe and pose the very real threat of an invasion of England. The Paris mob had became so threatening that in June 1791 King Louis XVI attempted to escape and go into exile but the coach in which he was travelling was stopped and he was sent back to Paris, a virtual prisoner. Concerned for the safety of Marie Antoinette, the king's Austrian wife, and under pressure from French emigrés to provide support for royal government in France, the Emperor of Austria entered into an alliance with the King of Prussia. This was seen by the revolutionaries in Paris as a threat against the people of France. In February 1792 the National Assembly declared war on Austria and Prussia. The French army was under-financed and most of its aristocratic officers had emigrated so it was no surprise that it was defeated in its first clash with the Austrian army. However the revolutionary ardour and patriotism of the people's army proved an overwhelming force and on 20 September 1792 the French defeated a Prussian army at Valmy, pushed them back across the Rhine and occupied Brussels.

Britain watched the movements of the French army with growing concern but it was the execution of the French king which led politicians and political commentators to realise that war with France was inevitable. Louis XVI was executed on the morning of Monday 21 January 1793 but it was four days before the news reached London. On 25 January *The Times* printed a detailed report describing the King's last hours. He had taken an affectionate farewell of his family at 6 am and had been driven through the hushed streets of Paris in the mayor's carriage to La Place de Révolution. The guillotine had been set up beside the pedestal which had formerly supported the statue of his grandfather. Dressed in a brown greatcoat, white waistcoat and black breeches, he mounted the scaffold with composure, attended by an Irish priest as his confessor. His attempt to address the crowds was drowned by the beating of hundreds of drums from the massed ranks of the soldiers surrounding the guillotine. The executioner laid hold of him and at a quarter past ten the blade came down. When his severed head was held up by the executioner the people threw their hats in the air and let out a great shout of 'Vive la Nation!'

Fanny Burney was living at Norbury Park, near Box Hill, when she heard the news. She was so devastated that for some days she lost any desire to read, write or even go walking. 'The dreadful tragedy in France has entirely absorbed me,' she told her father, 'Except the period of the illness of our own inestimable King, I have never been so overcome with grief and dismay for any but personal and family calamities. O what a tragedy! how implacable its villany, and how severe its sorrows!'[1]

Within two days of receiving the news in London the French ambassador was ordered to 'quit this kingdom before the first of February next, on account of the atrocious act lately perpetrated at Paris.'[2] And by the end of the first week of February the British government was informed that France had declared war on England and Holland. The Nootka Sound crisis and the threat of war with Spain had served as a useful dress-rehearsal for the Royal Navy, and the preparations for war against France followed similar lines. The Board of Admiralty sent off press warrants to the mayors and chief magistrates of the cities, boroughs and towns of England and Wales. Once again the press gangs went into action on the Thames and on the night of 4 March all homeward- and outward-bound merchant ships were stripped of their crews. Within a few days three tenders full of men were despatched from the rendezvous on Tower Hill to HMS. *Sandwich*, the guardship at the Nore.[3] Similar operations took place in Portsmouth and Plymouth. But the forcible recruitment of seamen did not go smoothly everywhere. In Newcastle and Sunderland the sailors kept together in large groups, and success-fully beat off the press gangs. They made it clear that they were refusing to enter His Majesty's service without an increase in the current rate of pay. The scandalously low pay of seamen was a source of much resentment in the navy and would eventually lead to mutinies throughout the fleet in 1797.

Along with the recruitment of seamen the Admiralty issued orders for ships in ordinary to be put back into commission. On 16 March, barely two weeks after the declaration of war, Captain Pasley climbed aboard the *Bellerophon* and commissioned the ship. It was a crisp spring day with a fresh breeze blowing across the river. There were some workmen from the dockyard on board and by the end of the day they were joined by a handful of seamen and several officers. More men continued to arrive during the next few days, some of them pressed men, some of them volunteers, and they were all set to work cleaning the ship and putting her back into working order.

On 25 March the ship was hauled alongside one of the two sheer hulks permanently stationed at Chatham. These were old warships which had been converted into floating cranes. With the aid of a capstan on the deck of the sheer hulk, and the combined muscle power of two or three dozen seamen and dockworkers, the three great masts and the bowsprit were lifted aboard and lowered into place. Over the next few days a team of riggers from the dockyard set up the standing rigging for the lower masts, and then helped the crew to raise the topmasts. Nearly 300 tons of iron and shingle ballast was heaved aboard, followed by a constant stream of provisions. On 26 April the *Bellerophon* sailed down the river to Blackstakes where the seventy-four guns were swung aboard, and secured on their carriages. The ship then sailed downstream to the anchorage at the Nore where she stayed for the next month. She was now ready for sea but was still short of seamen. Twenty-three of the pressed men rounded up on the Thames and held aboard HMS. *Sandwich* joined the crew on 14 May and, in an effort to get hold of more sailors, Pasley sent out the *Bellerophon's* boats with an officer and a gang of sailors to round up a few more men. At last on 13 June she

An engraving by E. W. Cooke of a sheer hulk which was a floating
crane used for hoisting masts in and out of ships.

left the mouth of the Medway and sailed around the North Foreland and down the Channel to Portsmouth where she joined a great gathering of warships.

The fleet gathered in the anchorage at Spithead that summer was formidable and included the combined might of Britain's navy. Many of the ships present would become household names in the coming conflict. The first to depart were the ships of the Mediterranean fleet, under the command of Vice-Admiral Lord Hood[4] in the *Victory*, which set sail down the Channel heading for Gibraltar and Toulon. They were followed a few days later by a squadron of seven warships which headed out across the Atlantic with orders to safeguard British possessions in the West Indies. And on 14 July the Channel fleet, under the command of Admiral Lord Howe, weighed anchor and set sail. There were fifteen ships of the line, including the *Bellerophon*, seven frigates and a fireship. Their orders were to destroy the French fleet from Brest which had left harbour and was believed to be cruising off Belle Isle.

On this, her first cruise outside home waters, the *Bellerophon* got no further than the seas to the south-west of the Scilly Isles. On 18 July the fleet was sailing in line ahead when the wind suddenly shifted and rose to gale force. The *Majestic*, which was sailing immediately ahead of the *Bellerophon*, with sails flapping and thundering in the wind, was driven across the bows of the *Bellerophon*. Captain Pasley described what happened next:

> At half-past three I was called in a great hurry and told the *Majestic* would be aboard of us. I ran out and found it was only too true, and past remedy. She came down on us in the act of wearing and ran over our bowsprit, which she carried away, with the head and stem. There being a good deal of sea, the foremast soon followed, carrying away with it the main topmast and main yard, with a dreadful crash. Not one life was lost nor man hurt, thanks to God.

Although the structural damage to the hull was limited to the smashing of the figurehead and cutwater, the ship was crippled by the loss of the bowsprit, foremast and main topmast and Pasley had no option but to return to England for repairs. The *Bellerophon* was taken in tow by the *Ramillies* and headed for Plymouth. In the years to come, the morale and fighting spirit of the *Bellerophon*'s crew became legendary and we get a glimpse of this spirit in their reaction to the collision. Although the crew were new and had only brief experience of working together, they managed to clear up the wreckage on deck, and within twenty-four hours they erected such an effective jury rig that they outsailed the *Ramillies* and were able to cast off the towing line. They sailed back to Plymouth unassisted and were soon alongside the sheer hulk where the ship was examined by officers from the royal dockyard. The damaged rigging was replaced, the topmasts set up again, and repairs were carried out to the ship's head.

Five weeks after the collision the *Bellerophon* was back with Howe's fleet patrolling the seas off the west coast of Brittany. She had not missed any action. The French fleet had retreated back into the great harbour at Brest, protected by the forts at the harbour entrance. There was nothing that Howe and his ships could do but watch and wait. It was the Mediterranean fleet, commanded by Lord Hood, which was the first to go into action against the forces of Revolutionary France. By chance both Napoleon and Nelson were directly involved in the consequences of this action.

Toulon, the principal French naval base in the Mediterranean, was a fortified town of 28,000 inhabitants. In the summer of 1793 the local people, sickened by the execution of the King and the rising tide of terror, threw out the Jacobins who had been running the town. They believed that the restoration of the French monarchy was the only hope for France and on 27 August they raised a white flag spangled with fleur-de-lis over the town and proclaimed the young Louis XVII as their king. When the Revolutionary government in Paris sent an army to restore control, the people of Toulon looked to the old enemies of France for help and opened the port to British and Spanish troops and ships. (Britain and Spain had patched up their differences following the Nootka Sound crisis.) Lord Hood sailed his fleet into the harbour and landed two regiments of British infantry and 200 marines. The Spanish sent an army across the frontier to defend the landward side of the town.

Nelson had joined Hood's Mediterranean fleet a few weeks before.

Like so many British naval officers he had been on half pay and without a ship for several years while the nation was at peace. He had spent much of this time staying at his father's country rectory in Norfolk. It should have been an idyllic interlude but he was impatient to get back to sea, and his wife Fanny felt cold and isolated after the tropical heat and social life which she had enjoyed in the West Indies. In January 1793, shortly before King Louis was sent to the guillotine, Nelson was given command of the 64-gun ship *Agamemnon*, the ship in which he would first make his name. Hood sent him to Naples to persuade the King of Naples and Sicily to send reinforcements to assist in the defence of Toulon against the advancing Revolutionary army. Nelson secured a promise that 2,000 troops would be immediately despatched to Toulon. He also struck up a warm friendship with the British envoy Sir William Hamilton and his wife Emma, Lady Hamilton. They invited him to stay with them at their house, a former palace on high ground overlooking the bay, its sunny rooms filled with fine paintings, exquisite statues and the Greek vases which were Sir William's passion. Nelson was charmed by them both and, although he must have been aware of Emma's colourful past, he wrote and told Fanny that 'She is a young woman of amiable manners and who does honour to the station to which she is raised.' He was entertaining them on board the *Agamemnon* when he received news that a French warship with a captured British merchantman was at anchor off Sardinia. 'I considered that the city of Naples looked to what an English man-of-war would do. I ordered my barge to be manned, sent the ladies ashore and in two hours my ship was under sail.'

There was no sign of the French warship off Sardinia so Nelson headed back to Toulon. When he arrived in the harbour on 5 October he found the British fleet under heavy bombardment. Directing the guns from the ramparts overlooking the harbour was the 24-year-old artillery officer Napoleon Bonaparte, now a major and soon to be promoted to brigadier-general. It was the only occasion that the two men, who were to play such a significant role in history, were ever in sight of each other. As far as Napoleon was concerned the sails of the *Agamemnon* were just another target for his guns, and Nelson had no idea who was organising the bombardment. 'Shot and shells are throwing about us every hour,' he wrote but he did not have to endure the shelling for long because within a week he was despatched to Sardinia and was soon in action against a squadron of French frigates.

Although Napoleon was not in command of the French forces at Toulon, his actions were largely responsible for the recapture of the city. Earlier in the year a civil war on the island of Corsica had resulted in the Bonaparte properties being ransacked and the family being declared outlaws. Napoleon rescued his family and took them first to Toulon and then settled them in Marseilles. He was therefore close at hand when the British and Spanish entered Toulon. He immediately made himself available to the commander of the French Revolutionary forces and was given a free hand to organise the artillery. He was aware that this was his big chance. He sent men to get guns from the forts at Monaco and Antibes, he brought in 100,000 sacks of earth on wagons from Marseilles to build parapets, and he organised an arsenal of eighty forges. The guns were set up behind the new defences which he built along the waterfront and he directed a continuous and devastating bombardment at the British ships in the harbour.

The chaotic conditions in the Revolutionary army led to the coming and going of several commanders until on 17 November an experienced and professional soldier, General Dugommier, arrived to take charge. Napoleon persuaded him to adopt a plan of attack which involved the capture of a key fort on high ground overlooking the harbour. The attack took place on 17 December in driving rain. While Napoleon's guns battered the fort, Dugommier led the first charge on the ramparts but he was repulsed. Napoleon, mounted on horseback, led the second charge of 2,000 troops. When his horse was shot under him he continued on foot, detached a battalion of light infantry to launch a flanking attack at the same time as his own, and succeeded in getting his men into the fort. After two hours of hand-to-hand fighting the fort surrendered. Napoleon was badly wounded by an English sergeant who thrust his pike deep into his left thigh, and he was lucky that the army surgeon who treated him decided not to amputate his leg.

As Napoleon had foreseen, the capture of the fort made the position of the British fleet untenable and Hood was forced to organise an immediate withdrawal. He set fire to the arsenal, burned nine of the French warships on their moorings, and under cover of darkness he embarked the allied troops and slipped out to sea, taking with him several French ships as prizes. However, he left behind eighteen French ships of the line, enough to provide the navy of the French Revolution with a powerful Mediterranean fleet. These were the ships which Nelson, leading a fleet which included the *Bellerophon*, would attack at the mouth of the Nile in five years' time.

While Admiral Lord Hood's fleet was in action at Toulon, Lord Howe's fleet continued to patrol the western approaches of the English Channel. During the course of two September cruises to Ushant and back, Lord Howe decided to race all his ships under full sail. This was a useful exercise which would enable him to group them according to their relative speeds when he took them into battle. The result was a triumph for the *Bellerophon*. As they passed Bolt Head on the Devon coast on 4 September, Howe made the signal 'for the fleet to take stations as most convenient'. The *Bellerophon* came up with and passed most of the ships with all sail set. The ships were then ordered to head for Torbay. Pasley piled on all sail, including the topgallant studding sails, and noted that even in the light breeze then prevailing the ship achieved a speed of 10 knots. On the second cruise the speed of the *Bellerophon* was proved beyond all doubt. As they headed back from Ushant at the end of September, Lord Howe again made the signal for each ship to make the best of her way into Torbay. The *Bellerophon's* log recorded the result: 'Set all sail, passed all the ships and about 5 was anchored in the Bay and all sails handed before any of the rest got a berth.'[5]

For the *Bellerophon* to outsail the entire fleet including the frigates was a considerable achievement and reflected well not only on her commander and crew but also on Edward Greaves who built her and on Sir Thomas Slade her designer. She now acquired the name 'The Flying Bellerophon' although no doubt the sailors continued to refer to her as plain 'Billy Ruff'n'. In fact we know the exact speed of the ship on all points of sailing because two of the reports on her sailing qualities have been preserved. These reports were printed forms which the captains completed at various intervals during the life of a ship. The forms consisted of a series of questions which covered the performance of the ship on different points of sailing and under various conditions of wind and weather, her draught before and after being loaded with stores for foreign service, and such details as the height of her lowest gunport above the surface of the water.

The first report on the *Bellerophon* was completed by Captain Darby in April 1800, fourteen years after her launch. From this we learn that her top speed was 12 knots which she achieved when running before the wind. 'With the wind two points abaft the beam and a stiff gale she will run 11 knots, with the wind on the beam, 10 knots, one point before the beam 9 knots, and close to the wind with a head sea 5 knots.'[6] Such speeds were not so remarkable for a vessel with a length on the waterline of 168 feet, and are put in the shade by the performance of the clipper ships in the second half of the nineteenth century which could achieve speeds of 15 or 16 knots for days on end, but of course the *Bellerophon*, like her fellow ships of the line, was not built primarily for speed but as a gun platform for 74 guns and as a bulk carrier for ammunition and water and provisions for 550 sailors and marines. In a second report on her sailing qualities completed by Captain Halsted in 1811 the *Bellerophon* was still achieving top speeds of 12 knots and in answer to the question of how her rate of sailing compared with other ships the answer was 'In general superior.'[7] Both reports commended her on being well built, and very weatherly. She steered very well, and in the trough of the sea 'she rolls deep but very easy'.

After the first race back to Torbay Lord Howe created a flying squadron of the fastest ships in the fleet and put Pasley in command of the squadron with the position of commodore. This gave an experienced or talented captain a temporary command over other captains in the squadron, even if they were his seniors. Pasley had held it once before when in command of the ships in the Medway. On that occasion he commanded the *Bellerophon* himself and drew no extra pay, but he was now given a captain under him to command the ship while he took command of the squadron. He was able to draw the pay and wear the uniform of a rear-admiral, and to fly a broad pennant on his ship which, according to the ship's log, was first hoisted on 11 September.

The man who became Captain of the *Bellerophon* under Commodore Pasley was William Johnstone Hope, a 28-year-old Londoner.[8] He had joined the navy at the age of ten, had served on a frigate under Prince William Henry (the future King William IV) and on the *Boreas* under Nelson. In 1790 he was given his first independent command, the *Rattler*, a sloop, and this was followed by command of a frigate and then a fireship. He was advanced to the rank of post-captain on 9 January 1794 and given command of the *Bellerophon*. Captain Hope and Commodore Pasley both arrived at Portsmouth early on the morning of 16 January 1794. Pasley had been away on leave, visiting his wife and two daughters in Winchester. It was a fine but cold winter's day with a light breeze. They were rowed out across the choppy waters of the anchorage to the *Bellerophon* and as they stepped onto the deck of the ship they were welcomed by the salutes of the ship's officers, the shrill whistles of the bosun's pipes, and the stamping feet of the line of red-coated marines as they presented arms. Back at his desk in the great cabin at the stern of the ship, Pasley wrote a letter to the Admiralty informing their lordships that he had returned to duty and asking them to give orders to the Navy Board 'to cause the Bellerophon to be fitted in the usual manner as a flagship, that proper accommodations may be made for the additional officers appointed.'[9]

At 10 am they weighed anchor and sailed to St Helen's Roads, the anchorage in the lee of the Isle of Wight, off Bembridge. The next day they were joined by the other ships in Pasley's squadron and on 17 January they sailed with the fleet out into the Channel, past the Eddystone rock, towards Ushant. During the next four months the *Bellerophon*, in company with other warships, made a series of cruises out to Ushant and back, just as she had the previous autumn. It was hard, gruelling work at the best of times but in the winter months the men had to endure bitterly cold weather and storms. The seas to the west of Brittany and in the Bay of Biscay are notoriously hostile for sailing ships. Gales sweeping across the Atlantic stir up long rollers which can change to breaking seas as they hit the shallow waters of the continental shelf. With the prevailing wind in the southwest, the rockbound coast of France becomes a dangerous lee shore, made more hazardous by numerous offshore islands and shoals, fierce currents and overfalls. The log-books of the British ships sent out to patrol this coast make little mention of the dangers and none at all of the hardships involved. The letters of Commodore Pasley occasionally provide a glimpse of the conditions. In January 1794 he was ordered to take a squadron of seven ships down the Channel to intercept some French frigates known to be sailing off Cherbourg. There was no sign of the frigates so, when they arrived off Ushant, Pasley decided to send two of his own frigates to reconnoitre the port of Brest, while he and the ships of the line took up station 6 to 10 leagues west of Ushant to cover their retreat if they ran into trouble. The frigates had only been gone a few hours when the squadron was hit by a fierce gale from the north-west.

'Twice I hauled the squadron to the westward,' Pasley wrote, 'and each time I met a violent gale from the NW. In the last attempt we carried away our bumpkin.'[10] When it became clear that there was going to be no let-up in the weather Pasley ordered the squadron to bear away and seek shelter in Torbay. He assured the Admiralty that the Channel was clear of enemy cruisers and promised to resume his station off the French coast as soon as the gales subsided. This he did but the squadron was again driven back to Torbay, this time by a strong south-westerly gale which caused the *Defence* to spring her main topmast. He concluded his report, 'Since I have had the honour of commanding a kings ship I never experienced such a continuance of boisterous weather as the squadron entrusted to my care has encountered from the 24th ult.'[11] And this came from a veteran sailor who had made several Atlantic crossings and sailed as far afield as Newfoundland and the Guinea coast of Africa.

Later, in the long war against France, and for limited periods, the British Navy mounted a continous blockade of the French coast but this was not a policy pursued in the early stages of the war. An effective blockade required a very large fleet in order to contain the enemy ships in their naval bases. Lord Howe, who was in command of the Channel fleet from 1790 to 1794, saw no point in wearing out his ships during the winter months and preferred to send squadrons out to patrol the western approaches while keeping much of the fleet in home waters, ready for action in the event of the French fleet putting to sea. This led to him being called 'Lord Torbay' by those who wanted to see quick results but Howe was old enough and experienced enough to shrug off criticism from landsmen who knew little or nothing of naval matters.

Richard, Earl Howe, Admiral of the Fleet, is little known today outside the small world of those interested in maritime history. He never achieved the fame of Nelson or Drake or Captain Cook, and yet in an age which produced a succession of brilliant naval commanders he was a revered figure, admired by his fellow officers and widely respected by the common sailors in his fleet. He had captured a French ship off the mouth of the St Lawrence River at the beginning of the Seven Years War and he later led Hawke's fleet into action in the Battle of Quiberon Bay in 1759. He had been Commander-in-Chief on the North American station during the American War of Independence and had fought a series of rearguard actions against superior French forces. He had led the fleet which recaptured Gibraltar from the Spanish in 1782. And for five years he had held the office of First Lord of the Admiralty. His reputation was built on his courage, his leadership and his mastery of all aspects of his profession. Nelson was among his admirers and after his victory at the Nile it was the letter of congratulation he received from Howe that he valued above all others.

'It is only this moment that I had the invaluable approbation of the great, the immortal Earl Howe,' he wrote, 'an honour the most flattering a Sea-officer could receive, as it comes from the first and greatest Sea-officer the world has ever produced.' He went on to describe Howe as 'our great Master in Naval tactics and bravery . . .' Howe would have been the first to disown such extravagant praise. He was a man of few words, as unshakeable as a rock, and as silent, according to Horace Walpole. His dour manner, his rugged, impassive features, his dark eyes and heavy, black eyebrows had earned him the name of 'Black Dick'. He was now aged sixty-eight and was shortly to lead his ships into battle in the first major fleet action of the war against Revolutionary France.

FIVE

The Glorious First of June

1794

On the morning of 28 May 1794 the *Bellerophon* was far out in the North Atlantic. The Isle of Ushant on the French coast was 400 miles to the east, and Plymouth, the nearest British naval base, was more than 600 miles away. The weather was fine, but high feathery clouds, a freshening south-westerly breeze and a heavy swell from the west warned of gales to come. In the pale light of dawn it was just possible to see the topsails of the frigates on the eastern horizon. They had been sent ahead to search for the enemy fleet which was known to be somewhere close at hand. Astern of the *Bellerophon* was the main body of the British fleet, sailing in two columns with Lord Howe in the *Queen Charlotte* leading the weather column. Sailing in company with the *Bellerophon* were the *Russell*, the *Thunderer* and the *Marlborough*. They were the fastest 74-gun ships in the fleet and together formed the flying squadron of Thomas Pasley who had recently been promoted to rear-admiral. Their job was to chase and intercept the enemy ships if and when they were sighted.

The British were on the lookout for a large convoy of merchant ships and their escorting warships. France had suffered a bad harvest in 1793 and was heavily dependent on supplies of grain from America. A convoy had been assembled in Virginia consisting of more than a hundred merchantmen: some of the ships were carrying produce from the French West Indies; most were carrying cargoes of wheat flour.

The convoy had set off from America on 2 April accompanied by two ships of the line and three frigates. Another squadron of five ships of the line, three frigates and a corvette, under Rear-Admiral Nielly, was sent out from France to meet them. To make doubly sure that the convoy did not fall into the hands of the British, the Brest fleet, under the command of Rear-Admiral Villaret-Joyeuse, was despatched on 16 May to bring the merchantmen safely into port. The Brest fleet consisted of twenty-six ships of the line, including three huge three-deckers of 110 guns, and one of 120 guns.[1]

The Channel fleet, under the command of Lord Howe, did not have the weight of guns of the French fleet but it had more supporting vessels. There were twenty-six ships of the line, seven frigates, two fireships, two armed cutters and a hospital ship. Anchored in port this would have been an impressive array of vessels but in the vastness of the Atlantic Ocean they were no more than a few white specks on the ruffled grey surface of the sea. Thanks to the prevailing foggy weather Villaret-Joyeuse had successfully avoided the watching British ships on his outward voyage towards the convoy and in theory he should have been able to evade them on his return. However, two French corvettes and various merchant ships had blundered into the path of Howe's fleet and had given him some idea of the whereabouts of the enemy. Instead of heading westwards out into the Atlantic, Howe had altered course and the fleet was now steering south-east.[2]

At 6 am on the 28th the frigate *Phaeton* sent a signal back to Admiral Pasley on the *Bellerophon*. She had sighted a strange sail to the south-east. She followed this with a second signal to the effect that there was a strange fleet to the south-south-west. Three hours passed by with no further news and the four ships of the flying squadron continued to sail south-eastwards, heeling before the rising wind, their bows dipping into the choppy seas and sending puffs of white salt spray into the air. At around 9 o'clock the lookouts on the *Bellerophon* saw for themselves the sails of a large fleet on the horizon to windward. As they drew closer they were able to count the individual ships. There were thirty-three ships in all and twenty-three of them appeared to be ships of the line. A young observer in Howe's fleet recorded that 'At 10 the Bellerophon 74 commanded by the bold

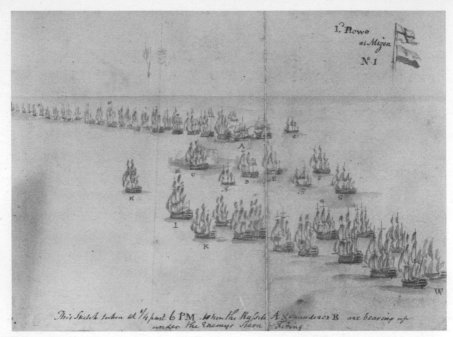

Sketch no. 1 from the notebook kept by Nicholas Pocock during the four-day action which culminated in the battle of the Glorious First of June. This shows the action on 28 May 1774 with the *Bellerophon* (C) near the centre of the picture firing at the stern ships of the enemy's fleet.

Sketch no. 2 by Nicholas Pocock showing the situation during the morning of 29 May. The *Bellerophon* (L) is following in the wake of Howe's flagship (K).

Sketch no. 3 by Nicholas Pocock showing the early stages of the action on 1 June 1794. The *Bellerophon* (B) is shown in the top left-hand corner of the picture.

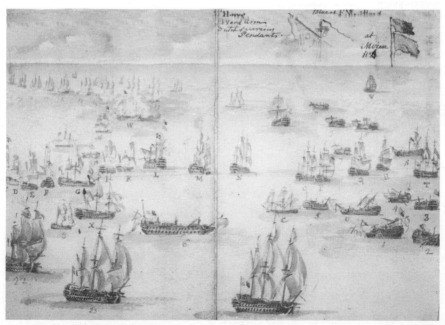

Sketch no. 4 by Nicholas Pocock showing the situation around 1.30 p.m. on 1 June when the firing had ceased. The *Bellerophon* (A) is on the left of the picture, 'Fore & Main Topmast gone & much shattered.'

Adml Paisley [Pasley] went per signal to reconnoitre the strange fleet.'[3] Accompanied by the other three ships of the flying squadron, the *Bellerophon* slowly and steadily gained on the fleet but it was not until noon that the lookouts in the tops were able to confirm what they already knew. Ahead of them was the French fleet. It was stretched out in a long line, 'standing on the larb'd tack under easy sail'.

What happened next, and in the three days which followed, was recorded in the log-books of every ship present and these provide a glimpse of the action from a variety of angles. Most of the log-book accounts are restricted to brief notes of the weather, sail changes, signals, damage sustained by the ships and a note of the numbers of dead and injured. However the events were also recorded in journals and notebooks by a number of people who were present on board the warships and these provide a more personal view of the proceedings. Among the most interesting are the notebooks of Edward Codrington, who was a midshipman in Howe's flagship and later became an admiral; the observations of two thirteen-year-old midshipmen – William Dillon of the *Defence* and William Parker of the *Orion*; and a letter from an ordinary seaman serving in the *Queen*.

There is an additional, and unusual, perspective on the events leading up to and culminating in the Battle of the Glorious First of June and this is an illustrated journal by the marine artist Nicholas Pocock. He was present on the frigate *Pegasus*, and not only kept a journal but illustrated the unfolding events with aerial views and dozens of sketches.[4] The son of a seaman, Pocock had risen to become a captain of merchant ships sailing out of Bristol. For ten years he recorded his voyages to South Carolina and the West Indies with delicate pen-and-wash drawings in his log-books. While still in his thirties he retired from the sea and set himself up as a painter of Bristol views and shipping on the Avon. His local success prompted him to move to London with his family in 1789 and he soon had a thriving practice as a painter of naval actions. His knowledge of ships and seamanship and his meticulous attention to detail much impressed his naval patrons who included senior captains and several admirals such as Lord Hood and Lord Bridport.

It is not known how Pocock came to be on board the *Pegasus* – we can only assume that he was invited along as a guest by her captain, Robert Barlow. But what is certain is that Pocock was in a good position to see the unfolding action. In fleet actions the battle was fought out between the ships of the line. The role of the frigates was to stand by and be ready to assist ships in trouble. They also had the vital task of repeating the signals made by the commander-in-chief whose flagship would usually be in the thick of the action, only her topmasts visible above the dense clouds of gunsmoke. On 1 June the frigate *Niger* was the repeating frigate for the van, the *Aquilon* for the rear squadron, and the *Pegasus* for the centre. Nicholas Pocock was fifty-two in 1794 but as a former seaman he would have had no qualms about going aloft and, from a position high up in the tops of the *Pegasus*, he would have had an aerial view of the whole scene.

Pocock's notes and sketches place considerable emphasis on the signals hoisted at various times by Lord Howe, and with some justification because these played a key part in the proceedings. The British Navy had used various forms of flag signals since the time of the Anglo-Dutch wars in the previous century, but these tended to be inflexible and became unwieldy as more and more flags were introduced to cope with the various orders and instructions issued by commanders. It was Lord Howe who first introduced a new system during the American War of Independence of 1776. While in command on the North American station he issued a book entitled *Signal Book for Ships of War* which was accompanied by explanatory instructions. During the next few years he and a number of other officers refined and experimented with different arrangements of flags. In 1790 Howe issued a revised *Signal Book for Ships of War* which was based on a numerical system. The numbers one to ten were each represented by a flag, and by using combinations of these, together with the explanations in the signal book, it was possible to issue a great variety of instructions with a limited number of flags. The flags were designed to be easily distinguished at a distance so there was only one with a diagonal cross, one with two vertical bands of colour and so on. They came into their own in the events which began on 28 May when Howe was in command of a large and extended fleet and needed to send signals to ships which were some-times 2 or 3 miles distant from his flagship.

By mid-afternoon the weather had turned nasty. The wind had risen to gale force and squally showers of rain were sweeping across the heaving surface of the sea. With the leading British ships now closing on the rear of the long column of French ships, Lord Howe hoisted signal 29 at the mizen masthead of the *Queen Charlotte*. In the first of his aerial views of the action Pocock shows the signal flags in the top right-hand corner of his picture – a flag with a blue cross on a white ground for the figure 2 and a flag with red, white and blue horizontal stripes for the figure 9. Captain Hope simply recorded this as 'the general signal for chase and battle' but it had a more particular meaning which was 'to attack or harass the rear of the enemy . . . to bring on a general action' which was exactly what the flying squadron proceeded to do. The *Russell* and the *Thunderer* were in the lead and, as they cut across the enemies' wake, they fired ranging shots at a distance of about a mile. These were the first shots in the first sea battle of the prolonged war against France: a war which would reach its climax at sea with the Battle of Trafalgar in 1805 but which was not finally concluded until Napoleon was defeated on the field of Waterloo in 1815. Thanks to a bold and well-timed manoeuvre by Admiral Pasley, the *Bellerophon* became the first ship in Howe's fleet to go into action in this opening battle. Midshipman Parker observed that 'At 8 o'clock Adml Paisley [Pasley] got within gun shot of the enemy's rear and gave them a very warm and fierce reception which the enemy returned with great vivacity.'[5] The *Bellerophon*'s adversary was a huge French three-decker, just as it would be in a more famous battle in four years' time.

Captain Vandongen, in command of the *Révolutionnaire* of 110 guns, believing that he had the firepower to overwhelm the 74-gun ships on his tail, dropped back into the path of the *Bellerophon*. Pasley judged his moment, tacked his ship and was soon exchanging fire with the Frenchman. He later wrote, 'On that day, and for some days before, the Bellerophon was the worst-sailing ship of the flying

Rochester in the late eighteenth century with Rochester Cathedral on the extreme left and the castle seen beyond the medieval stone bridge. The view is taken from the Frindsbury shore near the spot where the *Bellerophon* was built.

Sir Thomas Slade, Surveyor of the Navy, and the designer of a long line of successful 74-gun ships including the *Bellerophon*.

The young General Napoleon Bonaparte at Arcole in November 1796, painted by Antoine-Jean Gros. The battle for the bridge at Arcole near Verona led to the defeat of an Austrian army and was one of the key engagements of the Italian campaign.

Portrait by Lemuel Francis Abbott of Rear-Admiral Sir Thomas Pasley, the first Commander of the *Bellerophon*. He was made a baronet after the Battle of the Glorious First of June and later became Port Admiral at Plymouth.

Captain William Johnstone Hope, the 28-year-old Londoner who was Pasley's flag captain at the Battle of the Glorious First of June.

The Battle of the Glorious First of June, 1794, by Philippe Jacques de Loutherbourg. A dramatic depiction of the action showing Howe's flagship, the *Queen Charlotte* (centre left), engaged with the *Montagne*, the flagship of Admiral Villaret-Joyeuse.

Portrait of Lord Howe, Admiral of the Fleet, by John Singleton Copley. Howe, who commanded the British fleet at the Battle of the Glorious First of June, was an officer of vast experience and was admired and respected throughout the fleet.

Nicholas Pocock, the marine artist and former sea captain, who depicted the naval actions of the Nelson era. This engraving is taken from a portrait by his son Isaac Pocock.

A sketch made on the spot by Nicholas Pocock showing the desolate scene after the Battle of the Glorious First of June with damaged and dismasted ships including the *Queen Charlotte* (centre left) and the *Queen* (centre right).

Captain Henry D'Esterre Darby, the Irishman who commanded the *Bellerophon* at the Battle of the Nile. He ended his naval career with a knighthood and the rank of Admiral.

Captain Edward Rotheram who was Collingwood's flag captain at Trafalgar and was subsequently appointed to command the *Bellerophon* following the death in action of Captain John Cooke.

Shipping in the harbour at Portsmouth in the late eighteenth century with the buildings of the royal dockyard in the background.

Napoleon surveying the battlefield at Wagram, July 1809, by Horace Vernet. This hard-fought battle in the valley of the Danube near Vienna ended with the defeat of the Austrian army by Napoleon's troops.

British ships under fire from the guns of Fort Louis, Martinique, during the action in March 1794 which led to the capture of the island from the French. Fort Louis guarded the entrance to Fort Royal Bay where the *Bellerophon* anchored in March 1802.

Portrait of Captain John Cooke, by Lemuel Francis Abbott. Cooke was in command of the *Bellerophon* at Trafalgar and was shot dead shortly before Nelson was fatally wounded.

William Pryce Cumby, the heroic first lieutenant of the *Bellerophon*, who took over command of the ship when her captain was killed at the Battle of Trafalgar. He is shown here in the uniform of a captain, the rank he was promoted to soon after the battle.

A painting by Nicholas Pocock showing the capture of the French ships *Resistance* and *Constance* off the port of Brest by the British frigates *San Fiorenzo*, Captain Sir Harry Neale, and the *Nymph*, Captain John Cooke, in 1797.

A portrait by Samuel Woodford of Captain Frederick Maitland, the Scottish commander of the *Bellerophon* who accepted the surrender of Napoleon at Rochefort in July 1815.

Miniature portrait of Captain Maitland's wife Catherine. When Napoleon saw a picture of her in Maitland's cabin he remarked that she was very young and very pretty.

Engraving after a picture by Thomas Buttersworth showing the daring raid by the crew of the British frigate *La Loire*, Captain Maitland, on the shipping in the Spanish harbour at Muros in June 1805.

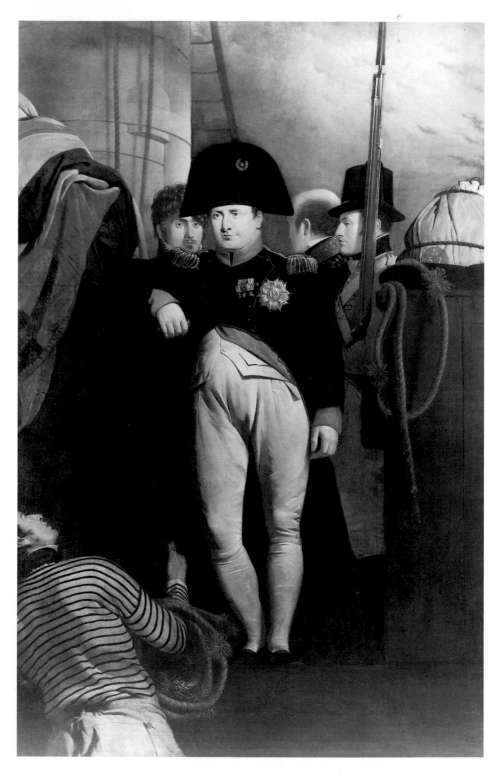

Napoleon on the Bellerophon *at Plymouth*, by Sir Charles Eastlake. The artist was among the thousands of spectators who came to see the former emperor and he painted this picture from sketches that he made on the spot.

squadron. Yet by embracing the moment for tacking after the enemy, she was enabled to bring them to action, with which she was engaged alone more than an hour and a half.'6

Lord Howe saw what was happening and, as the rest of his fleet was still some distance away, he made a signal to the other ships in the flying squadron to come to the *Bellerophon*'s assistance. The *Russell*, the *Thunderer* and the *Marlborough* headed towards the scene of the action which was conspicuous in the gathering gloom by the brilliant flashes of gunfire and the thunderous boom of the broad-sides. By the time they reached the embattled ships and swept past, firing their guns, the *Bellerophon* was in difficulties. The broadsides of the three-decker had caused a considerable amount of damage and her main topmast was about to go by the board. She was forced to signal her inability to continue in action and drifted clear of the French ship. As she did so, the leading ships from the main body of Howe's fleet at last arrived on the scene. The *Audacious* and the *Leviathan* engaged in a running battle with the French ship which had lost her mizenmast but continued to direct such devastating fire at her attackers that the *Audacious* was reduced to a crippled wreck.

It was now around 8 o'clock in the evening. A sea mist was reducing visibility and Lord Howe realised that he would be unable to bring on a general action before darkness fell and communication with his ships became difficult. He therefore made the signal to recall the fleet and form line ahead and astern of his flagship. During the night the much battered *Révolutionnaire* evaded the British fleet and made her way back to Brest escorted by a French seventy-four. The equally battered *Audacious* needed dockyard attention and headed back to England. The first round had ended in a draw.

With the coming of dawn on 29 May the enemy fleet was seen to be 4 or 5 miles away, sailing in a line ahead. It was a grey day, with cloudy skies and a mist hovering on the horizon. The wind was still blowing from the south-west and had lessened from gale force to a stiff breeze, but a heavy swell continued to roll across the ocean from the west. The French were to windward of the British and therefore had the advantage of the weather gauge. This meant that they could choose to run down on the British fleet with the wind behind them or try and avoid action altogether by maintaining their current course which was taking them away from the British. Howe was determined to bring on a general action but this meant sailing close-hauled and tacking his fleet to bring his leading ships into contact. The second of Nicholas Pocock's aerial views shows exactly what happened. Lord Howe hoisted signal 78 for the fleet to tack in succession, 'the head-most and weathermost ships to tack first'. At 11.30 am the French fleet is stretched out along the horizon. Most of the British fleet have already tacked and the leading ships have begun firing on the enemy. The *Bellerophon* is in the centre of the picture, following in the wake of Lord Howe's flagship.

If they stayed on the same tack the leading British ships would pass harmlessly to leeward of the French so Lord Howe hoisted the signal to cut through the enemy's line. Captain Hope in the *Bellerophon* observed that Howe 'tacked in the midst of a very heavy fire or cannonade and cut through between the 4th and 5th ship in their rear. We tacked and passed between the 2nd and 3rd ships.'

An engraving by Nicholas Pocock showing the action on 29 May 1794.
Howe's flagship, the *Queen Charlotte*, in the foreground, has just cut
through the French line and she is followed by the *Bellerophon*
on the right of the picture, firing on both sides.

He went on to provide a glimpse of the confusion as ships at close quarters poured broadsides into each other: 'In passing we brought down a ships topmasts and in the heat of the action it was difficult to know who was French and who was English. We was all firing thro one another.'[7] By sailing through the line of enemy ships, the *Queen Charlotte* and the *Bellerophon* exposed themselves to the full broadsides of the enemy before they were able to bring their own guns to bear. Captain Hope noted that 'in passing the line we had our sails and rigging cut to pieces' but they had succeeded in cutting off three French ships and isolating them from the rest of the French fleet. These ships received such a pounding from the British guns that one of them was totally disabled. Admiral Villaret-Joyeuse acted promptly. In the words of Pocock, 'The French Admiral seeing this ship must be taken if he stood on, wore his fleet in succession from the van and rallied in a very gallant manner and in good order towards our fleet.'[8] In the ensuing mêlée the French managed to rescue their damaged ships and tow them clear.

This second day of action, like the first, ended inconclusively. The French had fought valiantly but several of their ships were so badly damaged that they had to retire from the scene. Some of Howe's ships, notably the *Leviathan* and the *Queen*, had sustained heavy casualties and were badly damaged but they could be repaired by their crews on the spot. From a tactical point of view the British were now in a much stronger position. By tacking through the enemy line Howe had successfully manoeuvred his ships to windward of the French and now he had the weather gauge.

That night the sea mist, which had been lurking on the horizon, spread across the ocean and enveloped the two fleets in a damp haze. Howe's main concern was to prevent the French fleet from escaping. The French admiral's concern was to protect his crippled warships and to keep the grain convoy at a safe distance from the British. On the *Bellerophon* the crew used the interlude of night to carry out urgent repairs and were employed splicing lengths of rope and repairing sails and rigging. The gun crews remained at their quarters. Indeed, according to a seaman on another ship, 'we lay upon the

decks at our guns all night for two nights and three days.'[9] In spite
of their vigilance they lost sight of the French fleet and at one stage
the fog was so thick that visibility was reduced to a cable's length
(200 yards) and they could only glimpse three of their own ships in
the immediate vicinity. In the early hours of 31 May the mist was
accompanied by drizzling rain. Edward Codrington provides us with
a vivid picture of the scene on board the *Queen Charlotte* at dawn.
The ship was cleared for action and there was consequently only a
canvas screen between the Admiral's cabin and the quarterdeck.
Codrington was an officer of the watch at that early hour and by
lifting the canvas screen he was able to observe a brief exchange
between Lord Howe and his flag captain Sir Roger Curtis. He saw
Lord Howe sitting in an armchair in his greatcoat. Curtis came in
to make his report to the Admiral.

'My Lord, I am sorry to tell you that the fog is now so thick that
we cannot see anything beyond our ship, and God knows whether
we are standing into our own fleet or that of the enemy.'

'Well, Sir, it can't be helped,' Howe calmly replied, 'we must wait
with patience till the weather improves.' Codrington noted that the
Admiral showed no nervousness in the difficult circumstances but
'evinced a heroic fortitude which may have been equalled, but never
can have been exceeded.'[10]

The fog partly cleared at around 6 o'clock and the crew of the
Bellerophon were able to see most of the rest of the fleet but not the
Queen Charlotte which remained hidden in a fog bank. Not till around
1 o'clock in the afternoon did the fog clear sufficiently for the flagship to be able to rejoin the fleet and for them to be able to see the
French fleet which was now 8 or 9 miles to leeward. Lord Howe
hoisted the signal for the fleet to form the established line of battle
and they set a course for the enemy. By 6.30 in the evening the French
were still too far away and it was evident to Howe that he would not
be able to bring on a conclusive general action before nightfall. He
decided to hold his hand till the next day and gave the signal 'to haul
the wind on the larboard tack.' That evening the British crews
completed the repairs to the damaged ships and prepared for the
impending battle. Howe sent the frigates *Phaeton* and *Southampton*

along the line with orders to hail each ship and tell them that the *Queen Charlotte* would be sailing all night under a single foresail, reefed topsails, jib and main staysail. This enabled individual captains to judge the speed required to maintain their station in the line.

The morning of 1 June was cloudy with a fresh breeze from south-south-west and a continuing heavy swell from the west. On the *Bellerophon* they could see no sign of the enemy fleet at daybreak but the frigates had spotted them about 7 miles to leeward. Howe was determined to make the battle decisive and he therefore hoisted signal 34 which meant, 'having the wind of the enemy, the Admiral means to pass between the ships in the line for engaging them to leeward'. And in case there should be any doubt in his captains' minds he followed this up an hour later with signal 36, 'Each ship independently to steer for and engage her opponent in the enemy's line.' Although baldly expressed in the language of Howe's signal book, this order was similar in spirit and intention to the famous direction which Nelson was to give to his captains before Trafalgar when he told them that 'no captain can do very wrong if he places his ship alongside that of an enemy.'

By 9.30 the two fleets were within gunshot of each other and Lord Howe ordered the signal for close action to be hoisted at the mizenmast of his flagship. This was signal number 5, a distinctive red-and-white-quartered flag which signified 'To engage the enemy. If closer a red pennant will be shown over the flag.' Howe made sure that the red pennant was duly hoisted. Codrington was with the Admiral on the quarterdeck at this moment and observed him shut the little signal book which he always carried with him, and turn to the officers surrounding him, saying, 'And now, gentlemen, no more book, no more signals. I look to you to do the duty of the Queen Charlotte in engaging the French admiral. I do not wish the ships to be bilge and bilge, but if you can lock the yardarms so much the better, the battle will be sooner decided.'[11] He then took over conning the ship, just as he had done thirty-five years before at the Battle of Quiberon Bay when he had steered the *Magnanime* among the treacherous shoals on the French coast in a November gale. He now headed for the centre of the French line and selected as his adversary the *Montagne*, a three-decker of 120 guns and the flagship of Admiral Villaret-Joyeuse.

From his viewpoint on the frigate *Pegasus*, Nicholas Pocock was well placed to observe the opening stages of the battle. The third of his aerial views shows the scene at 10.30 in the morning. The battle has been raging for about an hour. The *Queen Charlotte* has hauled up under the stern of the *Montagne* and her foretopmast is going over the side. Dense clouds of gunsmoke have already hidden many of the ships of the line from view. Standing well clear of the action in the foreground are five of the British frigates, the fireship *Comet*, the cutter *Rattler*, and the hospital ship *Charon*. The *Pegasus* is in the centre of the picture, in a position where she can repeat Howe's signals.

In this picture, as in his other three aerial views, Pocock has taken a bird's eye view of the entire scene rather than a literal view of what he would have seen from the masthead of the *Pegasus*. It was his usual practice before he began work on a painting of a sea battle to produce a careful plan of the action so that he could check the positions of the ships and the direction of wind and tide with people who had been present. In his First of June Notebook he used his own observations to produce what amounted to three-dimensional plans of the action. A few years later, when he was commissioned to paint pictures of Nelson's famous victories at the Nile, Copenhagen and Trafalgar, he chose to paint similar aerial views of the actions, presumably because these gave the spectator a clear and easily understood view of the relative positions of all the ships involved.

In addition to the aerial views, Pocock also made dozens of sketches of the battle on 1 June from the decks of the *Pegasus*. Like his distinguished predecessor Willem van de Velde the Elder, who was present at several of the battles of the Anglo-Dutch Wars, he used pen and pencil with the addition of a rapidly applied grey wash. This enabled him to depict the flash of cannon fire, the billowing smoke, the falling masts and spars, and the choppy surface of the sea with a freshness and a sense of immediacy which is missing from so many of the battle pictures by his contemporaries. Unfortunately on 1 June the

Bellerophon was too far away from Pocock to be seen clearly and she only appears in his bird's eye views.

When the British fleet sailed down on the enemy in line abreast the *Bellerophon* was at one end of the line with only the *Caesar* outside her. As they neared the French line Captain Molloy in the *Caesar* began firing at long range but then held back. (This led to much hostile criticism afterwards and a court martial.) The *Caesar's* absence meant that the fire of several French ships was directed at the *Bellerophon* as she made her final approach. According to Captain Hope, 'in going down we received a very heavy fire from 3 or 4 of the enemies van'. The officers on the quarterdeck were always in a dangerously exposed position and they now came under a murderous hail of musket balls and cannon shot. Shortly before 11 o'clock Admiral Pasley was hit. According to Matthew Flinders, the future explorer who was a midshipman on the *Bellerophon*, 'our brave admiral lost his leg by an 18 pound shot which came through the barricadoes of the quarter-deck — it was in the heat of the action.'[12] When two of his seamen expressed their sorrow at seeing him wounded Pasley briskly replied, 'Thank you, but never mind my leg: take care of my flag.'[13]

The Admiral was taken below where Alexander White, the surgeon, found his leg was so shattered that it had to be amputated. We get a rare glimpse of what the atmosphere below deck must have been like at this time in a letter written by Jonathan Wilkinson, a 28-year-old seaman serving on another ship, the 98-gun *Queen*. Before joining the navy Wilkinson had worked on a farm in Nottinghamshire and his letter was addressed to his former employer.

'Sir, in the time of the action you would have thought the element had been all on fire and the shot flying about our heads 42 pounder and case shot and double-headed shot. It was all the same as a hail storm.' Wilkinson described how the *Queen* had to run the gauntlet through the French lines and 'at the gun that I was quartered at we had 4 shot come in and killed two men and wounded five ditto which I was wounded in my left arm and in my breast but thanks be to God I'm a great deal better and to let you know that our captain lost his leg and is since dead and the master of the ship he was killed right out in the time of action . . .'[14]

While Admiral Pasley was on the surgeon's makeshift operating table, Captain Hope continued to give orders from the quarterdeck and the *Bellerophon's* gun crews continued to thunder away at the enemy ships on either side. The bombardment was so effective that the captain of the French 74-gun ship *L'Eole* decided that his ship had taken enough punishment and withdrew from the line of battle. By this time the *Bellerophon* had lost all three of her topmasts, most of her lower shrouds were shot away, and her mainsail was shot to pieces. Unable to manoeuvre the ship any more, Captain Hope had to signal to the frigate *Latona* to come to her assistance and tow her clear. As they emerged from the pall of gunsmoke Captain Hope counted eleven ships without a mast standing, one of them being the *Defence*, a seventy-four designed by Slade and a sister ship of the *Bellerophon*.

Nicholas Pocock witnessed the heroic performance of the *Defence* and later produced a small oil painting of her under fire from two French ships. It is one of the most authentic depictions of a sea battle ever painted. It has none of the theatrical glamour of Philippe Jacques de Loutherbourg's vast canvas, *The Glorious First of June*, but it does have a deadpan realism and a mastery of significant detail which could only come from the hand of someone who had witnessed the occasion. Captain Gambier in command of the *Defence* had piled on so much sail during the approach to the enemy that his ship drew ahead of the British line and came under a concentrated hail of fire as she reached the French line. First she lost her mizenmast and then her mainmast, but even when her foremast was shot away and her deck was strewn with wreckage, her gun crews continued to keep up a barrage of fire. Midshipman Dillon observed that 'The lower deck was at times so completely filled with smoke that we could scarcely distinguish each other, and the guns were so heated that, when fired, they nearly kicked the upper deck beams.'[15] At one stage Dillon was standing next to a seaman called John Polly who was so short that he was confident that any shot would pass harmlessly over his head.

'The words had not been long out of his mouth when a shot cut his head right in two, leaving the tip of each ear remaining on the lower part of the cheek.' Dillon noted that 'The head of the seaman was cut so horizontally that anyone looking at it would have supposed it had been done by the blow of an axe.'[16] His words are a graphic reminder of the horrendous damage which could be inflicted by a single cannon ball. Codrington observed that one French shot went clean through 7 feet of oak timbers and then struck a gun with such force that it dented the barrel. On the frigate *Phaeton* a 36-pounder shot went through her quarter gallery, took off a man's head, broke both the thighs of another man and wounded several others.

The battle lasted for more than four hours. By 12.30 many of the ships had fought themselves to a standstill and Lord Howe hoisted the signal for ships to close and join the Admiral. The fourth of Pocock's aerial views shows the scene an hour later with those French ships which were not totally disabled retreating 'in tolerable good order'. Scattered across a wide expanse of ocean are dozens of wrecked and dismasted vessels. The *Bellerophon* can be seen on the extreme left of the picture, 'Fore and main topmast gone and much shattered.' On board the ship Captain Hope and his officers were attempting to produce some order from the chaos. The ship was strewn with the debris of shattered spars, sails and rigging and the boats and spars which were stored on the main deck were almost destroyed by shot and falling debris. The men began clearing away the wreckage, and carrying out urgent repairs to the standing rigging supporting the mainmast which was in a dangerous condition.

Considering the ferocity of the gunfire which she faced during the first part of the battle the *Bellerophon* suffered surprisingly few casualties, with four men killed and thirty wounded. Other ships did not fare so well. The *Queen* had thirty-six killed and over sixty wounded but the highest British death toll was the *Brunswick*'s which had forty-four men killed, including her captain, John Harvey. The *Brunswick* was engaged in a prolonged and ferocious duel with the French ship *Vengeur du Peuple*. According to Lieutenant Bevan, 'We did not fire a single gun untill we were within point blank shot and 10 minutes after ten we lay'd the Vengeur, an 84, alongside. Sometimes their guns running into our ports, at other times ours into theirs.'[17]

The anchors of the two ships had become hooked and the ships were so closely locked in combat that the *Brunswick* was unable to open her lower deck ports and had to blast them off with her guns. After four dreadful hours the *Vengeur* hauled down her flag and surrendered, her masts going by the board soon afterwards. The *Brunswick* succeeded in extricating herself from the wreckage and sailed clear of the *Vengeur* which was sinking. Boats from the *Culloden* and the *Alfred* managed to take off the French ship's captain and about 130 of her crew before she went down. Her final moments were vividly recorded by Mr Baker of the *Orion*:

> At half-past five o'clock, we were witness to the most shocking scene possible. Le Vengeur, being very much mauled between wind and water in the action, filled with water and lay upon her beam ends. Numbers of unfortunate wretches were seen clinging to her side. Soon they were floating in the water and crying for assistance. In a minute's time, she heel'd right over and went to the bottom. Numbers were seen floating in the water, of whom the *Rattler* cutter picked up several, but much the greater part of the crew were lost.[18]

The sinking of the *Vengeur* made a great impression on all present because it was extremely rare for warships of this period to be sunk by gunshot unless the magazine caught fire and exploded. Normally their massive oak hulls could take several hours of bombardment and still remain afloat. When news of the heroic defence of the *Vengeur* reached France her crew were hailed as martyrs in the cause of the Revolution and the ship became the subject of numerous pictures and patriotic ballads.

Before they retreated from the scene of the battle the French frigates succeeded in towing away four or five damaged ships of the line but they were unable to prevent six dismasted warships from falling into the hands of the British. Two of these, *Le Juste* and *Sans Pareil*, were 80-gun ships, the others were 74s. It was the largest number of prizes captured during a sea battle in the eighteenth century up till that date and was considered a glorious triumph when the news eventually reached England. But the victory was achieved at a heavy cost. The total casualty list for the British fleet was 287 men killed and 811 wounded. The French were reckoned to have lost 1,500 killed and 2,000 wounded, with 3,500 men made prisoner.

As the smoke drifted away and the prizes were taken in tow, Lord Howe retired to bed, totally exhausted. For four days running he had masterminded the movements of a large fleet by day and night. On three of those days his ships had been in action and on two of them his own flagship had led by example: on 29 May the *Queen Charlotte* was the first British ship to cut through the French line, and on 1 June she had to force her way between the 120-gun *Montagne* and the 80-gun *Jacobin* while under fire from both ships. It would have been a gruelling enough experience for a young man but for a man of sixty-nine it certainly took its toll. A few captains remarked at the time that the victory would have been even more spectacular if Howe had not called a halt to the fighting and had allowed his captains to chase down and secure more of the disabled French ships. With hindsight, and the knowledge of what Nelson was to achieve in the years to follow, there is clearly some truth in this. But in defence of Howe it has to be remembered that the battle was fought 600 miles out in the open ocean and a number of his ships required dockyard repairs before they could fight again. He had achieved a decisive victory over a French fleet whose officers and men may have lacked the experience and expertise of the British, but who fought, like the armies of the French Revolution, with a patriotic and almost fanatical fervour. Captain Collingwood, who was in command of the *Barfleur* and would later be Nelson's second in command at Trafalgar, considered the action on 1 June was 'as compleat a victory as ever was won upon the seas, more decided than we had just reason to expect, for the enemy was superior to us in strength and fought with a savage ferocity.'[19]

SIX

The Aftermath

1794

Twelve days passed before the people of London learnt of the battle which had taken place out in the Atlantic. News travelled at the speed of a galloping horse on land but at sea it all depended on the vagaries of wind and weather.[1] On the morning after the battle, Lord Howe had sat down at the table in his great cabin and compiled his report. He had headed it, 'Queen Charlotte at Sea, June 2, 1794. Ushant E.Half N.140 Leagues.'[2] He outlined the main events of the previous day and provided details of the French ships which had been captured. When he had completed the despatch he gave it to his flag captain, Sir Roger Curtis, to deliver to the Admiralty. Curtis boarded the frigate *Phaeton* and headed for England, leaving the fleet to limp slowly home with its prizes in tow. The *Phaeton* arrived in Plymouth at 5 pm on 9 June and was met by the *Cockchafer*, an armed lugger on hire to the navy, which carried Curtis ashore so that he could take an express postchaise to London. No other boats were permitted to approach the *Phaeton* which immediately weighed anchor and headed eastwards up the Channel under a crowd of sail.

In the haste to deliver Lord Howe's despatch, the postchaise overturned, causing Sir Roger Curtis to bruise his arm severely so that when he arrived at the Admiralty on the evening of 10 June he had his arm in a sling. Within a few hours the news had got around and the following day *The Times* published a brief report under the

headline 'IMPORTANT NAVAL VICTORY!!!!' which described how the
English had gained a victory over the French fleet by the capture of
six sail of the line 'after a severe conflict of many hours'. The next
day *The Times* published Lord Howe's despatch in full and recorded
the first reactions of the people of London:

> We never recollect to have witnessed more general joy, than was mani-
> fested on every countenance throughout yesterday, in consequence of the
> GLORIOUS VICTORY obtained on the 1st inst. by his MAJESTY'S NAVAL FORCES
> under the command of Earl Howe; – a victory, which we may say with
> confidence, has so crippled the navy of France, that it will be impossible
> for the French to send another grand fleet to sea, at least during the
> present campaign.[3]

England badly needed a victory. The most recent war had ended igno-
miniously with the defeat of the British armies in America and the
loss of the American colonies, and the country now faced an aggressive French nation which had executed its king, guillotined or driven
abroad thousands of its aristocrats, instituted a reign of terror, and
declared war on its neighbours in Europe. As news of Lord Howe's
victory spread across the capital the joyful sound of church bells rang
out from Shoreditch in the east to Westminster and Chelsea in the
west. Flags were hoisted everywhere, and from the ships moored in
the river came the sporadic booming of guns. At the Opera House
the band led the audience in a rousing rendition of 'Rule Britannia',
followed by 'God save the King'. At Lloyds a subscription was opened
for the relief of the widows and children of sailors who had died in
the battle and within two hours more than 1,000 guineas had been
collected. That night, the theatres and many of the public buildings
and streets were illuminated to celebrate the occasion.

Meanwhile Lord Howe's fleet was making the slow voyage home.
Some of the damaged British ships were sailing with jury masts
and rigs, and the six dismasted French prizes were so crippled that
they had to be towed all the way. The fleet was also slowed down
by several days of calms and light breezes. On board the *Bellerophon*
the crew continued to clear away the wreckage and had to heave

one of the boats overboard because it was shot to pieces. The already cramped conditions below deck were put under further strain when space had to be found for 174 prisoners from the French ship *L'Achille* and then another 24 prisoners who were transferred from the frigate *Venus*.

On Sunday 8 June, a week after the battle, Lord Howe gave the signal for the ships to close round the flagship. Under an overcast sky, with the surface of the flat, grey sea only lightly ruffled by a northerly breeze, the scattered fleet contracted to form a dense thicket of swaying masts and sails. To the accompaniment of creaking wooden blocks and the occasional flapping of heavy canvas, the men assembled for services of thanksgiving. The service on the *Bellerophon* was led by the ship's chaplain, the Reverend John Fresselicque. The chaplain had been educated at Queens' College, Cambridge, and had been domestic chaplain to Lord Northesk. He used the occasion to give a lengthy sermon which he later published to raise funds for the benefit of those members of the crew who had been wounded and disabled in the three days of fighting. His sermon was couched in language so tortuous and long-winded that it must have gone over the heads of most of the sailors and marines listening in respectful silence. He took as his text a verse from Psalm 115, 'Not unto us, O Lord. Not unto us, but unto thy name give glory for thy mercy and for thy truth's sake.' And he followed this by a sentence which set the tone for the rest of his sermon:

> The natural impulse of gratitude in the mind of men, is never more forcible, or its effects more pleasant, than when the Heart is warmed by the pleasing recollection of the recent benefit; this disposition is always attended with the most agreeable sensations and the spontaneous effusions of the grateful spirit are given and received with equal condescension and favor in proportion as the declaration is made with sincerity.[4]

Hidden amidst the chaplain's florid thanks to the Almighty were several references to the courage of the officers and men and also some pointers to the high morale and discipline of the crew. He noted that, during a conflict spread over five days and involving three separate actions with the enemy, 'no complaint of any kind, even for the most trifling omission was brought forward against any one of that ship's company, exceeding six hundred.' He also drew attention to the bravery, patience and resignation shown by the wounded Admiral Pasley: 'He fought like a hero – he bore his misfortune like a Christian.'

On 10 June observers at Plymouth spotted a three-decked ship on the horizon. She had damaged masts and rigging and was heading eastward up the Channel. It was presumed that she was one of Howe's fleet. This was confirmed when the next day eighteen of Howe's ships of the line and nine frigates sailed into Plymouth harbour. At dawn on 13 June the rest of the fleet, together with the French prizes, arrived at Portsmouth. Crowds rapidly gathered along the waterfront and, as Howe's flagship dropped anchor, the guns of the shore battery thundered out a salute. When Howe stepped ashore around midday the battery fired a second, deafening salute and the band of the Gloucester militia, which was drawn up on the lower end of the Grand Parade, played 'See the conquering hero comes'. By now there were people on the tops of buildings, at every balcony and window, filling the streets and packing the ramparts of the city's defences. As Howe passed through the cheering crowds he repeatedly thanked them but reminded them that it was 'the brave British seamen that did the business'.[5]

Earlier that morning the *Bellerophon* had dropped anchor in the fleet anchorage at Spithead. Shortly afterwards Admiral Pasley was helped down the ship's side and into his barge. It was almost four years since he had first stepped on board the *Bellerophon* as her first captain, and we can only guess at his feelings as he was rowed away from the ship for the last time. He was heading, not for the jubilant crowds and the military band at Portsmouth, but for Gosport on the other side of the harbour entrance in order to have his wound treated by the surgeons at Haslar Hospital. According to a newspaper report he looked much better than might have been expected and waved his hand to the people who cheered him as he came ashore.

Pasley had proved an extremely effective captain and had made his mark as rear-admiral commanding Howe's flying squadron in the recent battle. On 26 July he was created a baronet and he was granted a pension of £1,000 a year for the loss of his leg. He was now sixty years old and might have been tempted to retire to his house in Winchester and to live out his days quietly with his wife and family. However, four years after the First of June, he was appointed commander-in-chief at the Nore and in March 1799 took up the post of port admiral at Plymouth where he gained a reputation for his hospitality.[6]

The day after Pasley was rowed ashore some men arrived from the dockyard to examine the extent of the damage to the *Bellerophon*'s hull, masts and rigging, but there were so many demands on the dockyard's facilities that five weeks were to pass before she was hauled alongside the sheer hulk in the dockyard for repairs to be carried out. Meanwhile the celebrations over Lord Howe's victory continued unabated and came to a climax with a review of the fleet by the King. This was a surprisingly rare event. Charles II and his brother James, Duke of York, had both taken a keen interest in the navy back in the 1660s and Pepys's diary records their various visits to the fleet. Since then, British monarchs had preferred to follow the fortunes of the navy from a distance. However King George III was a warm admirer of Lord Howe. The moment he heard the news of the 1 June victory he wrote to Howe's wife, telling her that 'nothing can give me more satisfaction than that it has been obtained by the skill and bravery of Earl Howe,'[7] and he was determined to pay his respects to Howe, his officers and men in person.

The King and the rest of the royal family arrived at Portsmouth on Friday 27 June. At noon they were rowed out to the anchored fleet in Howe's barge, the red and gold colours of the royal standard flying from a flag staff at the stern. A procession of barges followed in their wake, carrying the Lords of the Admiralty and all the admirals and captains of the Channel fleet. Once again the deafening boom of guns echoed across the waters of the Solent as all the forts and all the anchored warships fired a royal salute. On the deck of the *Royal Charlotte* the King presented Howe with a magnificent sword set with diamonds. It was characteristic of Howe that he should later arrange for the sword to be shown to all the sailors on every ship in the fleet, together with a message to be read out from their commander-in-chief to the effect that the sword was proof of the King's admiration for all their exertions. The sailors were delighted by this gesture and Howe's message was greeted with three cheers from every ship.

The royal celebrations continued for the next four days and the festive atmosphere was greatly helped by a spell of fine and sunny weather. The King held a levee in the Commissioner's House to which all the naval officers were invited and he officiated at the launch of a first-rate ship in the dockyard. He and his family attended Sunday morning service in the dockyard church, and then boarded the frigate *Aquilon* and sailed across to Cowes and back. The following day they sailed from Portsmouth to Southampton, where they boarded their carriage and headed back to London.

One of the highlights of the King's visit was his inspection of the French prizes which were then anchored off the harbour entrance at Spithead but were later towed into the dockyard to be surveyed and then repaired for service in the British Navy.[8] They attracted a lot of local attention and were painted and drawn by several marine artists who showed their decks crowded by sightseers, and the union flag flying above the French tricolour at the stern. Four of the ships

Captured French ships at Portsmouth after the
Battle of the Glorious First of June.

were 74s and two of them were 80-gun ships. Although dismasted and mauled by gunshot, they were still an impressive sight and no doubt helped to underline the importance of Howe's victory in British eyes. And yet the French never regarded the First of June as a defeat because they had succeeded in their primary aim of safeguarding the vast grain convoy. Reporting to the Committee of Public Safety in Paris on 16 June, Barère presented the battle as a heroic victory by the sailors of the Republic over a superior British force. An ear of corn was produced as a symbol of the good news.

'The convoy of one hundred and sixteen vessels coming from America, has entered our ports,' announced Barère, 'and brings us subsistence of all kinds.'[9] He told them that the English had united all their forces to capture the rich convoy but they had been foiled by the French fleet who had fought a battle which had been one of the most glorious and bloody that ever occurred. This was indeed the case, but he then indulged in some shameless propaganda, claiming that the French fleet was fourteen ships inferior in number to the British, that one of the British three-deckers had been sunk and that the British had been obliged to abandon to the French the scene of the action. 'Let Pitt then boast of this victory to his nation of shopkeepers,' he concluded to loud applause.

The *Bellerophon* spent the rest of the summer of 1794 in the vicinity of Portsmouth, recovering from her recent ordeal. She was hauled alongside one of the sheer hulks and a gang of workmen from the dockyard lifted out her damaged masts, replaced them with new masts, and set up the rigging. She was heeled over and had the weed scraped and scrubbed from her copper bottom. Rafts of heavy timbers were floated alongside her and secured with lines. These were used as working platforms by teams of caulkers who hammered oakum into the seams between her planks and then filled the seams with hot tar. The caulkers were followed by painters who used the rafts to slap paint on the ship's sides. Heavy working boats came alongside loaded with barrels of beef and ship's biscuit which were swung aboard using the blocks and tackles on the ship's yard-arms. The same system was used to lift aboard the barrels of gunpowder brought across from the powder store at Priddy's Hard.

At the end of August she left the sheltered waters of the harbour and sailed across the Solent to the anchorage at St Helen's. The sailors, most of whom had not been allowed shore leave in case they should desert the ship, became increasingly restive. Captain Hope decided to make an example of the worst offenders. On Saturday 23 August he assembled the crew on deck and ordered James Aldridge to be flogged with twenty-four lashes for disobedience and David Pugh with forty-eight lashes for drunkenness. Ten days later they put to sea and sailed to Torbay with a fleet of thirty ships of the line. From there they sailed down the Channel and once again resumed the task of patrolling the seas between Ushant and the Scilly Isles, keeping a lookout for French ships. This continued until the end of November when she returned to Spithead. On 1 December Captain Hope handed over command of the *Bellerophon* to another captain. He had been presented with a gold medal for his part in the Battle of the Glorious First of June and he continued to enjoy a distinguished career in the navy. He was knighted in 1815, was a Vice-Admiral by 1819 and the following year became a Lord of the Admiralty. Three of his four sons followed him into the navy.

SEVEN

Lord Cranstoun and Billy Blue

1794–7

The new captain of the *Bellerophon* was a Scottish aristocrat who had the most glittering background of all the men who would command the ship during her eventful life. The Right Honourable James, the eighth Baron Cranstoun, was a descendant of the Lord of Teviotdale, and was born at the family seat at Crailing on the Scottish Borders. He entered the navy at an early age, was a lieutenant by 1776, and was in command of a frigate on the West Indies station during the American War of Independence. He was present at the battle of St Kitts in 1782 and three months later he was Admiral Rodney's flag captain at the Battle of the Saints. He boarded the French flagship *Ville de Paris* after her surrender and received the sword of the Comte de Grass on behalf of Rodney.

Lord Cranstoun was now aged thirty-nine, and recently married. His previous ship was the 64-gun *Raisonable*. On learning of his new command, he arranged for the clerk, the master's mates, the midshipmen and thirty seamen from that ship to be transferred to the *Bellerophon*. As he explained in his letter to the Admiralty, 'I brought them into the Service and they would prefer sailing with me without any rating to going with any other.'[1] This was a common practice and helps to account for the strong bond of loyalty which often existed between captains and their crews. However in this instance it did nothing to improve the morale of the rest of the ship's company which began to deteriorate following the departure of Admiral Pasley and Captain Hope. Whether this was the fault of Lord Cranstoun or was a symptom of the general discontent with pay and conditions which was to lead to the notorious fleet mutinies of 1797 is hard to determine from the surviving documents.

The gales which swept the anchorage during the winter of 1794–5 did not help matters. In February five men were flogged for various offences including gambling, drunkenness, and insolence to an officer, but this was nothing unusual. It was when the ship returned to Spithead after a cruise to Cape Finisterre that the rot set in. For three long months the *Bellerophon* lay at anchor in the Solent, off Portsmouth, and during that time there were floggings every three or four days. On 6 April four men were flogged with twelve lashes each for assisting a man to desert the ship; on 11 April two men were each given one dozen lashes for neglect of duty; on 14 April three men were punished with twenty-four lashes each for drunkenness and fighting and one man with twenty-one lashes for neglect of duty; on 17 April Tim O'Brian was given thirty-six lashes for theft, and on 22 April one man was given twelve lashes for leaving his post and another man twelve lashes for theft.[2]

It is hard to tell from the brief entries in the ship's log exactly what caused the unrest. Many of the crew were pressed men who had good cause to resent being confined in a warship for months on end. Even the volunteers must have felt they deserved some shore leave after their heroic efforts in the previous summer's battles. According to the surviving letters of Lord Cranstoun the focus of the unrest was a group of marines. On 16 April they wrote a letter to General Wemyss who was in overall command of the marines at Portsmouth:

Since the departure of the late Admiral Pasley and Capt Hope from this ship our situation has been and now is very different. In their time we were looked upon and received such usage as we flatter ourselves we deserved, but since whose departure their case is quite altered but for what reason we cannot conceive as we always endeavoured to perform the duty imposed upon us to the best of our power.

The men requested to be removed from the ship and said, 'we are very willing to go on board any other of His Majestys ships'.[3]

This was a serious challenge to the authority of Lord Cranstoun who immediately wrote to the Admiralty requesting that the marines should face a court martial to determine the truth or otherwise of their complaints. He maintained that the discipline on board the *Bellerophon* was milder than almost any other ship in the service, and went on to say, 'Had I known the situation of the *Bellerophon* latterly, I never would have accepted the command of her.' He blamed Sir Thomas Pasley for commanding a ship which was more like a privateer than a man of war and for allowing the ship's company to be drunk, quarrelsome 'and to do just as they pleased'.[4]

Before a court martial could be arranged the *Bellerophon* was ordered to sea. On 26 May 1795 she weighed anchor and the men put aside their grievances for the time being and got on with the business of running the ship. They joined a squadron commanded by Vice-Admiral William Cornwallis, a battle-hardened officer who had acquired the nickname 'Billy Blue'. He was the younger brother of General Cornwallis who had surrendered to Washington at Yorktown. He had fought the French on numerous occasions, most notably at the Battle of the Saints, but his nerves were shortly to be tested to the limit in an action which became known as Cornwallis's Retreat. This was a retreat in the face of a vastly superior force which, like the retreat of Sir John Moore's troops at Corunna in 1809, or the retreat of the British army at Dunkirk in 1940, acquired a lustre similar to that of a victory. And, just as the retreat and death of Sir John Moore were immortalised in a poem ('Not a drum was heard, not a funeral note, as his corse to the ramparts we hurried . . .'), so the action of Cornwallis and his squadron inspired a lengthy and patriotic ballad which joined the repertoire of songs and shanties sung by sailors over the years. The first two verses set the scene:

> It was just at break of day,
>   We were cruising in the Bay,
> With Blue Billy in the *Sov'ren* in the van,
>   When the French fleet bound for Brest

From Belle isle came heading west—
'Twas so, my lads, the saucy game began.
                                    Billy Blue—
Here's to you, Billy Blue, here's to you.

We'd the *Triumph* and the *Mars*,
And the *Sov'ren* – pride of tars,
Billy Ruff'n, and the *Brunswick*, known to fame;
With the *Pallas*, and the *Phaeton*,
Frigates that the flag did wait on—
Seven ships to uphold Old England's name.
                                    Billy Blue, etc.

The bay mentioned in the ballad was the Bay of Biscay and the squadron consisted of the *Royal Sovereign* of 100 guns which was the flagship of Cornwallis; the 74-gun ships *Triumph, Mars, Bellerophon* and *Brunswick*; and the two frigates, *Phaeton*, 38 guns, and *Pallas*, 32 guns. They arrived off Ushant on 7 June and the following day they intercepted a French convoy some 5 miles east of Belle Isle. They chased off the escorting French warships and captured eight of the merchant ships. So far, so good. But a week later they were cruising in the same area when they encountered a more formidable force. This was the entire Brest fleet under the command of Admiral Villaret-Joyeuse, the man who had put up such a fierce resistance to Howe's fleet at the Glorious First of June.

The first person to sight the French sails was the masthead lookout on the *Bellerophon*. At 9 o'clock on the morning of 16 June he reported a strange fleet east-south-east of their position. The *Phaeton*, under the command of Captain Stopford, was sent to investigate and at 9.25 she made the signal that the fleet was 'an enemy and superior force'. Cornwallis could not yet see the hulls of the enemy, so he did not know just how superior the enemy was in terms of ships and guns. He subsequently noted, 'I stood upon the starboard tack, with all our sail, keeping the ships collected. Upon enquiring by signal of the enemy's force, Captain Stopford answered, 13 line of battle ships, 14 frigates, 2 brigs, and a cutter; in all 30 sail.'[5] This represented a force roughly four times the size of the British squadron and there was clearly only one course of action possible, which was an orderly retreat. The wind dropped during the afternoon but not enough to hamper the French fleet which slowly gained on Cornwallis's ships, and divided into two divisions in order to attack them from both sides. Despite their reputation for being fast ships, the *Bellerophon* and the *Brunswick* began to lag behind the others, putting the entire squadron at risk. Cornwallis had no intention of abandoning them; he therefore slowed down the leading ships in order to maintain a tight formation.

As night fell the French were still some way astern but were continuing to close the gap. At 10 pm a boat from the frigate *Phaeton* came alongside the *Bellerophon* with orders from Cornwallis to lighten the ship by jettisoning the two bower anchors and cutting up the launch and throwing it overboard. These orders were promptly carried out but had little effect on the speed of the ship. The situation at dawn on 17 June was alarming and was recorded in graphic terms in the *Bellerophon*'s log-book:

Engraving of Cornwallis's Retreat with the *Bellerophon* in the foreground.
The *Royal Sovereign*, the flagship of Cornwallis, is on the right,
firing her starboard broadside at the advancing French fleet.

At daylight saw the French fleet coming up very fast in three divisions. The weather division, nearly abreast, three of the line and five frigates; the centre, six of the line and four frigates; the lee division, four of the line, five frigates, two brigs, and two cutters. Cleared ship for action. Started sixteen tons of water in the main hold to lighten the ship. At seven went to quarters. Served bread, cheese, and wine to the ship's company at quarters.[6]

Cornwallis ordered the *Bellerophon* and the *Brunswick* to the front of his squadron to avoid them being slowed down any further by damage to their sails or rigging from the shots of the leading French ships. He also wanted to keep them as a reserve force. He was aware that both ships had fought heroically at the First of June and could be relied on to fight to the death if necessary. As he later explained in his despatch to the Admiralty:

The Bellerophon I was glad to keep in some measure as a reserve, having reason at first to suppose there would be full occasion for the utmost exertions of us all . . . I considered that ship a treasure in store, having heard of her former achievements, and observing the spirit manifested by all on board when she passed me, joined to the zeal and activity shewed by Lord Cranstoun during the whole cruize.[7]

At 9.12 am the French opened fire on the *Mars* which was bringing up the rear of the squadron. The *Mars* returned the fire with her stern chasers, and at the same time the *Royal Sovereign* and the rest of the squadron hoisted their colours. These were the battle ensigns which were kept flying on every ship during an action and were only lowered if the ship was forced to surrender. Considering the overwhelming odds against them, the morale in the British squadron was extraordinarily high. As the *Bellerophon* sailed past the *Royal Sovereign* to take up her position at the head of the squadron, the entire crew cheered the Admiral. 'Billy Blue' was standing on the quarterdeck regarding the oncoming French ships with an indifference bordering on contempt, but as the *Bellerophon* passed under the lee of his flagship he raised his hat in response to the men's cheers. The firing from both sides became more general and the high-spirited cheering of the British crews became a feature of the action, each ship cheering other ships in the squadron as they fired their guns to keep the enemy at bay.

Around 4 in the afternoon the leading French ships made a determined effort to cut off and surround the *Mars* which had been injured by the enemy fire and was lagging behind. When Cornwallis saw several French 74-gun ships changing course towards her he pulled his flagship out of the line, swung her between the *Mars* and the French and let loose a thunderous broadside. The French ships immediately fell back out of range. 'This was their last effort,' he later remarked, 'if any thing they did can deserve that appellation.'[8] At the time Cornwallis presumed that they would return to the attack, and he had a last-ditch plan prepared which might or might not save his squadron. During the previous night he had arranged that Captain Stopford of the frigate *Phaeton* should resort to a classic *ruse de guerre* if no other British ships came to their aid the next day.

At 5 o'clock in the afternoon on 17 June the *Phaeton* was 2 or 3 miles ahead of the squadron, and from her position on the horizon she began sending signals. First she reported sighting one ship of the line. Then she hoisted the signal indicating that she had sighted three ships of the line, then five, and then nine. She followed this by letting go the topgallant sheets which was a signal the French would certainly have known and meant there was a strange fleet in sight. She then displayed a Dutch flag which indicated that the fleet was a friendly one.[9] The French naturally presumed that this must be the British Channel fleet, especially when the *Phaeton* altered course and headed back towards Cornwallis. When the topsails of some ships were sighted in the far distance (they were a convoy of English merchantmen which happened to be in the area) the French commander gave the order for the Brest fleet to break off the action and head for home. There was of course no Channel fleet and the successful deception added a final twist to Cornwallis's Retreat. When he sent a despatch to the Admiralty two days later Cornwallis was generous in his praise of the conduct of the captains, officers, seamen, marines and soldiers of all the ships in the squadron.

'It was the greatest pleasure I ever received to see the spirit manifested in the men, who instead of being cast down at seeing thirty sail of the enemy's ships attacking our little squadron, were in the highest spirits imaginable.' Their conduct throughout had made an indelible impression on his mind, and he said that had he let them loose on the enemy, 'I hardly know what might not have been accomplished by such men.'[10]

On 25 June the squadron returned to England and anchored in Cawsand Bay, the fleet anchorage at the entrance to Plymouth harbour. There they stayed for a few days to take in stores and victuals before returning to patrol the seas between Ushant and Belle Isle where they remained for the next three months. Mid-September saw them back at Spithead, giving Lord Cranstoun an opportunity to deal with the nine rebellious marines who had written the letter of complaint regarding their treatment on the *Bellerophon*. A court martial was arranged for 29 September. It was held on board the 80-gun ship *Le Juste*, which was one of the French ships captured at the battle of the Glorious First of June and was moored in Portsmouth harbour. The president of the court was none other than 'Billy Blue' or, to give him his formal title, the Honourable William Cornwallis, Vice-Admiral of the Red, and second officer in command of his Majesty's ships and vessels at Portsmouth and Spithead. Among the other officers present were four admirals and two captains. The nine marines were charged with 'attempting to make a mutiny amongst the whole party on board by complaining of harsh and improper treatment in the Bellerophon and being accessory to the writing a publick letter to the Commanding Officer of the Marines on shore.' This was a serious charge and if the court found the men guilty of mutiny they could face the death penalty.

Lord Cranstoun questioned Major Smith, captain of the marines on board the *Bellerophon*, about the regime on the ship and asked him whether it was too severe and whether any of the marines had ever complained to him about their duties. Major Smith replied that the regime was perfectly easy. Lord Cranstoun then asked:

'Is it my custom in carrying on the duty of the ship to swear or speak
in such a manner to any of the men as likely to hinder their coming
forward with their complaints?'
'Remarkable for the contrary.'
'Do I suffer the officers to speak harshly to the men?'
'I do not recollect that I ever heard Lord Cranstoun mention anything
to the officers as to the mode of speaking to the men.'

Admiral Cornwallis then intervened and asked Major Smith, 'To the
best of your knowledge then have the marines serving on board the
Bellerophon been treated in a harsh and improper manner?'

'I certainly do not think they have,' answered Major Smith.

Robert Daniel, the first lieutenant of the *Bellerophon*, was questioned along similar lines. He thought that the regime of the marines
on the ship was as easy as any in the navy. When asked whether
Lord Cranstoun had ever spoken harshly to the men he replied, 'I
have very seldom heard Lord Cranstoun swear and never saw him
strike a man or behave in a manner to prevent the people coming
forward with their complaints.' Some of the other officers of the
Bellerophon were questioned by Lord Cranstoun and came up with
similar answers.

All this put Lord Cranstoun in a favourable light and left the
marines in a difficult position because there seemed to be no
justification for their complaints. However, they were saved by Major
Smith who put in a passionate plea on their behalf. He told the
court, 'I have been nearly two years embarked with them on board
the Bellerophon, and I never felt myself so pleased with any party
I had the honour of commanding, as I have done with them till this
unhappy letter. Their attention and civility to every officer in
whatever station on board is not to be exceeded by any one set of
men afloat.'

He went on to praise their recent performance in the face of the
French fleet: 'I have also had the opportunity in being with them in
action and their courage and loyalty was never disputed. Lately in a
particular situation the prisoners in particular on the seventeenth of
June last, when not obliged to go to their quarters as being prisoners,

were amongst the first under arms as volunteers.' He concluded by declaring that the prisoners 'exerted themselves to the utmost in everything relative to themselves and the duty of the ship'.

The court adjourned to consider the evidence and then returned a verdict which honourably cleared both parties. The court could find no evidence of ill-treatment of the marines. It was felt that the writing of the letter to Major-General Wemyss was highly improper but, in consideration of the good character of the prisoners, and their having behaved in a most exemplary manner in the recent action with the enemy, they should receive no punishment and should return to their duties on board the *Bellerophon*.

Lord Cranstoun had been in command of the ship for less than ten months. He remained her captain for another year. As far as one can tell from the ship's log and his own correspondence he encountered no further problems with the crew, and the ship resumed her usual routine – which meant returning to blockade duty off the west coast of France. But first she needed a complete overhaul. Nine years had passed since her launch in October 1786 and, although she had been out of commission on the Medway for two of those years, much of the remaining time had been spent at sea in all weathers. Cranstoun had written to the Admiralty on 16 September with a list of defects needing urgent attention. The most serious of these was the copper on the ship's bottom which was in a very bad state, and no doubt explains why she was sailing so slowly during the cruise which culminated in Cornwallis's Retreat.

Repairing and, where necessary, replacing the copper plates on the bottom of a warship was a major operation because it usually meant taking the ship into dry dock. With a relatively large ship, such as a two-decker, this meant lifting out the masts, guns and most of the ballast in order to lighten her and reduce her draught. On Sunday 11 October the *Bellerophon* was moved from the anchorage at Spithead into Portsmouth harbour and was lashed alongside the *Essex* hulk. For the next six weeks her sailors, assisted by workmen from the dockyard, were engaged in a great deal of heavy lifting and hard manual labour. While autumn gales raged outside in the Solent and driving rain swept across the waters of

the harbour they systematically cleared the ship of almost everything that could be moved. The guns were hoisted out and lowered
into a barge alongside. The massive anchors and anchor cables were
stored in the *Essex* hulk, together with several hundred barrels of
stores; 150 tons of shingle ballast were removed, and most of the
running rigging was taken to the rigging store in the dockyard. On
26 October the ship was moved alongside the sheer hulk and her
three great masts were lifted out. The next day she was towed across
to the dockhead at the northern end of the dockyard and at high
tide she was floated into one of the dry docks and made secure. When
the water had drained out at low tide the gates were closed, and the
workmen from the dockyard got to work. The barnacles and the
thick weed trailing from the bottom of the ship were scraped and
burnt off. The copper plates were carefully inspected, and repairs
were carried out where necessary. Meanwhile a team of caulkers
started work on the lower deck. The smell of hot tar replaced the
dank odours from the bilges as the men worked their way through
the ship, hammering oakum into the seams and sealing them with
tar. Carpenters and plumbers brought their tools on board to make

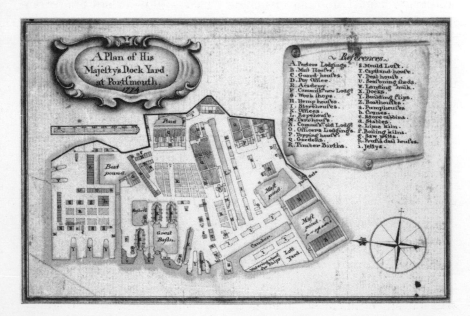

A plan of the royal dockyard at Portsmouth in the late eighteenth century.

good the defects on Cranstoun's list. They fitted new steps to the ship's sides, repaired ladders and gratings, and the lanterns on the poop, mended the fire hearth in the galley and replaced leaking lead pipes.

While the ship was in the dry dock most of her crew were given work in the dockyard or on other ships in the harbour. One party of men was despatched to the rigging loft to work on the standing rigging. Another work party was sent to Southsea beach and spent an exhausting three days loading shingle for ballast into a lighter. On one day alone they shifted 76 tons of shingle. The carpenters, joiners, caulkers and shipwrights finished most of their work on the hull in a little over two weeks; on 13 November the gates of the dry dock were opened and the *Bellerophon* was floated out. She was hauled back to the sheer hulk to have her masts lifted back in, and then moved alongside the *Essex* hulk for her guns, anchors, cables and stores to be hoisted aboard and manhandled back into their respective places. As soon as the rigging had been set up she was towed out of the harbour entrance to join the other warships swinging with the tide in the anchorage at Spithead.

January 1796 found her once again heading down the Channel to face the winter storms off Ushant and the grey Atlantic waves rolling across the Bay of Biscay. Two or three months at sea scanning the horizon for French ships, a few weeks respite in the Solent or at Cawsand Bay to take on water and provisions, and then back to sea for another two or three months: it was a pattern her crew, and the crews of the other British warships on blockade duty, had been living with for two years and would have to endure for years to come. The only change in the routine as far as the *Bellerophon* was concerned was that in September 1796 she got a new captain. Lord Cranstoun was evidently not happy with his command. He managed to pull some strings and was appointed Governor of Grenada, the West Indian island which lies between Trinidad and Barbados. A more welcome contrast to the Bay of Biscay in winter would be hard to imagine. Unfortunately he did not live to take up his new post. Soon after his appointment was announced he died at his home in Bishops Waltham, Hampshire, his death apparently caused by drinking cider which had been kept in a vessel lined with lead. His wife Elizabeth, who was only twenty-seven, died within months 'of a decline occasioned by her bereavement'.

The *Bellerophon's* fourth captain was Henry D'Esterre Darby, a 47-year-old Irishman. An engraved portrait of him shows a handsome man with a sardonic expression. He was not an aristocrat but came from the landed gentry. His father was a barrister whose family owned Leap Castle in King's County, some 50 miles west of Dublin. His uncle George was a vice-admiral. Henry joined the navy as a midshipman at the age of thirteen and spent several years serving in frigates. His progress through the ranks was slow compared to the meteoric careers of many of his contemporaries. He was twenty-seven when he became a lieutenant and, although he spent two years on the *Britannia*, the flagship of his uncle who was then in command of the Channel fleet, it was not until 1783 that he was appointed captain at the comparatively advanced age of thirty-four.

Captain Darby took over the command of the *Bellerophon* at a

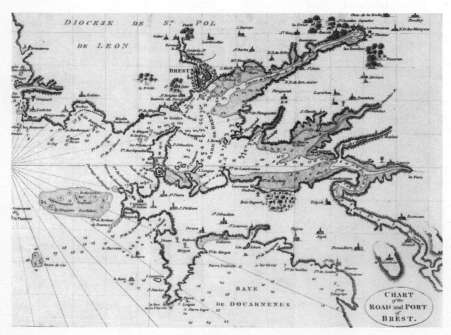

Chart of the port of Brest in 1800 showing the
numerous rocks and shoals off the entrance.

critical time. All the attempts of Prime Minister William Pitt to make peace with an increasingly aggressive France had come to nothing. The coalition of allies which he had established to counter the advancing French armies had fallen apart. Prussia, Holland and Spain had made peace with France during the course of 1795. In 1796 a French army commanded by Napoleon marched into northern Italy, crushed all opposition in the states ruled by Austria, and replaced the feudal regimes with republican governments modelled on the new French constitution. And in October 1796 Spain decided to throw in her lot with France and declared war on Britain. This was an extremely serious development. Britain's command of the seas, and in particular her control of the English Channel, had prevented the French from mounting an invasion. But Spain had a formidable navy and, while the British blockade had curtailed the movements of the French fleet up till now, it would be much more difficult to prevent the combined fleets of France and Spain from breaking out of their naval bases. They would then be able to sail up the Channel and provide cover for transport vessels which would ferry the French troops across and land them on the coasts of Sussex or Kent.

France's determination to take on Britain was demonstrated in December 1796. Encouraged by rebellious movements in Ireland, the French decided to mount an invasion of Ireland as a stepping stone to attacking England. On 15 December a fleet of forty-four ships, including seventeen ships of the line and thirteen frigates, set sail from Brest. The invasion force included 16,500 troops under the command of General Hoche and the plan was to land the troops in Bantry Bay on the south-west coast of Ireland, then march overland and capture Cork which was used as a naval base by the British. The whole venture was a disaster. One of the French 74-gun ships was wrecked off Brest on the day they sailed, and the remainder ran into fierce easterly gales off the coast of Ireland. Forced to beat back and forth for days on end, the ships began to run low on provisions, and abandoned all hope of landing the troops. Two ships were driven onto the Irish coast, two foundered in heavy seas, seven were captured, and the *Droits de l'homme*, another 74, was wrecked on the French coast – with great loss of life – after a running battle with two British frigates.

The French invasion plans had taken the British by surprise. The Channel fleet was anchored at Spithead 400 miles from the coast of Ireland. The *Bellerophon* was cruising with a squadron off Ushant but failed to sight the French fleet. When she returned to Plymouth, on 2 January 1797, she was ordered to join a squadron of three other ships of the line and to patrol the seas between Bantry Bay and Cork but it was a case of shutting the stable door after the horse had bolted. By the time they sighted the Old Head of Kinsale on 18 January the French were long gone. The squadron spent three weeks patrolling the south-west coast of Ireland in gales which were so strong that the *Bellerophon*'s mainsail was ripped to pieces. However this was all in a day's work for her crew and a new sail was soon bent onto the yard. On 4 February they put into Cork to take on water and provisions. Anchored in the sheltered waters of the harbour they found the 64-gun ship *Polyphemus* flying the flag of Admiral Kingsmill and five frigates. This was the navy's Irish squadron which had the job of patrolling the Atlantic coast of Ireland and the western approaches. The frigates had captured several French ships the previous summer but had been in harbour when the French invasion fleet had arrived off Bantry Bay. After ten days at Cork the *Bellerophon* set sail and was back at Spithead by the beginning of March.

Captain Darby now received orders which were to change the familiar routine of the *Bellerophon* and her crew dramatically. Instead of blockading the French coast she was to join the Mediterranean fleet under Sir John Jervis. The new enemy was the Spanish fleet, based at Cadiz. On 17 March 1797 the *Bellerophon* left the grey skies and chill winds of the Solent and headed for the sun and the warm waters of southern Spain. It would be more than two years before her captain and crew saw the shores of England again.

EIGHT

The Bay of Cadiz

1797

On 30 May 1797 the *Bellerophon* arrived in the Bay of Cadiz and joined the fleet of British ships blockading the port. The main body of the fleet was anchored in an extended line across the entrance of the bay but the *Bellerophon* was ordered to join the Advanced Squadron which was positioned some way ahead of the main fleet, close to the walls of the ancient city. Under a cloudless blue sky she worked her way across the choppy waters of the bay towards the four ships of the Advanced Squadron. When she was level with them she dropped anchor in 11 fathoms. Ahead lay Cadiz, shimmering in the heat of the summer afternoon. Situated at the end of a promontory, the city was protected by an encircling wall and several forts. Above the wall could be seen the tiled rooftops of houses, and the towers and domes of numerous churches and grand civic buildings. In the harbour beside the city walls were thirty Spanish warships, their colourful red and orange flags extended in the fresh breeze, the nearest of the ships almost within gunshot.

For two days the crew of the *Bellerophon* were kept busy carrying out minor repairs and taking on board water and provisions – including several basketloads of lemons, and six live bullocks. On the third day the ship's log noted that 'Rear Admiral Nelson came on board and mustered the ship's company.' Nelson had been given command of the Advanced Squadron and, although this was the only time that he set foot on the decks of the *Bellerophon*, the ship's fortunes were to be closely linked with his during the course of the next few years. Nelson was already a legend in the British Navy and the crew would have been intensely curious to see him. He was now thirty-eight years old. Since the siege of Toulon in 1793 he had made his mark as a ruthless and formidable commander in battle, and had begun to achieve the celebrity which he craved and believed was his destiny.

While taking part in the siege of Calvi on the coast of Corsica in 1794 he had been wounded and blinded in his right eye. The pupil was now a hazy blue colour and although he simply regarded it as one of the hazards of war, he could barely distinguish light from darkness with that eye, and admitted that 'as to all the purpose of use it is gone.' His hair was flecked with grey and his face was lined

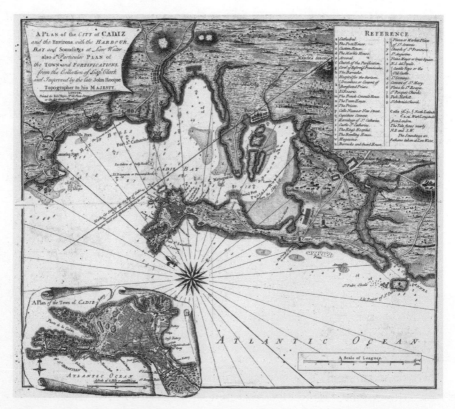

A chart of Cadiz Bay in 1762 with an inset plan of the city of Cadiz.

and gaunt, but he still had a restless energy. He had also acquired
an air of command. He had, after all, been a full captain since the
age of twenty and had recently demonstrated the fighting qualities
which were to make his name famous throughout Europe.

In 1795, while in command of the 64-gun *Agamemnon*, he had
engaged the *Ça Ira*, an 84-gun French ship, and had kept up such a
devastating fire on her that she subsequently surrendered, with the
loss of 400 men killed and wounded. And then on 14 February 1797
he had played a spectacular role in the Battle of Cape St Vincent. As
the British fleet, under Admiral Sir John Jervis, was going into action
against a Spanish fleet off the south-west coast of Spain, Nelson had
disobeyed orders by swinging his ship, the *Captain*, out of the line
of battle in order to hold apart the two Spanish divisions, an action
which directly contributed to the subsequent British victory. After
coming under fire from seven Spanish ships, Nelson had rammed the
San Nicolas, boarded her, and forced her surrender. Another Spanish
ship, the *San Joseph*, had become entangled with the *San Nicolas*.
Nelson shouted 'Westminster Abbey or victory!' and led a boarding
party onto her quarterdeck where 'extravagant as the story may
seem, did I receive the swords of the vanquished Spaniards . . . The
Victory passing saluted us with three cheers, as did every ship in the
fleet.'[1]

When the news reached England, that a British fleet had defeated
a Spanish force of almost double its strength, there was general
rejoicing and Nelson was rewarded with a knighthood. His father,
who was staying in Bath, reflected the mood of many when he wrote,
'The name and services of Nelson have sounded throughout the City
of Bath from the common ballad-singer to the public theatre. Joy
sparkles in every eye and desponding Britain draws back her sable
veil and smiles.'[2] Sir John Jervis was made an earl and became Lord
St Vincent. A few weeks after the battle he had taken the British
fleet south and commenced the blockade of Cadiz.

There is no record of the reaction of the *Bellerophon*'s crew to
Nelson's arrival on board, nor of his conversation with Captain Darby,
but the marine artist Thomas Buttersworth painted a number of
watercolours of the ships of the Advanced Squadron around this time

which show the *Bellerophon* anchored alongside the *Theseus*, Nelson's flagship. Buttersworth was a seaman on one of the ships in the main body of the fleet under Lord St Vincent and although his pictures are strangely lacking in atmosphere they are full of carefully observed detail. The anchored ships of Nelson's squadron are beautifully drawn; he notes the boats moored alongside their sterns, and the longboats and cutters coming and going in the foreground. His pictures clearly show how close the squadron was to Cadiz. According to Nelson, 'We are looking at the ladies walking the walls and Mall of Cadiz and know of the ridicule they make of their sea officers.'[3]

Compared to the hazardous job of patrolling the seas off Brest, the blockade of Cadiz should have been a relatively easy task but St Vincent imposed a strict regime and with good reason. He and his fellow officers were aware that there was unrest among the sailors of the fleet, much of it inspired by news of the two fleet mutinies which had recently taken place in home waters – the most serious in the navy's history. With the nation at war and under threat of invasion from France, such rebellion could have had the most disastrous consequences. There was much talk of the mutineers being influenced by the French Revolution and some may have been, but the British sailors' demands were much more basic than the republican ideals of Liberty, Equality and Fraternity. The grievances on the list drawn up by the sailors of the Channel fleet at Spithead on 17 April 1797 were entirely concerned with their pay, food and conditions. The pay of seamen in the Royal Navy had remained unchanged since 1653 and was fixed at 24 shillings a lunar month for able seamen and 19 shillings for ordinary seamen. Merchant sea captains in the Pool of London were offering wages of £3. 15s. a month around this time and a private in a cavalry regiment earned £3 a calendar month. In addition to an increase in pay, the sailors wanted better food and the full rations to which they were entitled; they wanted shore leave when ships returned to port so they could see their families (most captains refused shore leave on the grounds that their crews inevitably included large numbers of pressed men who were likely to desert); and they wanted better treatment and pay for men who were sick or wounded.

Senior officers in the navy were generally sympathetic to the men's requests and within eight days the Admiralty agreed to all the demands, but when the fleet was ordered to sea on 7 May, the men refused to obey their officers because they did not believe the promises that had been made. An Act of Parliament was hastily passed, and on 14 May Lord Howe arrived at Portsmouth with the news that all the men's demands would be met and a pardon would be provided for the Spithead mutineers. The jubilant sailors carried Howe on their shoulders to the governor's house and later manned the yards of their ships in celebration as he was rowed through the fleet.

Unrest had also spread among the ships anchored at the Nore. In addition to the concessions made to the men at Spithead (which had been extended to the whole navy by the Act of Parliament), the Nore seamen wanted a more equal distribution of prize money, the payment of arrears of wages before ships went to sea, and the removal of the harshest of the Articles of War. The mutiny at the Nore began on 12 May and rapidly extended to most of the ships in the Medway as well as the North Sea fleet along the coast at Yarmouth. The mutineers tarred and feathered several officers, looted local fishing boats and farms, and began intercepting shipping on the Thames with the aim of blockading London. However, when the government began to set up shore batteries and brought up warships with loyal crews, the mutiny rapidly collapsed. Officers resumed command of their ships, and Richard Parker, the leader of the mutiny, was handed over to the authorities. This time there was no mercy for the mutineers. Richard Parker and thirty-five other seamen were hanged.

The *Bellerophon* had been anchored in the Bay of Cadiz for nearly six weeks when an event took place which provoked a mutiny on one ship and might have led to a more general mutiny had it not been for the swift and uncompromising action taken by Lord St Vincent. Two young seamen from another ship in the fleet were charged with committing 'the unnatural and detestable sin of sodomy'. The court martial was held in the great cabin of the *Prince George*, a big three-decker of 90 guns. The two seamen had spent three days in confinement, and would have been only too aware that the punishment for breaching the Twentieth-ninth Article of War was death. After their cramped and gloomy quarters, confined in irons below deck, the atmosphere of the great cabin must have been extremely intimidating. They found themselves in an elegantly proportioned room filled with senior naval officers resplendent in their full dress uniforms with dark blue coats, white breeches and stockings, buckled shoes, and an impressive array of gold lace on sleeves and lapels. The room had a low, gently curving ceiling with the far wall almost entirely composed of windows. The sunlight streaming in through the curved arc of these stern windows was dazzling. It glistened on the polished mahogany chairs and tables, and on the gold epaulettes and brass buttons of the assembled officers. The president of the court was Charles Thompson, Vice-Admiral of the Blue, and the captains included Cuthbert Collingwood, Thomas Troubridge, Sir Robert Calder and the *Bellerophon*'s Henry Darby.

The first man to give evidence was Nicholas Tobin, the captain's coxswain of the *St George*, the 90-gun sister ship of the *Prince George*. He was sworn in and asked to relate what he knew of the business. He told the court that on the night of 27 June, between the hours of 9 and 10, he was on the main deck when seaman John Tipper came to him and said that there were two men connected together. Tobin told him to get a light and they went below to where they heard a man breathing very hard. This was in the area below the forecastle beside the door of the sick berth.

'I saw John Benson and Philip Francis laying with their trowsers down about their legs one hand fast held of John Benson's privates while several people standing by tried to get them up.' What happened next was described by John Tipper who was the next witness. For some reason Tipper had taken the light away for a few minutes and he recalled that, when he came back, he:

saw Philip Francis lying upon his belly and John Benson upon the top of him, making motions with his body as tho' he wished to have connections with him. I then went and laid hold of Philip Francis's jacket and said to him are you not ashamed to be laying here in this condition. He made me no answer at first, but muttered to himself. I then shook him again. He said, whats the matter, whats the matter, what are you about. I said get up. He made answer and said am I not in my hammock. No, I said. Get up and button your trousers about you. He then got up and leaned his head against a hammock that was over him. I then said to Nicholas Tobin, go aft and report them to the officer of the watch.

Tobin went to see Mr Cuthbert and told him 'there was a very horrid thing committed in the ship that night'. They returned with the Master at Arms and the two men were put into confinement.[4]

Other witnesses were called and repeated the same story. The court had to determine whether there was willing agreement and whether penetration had taken place. All the witnesses were asked the same question, 'Did you see they were connected one with another?' Tobin could not be certain, but Tipper said that to the best of his knowledge they were, and other witnesses confirmed this. The witnesses were also asked whether either of the accused men were drunk at the time. It transpired that Philip Francis was 'very much in liquor when he lay down there'. Indeed Francis's defence was that he was so drunk that he knew nothing of what had taken place.

The court was cleared, the assembled officers deliberated, and the prisoners were brought back into the great cabin. It was a solemn moment. Admiral Thompson told the two seamen that the court was of the opinion that the charge had been fully proved. Consequently it was agreed that they should be hanged by the neck until they were dead 'at the yard arm of such ship or ships of His Majesty and at such time or times as the Commander-in-chief shall direct.'

Lord St Vincent directed that they should be executed two days later from the yard-arm of their own ship. The *Bellerophon*'s log-book entry for Sunday 2 July simply notes, 'At 7.30 AM sent two boats and armed with an officer in each to attend an execution of two seamen on board HM.Ship St George.' Later that day Lord St Vincent sat down in the great cabin of his flagship and dictated the following letter to the Secretary of the Admiralty in London:

Sir,

I enclose the sentence and minutes of a court-martial on two seamen, late belonging to His Majesty's ship St George. The crime of which they were convicted was of so horrible and detestable a nature, and the times requiring summary punishments, I caused the sentence to be carried into execution at nine o'clock this morning in presence of the whole squadron.[5]

Within a week there were more hangings. The crew of the *St George* were discovered in a plot to mutiny and take over the ship. The mutineers' pretext was that they objected to the men convicted of sodomy being hanged on their ship but the truth seems to have been that they had been plotting mutiny for some months. At a court martial on 7 July, John Anderson, Michael McCann, John Hayes and James Fitzgerald were found guilty of 'seditiously, mutinously and traitorously conspiring to deprive Captain Peard and the rest of the officers of the *St George* of the command of the ship.'[6] In fact the mutineers' plans had been foiled by a loyal member of the crew who had warned Captain Peard that the ship's company had been planning to seize the ship during the night. The four ringleaders had previous records which caused them to be seen as villains with notoriously bad characters. Michael McCann had served on a French privateer before being captured by a British warship. The other three had been guilty of desertion for which John Hayes had received 300 lashes.

Lord St Vincent was a hard man at the best of times, but with the mutinies at Spithead and the Nore uppermost in his mind, he decided to make an example of the entire crew of the *St George* by insisting that they hang their own shipmates. And to make sure that everyone understood the significance of this unusual procedure he issued a General Order to the entire fleet:

The sentence is to be carried into execution by the crew of the St George alone, and no part of the boats' crews of other ships, as is usual on similar occasions, is to assist in this most painful service, in order to mark the high sense the Commander-in-chief entertains of the loyalty, fidelity and subordination of the rest of the fleet, which he will not fail to make known to the Lords Commissioners of the Admiralty and request them to lay it before the King. This memorandum is to be read to the ships companies of the fleet before the execution.[7]

As a further break with tradition the commander-in-chief refused to allow the men a few days to prepare themselves for death and ordered them to be hanged on the day after the court martial, even though this meant the execution would take place on a Sunday. So at 7.30 am on Sunday 9 July the *Bellerophon* again sent two boats across the bay. In addition to the sailors pulling at the oars, each boat had an officer and two red-coated marines armed with muskets sitting in the stern. As they rowed out from under the shadow of their ship, the men could see boats from the other anchored ships setting out towards the *St George*. By the time all the boats were gathered around the disgraced ship, the men were sweating in the morning sun. On the forecastle of the *St George* the four condemned men were listening to the prayers of the ship's chaplain while their shipmates stood by the ropes which had been rigged from the lower yard-arm of the foremast. The crews of every one of the ships of the line, the frigates, cutters and naval supply ships gathered in the bay, were assembled to witness the execution. More than 15,000 officers and men stood in silence on the decks of their ships awaiting the signal. At exactly 9 o'clock a single gun was fired. As the explosion echoed across the bay four bodies were hauled rapidly into the air, their legs kicking briefly before they hung lifeless, swaying to and fro as the *St George* rocked slowly back and forth in the low swell.

In reporting the executions to the Admiralty later that day Lord St Vincent said that he hoped he would not be censured by the bench of bishops for profaning the Sabbath. Although he was the last man to care what a few bishops thought of his actions he was no doubt heartened to receive an approving letter from Nelson who had not been able to attend the court martial because he and the men of his squadron had to remain at their posts and keep a continuous watch on the Spanish ships. Nelson wrote to congratulate St Vincent on finishing the *St George*'s business so speedily, 'even although it is Sunday. The particular situation of the service requires extraordinary measures. I hope this will end all the disorders in the fleet.'[8] The severity of St Vincent's response to any sign of disaffection prevented a general mutiny on the scale of those at Spithead and the Nore but did not end the unrest. Further plots were discovered, the most serious being on the 74-gun ship *Defence* where the boatswain was planning to seize the ship at night and deliver her up to the Spanish in Cadiz harbour. In the six weeks following the hanging of the *St George*'s men there were four more executions before the sailors settled down and resumed their usual shipboard routine.

The routine and the confinement of shipboard life at anchor in the bay ended on 7 October when Lord St Vincent took the fleet to sea. They sailed north, rounded Cape St Vincent and dropped anchor in the River Tagus. From November through to the following May the log-book of the *Bellerophon* makes dreary reading. Those seven months were like a repeat of the endless cruises off Ushant. In company with a squadron of six or seven warships the *Bellerophon* patrolled the coast between Cape Trafalgar and Cape St Vincent. After two or three weeks at sea the squadron returned to the Bay of Cadiz or the River Tagus to take in provisions and carry out any repairs necessary and then headed off into the rolling swell of the Atlantic – until Friday 25 May 1798 when there was a new development which was to lead to momentous times ahead. On that day the *Bellerophon* left Cadiz for the last time and joined a squadron under the command of Captain Thomas Troubridge. Their orders were to sail into the Mediterranean and meet up with Nelson and the *Vanguard*. Their mission was to find Napoleon who was reported to have left Toulon in command of a vast fleet of transport ships, a huge army and an accompanying fleet of French warships.

NINE

In Search of Napoleon

1797–8

Napoleon had come a long way since the recapture of Toulon in 1793. His role in the battle for the port had earned him the praise of his commanding officer and promotion to the rank of brigadier-general. The next milestone in his astonishing rise to power took place on a wet and windy day in Paris on 4 October 1795, when an armed and rebellious mob of some 30,000 royalists, anarchists and others opposed to the republican government marched on the Tuileries. Their aim was to overthrow the ruling Convention and overturn the Revolution. Napoleon, who was in Paris at the time, had been introduced the day before to Paul Barras, the newly appointed commander-in-chief. He agreed to take charge of the local forces and arranged for forty field guns to be rushed into the city. He carefully positioned them so that they commanded the approaches to the Tuileries and, when the rebels attacked, he fired round after round of grapeshot into their leading ranks. Grapeshot, or case shot, consisted of dozens of small iron balls enclosed in a canvas case which opened up when fired and scattered a murderous hail of missiles. It was particularly effective when fired into a packed crowd. The bombardment lasted only a few minutes and scattered the rebels, who fled, pursued by Government troops.

Napoleon's 'whiff of grapeshot' had proved decisive and Barras was able to announce to the Convention, 'The Republic has been saved.' Two weeks later Napoleon was made a full general and given command of the Army of the Interior. He was twenty-six years old. A few months later, in March 1796, the Directory of the French Republic, which had replaced the Convention, put him in command of the Army of Italy with orders to conquer northern Italy. This was to be achieved by attacking and defeating the armies of Austria and Piedmont and occupying the Austrian duchy of Milan. Within thirteen months Napoleon had not only achieved these objectives but had also occupied the Papal States. He had won a dozen major battles by using the tactics which later routed armies across Europe: he imposed a rigid discipline on his troops and was able to move them from place to place at a speed which astonished his enemies; he used a combination of flanking movements and clever feints with a devastating concentration of force; he made the best possible use of the terrain because, like Wellington, he knew how to read the topography of the landscape; and he used his training as an artillery officer to position and use his field guns to maximum effect.

We get a glimpse of the charisma and force of character which he demonstrated during the Italian campaign in the heroic portrait painted by the young French painter Antoine-Jean Gros around this time. Napoleon had given the artist three brief sittings and from these sessions Gros produced an iconic image of the young general advancing on the bridge at Arcole where one of the key battles of the campaign had taken place. The hawklike face, piercing glance, flowing hair and vigorous pose are in marked contrast to the later images of a stocky, plump figure with thinning hair and a glowering expression. Fanny Burney described meeting Napoleon in Paris in the summer of 1802: 'I had a view so near, though so brief of his face, as to be much struck by it. It is of a deeply impressive cast, pale even to sallowness, while not only in the eye but in every feature – care, thought, melancholy and meditation are strongly marked, with so much of character, nay, genius, and so penetrating a seriousness, or rather sadness, as powerfully to sink into an observer's mind.'[1]

After his victories on the battlefield Napoleon revealed his diplomatic and political skills during the negotiations which followed.

Having driven the Austrians out of Italy, his aim was to bring the liberties and benefits of the French Republic to the northern Italians. With the backing of the Directors in Paris he set up the Cisalpine Republic as a free and independent state with a constitution modelled on that of France. This proved so successful that the people of Genoa overthrew their feudal and aristocratic government and Napoleon set up the Ligurian Republic in its place. In May, following riots and disturbances in Verona, he marched his army from Milan and occupied Venice. And in October, after months of negotiations, he successfully concluded a peace treaty with Austria at Campo Fornio. When he returned to Paris in December he was greeted as a hero and cheered wildly in a public ceremony at the Luxembourg.

To the Directors who were now governing France, Napoleon must have seemed like a man who could achieve miracles. It was therefore not so surprising that they should give him his most challenging task to date. He was made commander of the Army of England and given the job of masterminding the invasion of the only country which was still at war with France. Accompanied by two aides, his secretary and a courier, he travelled north in a coach to inspect the ports and harbours of Normandy and Flanders. He reached the coast on 10 February 1798 and spent the next eight days visiting Boulogne, Calais, Dunkirk and Antwerp, as well as several of the smaller fishing ports like Etaples.

The weather was atrocious, with bitterly cold north-easterly gales sending flurries of snow and sleet across the heaving grey seas and breaking waves of the English Channel. Napoleon interviewed army officers and naval officers and cast a critical eye over the troops as well as the transport vessels and barges which were being built or converted to carry infantry and cavalry. He had told his aides that he wished his identity to be concealed during his visit but this did not prevent the Paris newspapers from printing details of his progress. Within twelve days of his arrival on the coast the readers of *The Times* in London learnt that General Napoleon had alighted from his coach at the Silver Lion Hotel in Calais and visited a coffee-house. They were informed that he intended to inspect a chain of military camps which had been established along the coast. 'It appears that the invasion of England will be a general attack, not partial ones.'

In London the threatened invasion seems to have had little effect on most people's lives. The King and Queen set the tone. During the week that Napoleon was inspecting the invasion troops, the royal family went on an excursion to Kew. The King took an airing on horseback and returned to Buckingham House to give an audience to the Duke of York. On the evening of 16 February their Majesties, accompanied by four of the princesses, went on one of their regular visits to the theatre, this time to Covent Garden to see a new comedy, *He's much to blame*, followed by a new production of *Joan of Arc*. The latter was 'a grand historical ballet of action', and was an odd choice of subject to stage in the circumstances. *The Times* thought that the principle of the ballet was bad and degraded British humanity. The horrific ending, in which the French heroine was burnt at the stake by the British, had been toned down by the time the royal family saw the show, and the ballet attracted a full house and was much applauded.

Although London society continued to enjoy itself there is no doubt that the invasion was regarded as a serious threat. In the City of London the Lord Mayor presided over a meeting of merchants and bankers at which it was unanimously resolved that 'in view of the enemy's purpose of utterly destroying the Constitutions of these Kingdoms' a subscription for voluntary contributions would be opened at the Bank for the defence of the country. The sum of £46,534 was raised by the end of the meeting and other patriotic funds were established and attracted considerable support.[2] The Admiralty decided that fifteen post-captains and seventy-five masters and commanders should be employed along the coast to command the Sea Fencibles: these were a maritime version of the later home guard and consisted of volunteers drawn from those local seamen who had escaped the activities of the press gangs – mostly fishermen, smugglers and seamen engaged in the coastal trade, who were armed, organised and given protection against impressment.

In the West Country, where he had recently moved with his wife and baby son, the poet Coleridge expressed his concerns about the invasion in a long and deeply felt poem, 'Fears in Solitude'. He was living in a cottage among the Quantock Hills beside the Bristol

Channel and the thought of his native land being rent by 'carnage and groans' filled him with dread:

> What uproar and what strife may now be stirring
>   This way or that o'er these silent hills –
>   Invasion, and the thunder and the shout,
>   And all the crash of onset; fear and rage,
>   And undetermined conflict . . .[3]

For Coleridge, as for most of his countrymen, it was Britain's 'fleets and perilous seas' which were seen as the country's strongest defence, and with good reason. The French and Spanish fleets were effectively penned into their respective naval bases by British ships, and the remains of the Dutch fleet, after being defeated by Admiral Duncan at the Battle of Camperdown the previous October, had retreated to the Texel. During the course of his tour of the Channel ports Napoleon rapidly came to the conclusion that it was too hazardous to send an army of 30,000 troops across the Channel. He sent a blunt report to the Directory in Paris:

> Whatever efforts we make, we will not, within a period of several years, gain the superiority of the seas. To perform a descent on England without being master of the seas is a very daring operation and very difficult to put into effect. If it is possible, it would be by surprise, by escaping from the squadrons blockading Brest or the Texel, then arriving in small boats during the night and after a crossing of seven or eight hours, at daybreak on the coast of Kent or Sussex. For such an operation we would need the long nights of winter. After the month of April, it would be increasingly impossible.[4]

He pointed out that there was a shortage of boats and of experienced seamen and he strongly recommended that the invasion should be postponed. Instead he suggested that France should mount an expedition to Egypt.

There were several reasons behind this startling proposition. Napoleon's principal argument was that an invasion of Egypt would open up a route to India and enable France to strike at England's richest possession. France had already conquered Corsica and Corfu; by occupying Egypt and turning it into a French colony she would fulfil her destiny and become the great power of the Mediterranean. And, from a practical point of view, an Egyptian expedition would be an easier and less dangerous operation than an invasion of England: the Mamelukes, the ruling caste in Egypt, were unlikely to put up much resistance and would be easily crushed by French troops; the summer weather in the tideless Mediterranean would offer fewer obstacles to an invasion fleet than the strong tides and frequent gales of the English Channel; and there was no threat from the British Navy which had withdrawn from the Mediterranean in the autumn of 1796 – this followed the Spanish declaration of war on Britain and the need to have the British Mediterranean fleet closer to home so that it could rapidly reinforce the Channel fleet at the first sign of the threatened invasion of England.

On 5 March the Directory in Paris gave the go-ahead to the Egyptian expedition. During the next three months the troops and ships were assembled at Toulon and nearby ports and harbours. On 19 May the bulk of the great armada set sail from Toulon and was joined during the next few days by convoys from Genoa and Corsica. There were thirteen ships of the line, six frigates and corvettes, and 400 transport vessels carrying 31,000 troops. The invading army included 2,810 cavalry soldiers, more than 1,000 horses, and 171 field guns. There was also a select band of 167 scientists, engineers and artists who were there at Napoleon's request to explore, observe and record the ancient civilisation of Egypt, and to bring the benefit of French knowledge to a backward and undeveloped country. Napoleon himself travelled on board the flagship of the invasion fleet, the impressive three-decker *L'Orient* of 120 guns.

The Admiralty in London had known since April that the French were planning some sort of amphibious operation in the Mediterranean. The British consuls at Leghorn and Naples sent home reports of ship movements and the French newspapers continued to be a valuable source of information. Lord St Vincent in the Bay of Cadiz had discovered from various sources that a fleet of thirteen

ships of the line had sailed from Corfu to Toulon, and that an
expedition was being assembled at Genoa, Marseilles and other ports.
But where and what was the objective? Naples and Sicily were
thought to be the most likely targets but other theories were that
the expedition was aimed at Portugal or Ireland or was intended to
drive the British fleet from Cadiz.

St Vincent decided to send a squadron into the Mediterranean to
investigate the French preparations at Toulon and to find out what
was going on. Both he and the Admiralty in London were agreed
on the man who should lead this critical but potentially dangerous
reconnaissance mission. 'The appearance of a British squadron in the
Mediterranean is a condition on which the fate of Europe may at
this moment be stated to depend,' wrote Lord Spencer, the First Lord
of the Admiralty, to St Vincent, 'I think it almost unnecessary to
suggest to you the propriety of putting it under the command of Sir
H. Nelson, whose acquaintance with the part of the world, as well
as his activity and disposition seem to qualify him in a peculiar
manner for that service.'[5]

The previous summer, while the *Bellerophon* had remained with
the rest of St Vincent's fleet blockading the Spanish fleet in Cadiz,
Nelson had sailed to the Canary Islands to attack the Spanish port
of Santa Cruz at Tenerife. The attack was made on a blustery night
and was a disaster. The British suffered heavy loss of life, and
Nelson, who insisted on leading the landing parties himself, was
hit by a musket ball as he scrambled ashore from his barge. He
suffered a compound fracture of the right arm just above the elbow
and was hastily rowed back to his flagship where the surgeon amputated the arm. In a letter to St Vincent accompanying his official
report on the unsuccessful action he requested a frigate 'to convey
the remains of my carcass to England.' He added a despairing post-
script to his letter: 'A left-handed admiral will never again be considered as useful, therefore the sooner I get to a very humble cottage
the better and make room for a better man to serve the state.'[6] St
Vincent was well aware of the difficulties posed by an amphibious
operation which involved landing a force on a beach under enemy
fire and was generous in his response. 'Mortals cannot command

success: you and your companions have certainly deserved it by the greatest degree of heroism and perseverance that was ever exhibited . . .'[7] and he arranged for Nelson to be sent home in the frigate *Seahorse*.

Nelson spent a restless six months in Norfolk and London convalescing. For his wife Fanny it was a happy time, indeed the last happy time she would have with Nelson who was now a naval hero and beginning to experience the celebrity which would soon become such a feature of his life. For the first few months after his return from Tenerife he was in considerable pain and was dependent on Fanny's love and attention. She dressed his wound, cut up his food for him at mealtimes and accompanied him to dinner parties and receptions. But, as always, Nelson was impatient to get back to sea and was greatly relieved when he received orders from the Admiralty to escort a convoy to Lisbon and then join the Mediterranean fleet off Cadiz. His flagship was the 74-gun ship *Vanguard* and his flag captain was Edward Berry. They set sail on 10 April and arrived off Cadiz at the end of the month. Nelson received a warm welcome from Lord St Vincent who was having to keep a tight rein on a fleet whose men continued to prove restless. 'The arrival of Admiral Nelson has given me new life,' he wrote to Lord Spencer. 'You could not have gratified me more than in sending him.'[8]

St Vincent now had the man he wanted to lead the reconnaissance mission to Toulon. Within a matter of days Nelson was on his way to Gibraltar and on 8 May he entered the Mediterranean with his squadron – the first British warships to do so for a year and a half. His squadron at this stage consisted of only six ships: the 74-gun ships *Vanguard, Orion and Alexander*, two frigates and a sloop. However, shortly after Nelson had left Cadiz, St Vincent received orders from London to send a more formidable force of not fewer than ten ships of the line. This would give Nelson a fleet capable of intercepting and attacking the French expedition, rather than simply observing and reporting on the enemy's movements. St Vincent deliberately selected the best ships and captains for the task and on 25 May his chosen ships weighed anchor and set sail to meet up with Nelson. The squadron was led by Thomas Troubridge in the *Culloden*, and the other ships were the *Bellerophon*, *Defence*, *Goliath*, *Zealous*, *Theseus*, *Swiftsure*, *Minotaur* and *Majestic*, heroic names which would soon become famous beyond the closed world of the navy.

We can follow the progress of the squadron in a decorative map of the Mediterranean which shows the tracks taken by the British ships and by Napoleon's invasion fleet. From Cadiz they sailed almost due south until they were a few miles off Tangier on the African coast. From there they sailed through the Straits of Gibraltar with all sail set and a following wind. Off Gibraltar they were joined by the *Audacious* and the *Leander*, both ships of the line, and by the brig *Mutine* of 18 guns. The brig was a French vessel which had been captured during the raid on Tenerife by boats led by Lieutenant Thomas Hardy. Following the action he had been promoted and given command of the prize. He was now twenty-nine years old and would later gain immortality as Nelson's flag captain at the battle of Trafalgar. The *Mutine* was to prove invaluable in the coming weeks because her appearance was less threatening than a ship of the line and she could be sent into ports and harbours to gather information.

From Gibraltar they sailed north-east towards the islands of Formentor and Majorca, keeping a sharp eye out for enemy ships. Although they were now a formidable squadron they were entering a hostile sea with no British naval bases to provide reinforcements or repairs. When they sighted two small vessels they flew Spanish flags to avoid arousing suspicion. By 1 June they were 50 miles east of Minorca, their progress slowed by several days of light and variable winds. All the ships took advantage of the calm seas to carry out gunnery practice. The sailors exercised the carriage guns and the marines their muskets. A week later they were within a few miles of Toulon and there, soon after dawn on 7 June, they sighted a single warship. The log of the *Bellerophon* recorded the moment: 'Light airs. Strange sail NW. AM. At 6 rear Admiral Nelson in the Vanguard under a jury foremast join'd the squadron. Hove to. The Captn went on board the Admiral at 8.'9

A map of the Mediterranean showing the tracks taken by Nelson's
fleet and the French fleet in the weeks preceding the battle of the Nile. From
A voyage up the Mediterranean in His Majesty's Ship Swiftsure, by the Reverend Cooper Willyams.

The *Vanguard* was still sailing under a jury rig because she and the *Alexander* and *Orion* had run into a freak storm which had hit them with the force of a typhoon. The frigates had been dispersed and returned to Gibraltar, which exasperated Nelson who needed frigates to help him locate the French. The *Vanguard* had been dismasted in the storm and nearly driven ashore and wrecked. She had been rescued by the *Alexander* and, with the help of the carpenters of all three ships, she had been re-rigged. The *Alexander* and *Orion* had then been despatched to chase some Spanish merchantmen, leaving the *Vanguard* to keep watch on the movements of shipping out of Toulon.

Nelson was expecting Troubridge and as soon as he had identified the strange fleet bearing down on him he ran up the signal for the approaching ships to heave to. With practised ease the sailors on each ship backed the necessary sails to bring them to a halt, and within a few minutes boats were being hoisted off the decks and lowered into the sea which was almost flat calm. Captain Darby and five other captains were rowed across to the *Vanguard* for a meeting with Nelson. Two days later the *Alexander* and *Orion* and the *Mutine* brig arrived and Nelson's squadron was now complete. They would spend the next two months searching the length and breadth of the Mediterranean for Napoleon and his armada of warships and transports.

On the same day that the *Alexander* and *Orion* joined Nelson's squadron the French armada arrived off the coast of Malta. This low rocky island was in a commanding position in the middle of the Mediterranean and had a fine natural harbour at Valetta. It would provide France with an excellent naval base and was the first target of the invasion fleet. Although the island was protected with massive fortifications, the resident garrison was poorly trained and too small in number to adequately defend the miles of defensive walls. The famous Knights of the Order of St John who ruled the island were no longer the formidable force they had once been, and in any case two-thirds of them were Frenchmen who proved reluctant to oppose their countrymen. The transport ships arrived off Malta on 6 June and the main force from Toulon arrived on 9 June. Some of the local soldiers put up a spirited resistance but were overwhelmed by the French landing parties. Within three days the Knights of St John agreed to cede Malta to the French Republic. Napoleon spent six days dismantling the existing regime and setting up a new constitution. He departed from Malta on 18 June, leaving behind a garrison of 3,000 French soldiers to guard the island. They now headed for Egypt and in doing so nearly ran into Nelson's ships.

The British squadron had sailed around the northern tip of Corsica, making for Naples. For a week they had experienced the rapidly changing and unpredictable weather which can make sailing in this part of the Mediterranean so alarming. Light airs and calms alternated with thunderstorms, heavy rain and sudden squalls. One of the squalls carried away the foretopmast of the *Bellerophon* and she lost the studding sail; it was still gusty and raining as they rounded the Isle of Ischia and entered the Bay of Naples. On this occasion Nelson did not go ashore but sent Troubridge in his place. While the squadron stayed several miles offshore, Troubridge boarded the *Mutine* brig in the early hours of the morning of 17 June and arrived in the harbour at Naples as the city was waking up at 5 am. He went ashore with Captain Hardy and the two of them were soon in a meeting with Sir William Hamilton and General Acton, the leading minister of the Kingdom of Naples. Hamilton was impressed by Troubridge's directness: 'We did more business in half an hour than should have been done in a week in the official way here. Captain Troubridge went straight to the point and put strong questions to the general, who answered them fairly and to the satisfaction of the captain.'[10]

By mid-morning Troubridge was back with the fleet and reporting to Nelson on the *Vanguard*. The results of his meeting were by no means as satisfactory as Sir William Hamilton imagined. The promises of assistance were too vague, the frigates were not forthcoming, and the information about the French expedition was not helpful. Sir William had been able to report that Napoleon had taken Malta but he had failed to pass on vital information from the French ambassador that Napoleon planned to land in Egypt and establish a French colony there. Presumably Sir William thought that the idea was too far-fetched and was intended to mislead the British, but if Nelson had received this information the eventual outcome might have been very different.

The British squadron hurried onwards, hoping now to catch Napoleon at Malta. With fresh breezes and fine weather they passed close to the island of Stromboli, and headed for the Straits of Messina between the southern tip of Italy and Sicily. The straits were famous for the rocky outcrops, fluky winds and dangerous currents which had given rise to the ancient Greek legend of Scylla and Charybdis but on this occasion they failed to live up to their reputation. The squadron took on board local pilots to guide them through and hoisted out the boats in case they should be needed to tow the ships out of danger but, although the waves echoed alarmingly in the confined space between the cliffs, they passed through without incident.

It was during the course of 22 June that the French and British fleets passed within a few miles of each other. At first light on that day the lookouts in the *Defence* sighted four ships to the south-east and Nelson despatched the *Leander* to investigate. Shortly afterwards Captain Hardy in the *Mutine* intercepted a merchant vessel whose master informed him that the French had already left Malta. Nelson ordered the fleet to shorten sail and summoned Troubridge, Saumarez, Ball and Darby to join him and his flag captain Berry in the great cabin of his flagship. They were the captains whose opinions he valued most highly and he wanted their views on the information they had received. Nelson had come to the conclusion that Napoleon must be headed for Egypt. They all thought he was probably right and Troubridge pointed out that the capture of Alexandria would seriously threaten British interests in India. This was enough for Nelson to act on. At 9 am he gave the signal for the fleet to make sail and head east.

By the time that the captains had returned to their ships the *Leander* had confirmed that the four ships on the horizon were frigates, but Nelson was now impatient to get to Alexandria. He did not wish to risk weakening his squadron by detaching ships to go chasing after a few frigates. It did not occur to Nelson or his captains that the frigates might be part of the vast and extended French armada which had sailed from Malta only two days before. As so often happened in his life, luck was on Napoleon's side. If Nelson's squadron had attacked the French armada at sea they would have inflicted crippling damage. The experienced British crews led by the most ruthless fighting admiral of his time would have caused mayhem among the lumbering transport vessels and the accompanying convoy of warships. It would have been the end of Napoleon's career, if not his life, because *L'Orient* would have been a prime target. Europe might have been spared nearly two decades of warfare.

Making good use of the favourable north-westerly winds, the British squadron drew rapidly away from the French armada and within a week they were nearing Alexandria. As the towers of the city came in sight Nelson ordered the squadron to prepare for battle but it soon became clear that there was no sign of the French invasion force. The only vessels in the harbour were a few Turkish warships and some fifty merchant vessels. Captain Hardy was sent ashore to speak to the British Consul but he found that he had been away on leave for three months. His deputy proved to be stupid and useless. However Hardy did manage to speak to the Egyptian military commandant of the city who was incredulous at the idea of an imminent French attack. 'It is impossible that the French should come to our country. They have no business here and we are not at war with them.' He went on to assure Hardy, 'If the French really think of invading our country as you pretend, we shall thwart their undertaking.'[11]

Hardy sailed back to the squadron, which was lying hove to, several miles offshore. Nelson was bitterly disappointed when he heard Hardy's news. Reason should have persuaded him to wait for a few days in case the French did arrive but such was his impatience to find the enemy that he had to be on the move again. The day following their arrival off Alexandria he ordered the squadron to set sail and head north towards Turkey. Once again luck was on Napoleon's side. At 11 am on 1 July, less than twenty-four hours after Nelson's ships had disappeared over the horizon, the first ships of the French armada arrived off Alexandria and began making preparations for an assault on the city.

The progress of the French expedition after leaving Malta had been slow and the more experienced naval officers in the warships were aware how vulnerable they were to a British attack. Their crews were lacking in seatime and had little or no experience of action, and all the ships were encumbered with troops, their baggage and equipment. They knew that enemy ships were in the Mediterranean because a French frigate had reported sighting sixteen British ships sailing down the coast of Italy. Napoleon seems to have been blithely unaware of the dangers they faced at sea, preoccupied as he was with the details of his historic venture to the Orient. During the voyage to Malta he had spent much of his time reading the Koran and books about the history of Egypt. In the great cabin of *L'Orient* he had frequent and sometimes heated discussions with the scientists and philosophers on board the flagship. Now he concentrated on the disposition of the ships and troops during the landing operation on the Egyptian coast. On 22 June, the day that the outlying frigates of his armada were spotted by the *Leander*, he issued a stirring proclamation to his troops:

> Soldiers! You are about to undertake a conquest whose effects upon the civilization and commerce of the world are incalculable. You are going to strike a blow against England more effective and more deeply felt than any other; a preliminary to her death-blow. We shall have tiring marches to make and plenty of fighting: but we shall succeed in every enterprise, for fate is on our side.

He urged them to treat the local people with respect and warned them that rape and pillage would create enemies and destroy their resources. He concluded, 'The first city we shall see was built by Alexander. We shall find at every step of our march memories fit to move Frenchmen to imitate his exploits.'[12]

Napoleon decided against a frontal attack on Alexandria. Instead he planned to land his army in the Bay of Marabout which lay 7 miles to the east of the town. This had a curving sandy beach with off-lying sandbanks which prevented the ships coming close in to the shore. The landing was a chaotic operation and Napoleon was fortunate that there was no opposition on the beach or from the sea. The merchant ships carrying the bulk of the troops anchored about a mile from the beach, and the warships anchored in deeper water to seaward of them. A brisk wind had stirred up a rough sea which made it difficult to transfer soldiers and their equipment from the ships into the boats in which they would be rowed ashore. Admiral Brueys advised Napoleon to delay the landing but Napoleon was determined to press on. The landing began around midday on 1 July and continued until well after dark. Napoleon himself did not get ashore until 11 pm. Many of the troops were seasick and abandoned their ration packs, and several boats were overturned in the surf. At least twenty men were drowned or lost during the landing but by midnight nearly 5,000 soldiers were safely ashore and the rest landed at daylight the next day.

Without further delay Napoleon led his wet and hungry troops along the hot, sandy track to Alexandria and at 10 am launched an assault on the walls of the town. The total population was only 6,000 and, although the small force of Egyptian soldiers put up a fight, they were overwhelmed. Within a few hours the town had fallen to the French. With his usual speed Napoleon pushed on with his invasion of the country. Two days after entering Alexandria, his troops had taken the nearby towns of Rosetta and Damanhour, and three weeks after landing at Marabout Bay he led his forces out on the plain by the Great Pyramids. There, on 21 July, his 25,000 men faced a warrior army of nearly 30,000 Bedouin and Mamcluke cavalry and infantry. The charges of the Mamcluke horsemen made little impression on the disciplined French troops and when the French heavy guns opened fire the Egyptian infantry fled. The next day Napoleon entered Cairo and completed the conquest of Egypt.

On the day that Napoleon won the Battle of the Pyramids the British squadron was at anchor in Syracuse harbour on the east coast of Sicily. Since leaving Alexandria they had searched the eastern Mediterranean, zig-zagging back and forth and intercepting passing merchant vessels in the hope of gaining information. After three fruitless weeks they put into Syracuse to stock up on provisions, and carry out necessary repairs. The *Bellerophon*'s heavy wooden launch was rowed ashore with empty water butts and returned with each of the butts filled with 100 gallons of water. Fresh vegetables and beef were loaded on board and lemons were distributed to the ship's company. The local people gathered in large numbers on the quay-side to gaze at the impressive squadron of foreign warships lying at anchor and to watch the activities of the sailors. On 25 July Nelson gave the order for the ships to prepare to sail and noted in his journal, 'the fleet is unmoored, and the moment the wind comes off the land shall go out of this delightful harbour where our present wants have been most amply supplied and where every attention has been paid to us . . .'[13]

The wind was so light that the ships had to be towed out of the harbour by the crews manning the ships' boats, but as soon as they were clear of the shore, they were able to hoist in the boats and take advantage of a light breeze from the north-west. Four days later they were sailing down the south-west coast of Greece. In the Gulf of Coron they shortened sail so that Troubridge could go ashore and seek information. They had learnt nothing useful during their stay at Syracuse but in the little Greek town of Coron they at last struck lucky. The Turkish governor told Troubridge that he had firm infor-mation from his government that the French were in Egypt. The *Bellerophon*'s log for 29 July records that 'At 5 the Admiral made the signal for having gained intelligence of the enemy.'[14] The squadron set all sail and with a favourable following breeze headed back to Alexandria.

TEN

Death at the Mouth of the Nile

1798

The *Alexander* and *Swiftsure* had been sent ahead of the squadron to see if the French fleet was anchored in the harbour at Alexandria. At 10 am on the morning of Wednesday 1 August 1798 the *Alexander* hoisted a signal to say that she had sighted land. As they drew closer the men high in her tops could clearly make out the towers and minarets of Alexandria and the low hills beyond the old town. By midday they could see the French flags flying over the forts and on many of the ships which were crowded in the harbour. This confirmed the rumours and the recent reports that Napoleon's great army had landed in Egypt and captured the city. But where was the army now, and was the French fleet still in the harbour? The *Alexander* sailed on and soon her lookouts were able to distinguish the ships anchored beyond the sandy spit of land and the lighthouse tower. The port was teeming with vessels. There were the distinctive local craft with their rakishly angled lateen rigs, there were several hundred transport vessels, and clearly visible were two ships of the line and six frigates flying the French tricolour. But there was no sign of the French battle fleet.[1]

The news was a bitter disappointment for Nelson and his captains. Saumarez expressed the feelings of many of them when he wrote that 'despondency nearly took possession of my mind, and I do not recollect ever to have felt so utterly hopeless or out of spirits as when we sat down to dinner.' We do not know how Captain Darby took the news. Life on board the *Bellerophon* had followed a familiar pattern in the week following their departure from Sicily. With a steady following wind they had sailed at 6 or 7 knots each day, making and shortening sail at intervals to maintain their position in the squadron. The Mediterranean sun burned faces and arms to a reddish mahogany and made walking on the deck painful in bare feet. The marines continued to cause trouble and on the morning that they sighted Alexandria two of them, together with a seaman, were flogged with twelve lashes each for drunkenness. The thirteen ships of the line maintained a loose formation, spread over several miles, with the *Alexander* and *Swiftsure* scouting ahead, and the *Culloden*, commanded by the energetic Thomas Troubridge, trailing some miles astern because she was towing a French merchant brig captured off the coast of Greece.

After finding that the French fleet was not at Alexandria the squadron headed east along the low sandy shore. This time the *Zealous* and the *Goliath* went on ahead and at 2.30 pm the *Zealous* made the signal for having sighted a strange fleet at anchor. At 2.45 she sent another signal with the details they had all been waiting for: '16 sail of the line at anchor bearing East by South.' Bursts of cheering broke out as the news spread through the squadron. Men below came rushing up on deck and the lookouts in the tops scanned the coast ahead with their telescopes. What they saw was a daunting sight. The French fleet was anchored in a long line in the middle of a great bay. There were thirteen ships of the line including a massive three-decker, and four frigates, and numerous gunboats. Viewed from the sea, the French fleet seemed to be in an impregnable position. As Captain Berry noted, 'The enemy appeared to be moored in a strong and compact line of battle close in with the shore,' a position which he thought presented the most formidable obstacles.

The obstacles were indeed formidable. Aboukir Bay lay at the mouth of the Nile and was protected from the north by a long peninsula a line of shoals, a small island and more shoals. There was a fort at the end of the peninsula and a gun battery on the island. The water beyond and behind the line of French ships was shallow; one British ship had a captured French chart but the rest of the squadron would have to take soundings as they approached to avoid running aground. In addition, it was usually difficult for ships under sail to dislodge and defeat an anchored fleet in a strong defensive position, as the Comte De Grasse had discovered in the West Indies when he had been decisively beaten off by Hood's ships anchored in Frigate Bay, St Kitts.

There was also the matter of timing. When the French fleet were first sighted Nelson's squadron were some 9 miles away. With the moderate northerly breeze the British seventy-fours could only travel around 5 knots and it would therefore take the leading ships nearly two hours to reach the enemy. By the time the trailing ships arrived in the bay the sun would be setting, and much of the battle would have to be fought in the dark. Apart from the obvious dangers of navigating in unknown waters in bad light, there was the hazard of mistaking one's own ships for the enemy in a night action. When the French admiral De Brueys was told that a British fleet had been sighted he certainly assumed that they would wait till the next morning before attacking.

However, in spite of the obvious dangers, Nelson was determined to attack immediately. This was not a rash or gung-ho decision but was based on a number of factors which he had in his favour. Critical was the fact that the wind was currently blowing steadily from north-north-west which meant that his ships would have the wind behind them as they headed into the bay. If he waited till the next day he not only gave the French many more hours to prepare for battle but he might find that the wind had dropped or had changed direction, forcing his ships to tack up to the enemy. Equally important was the fact that Nelson had total faith in his captains and the experience and morale of the men under their command. 'I knew what stuff I had under me, so I went into the attack with only a few ships, perfectly sure that the others would follow me, although it was nearly dark.'[2]

So at 3 pm he hoisted the signal: 'Prepare for battle and for anchoring by the stern.' On the *Bellerophon* the crew went into the much-practised routine of clearing for action, a routine which transformed the ship from a floating barracks into a fighting machine. A total of 550 men and boys went about their appointed tasks in a disciplined and orderly manner. Hardly any orders were necessary. (Years later Napoleon would tell the *Bellerophon*'s captain that he was astonished by the lack of shouted commands on the ship when she was getting under way.) Nets were rapidly rigged above the quarterdeck and upper deck to protect the crew from falling splinters, wooden blocks and rigging. Hammocks were brought up from below and stowed in rails around the decks as a shield against musket shot and flying splinters. The decks were scattered with sand to prevent bare feet slipping on blood, and were wetted to reduce the risk of fire. Under the forecastle the cook extinguished the galley fire as a safety precaution.

Below deck a visitor would scarcely have thought they were on the same ship so great was the transformation. In normal circumstances much of the after part of the ship was occupied by individual cabins in which the officers slept and worked or read when not on deck. Each cabin contained a hanging cot, a chair or folding stool, a small table or desk and perhaps a washstand. A hat and heavy weather coat were hung on a hook, and other clothes would be folded in a sea chest. Smaller items scattered around or held in racks might include a number of leather-bound books (many officers were avid readers), a sextant, quill pens, ink and notebooks, and perhaps a portrait miniature of the officer's wife or sweetheart. All this was swept away in a matter of minutes. The walls of most of the cabins were no more than canvas screens supported on wood battens. These were removed and, together with all the furniture, and personal possessions, were carried down below into the hold. Similarly the fine furniture in the great cabin occupied by the captain was removed and the cabin suddenly became a bare white room dominated by four guns.

In the forward part of the ship the hanging tables used by the seamen were lashed up to the ceiling, and benches were thrown down into the hold. The effect of this clearance was to open up the gun deck from end to end. A low, cavernous space previously densely hung with hammocks and cluttered with sea chests, pewter plates, chicken hutches, pet parrots, and pens containing a goat and a few cattle, was now dominated by the serried ranks of guns. The guns each weighed around 3 tons and were mounted on sturdy wooden carriages with wooden wheels. They were now released from the lashings which secured them, and the gun crews heaved on the gun tackles and ran out the guns through the gunports, ready for firing.

In the cockpit where the midshipmen normally slept, George Bellamy, the 25-year-old surgeon, and his two assistants prepared a makeshift surgery. Bellamy had seen action before (as an acting surgeon at the Battle of the First of June) and had experienced the horrors of a French jail, but he was going to be tested to the limit before the night was over.[3] The midshipmen's table was covered with a sheet and the surgical instruments were laid ready to hand. These included forceps, scalpels, probes and amputating knives and saws. There were buckets to hold blood and amputated limbs, and there were gags and bottles of laudanum and rum to take the place of anaesthetics.

Nelson's order to prepare to anchor by the stern was no surprise to Captain Darby in view of the position of the anchored French fleet but it involved a fairly arduous operation. One of the massive anchor cables had to be hauled out of the cable tier in the hold, manhandled the length of the ship, fed out of one of the stern ports, passed along the outside of the ship and then made fast to one of the great anchors suspended from the catheads at the bows. Springs were attached to the cable. These were smaller ropes which could be hauled on to alter the angle at which the ship was anchored and enable her to bring her broadside guns to bear on the enemy.

Shortly before 4 pm the leading ships in the British squadron rounded the shoals off the end of Aboukir Island and headed south into Aboukir Bay. As they passed the island the French guns and mortars fired some long-range shots but failed to score any hits. The British ignored them. They now had an unobstructed view of the line of French ships anchored some 3 miles away. From this angle they found themselves looking directly at the starboard broadside guns of thirteen ships of the line, a total of more than 500 guns aimed directly at them. However Nelson's plan was for his ships to head for the northern end of the French line, and then to turn, sail along the line and anchor. By concentrating his force at one end of the line so that two British ships attacked each one of the enemy, he intended to overwhelm those ships before moving

A plan of the Battle of the Nile from *The Life of Admiral Lord Nelson*, by Clarke and MacArthur, 1809. **British ships** A *Goliath*, B *Zealous*, C *Orion*, D *Audacious*, E *Theseus*, F *Vanguard*, G *Minotaur*, H *Bellerophon*, I *Defence*, K *Majestic*, L *Alexander*, M *Swiftsure*, N *Leander*, O *Culloden*, P *Mutine*

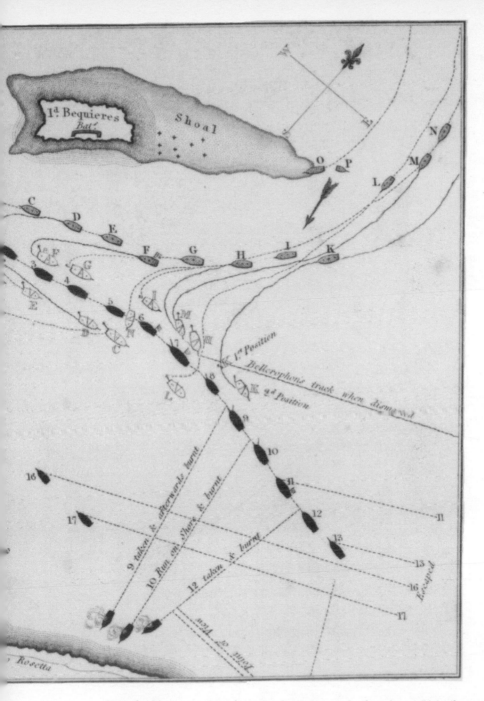

French ships 1 *Le Guerrier*, 2 *Le Conquérant*, 3 *Le Spartiate*, 4 *L'Aquilon*,
5 *Le Peuple Souverain*, 6 *Le Franklin*, 7 *L'Orient*, 8 *Le Tonnant*, 9 *L'Heureuse*,
10 *Le Timoleon*, 11 *Le Guillaume Tell*, 12 *Le Mercure*, 13 *Le Genereux*,
14 *La Serieuse*, 15 *L'Artemise*, 16 *La Diane*, 17 *La Justice*

on to deal with the rest. With the wind against them, the French ships at the far end of the bay could not come to their assistance. At 5 pm he issued the signal: 'I mean to attack the enemy's van and centre'; and half an hour later: 'Form line of battle as convenient.'

The plan of the battle reproduced in Clarke and M'Arthur's official biography of Nelson provides an admirably clear picture of the contours of the bay, the off-lying shoals, the position of the anchored French fleet and the routes taken by each of the British ships. As an explanatory diagram it is excellent and was compiled with input from those who had taken part, but the approach of the British fleet was not quite as tidy as is suggested by this plan. Nelson and his captains were in a hurry to get into action before nightfall, and there was no time to wait for the slower ships trailing behind to form an orderly line of battle. They therefore bore down on the French in an irregular line, the leading ships vying with each other to get into action first. The *Bellerophon* was the eighth ship in the British line, with the *Minotaur* ahead of her and the *Defence* astern of her. In common with five other ships in the British line of battle that day they had all been built to Sir Thomas Slade's designs, and had been launched within two or three years of each other. As they swept down on the waiting enemy ships, the *Goliath*, commanded by Thomas Foley, edged into the lead. She had the advantage of a captured and reasonably accurate French chart but, like all the leading ships, she had a sailor taking soundings with a lead line and shouting out the depths as they went. The sun was now low in the sky, dipping behind the castle on Aboukir Point and glittering on the waves breaking on the line of shoals which stretched out towards Aboukir Island. A steady breeze tempered the heat of the Egyptian evening and caused the tricolour flags on the motionless French ships to billow out and catch the last of the sunlight.

The *Goliath* was within musket shot of the *Guerrier* at the head of the French line when Thomas Foley made a discovery which played a key part in the outcome of the battle. He realised that, because the French ships were only anchored by the bow (and not anchored at bow and stern), there must be sufficient depth beyond for them to swing without grounding on the shoals. There must also therefore

be enough depth for a ship to sail past them on the inside. The
French would not be expecting an attack from this side and, as it
proved, many of their ships were totally unprepared for this. On the
Guerrier the lower deck guns were not run out and there were a lot
of boxes and lumber blocking the upper deck ports. So the *Goliath*,
followed by four other British ships, steered to pass round the head
of the French line and sail down the far side.

The peace of the evening, already disturbed briefly by desultory
gunfire from the battery on Aboukir Island, was now shattered by
the booming explosion of ships' broadsides. The French ships at the
head of their line began firing as the leading British ships came into
range, but the battle proper commenced as the *Goliath* completed her
turn round the bows of the *Guerrier* and fired a broadside at close
range. The gathering dusk was illuminated by the brilliant flashes of
guns. It was now around 6.45 pm. The *Bellerophon* had turned and
was heading for the centre of the French line. She had hauled up her
lower sails, the courses, and was sailing under topsails alone, as was
usual when going into battle. This gave her officers an unobstructed
view of the action and meant that her sailors could take in the
remaining sails rapidly when the time came to anchor. She was already
under fire from the enemy as she headed down their line. The sun
had now dipped below the horizon and she made her final approach
in a dim twilight made murky by clouds of drifting gunsmoke.

Whether Captain Darby intended to lie alongside *Le Franklin*,
which was the ship anchored ahead of the French flagship, or hoped
to position the *Bellerophon* so that she could fire her broadsides at the
vulnerable bows of *L'Orient* is not clear and was never explained.
What subsequently happened was disastrous. At 7 o'clock she let go
her best bower anchor which splashed into the water, hauling the
anchor cable down and along the ship's sides until it was stretching
out in a long line from one of the stern ports. The sailors out on the
yards heaved up the topsails as the anchor cable streamed out astern.
The ship began to swing stern into the wind but continued her forward
progress. Either the anchor was dragging on the seabed or the sailors
failed to check the cable and let out too much. When the anchor
finally brought the ship to a halt she found herself, not at the bows

of the enormous French flagship, but exactly alongside her, facing the entire weight of her broadside guns. *L'Orient* had three gun decks so she towered over the two-decked *Bellerophon*, but more critically she had almost twice the firepower. Not only did she have 120 guns to the *Bellerophon's* 74 but her guns fired a heavier weight of shot.

To add to Captain Darby's problems, *L'Orient* had three high-ranking officers on board who were to prove steadfast under fire. The most experienced was the man commanding the anchored French fleet, Vice-Admiral François, Comte de Brueys. He had fought the British in the West Indies and had proved a capable commander of the naval forces during the French landings in Egypt. His flag captain was Commodore Casabianca who had his ten-year-old son on board serving as a cadet. De Brueys's chief of staff was Rear-Admiral Honoré Ganteaume, the only one of the three who would survive the night.

As the *Bellerophon* came alongside *L'Orient*, and before she brought her guns to bear, Captain Casabianca fired two broadsides at her with devastating effect. The *Bellerophon* held her ground and, according to Ganteaume, came so close as almost to touch ('presque toucher') the French flagship, but it was at a terrible cost. On the English ship gun barrels were hurled off their carriages, rigging was torn apart, and men were dismembered by cannon shot. The *Bellerophon* responded with a rapid and disciplined series of broadsides from close range. This was what her crew had trained for. During the weeks of searching for the French fleet they had regularly 'exercised the great guns' and they now exercised them in earnest. The scene below deck was like something from Dante's Inferno: a low, confined space, sweltering hot and filled with acrid smoke, deafening explosions, and toiling, sweating bodies. The darkness was faintly illuminated by a few lanterns and the regular flash of gunfire, and by this light the gun crews, stripped to the waist, heaved the guns into place, and then stood clear as the guns fired and violently recoiled on their wooden carriages. Small boys ran back and forth with boxes containing cartridges of gunpowder brought up from the powder store in the hold. The dead were dragged out of the way of the guns and wounded men were helped to the cockpit by their shipmates.

There Bellamy and his two assistants were already up to their elbows in blood as they attempted to deal with men who had horrific wounds from cannon shot, musket shot and the lethal effects of flying wood splinters. Bellamy's scrawled notes of the killed and injured have survived and they make gruesome reading.[4] Sergeant Maxey had both legs broken in pieces and died from loss of blood before he could be attended to. Five other seamen lost both legs and died. Seaman Nieley lost both legs and one arm. Lawrence Curren had his abdomen ripped open and his bowels exposed. One man had half his head off. Robert Reeden was shot through the chest. Some had suffered head wounds and fractured skulls, others had fractured ribs, broken knees and wounds to hands and feet. Many were killed outright or died in the cockpit while waiting for the hard-pressed surgeons to attend to them.

Up on deck it was cooler but in many ways more alarming because the massive hull and masts and rigging of *L'Orient* towered alongside. Every time she fired her upper deck broadside she wrecked more of the *Bellerophon*. The boats stored on the booms in the waist of the ship were smashed to pieces, most of the guns on the quarterdeck were dismounted and the standing rigging was so shot through that the masts were increasingly precarious. The marines on the French flagship were able to pick out their targets from their higher vantage point. The first of the officers to be hit was Captain Darby who received a head wound which knocked him to the deck unconscious. He was carried below to the surgeons. Lieutenant Daniel, the first lieutenant, and Lieutenant Lander, the second, were both wounded but were able to remain at their posts for a while. Then Daniel was hit by a cannon ball which took off his right leg. As he was being carried towards the cockpit he was hit again, this time by a lethal round of grapeshot which killed him and also killed the seaman who was carrying him. John Hadaway, the fourth lieutenant, was hit and had to be taken below. George Jolliffe, the fifth lieutenant, was killed outright.

The *Bellerophon* had been fighting *L'Orient* single-handed for nearly an hour when, around 8 pm, her mizenmast was shot away and came crashing across the stern. Shortly afterwards her mainmast toppled and fell across the starboard side of the upper deck, most of it coming to rest on the booms and the forecastle. The mainmast brought down with it the topmast, the yards and heavy canvas sails, the tarred rigging of the shrouds, and a tangle of ropes and heavy wooden blocks. It killed Lieutenant Lander and several seamen and produced a scene of chaos on deck. Robert Cathcart, the third lieutenant, now left his post on the main deck and came up to the quarterdeck to take over command of the ship. There was no question of surrendering and the gun crews continued to load and fire, but the wreckage of the two fallen masts had to be cleared, and a new danger had arisen which was potentially even more hazardous than the bombardment of cannon and musket shot from *L'Orient*. This was a fire which had broken out in the stern part of the French flagship.

The *Alexander* and *Swiftsure* had been delayed by their reconnaissance of the port of Alexandria and came late on the scene. When they did so they headed for *L'Orient*. The *Alexander* was the first to arrive. She cut through the line of French ships astern of the flagship and anchored off her in a good position to do maximum damage. She was able to fire into the vulnerable stern of *L'Orient*, her shot smashing through the stern galleries and stern windows and causing carnage the length of the ship. This onslaught started a fire in the stern cabin which rapidly spread to the poop and the rest of the ship. A wooden warship of this period was a floating fire hazard. Almost everything was highly inflammable at the best of times but the Mediterranean sun had dried out sails and rigging, and softened the tar used to caulk the planking of decks. The liberal use of paint and tar as preservatives increased the fire risk and the barrels of gunpowder stored in the magazine had the potential to act as a bomb which could destroy the entire ship. As the fire on *L'Orient* spread out of control the disabled *Bellerophon* alongside her was in an exceedingly dangerous position. The ship's log provides a glimpse of what happened next: 'At 9, observing our antagonist on fire on the middle gun deck, cut the stern cable and wore clear of her by loosing the spritsail – shortly, the fore mast went over the larboard bow. Employed clearing the wreck and putting out the fire which had caught in several places of the ship.'[5]

This is a typically terse and shorthand account of an exceedingly difficult operation. With two of her masts gone, her deck a shambles, and many of her crew dead or wounded, it was not easy for her one remaining officer to get the ship clear of the burning flagship. After the anchor cable had been hacked through with axes the ship was free to drift but until she got some sail up she could not be manoeuvred clear of *L'Orient*. Lieutenant Cathcart dared not risk setting any sail on the foremast because most of the supporting rigging had been shot through. He therefore ordered the men to set the spritsail, a relatively small sail which was set on a yard from the ship's bowsprit. Even this put too much strain on the foremast because, as the *Bellerophon* gathered way, the mast toppled forward and came crashing down. The ship was now totally dismasted but, to the relief of her shattered crew, she continued to move slowly clear of *L'Orient* and out of the line of battle. The map in Clarke and M'Arthur's biography of Nelson shows her track. What it does not show is how the *Bellerophon* nearly became the victim of friendly fire.

The *Swiftsure* was bearing down on the enemy under a press of sail when her commander, Captain Hallowell, saw a dismasted ship moving out of the line of battle. In the darkness it was difficult to identify her but he noted that she was not displaying the four lanterns at her mizen which were the distinguishing lights of a British ship. The Reverend Cooper Willyams, who was the chaplain on board the *Swiftsure*, later described how Captain Hallowell, presuming the ship to be the enemy, felt inclined to fire into her,

> but as that would have broken the plan he had laid down for his conduct, he desisted: and happy it was that he did so; for we afterwards found the ship in question was the Bellerophon, which had sustained such serious damage from the overwhelming fire of the French Admiral's enormous ship L'Orient, that Captain Darby found it necessary for him to fall out of action, himself being wounded, two lieutenants killed and near two hundred men killed and wounded. His remaining mast falling soon after, and in its fall killing several officers and men (among the former was another of his lieutenants) he was never able to regain his station. At three minutes past eight o'clock the Swiftsure anchored, taking the place that had been occupied by the Bellerophon.

In fact the *Swiftsure* did not anchor in the *Bellerophon*'s place but selected a spot somewhat ahead of *L'Orient*. From there she could direct her fire at the bows of the burning flagship and at the stern of *Le Franklin*. She was in no immediate danger from the flaming debris falling from *L'Orient* because she was upwind of her and Captain Hallowell reckoned that if and when the flagship did explode 'the greater part of the fragments would naturally be projected over and beyond her.' Meanwhile the *Bellerophon* was moving further and further away from the battle and into the darkness beyond, her progress impeded by the shattered masts, torn sails and rigging trailing next to her battered hull. The most urgent task of her crew was to extinguish the fires which had broken out and when this had been done they turned their attention to cutting away the wreckage of the three masts. It was while they were hacking at the chaotic jumble of ropes and sails that the French flagship exploded.

Admiral de Brueys was dead before his ship blew up. His heroism became a legend in the French Navy. He had been hit in the face and left hand by musket shot fired from the *Bellerophon* but he had the wounds bound up and continued to direct operations. Both his legs were then shot away but still he refused to leave the deck. According to some French accounts he had tourniquets tied around the stumps, got himself strapped in a chair and was heard to say that a French admiral ought to die on his own quarterdeck. His bravery proved fatal because he was in an exposed position. He was hit again, this time by a cannon ball which nearly cut him in two. His flag captain, Commodore Casabianca, was also mortally wounded. His young son refused to leave his side, and this later inspired the poem by Felicia Hemans with the familiar opening lines, 'The boy stood on the burning deck / whence all but he had fled.' Father and son took to the water and were last seen clinging to a floating mast. Admiral Ganteaume, several other officers, and many of the crew also abandoned ship, realising that it was only a matter of time before the fire reached the gunpowder in the magazine.[6]

Many accounts have survived of the devastating noise of the explosion, and numerous pictures were later painted showing the night sky illuminated by the blinding light at the centre of the blast as the great ship disintegrated. One of the most graphic descriptions of the scene was provided by a French onlooker who was several miles away in the town of Rosetta at the mouth of the Nile. Monsieur Poussieulque was Comptroller-General of the Eastern Army in Egypt and two days after the battle he wrote to a friend in Paris about the battle which he had witnessed. The ship carrying his letter, together with the latest despatches from Napoleon, was intercepted in the Mediterranean and nine weeks later the letter was published by *The Times* in London. Poussieulque described how he and his companions heard the firing of cannon at 5.30 in the evening:

> We immediately got upon the terraces, on the tops of the highest houses, and on the eminences, from whence we plainly perceived 10 English ships of the line; the others we could not see. The cannonade was very heavy until about a quarter after 9 o'clock, when, favoured by the night, we perceived an immense light, which announced to us that some ship was on fire. At this time the thunder of cannon was heard with redoubled fury and at 10 o'clock the ship on fire blew up with the most dreadful explosion, which was heard at Rosetta in the same manner as the explosion of the *Grenelle* at Paris. When this accident happened the most profound silence took place for the space of about 10 minutes; from the moment of the explosion until our hearing it might take up about two minutes. The firing commenced again, and continued without intermission until 3 o'clock in the morning . . .[7]

It is difficult to be certain exactly where the *Bellerophon* was at the time of the explosion. Her log-book simply states, 'at 10 L'Orient blew up. Got up jury sails on the stumps of the masts, the winds favouring us enabled us to clear the French fleet.' In some of the pictures of the battle she is shown a few hundred yards away from *L'Orient* but with the favourable breeze driving her along under the spritsail she could have made a steady 1 or 2 knots which would have taken her a mile or more from the scene. Even at that distance she would have felt the shock waves which the other ships experienced and her crew must have paused in their clearing-up operations as the burning fragments of *L'Orient*, blown high in the air, rained down on

the battlefield. Recent excavation of the seabed by French archaeologists has revealed the force of the explosion. Divers have discovered
that a cannon weighing 2 tons was hurled more than 400 yards.

Captain Darby had by this time recovered sufficiently to resume
command of his battered ship and, under his directions, the makeshift
jury sails were erected. The next step was to drop anchor so that
they could concentrate on clearing away the wreckage and repairing
the honeycomb of holes in the ship's sides. Lord St Vincent later
remarked that he had never seen a ship so mauled. The only problem
was that the anchor cables had been cut through by the broadsides
of *L'Orient*. It took them several hours to splice the remnants together
and it was not till 4 o'clock the next morning that they were able
to bend a length of cable to the small bower anchor and let it go in
7 fathoms. By this time they had partly sailed and partly drifted away
from the scene of the battle. They were now a mile or so offshore,
at the eastern end of Aboukir Bay, close to the mouth of the Nile.
As the sky lightened in the east they could clearly see the houses
and towers of Rosetta. In a letter to his wife after the action Captain
Miller of the *Theseus* recalled that after the *Bellerophon* had broken
off the action with *L'Orient* she had drifted along the French line
and anchored 6 miles to the east 'where we discovered her next
morning (without a mast standing) with her ensign on the stump of
the mainmast.'[8]

For the next few hours they took stock, carried out repairs, and
buried the dead. They found that all the ship's boats stored on the
booms in the waist of the ship were shot to pieces. Seven of the
quarterdeck guns, six of the main deck guns and two of the lower
deck guns were so damaged as to be useless, and one of the carronades
on the poop deck was shattered. Virtually all the hammocks stored
in the rails were cut and shredded by gunfire. At daybreak the
exhausted crew paused in the clearing-up operations and gathered
on deck to bury the men killed in the battle. The melancholy
ceremony was conducted by the chaplain, the Reverend John
Fresselicque, the same man who had preached a lengthy sermon to
the assembled crew on the Sunday after the battle of the Glorious
First of June. There were twenty-six bodies to be buried. Each body

was sewn into the torn remnants of a hammock, weighted with two cannon balls, and slipped overboard.

At 8 am a French frigate was spotted heading their way. Captain Darby gave the order to beat to quarters. The weary crew made their way to their stations, and the remaining guns on the main deck and lower deck were cleared for action. The approaching vessel was the 40-gun frigate *La Justice* which had spotted the dismasted British 74 and evidently hoped to capture her and salvage something from a night of French disasters. However she was still 2 or 3 miles away when she was intercepted by the *Zealous*. She turned back to rejoin the ships at the rear of the French line which had taken no part in the action. These were under the command of Rear-Admiral Villeneuve, in the *Guillaume Tell*, who had been agonising as to whether to remain at anchor or to attempt to escape with any other French ships able to do so.

Villeneuve was an ambitious 34-year-old officer who had enjoyed rapid promotion during the years of the Revolution. He had no orders to move up the line and assist the beleaguered ships ahead of him and in any case the wind direction made this difficult. Around midday he made his move. He cut his anchor cable and headed north-east out of the bay, followed by the *Généreux*, and the frigates *Diane* and *Justice*. The men on the *Bellerophon* looked up from their work and watched their progress. They saw them exchanging broadsides with the *Zealous* who attempted to bar their escape but was unable to do so. The four ships, heeling under all the sail they could set, passed beyond the low sandy mound of Aboukir Island and escaped into the blue waters of the Mediterranean beyond. Of the seventeen French warships present at the battle, they were the only ones not burnt, sunk or captured by the British. Seven years later Villeneuve commanded the combined French and Spanish fleet at the Battle of Trafalgar.

During the next five days the *Bellerophon* remained at anchor off the mouth of the Nile. The carpenters' crew repaired the shot holes and other damage; the sailmakers mended torn sails and made new ones; and the seamen rigged up jury masts and yards. On 6 August they weighed anchor and as they tacked slowly back and forth towards the main body of the fleet, they found that the ship behaved well under her jury rig. Other ships now came to their aid and supplied them with much-needed gear and equipment. The *Swiftsure* supplied them with a topgallant sail, and the *Culloden* sent across three coils of rope, a five-inch hawser, a foretopmast, a spritsail and a topgallant mast.

And every day more bodies were committed to the deep. On Friday 3 August Captain Darby had mustered the ship's company and 'found we had 3 lieutenants, 1 masters mate, 32 seamen & 13 marines killed – the captain, master, captain of marines, one midshipman, 126 seamen and 17 marines wounded; in all 49 killed, 143 wounded.' Eight more men died of their wounds during the next week. Only one other British ship, the *Majestic*, had comparable casualties, with 50 killed and 143 wounded. The British casualties overall were reckoned to be 218 killed and 677 wounded, making a total of 895 or roughly 10 per cent of the men who took part in the action. The French casualties were far worse. Nelson reported that some 5,235 of the enemy were killed or missing, and it was estimated that 3,305 French prisoners were taken, 1,000 of them wounded.[9]

ELEVEN

The West Indies

1798–1804

More than two months passed before the news reached London that Nelson's squadron had annihilated the French fleet at the mouth of the Nile. The first despatch which Nelson sent was intercepted by the enemy. On 6 August he had sent his flag captain Edward Berry in the *Leander*, under the command of Captain Thompson, with his official report addressed to Lord St Vincent at Cadiz. In light winds off the coast of Crete the *Leander*, a 50-gun ship, was attacked by a powerful French warship, *Le Généreux* of 74 guns, one of the ships which had managed to escape from Aboukir Bay the day after the battle. In the ferocious action which followed, the *Leander* was reduced to a dismasted wreck and forced to surrender. Tim Stewart, one of her lower deck gunners, was scathing about the way the French ship was handled. Long before she was in range she wasted powder and shot by blazing away to left and right:

> We fought six hours; just think of that. Why, if she had handled her guns in a seamanlike manner, she ought to have sunk us in little more than six minutes. We had to cut through the main topsail, lying over our larboard side to make room for the muzzles of the guns, for our ship was quite a wreck – not a stick standing – but still the brave hearts would not give in.[1]

The effectiveness of the *Leander*'s gunnery was grimly demonstrated by the fact that *Le Généreux* lost about 100 dead and more than 150 wounded from her enormous crew of more than 900 men. The *Leander*, with a crew of 282, lost 35 killed and 57 wounded, and when Captain Thompson eventually faced a court martial for the loss of his ship he was praised for his 'gallant and almost unprecedented defence' against a far superior force.

Nelson had initially sent only one copy of his despatch because he was short of frigates but on 12 August he decided to send a duplicate copy to Sir William Hamilton in Naples. He promoted his flag lieutenant, Thomas Capel, to the rank of master and commander and sent him on his way in the brig *Mutine*. Capel arrived in the Bay of Naples on 4 September where his news was received with a sense of relief and rejoicing which was soon to be echoed all over Europe. Capel wrote, 'I am totally unable to express the joy that appeared in everybody's countenance and the burst of applause and acclamation we received.'[2] Sir William Hamilton wrote to Nelson, 'It is impossible, my dear Sir Horatio, for any words to express, in any degree, the joy that the account of the glorious and complete victory you gained . . . occasioned in this court and in this city.'[3] Lady Hamilton fainted when she heard the news and then she too wrote to Nelson to tell him she was delirious with happiness: 'Good God, what a victory! Never, never has there been anything half so glorious, half so compleat . . .'[4]

In Vienna the Chancellor 'manifested the greatest pleasure at this memorable event' and in Berlin a British diplomat passed the news on to the King of Prussia and reported that the joy was universal. It was widely recognised that Nelson's action was more than a decisive naval victory. It was the first serious check to the hitherto invincible French nation and gave fresh heart to all the opponents of revolutionary France. During the course of one long night Nelson's squadron had eliminated French naval power in the Mediterranean and, although Napoleon would later institute a massive shipbuilding programme, the French Navy never recovered from the blow.

When Capel eventually arrived in London on the morning of 2 October and delivered Nelson's despatch to the Admiralty the reaction and the rejoicings eclipsed the celebrations which had greeted the news of the Battle of the Glorious First of June four years previously. Lord Spencer, the First Lord of the Admiralty, immediately passed on the news to the Lord Mayor of London and by midday the church bells were ringing all over the capital and guns were firing salutes in Hyde Park and the Tower. Lady Spencer wrote, 'My heart is absolutely bursting with different sensations of joy, of gratitude, of pride, of every emotion that ever warmed the bosom of a British woman,' and she reported that huge crowds had gathered in the streets. 'London is mad – absolutely mad – Capel was followed by a crowd of several thousands, huzzaring the whole way . . .'[5]

Lord Spencer sent a messenger to convey the news to Weymouth where the King was taking the waters. According to the newspapers the messenger was held up on the road by a highwayman who decided not to rob him when he learnt of the contents of the despatches and told him 'to proceed with all possible expedition with the good news to his Majesty'.[6] The King was so delighted by the news that he read Nelson's letters aloud four times to different noblemen and gentlemen on the esplanade at Weymouth. All over the country there were celebrations. Hotels and shops were illuminated, and patriotic songs were sung by audiences in theatres. In Norwich an ox was roasted in the Market Place and in the village of Chew Magna, near Bristol, 'a sheep was roasted whole and given, with plenty of beer, to the populace'.[7]

One of the few people to take the news calmly was Napoleon who was now marooned in Egypt with an army of 30,000 troops. 'Well, gentlemen, now we are obliged to accomplish great things,' he told his companions, 'The sea of course, of which we are no longer master, separates us from our homeland, but no sea separates us from either Africa or Asia.'[8] He told them that they had the men and the munitions and they would found a great empire. This he signally failed to do, but in a matter of months he left his mark on Egypt. He began work on a hospital for the poor, and established quarantine stations to check the spread of bubonic plague which was endemic in the country; he built windmills to raise water and grind corn; he set up a postal service; and he erected the first street lamps in Cairo. He also established the Institute of Egypt and it was the work of the French scientists, historians and archaeologists working for the institute which was to prove his most lasting legacy. They measured the Pyramids, they studied the history, zoology and anthropology of Egypt and eventually published their findings in ten magnificently illustrated folio volumes. Above all they discovered at Rosetta a basalt stone with inscriptions which led to the deciphering of Egyptian hieroglyphs and revealed for scholars and the Egyptian people themselves the hitherto unknown world of ancient Egypt.

Napoleon's attempt to govern a Muslim country which was twice the size of France was never likely to succeed and was doomed when he had to return to the battlefield within months of his arrival in Egypt. In October 1798 the Turks declared war on France and that winter they assembled an army in Syria and prepared to invade Egypt. Napoleon marched his army northwards, captured the fortress at Gaza, took the town of Jaffa, and then laid siege to the medieval fortress of Acre. A British force under the command of the dashing Sir Sydney Smith reinforced the Turkish troops defending the town and between them they successfully resisted the French bombardment. After two months Napoleon withdrew his troops, crossed the Sinai desert and returned to Cairo. His soldiers were demoralised and, although they went on to defeat the Turks at Mount Tabor and at Aboukir, Napoleon decided he must abandon them and return to Paris. He had learnt that the French republic was in serious danger from within and without. France's economy had collapsed, civil servants were unpaid, most of the artisans in Paris were unemployed, and bandits were roaming the countryside. And a new coalition of France's enemies, including Austria, Britain and Russia, was threatening her borders. On 22 August 1799, a year after the Battle of the Nile, he embarked on a frigate and arrived in Paris on 16 October. Within three weeks he had organised a coup, disbanded the ruling Directorate, and set himself up as First Consul. Far from being finished by the ill-fated Egyptian expedition he was on the threshold of an era which would lead to him extending his rule across Europe and being proclaimed Emperor of France.

Seven years passed between the Battle of the Nile and the next major event in the *Bellerophon's* life which was the Battle of Trafalgar. During those seven years she cruised the Mediterranean, escorted convoys of merchant ships, and resumed her old task of blockading the French coast. Her log-books for these years are a monotonous repetition of earlier log-books: daily notes of the wind and the weather; the passing of other ships, sail changes, taking on board water and stores, carrying out repairs to sails and rigging, and the punishment of crew members with floggings for drunkenness or neglect of duty. The only break in the routine was a spell of two years in which the ship was based on the Jamaica station in the West Indies.

The economic rivalry between Britain and France in the Caribbean had begun in the seventeenth century. During the eighteenth century it led to a series of military expeditions and sea battles as both nations attempted to capture and recapture islands whose sugar and tobacco plantations were a major source of wealth. Britain developed two naval bases to service the ships engaged in the long-running conflict. English Harbour in Antigua became the base for ships operating in the eastern Caribbean, and in particular for the ships of the Leeward Squadron which were stationed out there. Port Royal, on the south coast of Jamaica, was the base for the Jamaica Squadron and for ships patrolling the western Caribbean.

On 2 March 1802 the *Bellerophon*, in company with five other ships of the line, weighed anchor and proceeded slowly out of Torbay. The day was so calm that it was necessary for the boats of the squadron to tow the ships clear of the land until they picked up a light breeze off Berry Head. Two days later they were sailing past the Lizard and a week later they were off Madeira and heading for the West Indies. With the trade winds behind them all the way from the Azores they made good progress and sighted Barbados on the morning of 27 March 1802. They had covered the 4,700 miles from Plymouth in twenty-five days. This was an average of 188 miles a day, travelling at between 7 and 8 knots most of the time – a good average for a cruising yacht today and a surprising, though by no means unusual, speed for sailing warships each carrying more than 500 men and loaded with 74 guns, 300 tons of ballast and more than 700 tons of ammunition, stores and equipment.

On 28 March they saw the twin peaks of St Lucia on the horizon and the next day they sailed into Fort Royal Bay at Martinique to stock up on water and provisions before sailing the final leg of the journey to Jamaica. They arrived during the brief period when the island was under British rule. For nearly 200 years Martinique had been a French colony but in 1794 a British expedition had captured the island and for eight years the British flag flew over the fort which guarded the entrance to one of the most beautiful bays in the Caribbean. Napoleon's wife Josephine had been born in a house over-looking the bay in 1763 and had spent the first sixteen years of her life on the island. She had enjoyed a genteel upbringing as the daughter of a noble French family but after completing her convent education she had been sent to Paris to marry a rich aristocrat. Her husband had been guillotined during the Reign of Terror in 1794 but Josephine (then called Rose de Beauharnais) had survived and rejoined the fashionable life of the capital. She had met Napoleon during the summer of 1795 and had so enchanted him that he persuaded her to marry him the following spring. She was then thirty-two years old with two children. Napoleon was twenty-six and had just been put in command of the Army of Italy.

The chief concern of the *Bellerophon*'s crew was to provision the ship for the next stage of the journey and carry out essential repairs. The launch was hoisted overboard and sent ashore to fill up the water casks. Barrels of fresh beef were brought across in boats and stored down below. Fruit and vegetables were purchased from the local men and women in the bumboats which swarmed around every ship which arrived in the port. The sails on the yards were loosed and allowed to flap in the light breezes to dry out. Damaged and torn sails were spread out on the decks so the sailmaker could carry out repairs, and the standing rigging was overhauled and set up. Within a few days the *Bellerophon* was ready to set out. On 7 April she weighed anchor and beat out of the bay in company with the 74-gun ship *Audacious*, heading for Jamaica.

The weather kept the sailors busy during the passage. Fresh breezes alternated with sudden fierce squalls, constantly forcing them to shorten sail and take in reefs, then shake out the reefs and set more sail. One squall carried away the head of the mizenmast and the main topsail yard of the *Audacious* and another squall tore the main topsail of the *Bellerophon*, but these were minor problems for ships used to coping with the winter storms in the Bay of Biscay. The damage was repaired and, with the wind on the beam, they made rapid progress. On the afternoon of 11 April they sighted the mountains of Jamaica on the horizon, and early the following morning they sailed past the rocky islets strung across the approaches to Port Royal, rounded the low promontory dominated by the stone walls of Fort Charles and headed into the vast, glittering expanse of Kingston Harbour. A fleet of eleven ships of the line, and several frigates and smaller vessels were riding at anchor in the middle of the bay, their decks shaded from the tropical sun by canvas awnings, their colourful flags streaming out in the breeze.

As the guns of the *Bellerophon* boomed out a salute to the port admiral, a flock of pelicans took off and headed across the water, flying low with steady, rhythmic wingbeats. Beyond the flight of birds and the anchored ships lay the distant town of Kingston. And, rising up behind the town, and providing a dramatic backdrop to the harbour, were the thickly wooded slopes of the Blue Mountains, their highest peaks hidden in the clouds. At 8.30 am the *Bellerophon* dropped anchor in 9 fathoms of clear water. For the next two years the great natural harbour and the dockyard at Port Royal would be her base. Here her crew would provision the ship and from here they would set off to patrol the Jamaica Passage and embark on an extended cruise up the American coast to Nova Scotia.

Port Royal today is a shadow of the town it once was. It is off the beaten track for most tourists and remains what it has been for a century or more, a sleepy fishing village set at the end of a long, snaking promontory. The ramparts of the old fort and the naval hospital are the most prominent of the few elderly structures which have survived the onslaught of earthquakes, fires and hurricanes. It is hard to believe that in the 1660s it was the richest of all the towns in the British colonies across the Atlantic. The daring raids of Sir Henry Morgan and the buccaneers on the Spanish treasure ports had brought fabulous wealth to a town already rich on the profits of the slave trade and the sugar plantations. The harbour swarmed with merchant ships, and the taverns and brothels along the waterfront did a roaring trade. All this ended dramatically in 1692 when a devastating earthquake shook the town to pieces. The old stone church, where the funeral of Sir Henry Morgan had been held, crumbled and collapsed. Two entire streets along the waterfront with shops, houses and wharves slid beneath the sea. A tidal wave following in the wake of the earthquake caused further devastation. It was estimated that 2,000 people died that day and a further 2,000 died later from their injuries or from disease.

The town never recovered its former prosperity as a trading port but developed instead into a British naval base. The damaged and derelict waterfront was transformed into a small but remarkably efficient naval dockyard. When Admiral Vernon visited Port Royal in 1740 to refit his squadron he was able to write approvingly, 'I believe I may say never more work was done in less time, and with fewer hands, than what has been done since my coming in.'[9] By the time the *Bellerophon* dropped anchor in the harbour in April 1802 the dockyard had expanded further and was capable of repairing and victualling a fleet. Protected behind a retaining wall were blacksmiths' shops, sawpits, a mast house, a boat house, a pitch house, and a shed for the coopers to make and repair barrels. There was a fine house for the port admiral and a row of houses for visiting naval captains. And although there were no dry docks there were two careening wharves with capstan houses. Ships were hauled alongside these wharves, and then heaved on their sides with the aid of the capstans. The weed, worms and barnacles which grew so rapidly on ships' bottoms in the warm tropical waters were then burnt and scraped off, and the copper plates were repaired.

The *Bellerophon* remained just over a week at Port Royal before setting sail to join a squadron of warships which was stationed in the Jamaica Passage. Although hostilities between Britain and France had been temporarily suspended, following the signing of the Peace of Amiens on 25 March, the Admiralty had no intention of easing up on the patrols of a region so critical for Britain's trade. Spread out in a line in the vicinity of Navassa Island, the squadron commanded the eastern approaches to Jamaica and was in a good position to keep an eye on French warships based at San Domingo, as well as providing some protection for the numerous British merchant ships using the Windward Passage and voyaging to and from Jamaica.

After only four months on the Jamaica station the *Bellerophon* was despatched to Halifax, Nova Scotia, with a squadron of ships of the line. This was to avoid the worst of the hurricane season in the Caribbean, to show the flag in northern waters, and to remind France that Britain still maintained a presence in North America. The British had established a fortified naval base at Halifax back in 1749 in order to counter the threat to Britain's interests posed by the massive fortress which the French had built at Fort Louisbourg on the northern tip of Nova Scotia. With the loss of the American colonies in 1782, Halifax assumed a special importance as a base from which to defend British merchant ships trading with America and the fishing fleets operating off Nova Scotia and Newfoundland.

The voyage from Jamaica, through the scattered islands of the Bahamas and up along the coast of America, took three weeks. On 14 September 1802 they sailed past the rocky headlands guarding the approaches to Halifax and dropped anchor among the ships gathered in the harbour. They were greeted by a steady downpour of rain, and the weather continued damp and overcast for the next few days. The squadron remained at Halifax for just under a month before heading back to the West Indies.

By 8 November they were once again moored off Port Royal. For the next eighteen months the routine for the *Bellerophon* and for the other ships of the line on the Jamaica station settled into a regular pattern: two or three months at sea patrolling the stretch of the Caribbean which lay between Jamaica, Cuba and San Domingo, and then two or three weeks at anchor off Port Royal. The tasks were much the same as they would have been at Portsmouth or Plymouth: taking in stores, carrying out repairs, and providing assistance to the workers in the dockyard. However, there were a few additional tasks due to the climate. The heat caused the planking of the decks and sides to open up and the caulkers were kept busy caulking the seams; for a similar reason canvas covers were made for the ships' boats when they were stored on deck to prevent their planks opening in the heat; and windsails were erected to catch the breeze and provide some ventilation below decks.

The routine was interrupted when news reached Jamaica that the Peace of Amiens had come to an end on 16 May 1803 and Britain and France were once again at war. The peace had never been more than an uneasy truce. For Britain it had provided a much-needed breathing space and an opportunity to tackle her economic difficulties. Her national debt in 1802 amounted to £507 million and the gold reserves at the Bank of England were dangerously low. Large numbers of British tourists had crossed the Channel to visit Paris and to see for themselves the changes brought about by the French Revolution but the terms of the peace treaty were so unfavourable to Britain that there was little chance of a lasting peace. Under the terms of the treaty, signed on 27 March 1802, Britain had agreed to return to France, Spain and Holland all her recent conquests except Trinidad, Ceylon and the Spice Islands. So Minorca went back to Spain; and St Lucia, Tobago, Martinique and St Pierre went back to France. It was agreed that Malta, which Britain had captured from the French in 1800, should be returned to the Knights of Malta.

While Britain used the peace to take stock, Napoleon took advantage of the cessation of hostilities to pursue his territorial ambitions. In the words of his biographer J.P. Thompson, 'Bonaparte was conscious of a revolution behind him, a republic beside him, and an empire ahead of him.'[10] During the summer and autumn of 1802 he annexed Elba and Piedmont, he incorporated Parma into the French Republic, and he invaded Switzerland. By December he was blocking British exports to Italy and Holland, and by March 1803 he had set in train a shipbuilding programme for warships as well as for large numbers of landing craft. These aggressive actions caused increasing suspicion and resentment in Britain. In his speech from the throne on 8 March 1803 George III announced that 'as very considerable military preparations are carrying on in the ports of France and Holland, he has judged it expedient to adopt

additional measures of precaution for the security of his domin-
ions.'[11] Britain had already delayed the evacuation of Malta, which
was a strategically valuable naval base in the Mediterranean, and
by the time she declared war on 16 May she had passed two Militia
Acts to raise men for the army and had fifty-two ships of the line
in commission.

When the news of the resumption of hostilities reached Jamaica
the British squadron immediately went on the offensive. On 29 June
they captured the French corvette *Mignonne* and a French brig. And
in July they gave chase to two French ships of the line as they left
the shelter of their harbour at San Domingo. The *Bellerophon* captured
the 74-gun *Duquesne* after a few shots had been fired, but the second
warship, the *Duguay-Trouin*, escaped and set sail for France. Apart
from the capture of an American schooner in March 1804 this was
the only action seen by the crew of the *Bellerophon* during their two
years in the Caribbean.

The ship had lost only one man in the taking of the *Duquesne*
but her crew had not been able to escape the ravages of disease. In
this they reflected the experience of almost every ship and army
unit which served in the West Indies. The greatest killer in the
navy in this, as in earlier periods, was not enemy action but the
ravages of scurvy, typhus, malaria and yellow fever. It has been
calculated that during the wars against Revolutionary and
Napoleonic France of 1793 to 1815 approximately 100,000 British
seamen died. Of this number, 1.5 per cent died in battle, 12 per
cent died in shipwrecks or similar disasters, 20 per cent died from
shipboard or dockside accidents, and no less than 65 per cent died
from disease.

Scurvy, caused by a lack of vitamin C in the diet, had decimated
the crews of ships on long ocean voyages in the past but, thanks
largely to the work of Dr James Lind, physician to the Royal Naval
Hospital at Haslar, much progress had been made in tackling this
horrible disease. By following most of Lind's recommendations,
Captain Cook had almost eliminated deaths from scurvy on his
three great voyages of discovery although he had not realised that
citrus fruits were the most effective cure. In 1795 the Navy started

issuing ships with lime and lemon juice on a regular basis and
captains were expected to see that every crew member got his share.
On 1 June 1797, for instance, a few days after the *Bellerophon* arrived
at Cadiz, there is a note in the captain's log which reads, 'Served
lemons to the ships company,' and on 26 August 1803, when the
ship was at anchor in Port Royal harbour, '220 gallons of Lime
Juice was received on board to which 40 gallons of rum was added
for its preservation.'

Scurvy continued to affect naval crews during the course of long
cruises but deaths from the disease dropped dramatically. Alexander
White, who had taken over from George Bellamy as the *Bellerophon*'s
surgeon, noted that thirty-one men were sick with scurvy during
the course of the year from June 1803 to June 1804 but none of them
died. Malaria and yellow fever were a different matter and during
that same period White's journal records that 212 members of the
crew were ill with fever. Seventeen of these men died on board and
the rest were sent to the naval hospital. White's entry for 4 February
1804 records their fate: 'This morning sailed from Port Royal where
we have been near 9 weeks at our anchor; during which upwards of
one hundred men have been sent to Port Royal Hospital with fever,
about 40 of which have already died.'

Many ships suffered even higher death rates. In 1801 James
Gardner went out to the West Indies on the *Brunswick*, which had
fought with the *Bellerophon* at the Battle of the Glorious First of
June. The *Brunswick* soon had 287 men sick 'and buried a great many'
but worse still was the fate of the frigate *Topaze* which had a crew
of 255. Gardner wrote that 'a short time before we arrived, the *Topaze*,
36, on a cruise, buried all hands except fifty-five; the captain (Church)
and all the officers died, and the ship was brought in by the gunner.'

It would be many years before the medical profession realised that
malaria and yellow fever were spread by mosquitoes. At this period
there was no known cure so it is little wonder that a posting to the
West Indies was regarded by many sailors as a death sentence and
that officers with influence did their best to avoid it. The crew of
the *Bellerophon* must have been greatly relieved when they received
the news that the ship had been ordered home.

TWELVE

Prelude to Trafalgar

1804–5

In the early hours of Sunday 17 June 1804 the crew of the *Bellerophon* hoisted in the launch and got up the topsail yards ready for sailing. In the darkness all around them, the shouted commands and curses from other ships, and the creaking of ropes being hauled through wooden blocks, interrupted the insistent background chorus of the tree frogs. When the first rays of sunlight illuminated the upper slopes of the Blue Mountains a breeze sprang up and heavy canvas sails began flapping as the fifty or more merchant ships scattered across the harbour prepared to get under way. By mid-morning all except a few stragglers had weighed anchor and proceeded slowly past the fort at the harbour entrance, past Gun Cay, the rocky islet where the tarred bodies of pirates had hung until pecked clean by the circling vultures, and sailed out into the brilliant blue-green waters of the Caribbean. Once clear of the entrance the convoy headed westward along the southern shores of Jamaica towards Negril Bay. There, off the deserted beach and the mosquito-infested mangrove swamps, they were joined by the merchant ships and escorting vessels from the north side of the island. By the time they left Jamaica there were 172 vessels in the convoy.

They proceeded north through the Windward Passage and by 3 July, when they left behind them the mountains of Cuba and headed out into the Atlantic, the convoy had grown to 178 sail, and extended for nearly 6 miles. In overall command of the convoy was John Loring, captain of the *Bellerophon*, and to assist him in protecting the convoy were no fewer than seven warships. Apart from the *Bellerophon* there was only one other ship of the line, the 74-gun *Duquesne*, the French ship captured off Santo Domingo. The other ships in the escort were the *Desirir*, 40 guns, and the *Renard*, 16 guns (both were French prizes captured several years earlier and commissioned into the British Navy); the *Echo* and the *Snake*, ship-rigged sloops of 18 guns; the *Hunter*, a 16-gun brig; and the armed schooner *Pickle*. This formidable escort was necessary to protect the vulnerable merchant ships from attack by French privateers. Although the ships of the French Navy had been subjected to humiliating defeats on the few occasions they had escaped the British blockade and ventured out to sea, the French privateers had proved a menace to British merchant shipping. Some of the most successful privateer captains, such as Robert Surcouf, had become legendary heroes, and had notched up some spectacular captures in the Indian Ocean and the Caribbean.

Britain, being far more dependent on her overseas trade than France, could not afford to lose valuable cargoes and the 1798 Convoy Act made it compulsory for all merchant ships, except the powerful, armed ships of the East India Company and Hudson's Bay Company, to travel in convoys protected by British warships. The dates for the sailing of the outward-bound convoys were determined by the Admiralty, and the merchantmen usually assembled at the Nore or in the sheltered waters of the Solent. The homeward-bound sailings were determined by the admirals commanding the overseas stations.

Most naval captains hated convoy duty because the merchant ships were so difficult to control. The merchantmen were usually undermanned, varied enormously in speed, and were often commanded by bloody-minded individuals who objected to being bossed around. Thomas Pasley spent several years escorting convoys before commanding the *Bellerophon* and his journals are full of scathing comments. 'How can I pretend to answer for the safety of ships commanded by such a set of mules,' he wrote on one occasion.[1] But the convoy system proved remarkably successful and in the period of the war against France, from 1793 to the Peace of Amiens in 1801, the losses of merchant shipping amounted to no more than 3.4 per cent of all sailings.[2]

The *Bellerophon*'s convoy took just under five weeks to cross the Atlantic. They sailed up the Channel with a strong south-westerly wind behind them, passed Beachy Head in drizzling rain and dropped anchor in the Downs on the afternoon of 11 August. Having delivered her convoy safely, the *Bellerophon* returned to Portsmouth for a thorough overhaul following her two-year assignment in the tropics. Her guns and ballast were removed, her masts taken out, and on 5 September she went into dock where she remained until 8 October. For a total cost of £11,914 she was re-coppered, her masts and spars were repaired or replaced, and she was re-rigged and fitted out, ready to rejoin the fleet.[3] Within a week of leaving Portsmouth Harbour she was heading back down the Channel to resume her old task of blockading the French coast off Ushant. Apart from brief return visits to Cawsand Bay, off Plymouth, to repair storm damage and load up with water and provisions, she spent the rest of the winter months and the spring of 1805 with the squadron which was charged with blockading the French naval base at Brest.

When the *Bellerophon* returned to Britain in the summer of 1804 the country was facing the most serious threat of invasion since the days of the Spanish Armada. Much had happened on both sides of the English Channel during the two years that the ship had been away. Napoleon was no longer a mere general. In August 1802 he had been proclaimed First Consul for life and had begun the sweeping reforms of French institutions which were to leave a lasting mark on the country. He had reformed the financial and legal systems, revolutionised the educational system, and instituted a major programme of road building and canal construction. In May 1804 he was proclaimed Emperor of the French and before the end of the year crowned himself at Notre-Dame in the presence of the Pope.

Many in Britain had welcomed Napoleon's rise to supreme power. However enthusiasm for the First Consul began to ebb away when news of his ambitious plans for an invasion of England became known. When Napoleon had been put in command of the Army of England back in 1798 he had inspected the troops and ships assembled in the French ports and had wisely decided that they were not capable of mounting a successful invasion. He now had the power and resources to assemble an invasion force on an altogether different scale, and he approached the task with his usual energy and attention to detail. Within days of the resumption of hostilities following the breakdown of the Peace of Amiens, orders were sent out for the building of 150 landing craft, and on 24 May 1803 contracts were placed for a further 1,050 vessels. 'We must have a model of a flat-bottomed boat able to transport 100 men across the Channel,' Bonaparte wrote to Rear-Admiral Decrès, the Minister of Marine, on 29 May. 'There should be a mortar in the bows and stern. Such a boat should not cost more than £200 to £250.'[4] On 5 July Napoleon issued orders for the purchase and construction of 2,410 more vessels, including shallow-draught troop carriers, bomb vessels and fast coastal luggers.[5] Private shipyards all over France and Belgium were engaged in the work and invasion craft were even built on the Quai D'Orsay in the centre of Paris.

To accommodate this armada of invasion craft, Napoleon ordered many French harbours to be enlarged and protected by additional forts. At Boulogne, extensive new quays were built and a large artificial basin was excavated, and less ambitious works were carried out at the smaller ports such as Ambleteuse and Etaples. Ten new gun batteries were built along the Normandy coast in an effort to protect the invasion vessels from the frequent attacks made by British ships. The biggest concentration of troops, the Grand Army of 114,000 men, was assembled on the hills above Boulogne, creating an extended town of military huts, clearly visible in contemporary pictures on the green hills above the port. Napoleon made a number of surprise visits to the various ports and harbours to check on progress, and inspect the troops.

'I went on Friday to visit the harbour at Boulogne, and arrived quite unexpectedly,' he wrote on 5 November 1803. 'I took the greatest interest in inspecting all the works and preparations for the great expedition.'[6] Two days later he was writing, 'On Sunday I spent the day visiting the new ports of Ambleteuse and Wimereux,

(Top Left) Bow view of an eighteenth-century model of the *Bellona*, a 74-gun ship designed by Sir Thomas Slade and almost identical to the *Bellerophon*. She is shown on her launching cradle ready to be launched with the copper plates on her bottom clearly visible.

(Top Right) Shown here are a selection of the traditional tools used by shipwrights and caulkers for building wooden ships. They include an axe, an adze (the tool with the blade set at right angles to the strongly curved handle); an auger for drilling holes; a chisel, a small smoothing plane, a caulking mallet and two caulking irons.

(Bottom Left) Stern view of the *Bellona* showing the decorative carving and finely proportioned stern windows. The captain used the upper cabin with its elegant stern gallery. The lower line of windows illuminated the ward room used by the ship's officers.

A painting by Robert Wilkins of the royal dockyard at Chatham in 1777. The ship in the background flying large flags is ready to be launched. To the right of her is a ship under construction and just beyond is the Commissioner's house.

The dismasted British 74-gun ship *Defence* under attack from two French warships at the Battle of the Glorious First of June, 1794. Painted by Nicholas Pocock who was an eye-witness of the action.

A book of flag signals issued by Lord Howe to Rear Admiral Bowyer of the *Barfleur* in May 1793 and used at the Battle of the Glorious First of June, 1794.

A caricature by Thomas Rowlandson of Rear Admiral Sir Thomas Pasley who lost his leg at the Battle of the Glorious First of June. Preserved with the drawing is an inscription, 'The tough old commodore. The bullets and gout / have knocked his hulk about.'

Thomas Buttersworth, a seaman in the British fleet, painted this watercolour of the inshore squadron off Cadiz in 1797. The British ships are, from left to right: *Bellerophon*, *Orion* (broadside view, under sail), Nelson's flagship *Theseus*, *Colossus*, and *Irresistible*.

The midshipmen's quarters on a British warship, painted by Augustus Earle from sketches made on the frigate *Hyperion* in 1822. Note the navigational instruments, the books, the parrot, and the lad on the right with his violin and pet monkey.

(Previous page) *The Battle of the Nile*, 1798, with the French flagship *L'Orient* on fire, by Thomas Whitcombe. The dismasted *Bellerophon* is just beyond and to the right of the doomed French ship, and is about to withdraw from the action.

(Left) A preliminary oil sketch by John Hoppner for a full-length portrait of Nelson. It was painted in 1800 by which time Nelson had lost his right arm and the sight of one eye and become an international hero following his crushing victory at the Battle of the Nile.

(Below) Napoleon visiting Boulogne in July 1804 to inspect the troops and the fleet of landing craft, gunboats and warships assembled in the harbour for the planned invasion of England. The painting by Jean-Francis Hue is in the Palace of Versailles.

and making the troops quartered there go through their manoeuvres. The works are progressing satisfactorily.'[7] It was a refreshing change from his administrative duties in Paris and he was in his element. Returning to Boulogne on 12 November he noted, 'I spent the whole of yesterday at the harbour, either on horseback or in a boat, which means that I was soaked the whole of the day. But unless one is prepared to face the rain at this season, one would never do anything; fortunately for me, it suits me perfectly, and I have never been better in my life.'[8]

In addition to assembling his invasion craft he ordered a company of guide-interpreters to be formed to accompany the invading army, and even instructed Chaptal, the Minister for Home Affairs, to get a special song written for the invasion, to be set to the music of the *Chant du départ*. 'And while you are about it,' he instructed, 'have a number of songs written on the same subject, to go to different tunes.'[9] By May 1804 there were more than a thousand landing craft and gunboats available and he was planning the invasion for the late summer of that year. In July he made another tour of the invasion ports and on this occasion revealed his inability to understand the real problems of mounting an amphibious operation. In addition to his genius as a military commander Napoleon had an extraordinary ability to get things done, but he consistently failed to understand what every sailor and fisherman understood and that was the crucial importance of the weather and the tides in any operation involving sailing ships.

Early on the morning of 20 July he decided to hold a general review of the fleet at Boulogne. He sent orders to Vice-Admiral Bruix, who was in command of the invasion flotilla, to take the fleet to sea and anchor in the roadstead while he went for his daily ride on horseback. A strong south-westerly wind had been blowing the previous day and there was a heavy swell off the harbour entrance but it was evident to any experienced seaman that a strong gale was imminent. Admiral Bruix therefore decided that the review would have to be postponed to another day. When Napoleon returned from his ride to inspect the fleet he was furious to find that his orders had been disobeyed. Bruix explained that there was a storm on the way and he did not wish to risk the lives of his men. Napoleon over-ruled him and they nearly came to blows. Rear-Admiral Magon took the fleet to sea and anchored offshore.

During the afternoon the wind swung round to the north-east and rose to gale force, accompanied by thunder and lightning. The fleet was ordered to weigh anchor and seek shelter but the breaking waves at the entrance of Boulogne Harbour made it too dangerous to enter and so most of the ships and boats headed for Etaples. Forty-two of them reached it safely but four gunboats, two shallops and two caiques were driven ashore at Boulogne and wrecked. More than 200 men were drowned. Napoleon insisted on getting into a boat and leading the rescue efforts and was nearly drowned himself. A report sent to the Minister of War two days later by Marshal Soult played down the disaster and made much of Napoleon's rescue attempt. Soult described 'an extremely unfortunate event which caused the loss of a few soldiers and damaged several of the ships . . . His Imperial Majesty himself passed the night on the shore, and in the surf, directing the salvage operations, and his august presence was of the greatest comfort to the unfortunate men on the wrecks.'[10]

By August it was evident that the invasion would have to be delayed to the following year. Napoleon returned to Fontainebleau to embark on negotiations with the Pope and the arrangements for his coronation as emperor. However he remained as determined as ever to land his invincible French soldiers on English soil and march on London: 'With God's help I will put an end to the future and very existence of England.' During the winter of 1804–5 he drew up fresh plans for the invasion. Apart from the weather, and the problem of getting large numbers of vessels out of the various French ports on a single tide, the greatest obstacle was the British Navy. Small sailing vessels loaded with soldiers were extremely vulnerable to attack from patrolling frigates, let alone from a fleet of ships of the line. It was therefore essential that the French gain control of the Channel for at least twenty-four hours while the armada of invasion craft made the crossing. Napoleon's solution was a Grand Strategy which was admirable in theory but fatally over-estimated the capabilities of the French Navy. He planned that the French fleets would break out of their naval bases, cross the Atlantic and recapture from the British a number of West Indian islands, including Martinique, St Lucia and St Dominique. This would cause the British to send a major naval force across the West Indies. While they were away from Europe, the French fleets would combine forces, hurry back across the Atlantic and sail up the English Channel. He believed that their superior numbers would enable them to sweep aside any opposition and provide cover for the invasion flotilla.

The first stage of the strategy was partially successful. On 11 January 1805 a squadron of French ships under the command of Admiral Missiessy slipped out of Rochefort in a snowstorm, crossed the Atlantic, and captured Martinique and the small islands of Nevis, St Kitts and Montserrat. However when they returned to France in May they found Napoleon outraged that they had not also taken Dominica, Barbados and St Lucia. Meanwhile Villeneuve had made a sortie out of Toulon on 14 January with a fleet of eleven ships of the line and several frigates. He had been driven back by storms but on 30 March 1805 he was encouraged by favourable winds to make a second attempt.

He managed to evade Nelson's Mediterranean fleet, which was re-victualling in Majorca, and sailed through the Straits of Gibraltar to Cadiz, where he ordered some of the ships of the Spanish fleet to put to sea and follow him to the West Indies. The French fleet arrived in Martinique on 14 May and the Spanish ships arrived two days later. When Nelson learnt from his watching frigates that Villeneuve and a large French fleet was at sea, he set off in pursuit, just as Napoleon had planned. In the Gulf of Cadiz he found that the enemy fleet had headed out across the Atlantic. Although they had a month's lead on him, Nelson immediately headed west and arrived at Barbados on 4 June. He chased from island to island, and off Montserrat he received information that the French were intending to attack Antigua. But when he arrived at Antigua on 12 June there was no sign of them.

Villeneuve and his fleet had set off for France four days earlier. On 8 June his fleet had intercepted and captured a homeward-bound convoy of fifteen British merchant ships. This was a lucky break but when he learnt from the merchantmen that Nelson was in the West Indies, and was searching for him with a fleet of warships, he seems to have lost his nerve. He had received orders from France to capture Antigua, Grenada and other islands but he now abandoned his mission and headed for home. On 22 July in misty conditions off Cape Finisterre he encountered a fleet of fourteen British ships of the line under the command of Vice-Admiral Sir Robert Calder. A confused and inconclusive battle took place which came to be known as Calder's Action. The British captured two ships but failed to prevent the remainder of the French and Spanish ships from escaping in the mist and seeking refuge in the port of Vigo. Calder had to face a court martial later for failing to bring about a decisive action but at least he had successfully prevented the enemy fleet from heading up the Channel.

Napoleon had hoped to launch his invasion between 10 June and 10 July and was getting impatient. On 3 August he arrived at Boulogne to supervise the embarkation of the troops, and sent increasingly urgent letters to his admirals. He urged Villeneuve to 'sweep everything before you, and arrive in the Channel, where we are anxiously awaiting you . . . If you are here for three days, indeed if you are here only for twenty-four hours, your mission will be accomplished.'[11] And to Admiral Ganteaume at Brest he wrote, 'I wish you to put to sea at once, for the fulfilment of your mission, and to proceed with all your forces to the Channel . . . Start at once, and come here. We shall have avenged the insults of six centuries. Never have my soldiers and sailors risked their lives in a nobler cause.'[12]

The British took the invasion threat extremely seriously, particularly in the southern counties which were most vulnerable to attack. Their cruising frigates could see the enemy's vast encampment on the hills above Boulogne, and from the cliffs at Dover and Folkestone the people watched the comings and goings of brigs and luggers and gunboats as the invasion flotilla was assembled. The countermeasures undertaken in Britain were impressive and would have made it extremely difficult for the French forces to effect a landing

without massive loss of life. Lord St Vincent, who had been appointed
First Lord of the Admiralty in 1803, was responsible for the sea
defences of the kingdom. He established a triple line of maritime
defences. The first line consisted of frigates and gun-vessels which
were deployed along the French coast to blockade all French
shipping in port, including merchantmen and fishing boats. The
second and most formidable line of defence was a squadron of
warships based in the Downs whose job it was to intercept and
attack the invasion forces if and when they escaped the blockading
ships and put to sea. The third line of defence consisted of gunboats
and armed fishing vessels stationed in all the harbours, estuaries
and inlets along the south and east coast of Britain. They were
manned by the Sea Fencibles, the body of volunteer sailors and
fishermen set up by Lord Keith during the previous emergency in
1798 and re-established following the end of the Peace of Amiens.
To protect the Thames a line of old warships was anchored across
the lower reaches with orders to link up and form a continuous
barrier in the event of an impending invasion.

An engraving from *Stanfield's Coast Scenery* showing
a Martello tower on the coast near Hastings.

Behind the sea defences were the land defences. The most visible of these were the Martello towers. These were based on the design of a fort at Cape Mortella in Corsica which had impressed the navy and army engineers by standing up to prolonged bombardment from ship and shore in 1794. More than a hundred of them were built between Seaford in Sussex and Aldeburgh in Suffolk; some forty of them remain today as the most visible reminder of the Napoleonic threat to Britain.[13] In addition to the Martello towers there were batteries of guns established overlooking beaches and landing places. Existing forts and castles, like those at Dover and Walmer, were strengthened and manned with troops. If and when the invasion was imminent the news would be spread by the lighting of beacons on hilltops and the ringing of church bells; details would be transmitted by the chain of wooden shutter telegraph stations which linked the Admiralty with the dockyards at

The telegraph station on Southsea Common, 1805.
Overlooking the fleet anchorage at Spithead this
was one of a line of shutter telegraph stations which
linked Portsmouth with the Admiralty in London.

Chatham and Portsmouth. The regular army had around 80,000 men stationed in Britain at the resumption of hostilities and this was augmented by the militia and by volunteer regiments. Recruiting offices were inundated with men and boys wishing to join up. Although large numbers had to be rejected because they were too old, too young or hopelessly unfit, it was reckoned that by 1804 some 380,000 men, or 7 per cent of the adult male population, had joined the militia.[14]

The descriptions of the army manoeuvres which took place on the hills and valleys of Kent, Surrey and Sussex suggest that they were a source of entertainment to the local population as well as those who took part. Sham fights were particularly popular. On 2 August 1805, for instance, several regiments took part in a fight under the orders of the Earl of Harrington. The main body of the troops was stationed at Dulwich with small groups of men on Denmark Hill, on the village green in Half Moon Lane and at the cross roads by the Half Moon public house. After the fight the men marched past and saluted the Earl of Harrington and then settled down for a picnic. According to *The Times*, 'The Earl and Countess of Harrington, and

A drawing by Thomas Rowlandson of British troops guarding the coast when the country was threatened with invasion.

other ladies and gentlemen partook of a cold collation in a large
marquee pitched at the entrance of the common. Great numbers of
spectators were present.'[15] The royal family meanwhile were going
about their usual business. The King, the Queen and the princesses
were staying in Weymouth where they attended the theatre, and
went for cruises on the royal yacht. The Prince Regent was in
Brighton attending the races. On 30 July his horse won the Egremont
Stakes by a neck, and afterwards he went to a ball with his mistress,
Mrs Fitzherbert. Three weeks later he was still in Brighton and,
together with a number of noblemen and gentlemen, he watched
6,000 troops from Lewes, Shoreham and the surrounding area skir-
mish across the South Downs.[16]

While the regular army and the volunteer soldiers carried out
military exercises, and the Sea Fencibles kept watch from every signal
station, clifftop and harbour entrance, the British Navy continued to
blockade the French ports and guard the entrance of the Channel.
It was the vigilance and constant presence of the warships cruising
off the coasts of France and Spain which was the greatest obstacle
to Napoleon's plans. This was the period when the ships truly earned
the title of 'the wooden walls of England'. On her return from the
West Indies in the late summer of 1804 the *Bellerophon* once again
became part of those wooden walls. She joined the squadron
blockading the port of Brest, and for seven months she endured the
familiar hardships and perils of the rock-strewn coast of Brittany
with its fierce tidal streams, overfalls and breaking seas. On 24 April
1805, while she was back in Plymouth taking on water and provisions in between cruises out to Ushant, Captain Loring was replaced
by Captain John Cooke, the man who would command her at
Trafalgar. Cooke was forty-two and had been in the navy since the
age of eleven. He had seen action in the East Indies and then in the
West Indies where he had fought at the Battle of the Saints. Later,
when captain of the *Nymphe*, a 36-gunner, he had taken part in the
daring capture of two French frigates within sight of the French
fleet at Brest, an action commemorated in a sparkling painting by
Nicholas Pocock.[17]

Cooke's first lieutenant was William Pryce Cumby. He was

thirty-four and, unlike his captain, he had no previous experience of enemy action. He had served in frigates and ships of the line, and spent several years with the Mediterranean fleet under St Vincent engaged in the blockade of Cadiz. Before joining the *Bellerophon* in November 1804 he had commanded a naval cutter on the east coast and served briefly with the Sea Fencibles at King's Lynn.[18] He was to prove heroic under fire at Trafalgar when he had to take over command of the ship from the captain, and his account of the action (written at the request of his son Anthony) is one of the most vivid and personal of the many eye-witness descriptions.[19]

When the news reached England in May 1805 that Villeneuve had escaped from Toulon, Captain Cooke and the *Bellerophon* were despatched to the Straits of Gibraltar with a squadron led by Vice-Admiral Collingwood. They arrived off Cadiz on 31 May only to learn that Villeneuve had set off for the West Indies, taking with him several of the Spanish ships from Cadiz. While Nelson set off in pursuit of the enemy fleet, Collingwood and his squadron took up a position off the port to keep watch on the remaining Spanish warships in the harbour. They were there when Villeneuve returned from the West Indies, fought Admiral Calder off Finisterre and retreated into Ferrol. They were still there on 20 July when Nelson came back exhausted after his fruitless pursuit of the enemy fleet and stepped ashore at Gibraltar. He had been at sea without a break for two years and returned to England to recuperate, leaving Collingwood to take charge of the fleet.

In mid-August Villeneuve again managed to evade the blockading squadrons. He led his fleet out of Ferrol and headed south to join his forces with the Spanish ships in Cadiz Harbour. The *Bellerophon* and several other ships of the squadron were in Gibraltar and others were scattered along the coast when Collingwood, with only three ships of the line, a frigate and a bomb vessel under his command, found thirty enemy warships bearing down on him. He had no option but to make a hasty withdrawal but as soon as Villeneuve's fleet had entered Cadiz Harbour he resumed his position off the entrance. He sent a message back to England to warn the Admiralty of the current position of the Combined Fleet and proceeded to make signals to an imaginary fleet on the horizon to encourage Villeneuve to remain in harbour until reinforcements arrived.

The *Bellerophon* sailed from Gibraltar early on the morning of 23 August and rejoined Collingwood's squadron off Cadiz later the same day. By the time Nelson came out from England on 28 September the squadron had grown to a fleet of twenty-seven ships of the line. Nelson had orders from the Prime Minister and the Admiralty to engage and destroy the Combined Fleet of France and Spain. 'It is, as Mr Pitt, knows, annihilation that the country wants – not merely a splendid victory.'[20] The only problem was luring the enemy fleet out of Cadiz Harbour. The problem was solved by Napoleon, who became so impatient with Villeneuve's failure to head north and support his planned invasion of England that he despatched Vice-Admiral Francis Rosily to replace him. When news of this reached Villeneuve he decided that he had no option but to take his fleet to sea and face the consequences.

THIRTEEN

Victory or Death

1805

No other fleet in Britain's long naval history approached a major battle with a keener sense of anticipation or with a greater confidence in its ability to win than did the British fleet off Cape Trafalgar in October 1805. Many of those present had already taken part in sea battles or single-ship actions and were fully aware of the dangers but, as one of the *Bellerophon*'s crew later wrote, 'I can assure you I felt not the least fear of death during the action, which I attribute to the general confidence of victory which I saw all round me.'[1]

There were many reasons for this widespread feeling of invincibility. The first and most obvious was that the British seamen knew that they were superior to their enemy in every essential respect. In particular they were superior in seamanship, shiphandling and gunnery, all of which were crucial in the confusion of a sea battle. Unlike the ships of France and Spain which, apart from the brief and desperate foray to the West Indies, had spent years blockaded in their naval bases, the British ships at Trafalgar had been more or less constantly at sea since the outbreak of the war with France. Their officers were experienced in navigating and keeping station in all weathers and in some of the most treacherous waters in the world. Their crews were constantly drilled in gunnery and their accuracy in firing from a moving platform and their rate of fire were formidable. Moreover the British not only knew the weaknesses of their enemy but were used to winning. In the past ten years British fleets had been victorious in a succession of battles, notably those of the Glorious First of June, Cape St Vincent, Camperdown, the Nile and Copenhagen. And in Nelson they had a commander-in-chief in whom they had total confidence and who inspired a devotion and loyalty among all ranks which had a remarkably unifying effect.

A less obvious but equally powerful reason for the determination and spirit of the British seamen was that they truly believed that they were fighting for the defence of their country and for their homes and families. When the *Bellerophon* left Plymouth in September 1804 the entire south coast was in a state of readiness to repel the invasion flotilla which Napoleon had gathered in the French ports. Every English sailor knew that the navy was all that stood between Napoleon's armies and the conquest of their country. Collingwood spoke for many when he wrote that he felt 'as if the welfare of all England depended on us alone'. There was also a strong feeling among British sailors that they wanted to put an end to the dreary task of blockading the enemy ports, and to confront and defeat the enemy once and for all so that they could return home to their anxiously waiting families. What they dreaded was that the enemy would elude them. Much of this is summed up by the reaction of the *Bellerophon*'s Lieutenant Cumby when the combined fleet of French and Spanish ships was first sighted coming out of harbour:

> Our joy at the prospect this afforded of an opportunity of bringing the enemy's fleet to action, and consequently terminating the blockade which we had been so long and so disagreeably employ'd was considerably checked by the apprehension that it was merely a feint on their part and having no intention of giving us battle that they would re-enter the harbour of Cadiz so soon as they discovered us in pursuit.[2]

Cumby was not to be disappointed. Indeed he was the first man in the fleet on 19 October to observe the signal from the British ship on the horizon that the enemy had put to sea. Nelson had deliberately kept his fleet of twenty-seven ships of the line out of sight of Cadiz in order to encourage them to venture forth and to prevent them knowing how many British warships were in the vicinity. He relied on a line of frigates and an advanced squadron of ships of the line to keep him informed of any enemy movement.

At dawn on 19 October the frigates *Euryalus* and *Sirius* were keeping their usual watch on the masts of the enemy ships gathered in the harbour of Cadiz. They were so close to the shore that a midshipman in one of the frigates was able to see the ripples of waves breaking on the beaches of the bay. As the sky lightened in the east the lookouts on the frigates noted that the enemy ships had their topsails hoisted, a sure sign that they were preparing to get under way. At 7 o'clock the *Sirius* hoisted the signal flags 370, which, in the revised signal code devised by Popham, signified: 'Enemy ships are coming out of port.' The *Euryalus* passed the signal on to the frigate *Phoebe* waiting on the horizon, and from the *Phoebe* the message was passed on to the *Naiad*, then on to the ships of the advanced squadron: first the *Defence*, then on to the *Colossus* and then the *Mars* which was the last in the long line stretching from Cadiz to the main fleet 50 miles away.

It was such a lovely morning, with a clear sky and light winds, that Nelson had invited Collingwood and several of his captains, including John Cooke, to come on board the *Victory* and dine with him. In answer to Nelson's signal the *Bellerophon* had left her station and was setting sail towards the flagship when Lieutenant Cumby spotted the signal flags flying at the masthead of the *Mars* on the distant horizon. He distinctly made out the numeral signal 370 and immediately passed on this crucial information to Captain Cooke, asking his permission to repeat it. Cooke carefully examined the distant ship with his telescope but only the topgallant masts of the *Mars* were visible above the horizon and he could not make out the colour of the signal flags. He was unwilling to repeat a signal of such importance while a doubt remained but said he would do so if any of the other people who were staring at the *Mars* through their telescopes would confirm Cumby's interpretation of the signal. Cumby was convinced of what he had seen because he knew from long experience that he had unusually strong eyesight but unfortunately none of the other officers or signalmen were prepared to endorse his opinion. And so he had 'the mortification to be disappointed in my anxious wish that Bellerophon should be the first to repeat such a delightful intelligence to the Admiral.'[3]

Cumby knew that the *Mars* would now make the distant signal 370 which was made with a flag, a ball and a pennant at different mastheads and was much easier to make out because it did not depend on the colours being recognised. Sure enough the *Mars* hauled down the coloured flags, fired several guns to attract attention and hoisted the distant signal which left no one in any doubt of the message. Before the *Bellerophon* could repeat this the *Victory* acknowledged the signal and then hoisted the signal for a general chase to the south-east. The time was 9.30 am. Every ship in the fleet shook out the reefs in their sails, made all sail possible and headed for the Straits of Gibraltar because, with the wind from the north-west, Nelson presumed that Villeneuve was heading for the Mediterranean. Throughout the rest of the morning and all through the afternoon the British sailed in pursuit of an enemy which was only visible to the most distant of the British frigates. At sunset Nelson instructed the *Bellerophon* and four of the fastest ships in the fleet to sail on ahead during the night, each carrying a light in order to keep in touch. There was an air of impatience on every vessel and Captain Cooke was so concerned at missing the enemy that he suggested to Cumby that one or other of them should remain constantly on deck until they brought the enemy to action. Cumby agreed, and volunteered to take the first two watches. He remained on the quarterdeck until midnight when Cooke came up to relieve him.

At daylight on 20 October there was no sign of the enemy and Nelson ordered the fleet to haul the wind and head northwards. During the course of the morning the weather closed in. A fresh breeze brought rain and an enveloping, thick, damp fog. The ships hove to, each adjusting their sails and taking in reefs where necessary so they could keep their correct stations. By midday they were heeling over under squally showers, the rain sweeping across the decks, pouring off sails and dripping off the hats of the officers huddled on the quarterdecks. On the *Bellerophon* they were unable to see the signals of the distant frigates but Cumby was heartened to see the *Victory* send a signal to Captain Blackwood of the *Euryalus,* ordering him to keep the enemy in sight during the night. 'This cheered us with the hope of an action in the morning and according to our previous arrangement Captain Cooke remained on deck till twelve o'clock and he relieved me again at four without anything happening.' During the night the rain died away and the wind dropped to the lightest of airs but there was an increasingly heavy swell from the west, the forerunner of a storm which was heading across the Atlantic. Those on deck observed the frequent flashes of blue lights and fires from the frigates which indicated that they could see the lights of the enemy fleet.

Cumby had retired to his cabin and had been asleep for less than two hours when he was rudely awakened by his friend Overton, the ship's master: 'Cumby my boy, turn out,' he shouted. 'Here they are all ready for you; three and thirty sail of the line close under our lee . . .' Cumby hurriedly got dressed but before going on deck he knelt down by the side of his cot and prayed to the great God of battles for a glorious victory and 'committed myself individually to his all wise disposal and begging his gracious protection and favour for my dear wife and children, whatever his unerring wisdom might see fit to order for myself.'[4] He was later to reflect with a feeling of pride that his own prayer was remarkably similar to the prayer which Nelson committed to paper before the battle.

Lieutenant Cumby came on deck to find the crews of every ship staring at the eastern horizon which was filled with the masts and sails of warships silhouetted against the soft light of dawn. As the sun rose and illuminated the enemy fleet, the watching sailors could clearly see the colours of the flags and ensigns flying above the extended line of white sails: the blue, white and red of the French flags mingling with the rich red and amber of the Spanish flags. They were nearly 12 miles away and although the British fleet had the weather gauge the wind was so light that it was evident to all present that it would be several hours before the two fleets met. The *Bellerophon*'s log-book gives no hint of the excitement felt on board the ship but simply notes, 'at daylight observed the Enemy's Fleet to leeward bearing ENE' and follows this with a list of the signals hoisted by the *Victory* as Nelson prepared his fleet for the long-awaited encounter.[5] At 6.10 he ordered them to form the order of sailing. This was followed by an order to 'Bear up in succession on the course set by the Admiral.' The *Victory* slowly swung round and headed east-north-east in the direction of the enemy ships on the horizon. As the other ships followed her example a third signal was hoisted to the masthead of the flagship. It was signal 13: 'Prepare for battle.' On the *Bellerophon* and on every other ship in the fleet the orders were given to beat to quarters and clear for action.

Villeneuve was also preparing for action. Ever since he had heard the news that Napoleon intended to relieve him of his command and that Vice-Admiral Rosily was on his way to replace him, he had determined to venture forth and save his reputation by leading the Combined Fleet into battle. But he did so with a heavy heart. In theory his thirty-three ships of the line should have been more than a match for Nelson's twenty-seven but he knew only too well how unprepared his forces were. Writing from Cadiz to Decrès, the Minister of Marine, back in August, he had revealed his deep concerns about Napoleon's ambitious plans: 'I beg of you to believe that nothing can equal the despair that I am suffering from them and the horror of the situation in which I find myself.'[6] He warned that the state of equipment of his ships, and the lack of co-operation and intelligence 'did not allow of encountering the slightest obstacles without suffering irreparable injuries, dispersion and the ruin of the project, making us the laughing-stock of Europe.' His forebodings were backed up by the conclusions of a Council of War which he called on board his flagship *Bucentaur* on 8 October: 'All present recognised that the ships of the two allied nations are for the most part badly armed, through the weakness of their crews; that many of them have not yet exercised their crews at all at sea . . . and that the enemy in the offing is much more powerful than ours.'[7]

Now that he was at sea Villeneuve put a brave face on the situation. His final instructions to his captains issued on the morning of the battle were as resolute as could be expected in the circumstances. What is particularly interesting about these instructions is that he anticipated with remarkable accuracy the method of attack which

Nelson would adopt: 'The enemy will not confine himself to forming in a line of battle parallel with our own and in engaging us in an artillery duel.' This of course was the traditional way in which sea battles were fought. Recalling, perhaps, the tactics used by the British in previous actions, he warned his captains that the enemy 'will endeavour to envelop our rear, to break through our line and to direct his ships in groups upon such of ours as he shall have cut off, so as to surround and defeat them.' He reminded them that 'a captain who is not under fire is not at his post', and concluded, 'every effort must be exerted to go to the assistance of the ships assailed and to close on the flagship, which will set the example.'[8]

In the great cabin of the *Bellerophon* Captain Cooke and Lieutenant Cumby had breakfast together as they usually did at 8 o'clock. When they had finished their meal and the captain's servants had removed their plates Captain Cooke told Cumby that he had something which he wanted to show him. He unfolded a piece of paper and handed it to Cumby. It was Nelson's memorandum to all his captains in which he set out his instructions for the conduct of the battle. It began, 'I have made up my mind that the order of sailing is to be the order of battle . . .' and went on to describe how he intended to cut through the enemy line near the centre and then turn and overpower all the enemy ships from the centre to the rear of their line before the vessels at the front of the line could come to the rescue of their beleaguered and outnumbered ships at the centre and rear. Nelson had originally intended to attack with his fleet arranged in three lines but, as both fleets were smaller than he anticipated, he changed this to two lines. He would lead the weather column into action and Collingwood would lead the lee column. His memorandum concluded, 'Captains are to look to their particular Line as their rallying point. But, in case Signals can neither be seen or perfectly understood, no Captain can do very wrong if he places his Ship alongside that of an Enemy.'[9]

When Cumby had finished reading the document Cooke asked him whether he understood the Admiral's instructions. Cumby told him that they were so distinct and explicit that it was quite impossible that they could be misunderstood. Cooke expressed his satisfaction at this and said that he wanted Cumby to be aware of the instructions so that he would know how to proceed in case he, the captain, should be 'bowl'd out' during the action. Cumby recorded his reply: 'On this I observed that it was very possible that the same shot which disposed of him might have an equally tranquilizing effect on me and under that idea I submitted to him the expediency of the Master (as being the only other officer who in such case would remain on the Quarter Deck) being also apprised of the Admiral's instructions.' Cooke immediately agreed with this and Overton was summoned to the great cabin and he too read through Nelson's memorandum. Only one of the three men present would live to see the day out.

It was now time for the first lieutenant to carry out his duty of inspecting the ship, so that he could report back to the captain that all was in order and the ship was ready for action. Most of the gun crews had stripped to the waist and had handkerchiefs bound tightly around their heads and over their ears to deaden the noise of the guns. Some of the men were sharpening their cutlasses in readiness for boarding or repelling boarders when the time came. On reaching the lower deck Cumby made his way along the line of guns and gun crews until he reached George Saunders, the ship's fifth lieutenant, who was in charge of the seven foremost guns. Saunders drew his attention to some of the gun barrels 'where the zeal of the seamen had led them to chalk in large characters on their guns the words, "Victory or Death": a very gratifying mark of the spirit with which they were going to their work.'[10]

The same spirit was evident throughout the ship. One of the midshipmen later wrote, 'One would have thought that the people were preparing for a festival rather than a combat, and no dissatisfaction was expressed except at the state of the weather, which was calm, and prevented our quickly nearing the enemy.'[11] The slow speed at which the two opposing fleets approached each other was one of the most memorable features of the battle for those who took part in it. With the westerly breeze behind them, the British ships set all possible sail but so light was the wind that most of them were averaging no more than 2 or 3 knots. This meant that six hours elapsed between the first sighting of the Combined Fleet and the moment when the ships were close enough to open fire.

Surprisingly, with such an extended time to wait for battle to be joined, the British sailors remained remarkably cheerful. The music no doubt helped. Several ships had bands on board. These varied considerably in size and quality: a few captains had bands made up of professional musicians and several ships were able to muster some volunteer musicians from their crews, but everyone later recalled the sound of stirring tunes thumping across the calm water. 'Rule Britannia', 'Hearts of Oak' and 'God Save the King' were played with patriotic fervour and it is recorded that the band on the *Tonnant*, the ship immediately ahead of the *Bellerophon*, played 'Britons, Strike Home', a tune popular among the seamen at the time. No doubt the thought of prize money also kept many sailors' spirits up. The midshipman who remarked that people seemed to be preparing for a festival also noted that, 'so confident were our people of success, that though we were bearing down on a superior fleet, they were employed in fixing on the number of their prizes, and pitching upon that which should fall to the lot of each of our ships.' Although an ordinary seaman could expect no more than a tiny proportion of the value of any ship captured (for every £1,000 of a captain's share of a prize, a seaman's share in a 74 was around £2) there was always the hope that it would be enough for them to retire from the sea and find an easier life ashore.

At 11 o'clock the enemy fleet was still some 3 miles distant. Captain Cooke reckoned that they would not be in action for an hour or more and so gave the order for the men to be piped to dinner. The ship's cook and his assistants had been warned to have a meal ready around this time, on the basis that 'Englishmen would fight all the better for having a comfortable meal.' While the men ate their meals crouched beside the guns, Captain Cooke joined the officers in the wardroom. Situated below the great cabin this was normally lined with cabins and dominated by a long table in the centre of the room. With the bulkheads forming the cabins removed and the table and chairs stowed below, the space was eerily empty, apart from the six guns run out at the gunports and made fast, ready for action. The only flat surface was the rudderhead and they used this as a table for their makeshift meal of cold meats.

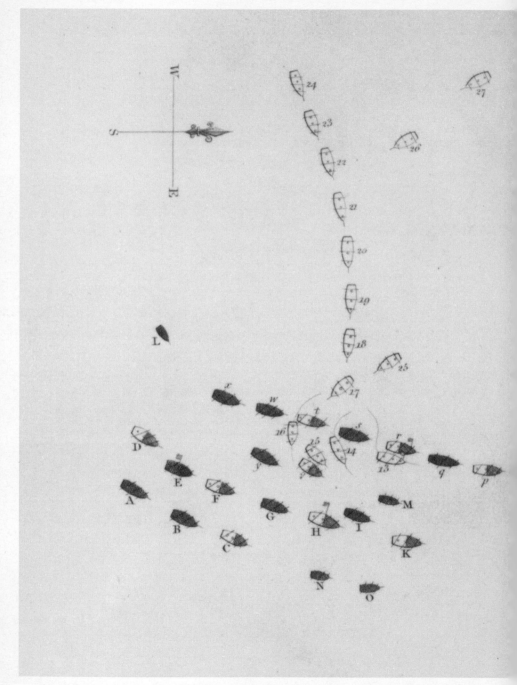

A plan of the commencement of the Battle of Trafalgar from *The Life of Admiral Lord Nelson*, by Clarke and MacArthur, 1809. The action is shown around 12.30 pm. The *Bellerophon* (17) is approaching the the enemy line and is under fire from the *Monarca (t)*.

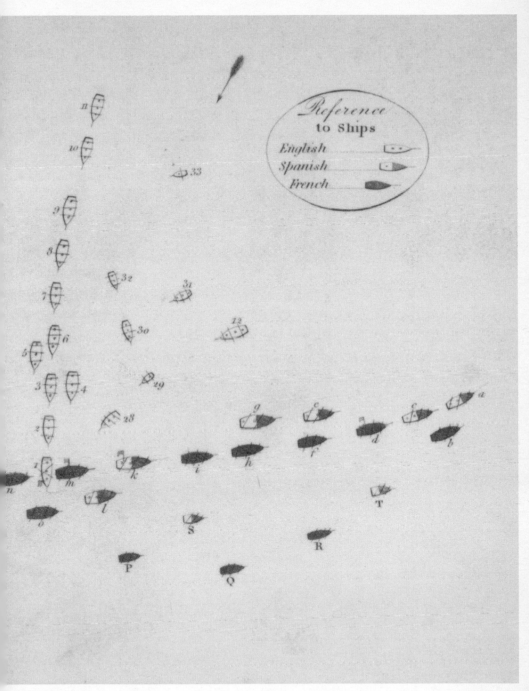

She will then encounter *L'Aigle* (I), the *San Juan Nepomuceno* (D), the *Bahama* (C) and the *Swiftsure* (G). Collingwood's *Royal Sovereign* (13) is alongside the *Santa Ana* (r). Nelson's *Victory* (1) is shown breaking through the enemy line between the *Redoubtable* (n) and the *Bucentaur* (m).

Most of the crew were still eating when there was the sound of cheering from those on deck and more distant cheering from other ships in the fleet. A signal had been hoisted on the *Victory* which had caused some excitement. The 19-year-old John Franklin (later to make his name as an Arctic explorer) was the signal midshipman in the *Bellerophon* and from his position on the poop he had noted the signal flags and worked out the message. It read 'England expects that every man will do his duty.' In some quarters the message was received with impatience, the seamen muttering that they had always done their duty and Collingwood complaining that he wished Nelson would stop signalling because they all knew what they had to do. However Lieutenant Cumby recorded that the message 'produced the most animating and inspiriting effect on the whole fleet'.

They were now only a mile or so from the enemy's line. A slight shift in the wind direction earlier had prompted Villeneuve to order the Combined Fleet to wear and form a line of battle on the port tack. This manoeuvre would have been carried out with military precision by the British fleet but it had led to considerable confusion among the Allied ships and their line was in still in some disorder. Nevertheless the spectacle of thirty-three line of battle ships, viewed broadside on and stretching across the calm water for nearly 2 miles, was both daunting and magnificent. The enemy ships were illuminated by the full glare of the midday sun, which glinted on the barrels of hundreds of guns emerging from rows and rows of gunports. The formidable power of the massive black hulls, enlivened with horizontal bands of yellow and white and red, provided a sharp contrast with the carnival spirit of the multi-coloured flags and pennants. 'I suppose no man ever before saw a sight of such beauty' wrote Captain Codrington of the *Orion* and he called all his lieutenants up on deck to witness a scene they were unlikely ever to see again.

At 2 minutes before noon the French ship *Fougueux* opened fire on the *Royal Sovereign* with a full broadside. Collingwood's flagship was fresh from the dockyard and her clean copper bottom enabled her to draw ahead of the slower ships following her. On the *Bellerophon* they watched her break through the enemy line and singlehandedly engage the *Fougueux* and the *Santa Ana*, the flagship of one of the

Spanish admirals. The *Belleisle, Mars* and *Tonnant* followed her into action, and then it was the turn of the *Bellerophon* to face the enemy broadsides. Captain Cooke had originally decided that he would hold his fire until they were in the act of passing through the enemy's line but, while still some distance away, the *Bellerophon* came under such fierce and accurate fire that men were going down and masts and rigging were in serious danger. Cooke gave the order to open fire without further ado. This gave the beleaguered crew a chance to retaliate and also provided a protective screen of gunpowder smoke so that the ship was not such an easy target for the enemy gunners.

The *Bellerophon* cut through the enemy line at 12.30, receiving fire from both sides and passing close under the stern of the Spanish 74-gun ship *Monarca*. The Spaniard received the full force of the pent-up energy of the *Bellerophon*'s crew. Two broadsides from the carriage guns and three devastating salvoes from the deadly carronades on the upper deck caused crippling damage and temporarily silenced her. The *Bellerophon* was moving in for the kill when the topgallant sails of another ship appeared above the billowing smoke to leeward. They were on a collision course. Captain Cooke ordered the sails to be backed in order to check their progress but it was too late. They just had time to read the name *L'Aigle* inscribed on her stern before they crashed into her, the *Bellerophon*'s starboard bow hitting her port quarter, and the yards of both ships becoming entangled.

L'Aigle was one of the new batch of French 74-gun ships and, while nothing like as powerful as the flagship *L'Orient* which the *Bellerophon* had faced at the Nile, she was a formidable opponent. She was bigger than the *Bellerophon*, had higher calibre guns (40- and 24-pounders compared with the *Bellerophon*'s 32s and 18s) and was commanded by Captain Gourrege who proved a determined and heroic commander. She also had 150 soldiers on board who lined the bulwarks and were posted in the tops, and subjected the *Bellerophon* to a hail of musket fire and grenades. On the poop deck, the quarterdeck and in the waist of the *Bellerophon* men were falling fast. The officers were always prime targets in such circumstances and when Cumby looked up and saw that the French soldiers had marked out Captain Cooke and were directing their fire at him, he urged him to remove his distinctive

The Battle of Trafalgar showing, 'The situation of the *Bellerophon*
at the moment of the death of her gallant commander
Captain Cooke.' The *Bellerophon*, in the centre of the
picture, is under fire from four enemy ships.

epaulettes. Cooke's reply was, 'It is now too late to take them off. I
see my situation, but I will die like a man.' Cooke then sent Cumby
below to give directions to the gun crews.

The *Bellerophon* was now under sustained fire from three enemy
ships in addition to *L'Aigle*. They were the Spanish ships *San Juan
Nepomuceno* and *Bahama* and the French ship *Swiftsure*.

To be attacked by the *Swiftsure* was a strange stroke of fate. She
was a sister ship of the *Bellerophon*, having been built to a Slade design
of the Elizabeth class and launched at Wells shipyard at Deptford in
1787, the year after the *Bellerophon's* launch. She had fought at the
Battle of the Nile and had taken the place of the *Bellerophon* alongside the massive French flagship *L'Orient* when the dismasted
Bellerophon had been forced to break off the action. In 1801 she had
been captured in the Mediterranean by a squadron led by Admiral
Ganteaume and the French had retained her British name.[12]

It is unlikely that there was anyone on the *Bellerophon* who was
aware of, or cared too much about, the past history of the *Swiftsure*

at this moment. She was flying a French ensign and, together with *L'Aigle* and the Spanish ships, she was rapidly reducing the *Bellerophon* to a shambles.

The ship's log-book records that at 1 pm the main and mizen topmasts fell over the side. This would have caused a chaotic scene, with a tangle of rigging, yards and sails strewn across the deck and dragging alongside. Captain Cooke was hit at precisely 1.11 pm according to the log-book. An eye witness described the moment of his death:

> He had discharged his pistols very frequently at the enemy, who as often attempted to board, and he had killed a French officer on his own quarterdeck. He was in the act of reloading his pistols (and upon the very same plank where Captain Pasley lost his leg on the 1st of June) when he received two musket balls in the breast. He immediately fell, and upon the quartermaster going up and asking him if he should take him down below, his answer was, 'No, let me lie quietly one minute. Tell Lieutenant Cumby never to strike.'[13]

Having checked on the gun crews below deck, Cumby was returning along the main deck when he met his friend and messmate Edward Overton, the master. His leg was dreadfully shattered and he was being carried by two men. Cumby had to turn aside and give some directions and was about to climb the ladder to the quarterdeck when a quartermaster told him that the captain was very badly wounded and he believed he was dead.

Cumby now assumed command of the ship. There was no question of surrendering but things did not look promising. In fact the *Bellerophon* was in a more perilous situation than any other British ship in the battle with the possible exception of the *Belleisle*. The *Bellerophon* was under fire from a ship astern of her, another ship ahead of her, and a ship on her port beam. She was hampered by the wreckage of two topmasts, and on her starboard side she was still entangled with *L'Aigle* whose crew continued to rake the decks with musket fire and to hurl grenades through gunports, before preparing to board. Because the upper deck and poop deck of *L'Aigle* were considerably higher than the *Bellerophon*'s decks the French soldiers were able to pick off the British sailors one by one and Cumby found that there were only a handful of his crew still standing on the exposed upper decks. He immediately ordered these survivors to take cover below and mustered a group of armed seamen and marines under the half deck in readiness to repel the boarders who were massing along the sides of the French ship.

Five of the French seamen climbed onto the *Bellerophon*'s spritsail yard and were heading towards her bowsprit when a seaman named McFarlane had the presence of mind to release the spritsail brace which supported the spar. The yard-arm tipped down under the weight of the boarders and they were all thrown into the sea. John Franklin, who had miraculously survived the hail of musket balls on the poop, observed a number of French sailors grabbing hold of the *Bellerophon*'s rail in an attempt to board her but their hands were so savagely beaten by the British sailors that they were forced to let go and fell between the ships and were crushed or drowned. Franklin also recorded an act of manic bravery typical of that day. Christopher Beaty, a veteran sailor who was yeoman of the signals, became so exasperated at seeing the *Bellerophon*'s ensign shot away three times, that he grabbed hold of the largest Union Jack he could find, climbed up the mizen rigging, spread out the flag as wide as possible and made fast the four corners to the shrouds. According to an eye-witness account, 'The French riflemen in the tops and on the poop of *L'Aigle*, seeing what he was about, and seemingly in admiration of such daring conduct, suspended their fire for the few seconds that he remained aloft; this forebearance on the part of the enemy being the more noble, as they had previously picked off every man that appeared before the Bellerophon's mizen-mast.'[14]

Meanwhile the gun crews below deck were working with the same disciplined and deadly effectiveness which they displayed when engaged in gunnery practice. Amidst the swirling clouds of gunsmoke, the flash and thunderous explosions of each gun and the savage recoil of the guns on their carriages, the men went through their well-rehearsed routine of loading, aiming and firing, with devastating effect on the enemy ships who came within range. So close were some of the gunports to those of *L'Aigle* on the lower deck that men were fighting hand to hand at the ports, seizing each other's ramrods and attacking each other with cutlasses. In addition to the gunfire of the ships on all sides the *Bellerophon*'s crew was at the mercy of the grenades which were being lobbed through the ports, causing devastating injuries. One grenade which exploded in the lower deck killed or injured twenty-five men, some of whom were dreadfully scorched. One of the men was so horribly burnt that, instead of going to see the surgeon, he ran aft screaming and threw himself out of one of the stern ports into the sea.

Cumby intercepted a grenade which he found on the gangway with its fuse burning and threw it overboard, but another grenade nearly ended the life of the *Bellerophon* and her entire crew. It was thrown into a gunport on the lower deck and exploded in the gunner's store room. The blast blew off the door of the store, set fire to the contents, and also blew open the door of the passage leading to the ship's magazine. Cumby described what happened next: '*most providentially* this door was so placed with respect to that opening from the passage into the magazine that the same blast which *blew open* the store-room door, *shut to* the door of the magazine otherwise we must all in both ships inevitably have been blown up together.'[15] The gunner acted with remarkable coolness in the circumstances. He was aware that if word spread that there was a fire in the vicinity of the magazine there was likely to be widespread panic. He therefore sought out Lieutenant Saunders, quietly explained the problem and requested some men to bring buckets of water to extinguish the fire. Saunders promptly detailed a few men to accompany the gunner back to the store room. They managed to put out the fire without anyone else being aware of the acute danger the ship had been in.

In spite of the devastation caused by the muskets and grenades of *L'Aigle*, the disciplined gunnery of the *Bellerophon*'s crew began to take its toll, the 32-pounders tearing into the hull and gunports of the French ship at point-blank range, dismounting their guns and causing carnage among their gun crews. After a while the gunports of the *L'Aigle* were lowered and she stopped firing altogether from her lower deck. At 1.40 pm her crew hoisted her jib and she slowly pulled clear, enduring a tremendous raking fire from the *Bellerophon* as she went. She drifted down onto the *Revenge*, fired two broadsides at her, and then found her way barred by the *Defiance*, whose captain, Sir Philip Durham, later recalled, 'L'Aigle appeared to have been severely handled by some other ship. She was, however, quite ready for action and defended herself most gallantly for some time.'[16] Cumby noted that soon after 2 o'clock the French ship hauled down her colours and surrendered to the *Defiance*. Her commander Captain Gourrège was mortally wounded and 270 of her crew were killed or wounded.

The *Bellerophon* was by now totally unmanageable. Not only were the main and mizen topmasts hanging over the side, but the jib-boom, the spanker boom and gaff were also shot away and not a single brace or bowline was serviceable. However, as the smoke cleared away in the lull following the departure of *L'Aigle*, Lieutenant Cumby saw that the *Monarca*, the first ship which they had engaged as they cut through the enemy line, was drifting nearby and had hauled down her colours. He immediately ordered a prize crew to take a boat, row across and take possession of her. The surgeon took the opportunity of the break in the gunfire to send a message to Cumby. He said that the cockpit was so crowded with wounded men that it was impossible for him to undertake any major operations. He begged to be allowed to bring those wounded men requiring amputations up into the captain's cabin. Cumby gave him permission to do so on the understanding that he must take the wounded men back to the cockpit if they were approached by any enemy ships.

One of the wounded men was Captain Wemyss, the captain of the *Bellerophon*'s marines and a good friend of Cumby. Wemyss had survived the first onslaught of the musket fire from *L'Aigle* and had remained at his post on deck until he was hit in the arm. He was coming up the quarterdeck ladder with blood streaming from his shattered arm when he met Cumby who was trying to avoid speaking to any friends and messmates who were wounded in case his distress at their plight distracted him from carrying out his duty as commanding officer. However he felt it would be unkind not to speak to his friend.

'Wemyss, my good fellow,' he said, 'I'm sorry you've been wounded but I trust you will do well.'

To which Wemyss replied cheerfully, 'It is a mere scratch and I shall have to apologise to you by and by for having left the deck on so trifling occasion.' He was then entering the cabin to have his arm amputated. He later died from his wound. While the surgeons struggled to deal with the dozens of wounded sailors and marines, the officers organised groups of men to clear the wreckage on the deck and cut away the shattered topmasts and sails which were hanging overboard on trailing lengths of rigging. At 4 o'clock Cumby spotted five enemy ships from the unscathed van of their fleet tacking and making off to windward. He ordered the captain's cabin to be cleared and at 4.10 they fired every gun which could be brought to bear on the fleeing ships. One of them, a Spanish two-decker, was cut off and surrendered to the *Minotaur*, but the remaining four escaped. Shortly after 5 o'clock the *Bellerophon*'s guns finally fell silent. The battle was effectively over.

Cumby noted that no fewer than nineteen of the enemy's line of battle ships had surrendered. One of them, the 74-gun *Achille*, was on fire, with flames and black smoke belching from her decks and gunports. Her crew were frantically abandoning ship and the British ship *Prince* had lowered her boats to pick up men from the water but the fire reached the magazine before everyone got clear. An eye witness recorded the horrific scene which followed:

In a moment the hull burst into a cloud of smoke and fire. A column of vivid flame shot up to an enormous height in the atmosphere and terminated by expanding into an immense globe, representing for a few seconds, a prodigious tree in flames, speckled with many dark spots, which the pieces of timber and bodies of men occasioned while they were suspended in the clouds.[17]

At 5.30 the *Bellerophon* took possession of a second prize, the Spanish 74-gun ship *Bahama*.[18] This was one of the ships which had fired on the *Bellerophon* as she cut through the enemy line and she had subsequently been on the receiving end of some devastating gunfire from the *Bellerophon* when approaching her from the stern at the height of the battle. The *Bahama* had then been attacked by the *Colossus*, had lost her mainmast and suffered the death of her captain who was shot in the head. The ship was such a shambles and had suffered such heavy casualties that her surviving officers decided to haul down her colours and surrender.

During the height of the battle a dense cloud of gunsmoke had blanketed the fighting ships as effectively as sea fog so that it was impossible for their crews to see anything clearly beyond the ships in the immediate vicinity. But, as the light westerly breeze blew away the smoke, a scene of utter devastation was revealed. The Combined Fleet, which had presented such a magnificent and colourful spectacle in the morning sunlight, was no more. Great ships with towering sails had been reduced to crippled hulks drifting helplessly on the Atlantic swell. The magnificent Spanish flagship *Santisima Trinidad*, of 140 guns, had been totally dismasted, and so had Villeneuve's flagship the *Bucentaure*, and the French ships *Algeciras* and *Intrepide*. The hulls of most of the enemy ships which had been on the receiving end of British gunnery were smashed and disfigured, their decks littered with dead and wounded bodies, the blood streaming from the scuppers. There was wreckage everywhere floating among the ships: broken masts and spars, hatches, capstan bars, gunport lids, hen coops, and barely recognisable fragments of figureheads, balustrades and stern decorations. Rowing among the wreckage were numerous boats searching for survivors, the sailors following the cries for help and heaving the bedraggled bodies aboard.

It was not till dusk that they became aware on the *Bellerophon* that Nelson had been killed. Collingwood had been forced to shift his flag to the frigate *Euryalus* because the *Royal Sovereign* had lost two of her masts, making it impossible for him to hoist signals. In the gathering dusk Cumby observed that the *Euryalus* was now carrying the lights of commander-in-chief and that there were no lights on board the *Victory*, 'from which we were left to draw the melancholy inference that our gallant our beloved Chief the incomparable Nelson had fallen.' Nelson had received his fatal wound at 1.35, half an hour after Captain Cooke had fallen. He had been walking on the quarterdeck of the *Victory* with Captain Hardy at his side when he was shot by a musketeer stationed in the mizentop of the French ship *Redoubtable.* The musket ball had entered his left shoulder, penetrated his chest, punctured his lung and lodged in his spine. He fell to the deck and when Hardy turned he was being lifted up by two seamen and the sergeant-major of marines. He told Hardy that they had done for him at last and that his backbone had been shot through. He was taken below to join the other wounded men in the cockpit and died three hours later at 4.30 pm.

The news spread slowly from ship to ship and had a profound effect on officers and men alike. One sailor later wrote that he was both sorry and glad that he had never set eyes on Nelson because 'all the men in our ships who have seen him are such soft toads, they have done nothing but blast their eyes, and cry, ever since he was killed.'[19] Others were so stricken by his death that they could scarcely bring themselves to talk about it. There is a revealing passage in Cumby's letter to this effect: '. . . but so unwilling were we to believe what we could scarcely bring ourselves to doubt that I actually went on board the Euryalus the next morning and breakfasted with Admiral Collingwood from whom I received orders without being once told or even once asking the question whether Lord Nelson was slain.'

Collingwood had known Nelson for nearly thirty years and they had developed a mutual respect and affection for each other. It seems likely that he was so heartbroken by the death of his friend that he could not bring himself to speak of it for fear of breaking down in front of a subordinate officer. He showed his true feelings in his official despatch to the Admiralty which, like his letters home, reveals a sensitivity and warmth which he rarely betrayed to those around him. He wrote, 'My heart is rent with the most poignant grief for the death of a friend, to whom, by many years' intimacy . . . I was bound by the strongest ties of affection – a grief to which even the glorious occasion in which he fell does not bring the consolation which perhaps it ought.'

On the *Bellerophon* they had worked steadily through the night, clearing away the wreckage strewn across the deck. The carpenters stopped up the holes caused by enemy gunfire and carried out emergency repairs, and the seamen refitted the damaged rigging. During the course of the morning after the battle they managed to get up jury topmasts and set sail. The ship was manageable again, which was just as well because the weather was deteriorating fast. The wind had risen during the night and was now blowing a fresh gale with frequent squalls of rain. By the evening it was evident, from the increasingly ominous swell from the west and the racing clouds overhead, that a big storm was heading their way. Before darkness fell Lieutenant Cumby ordered the crew to assemble on deck where he had the painful duty of reading the funeral service over the bodies of his friend Overton, and Captain John Cooke of whom he later wrote, 'more zeal, judgement and gallantry could not have been displayed than marked his conduct from the moment we saw the enemy to the close of his honourable and valuable life.' The two bodies were committed to the deep and the men wept for them and for the other shipmates they had lost during the battle. Out of a crew of 540, the *Bellerophon* had lost 27 men killed and 123 wounded. It was not the highest casualty list on the British side (the *Victory* had lost 57 killed and 102 wounded, the *Colossus* 40 dead and 160 wounded) but it was higher than average and reflected the fact that, for the third time in her life, the ship had been at the heart of the action in a major sea battle.

The total number of casualties on the British side was 449 killed and 1,242 wounded, out of a total strength of some 18,000 men. The French and Spanish losses were reckoned to be 4,408 dead and 2,545 wounded, the unduly high number of fatalities being partly explained by the fact that hundreds of men both fit and wounded were drowned when their ships sank or were wrecked in the storm after the battle. As John Keegan has pointed out in his masterly analysis of the battle, the casualty toll on both sides (about 8,500 killed and wounded, or 17 per cent of those present) was very much lower than the horrendous number of casualties suffered in Napoleon's land battles. There were 55,000 dead and wounded at Waterloo, out of 192,000 soldiers who took part (29 per cent of the total), and 78,000 casualties (35 per cent of those present) at Borodino.[20] Nevertheless, as

Keegan also points out, the Battle of Trafalgar was a massacre in terms of sea battles. Nelson's tactics, designed to produce a decisive and overwhelming victory, succeeded in doing just that, and in the process more men were killed and wounded than in any sea fight in the previous 250 years.

FOURTEEN

Voices from the Lower Deck

1805–7

The storm which followed the battle lasted for nearly five days and was one of the worst that even the most experienced seamen could remember. More than fifty ships, many of them dismasted and severely damaged, were exposed to the full force of a westerly gale less than 7 miles from a dangerous lee shore – the rocks and shoals of Cape Trafalgar. Collingwood later wrote, 'I can only say that in my life I never saw such efforts as were made to save these ships, and would rather fight another battle than pass through such a week as followed it.'[1] The entries in the *Bellerophon*'s log-book describe several days of fresh or strong gales with squalls, lightning and rain, with a heavy swell from the westward, but give little idea of the peril that faced so many of the ships. Captain Blackwood, of the frigate *Euryalus*, summed up the dangers in a letter to his wife Harriet. 'It has blown a hurricane,' he told her. 'All yesterday and last night the majority of the English fleet have been in the most perilous state; our ships much crippled, with damaged prizes in tow; our crews tired out, and many thousand prisoners to guard; all to be done with a gale of wind blowing us right on the shore . . .'[2]

Those ships which were dismasted and unable to hoist any sail were at the mercy of the wind and waves unless they could secure a tow from an operational ship, but securing a tow in the heavy seas was a difficult and dangerous operation. The *Belleisle* had been reduced to a hulk by the sustained fire of no fewer than nine enemy ships and had lost all three masts, her bowsprit, her figurehead and her anchors. The frigate *Naiad* managed to get a cable across to her but the cable parted and when they attempted to get another line across to her the *Belleisle* collided with the frigate and carried away most of her starboard quarter gallery. According to the *Naiad*'s log they had to abandon any further attempt to take a line across with boats because the sea was running so high. The *Naiad*'s main topsail then split across and had to be hacked free to save the topsail yard. The sail went overboard and soon afterwards the foretopmast stay-sail was blown to pieces. By the time they had sorted things out the *Belleisle* was far away, drifting perilously close to the shore to the eastward of Cape Trafalgar and in sight of breakers. At the last moment her crew managed to set a boat's sail on a jury foremast and beat clear of the immediate danger. When the wind moderated, the *Naiad* finally managed to get a boat alongside and take her in tow.

All the British ships survived the storm but many of the French and Spanish ships did not. The British prize crews were horrified by the sights which faced them when they boarded the enemy ships which had surrendered. Midshipman Badcock, who went aboard the *Santisima Trinidad*, found her beams covered with blood, brains and pieces of flesh, and her decks littered with the dead and dying, some without legs and some missing arms. On the *Bucentaur* the dead were lying on the decks in heaps where they had fallen. Captain Atcherley, a marine who had been sent to secure her magazine, reckoned that more than 400 had been killed, 'of whom an extraordinary propor-tion had lost their heads.' A raking shot had entered the lower deck, and had glanced along the beams causing carnage among the men working the guns. A French officer declared that this one shot alone had killed or wounded nearly forty men.

Henry Walker, one of the *Bellerophon*'s midshipmen, was a member of the prize crew which Lieutenant Cumby had sent across to the Spanish ship *Monarca* during a brief lull in the action and he later described the dangerous situation which he and his shipmates had to face: 'Our second lieutenant, myself, and eight men, formed the party that took possession of the Monarca: we remained until the morning without further assistance, or we should most probably have saved her, though she had suffered much more than ourselves.' At no point during the battle itself, Walker said, had he felt any fear of dying:

but in the prize, when I was in danger of, and had time to reflect upon the approach of death, either from the rising of the Spaniards upon so small a number as we were composed of, or what latterly appeared inevitable, from the violence of the storm, I was most certainly afraid, and at one time, when the ship made three feet of water in ten minutes, when our people were almost lying drunk upon deck, when the Spaniards, completely worn out with fatigue, would no longer work at the only chain pump left serviceable, when I saw the fear of death so strongly depicted on the countenances of all around me, I wrapped myself up in a Union Jack, and lay down upon deck for a short time, quietly awaiting the approach of death; but the love of life soon after roused me, and after great exertions on the part of the British and Spanish officers, who had joined together for the mutual preservation of our lives, we got the ship before the wind, determined to run her on shore.

After four dreadful days in the storm they were rescued by the *Leviathan* which sent boats across and took off the prize crew and all the Spanish crew except for 150 men who were afraid of getting into the boats. Soon afterwards the *Monarca* was driven ashore and wrecked. Altogether ten enemy ships were wrecked in the storm and three were scuttled or burnt. The *Redoutable* and the magnificent 140-gun *Santisima Trinidad* foundered at sea with great loss of life. Of the fifteen ships taken during the battle, only four weathered the storm and were towed into Gibraltar.

The *Bellerophon* sailed into Gibraltar Bay on 28 October in company with the *Agamemnon* and the *Colossus*. There was still a heavy swell running but the westerly wind had moderated. She dropped anchor in 15 fathoms beneath the soaring crags of the Rock of Gibraltar. The strongly fortified harbour commanding the entrance to the Mediterranean was filled with warships and merchant vessels of all types. Coleridge had called in the year before, en route to Malta, and had noted the extraordinarily colourful, polyglot atmosphere of the naval base and the town. Soldiers of all regiments, naval officers and runaway sailors mingled with Arabs, Jews, Spaniards, Italians and Greeks. He had climbed to the summit of the Rock and found it to be a mysterious place full of warlike shapes and impressions: 'What a complex thing! At its feet mighty ramparts establishing themselves in the Sea with their huge artillery – hollow trunks of Iron where Death and Thunder sleep; the gardens in deep Moats between lofty walls; a Town of all Nations & all languages . . .'[3]

The day after the *Bellerophon* arrived at Gibraltar the *Victory* was towed into the bay by the *Neptune*. The sun, breaking through the clouds for the first time for a week, illuminated her battered hull. She had lost her mizenmast and her foretopmast; her main mast was severely damaged; her main yard and her main topsail yard had been shot away; and her rails, gunports and the timbers of the head and stern were much cut by cannon shot. The white ensign flying from the staff at her stern was at half mast in honour of Nelson whose body lay below. Dr Beatty, the surgeon, had carried out a brief autopsy and then put the body in a cask of brandy to preserve it. The cask was lashed securely on the middle deck and was watched over by a marine sentry.

After less than a week in Gibraltar, where emergency repairs were carried out to her hull, masts and rigging, the *Victory* was ready to put to sea again. On 4 November she weighed anchor and set sail for England. She was accompanied by the *Belleisle* and the *Bellerophon*. Both ships needed urgent attention from the shipwrights and riggers of the royal dockyards but in view of the heroic performance of their crews in the recent action it was appropriate that they should accompany the flagship which carried Nelson's body on the voyage back home.

The *Bellerophon* was now under the command of Captain Edward Rotheram. He took over from Lieutenant Cumby on the morning they sailed from Gibraltar. Rotheram had been Collingwood's flag captain on the *Royal Sovereign* and, although he had put up a brave performance during the battle, Collingwood was no doubt glad to see the back of him because he thought him a stupid man. They had got on so badly that they had to be reconciled by Nelson before the battle, and afterwards Collingwood wrote, 'but such a captain, such a stick, I wonder very much how such people get forward . . . Was he brought up in the Navy? For he has very much of the style of the Coal Trade about him, except that they are good seamen!'[4] As it happened, Rotheram, who was the son of a Newcastle doctor, had spent his early years on colliers before joining the navy but unlike Captain Cook, the celebrated explorer, he had evidently not benefited from the exacting demands of the coal trade which involved navigating the shifting shoals and mudbanks of the East Coast in all weathers.

They sighted the coast of Devon on 2 December. When they were off Start Point the *Victory* parted company and headed eastwards up the Channel towards Portsmouth. The *Belleisle* and the *Bellerophon* made for Plymouth and dropped anchor in Cawsand Bay. Three weeks later the *Bellerophon* was alongside the sheer hulk and the riggers from the dockyard came aboard, stripped down the rigging and hauled out the main and mizen masts. On Boxing Day Lieutenant Cumby left the ship. In recognition of his conduct at Trafalgar he had been promoted to the rank of post-captain, with effect from 1 January 1806. In theory this was great news but it was a bad time to be a captain because there were not enough ships available. He lacked influence and for eighteen months was unemployed (and on half pay) before being given temporary command of a frigate on the Irish station.[5]

The *Bellerophon* remained under the command of Captain Rotheram for the next two and a half years. For much of the time the ship was stationed off Ushant with the squadron blockading Brest, and it was back to the familiar routine of two months patrolling the coast of Brittany and two or three weeks back in Torbay or Cawsand Bay to take on provisions and carry out repairs. At some point during this period Rotheram produced a remarkably detailed survey of the *Bellerophon*'s crew.[6]

He concentrated his attention on the 387 seamen in the ship's company. He did not include the marines, and although he listed the names of the officers and warrant officers he did not record any details for them.[7] However the resulting survey provides a unique picture of the composition, background and outward appearance of the crew of a British ship of the line in the years immediately following Trafalgar. Exactly why Rotheram decided to embark on such a survey is a mystery. Was it simply an exercise to pass the time during the monotonous days and weeks spent on blockade duty, or was there a more serious purpose? The two volumes of his journals and letters in the National Maritime Museum provide no obvious explanation. He was in the habit of making detailed notes on harbours and anchorages visited during the course of his voyages but this was a seamanlike exercise which many officers carried out, some even illustrating their notes to help them identify landmarks and coastal features on future occasions. A possible explanation for the survey is that it was carried out as an academic exercise. Rotheram's father, who was for a time the Senior Physician of a Northumberland infirmary, was described as 'a gentleman of high estimation . . . and a person of general science', and his brother John Rotheram studied under Linnaeus in Sweden and became Professor of Natural Philosophy at St Andrews University. It was Linnaeus who devised the system for classifying animal and plant species.[8] It is therefore possible that his brother's researches may have prompted Captain Rotheram to carry out his survey in the spirit of scientific enquiry, although he does not appear to have made any attempt to analyse the data he gathered.

Whatever the reasons behind Captain Rotheram's survey, the results are fascinating. We find that most of the men are surprisingly short. The average height is 5 foot 5 inches. There is nobody of 6 foot or over and several men are under 5 feet tall. Since the effective standing headroom on the gun deck of the *Bellerophon* was only 5 feet 8 inches, Captain Rotheram's crew would have found it much easier to work in the confined space than the taller men likely to be found on a naval ship today.[9] This also puts Nelson's height in perspective. It is commonly believed that Nelson, like Napoleon, was an unusually small man. In fact recent research has shown that he was between 5 foot 6 inches and 5 foot 7 inches tall, which means that he was above the average height of his seamen, and confirms the observations of many of his contemporaries. His nephew George Matcham, for instance, wrote, 'He was not as described, a little man, but of the middle height and of a frame adapted to activity and exertion.'[10]

A breakdown of the nationalities of the crew reveals that nearly half were English (49 per cent), and the rest were made up of a large contingent of Irishmen (24 per cent); a number of Scotsmen (12 per cent), and Welshmen (7 per cent); and a variety of foreigners (8 per cent). The foreigners included 13 black sailors (9 from the West Indies, 3 from Africa, 1 from America) as well as 2 Dutchmen, a Frenchman, a Swede, a Portuguese, a Maltese, a Bengal Indian, one man from Guernsey and one from the Isle of Man. It is not surprising to find that more men came from coastal towns and cities with ports than came from inland towns: 30 men came from Dublin, 26 from London, 10 from Bristol and 10 from Liverpool, with other ports like Swansea, Newcastle, Cork and King's Lynn being well represented.

The average age of the crew in Rotheram's study is thirty. There were 55 men in their forties, 11 in their fifties and the oldest man in the crew was 56. Since the life of a seaman in the age of sail was extremely tough and physically demanding, particularly for those hands required to work aloft, we find that most of the older men had less demanding duties. James Gill, aged 51, and Thomas Nichols, 50, were both quartermasters – experienced petty officers – whose job it was to keep an eye on the helmsman at the wheel and relay the orders of the officer of the watch. The majority of the crew (72 per cent) were unmarried, and 6 were widowed. The 102 seamen on board who were married would have had little chance to see their families during the long period of the war against France. Some wives made heroic effforts to travel to Portsmouth or Plymouth for a chance to see their husbands but all too often the men were refused shore leave in case they deserted. One of the later captains of the *Bellerophon* gave specific orders to his lieutenants to prevent any men getting away from the ship when she was anchored off Spithead. No boats were to go ashore unless absolutely necessary and those that went were to have a sufficient number of officers 'to prevent the men from running'.[11] This was one of the biggest sources of grievance for many sailors. William Richardson, who was pressed from a merchant ship and served on several warships between 1790 and 1815, spoke for many when he wrote, 'I think it only fair and just, that when seamen are pressed, in coming home from a long voyage, they should be allowed a few week's liberty on shore to spend their money among their friends and relations; when that was gone, they would soon be tired of the shore, return more contented to their ships, and by such means there would not be half so much desertion.'[12]

The outward appearance of the seamen was as varied as might be expected in a crew drawn from all over Britain and beyond. Standing on the quarterdeck and looking down on the assembled crew for a Sunday service, Captain Rotheram would have seen a sea of faces of all shapes and colours. According to his survey their complexions ranged from pale, fair and fresh to sallow, swarthy, dark and negro. There were thin faces, long faces, round and full faces, and a large number of faces pitted from smallpox. There were men who were thickset, strong-made, very stout and muscular, and 'well looking' and there were men who were ill-looking, thin, emaciated and 'very infirm, good for nothing'. A lot of men had tattoos. John Nichols, a 22-year-old Londoner, had a centaur, a heart and the initials 'MS' on his left arm and a crucifix, a sun, moon and stars on his right arm. Robert Stewart, a 50-year-old Irishman, had a fish and anchor on one arm and a mermaid and a woman with an umbrella on the other arm. Most had a few initials and the traditional anchor or mermaid. Thirty men had scars or various injuries: six had lost the sight of one eye; six had lost fingers, two had wounds from musket balls and several had injuries or disfigurements caused by falls.

One of the most interesting aspects of Captain Rotheram's survey is the information which it provides about the occupations of the men before going to sea. Twenty men had worked in dockyard trades (as shipwrights, sailmakers, coopers, caulkers, ropemakers and anchorsmiths) and most of these were employed in the same capacities on board the *Bellerophon*. No fewer than 174 men (or 45 per cent of the men in the survey) had previously been merchant seamen, mostly in the West India trade or the coal trade. There were also 8 fishermen, a Thames waterman, a Swansea boatman and a Dover pilot. Most of these men were probably victims of the press gang.[13] The navy urgently needed professional seamen and the press gangs therefore concentrated their efforts on seaports and harbours. They frequently intercepted homecoming merchant ships and stripped them of large numbers of sailors.

The survey also reveals that there were 119 landsmen in the crew with no previous experience of the sea. Twenty-seven of them listed their previous occupation as labourers, 16 had been weavers, 14 were farmers and 11 were shoemakers. The rest included almost every trade and working-class occupation current at the time, from bricklayers and blacksmiths to masons and miners. There were representatives from every shop to be found in a typical high street (a hatter, a tailor, a butcher, an ironmonger, a mercer and a haberdasher) but, apart from one lawyer, there were no men from the middle-class professions such as teachers, bankers, merchants or the clergy.[14]

This miscellaneous bunch of men had to be moulded into a disciplined team able to respond immediately to a variety of situations ranging from preparing for action to working to windward in a gale. This was achieved by constant practice in shiphandling and gunnery and by the establishment of a regular routine when the ship was at sea. We get a glimpse of the daily routine on board the *Bellerophon* from a surviving order book kept by Captain Edward Hawker, who commanded the ship from 1813 until the spring of 1815.[15] Hawker was the son of a naval captain. He had seen action in the West Indies and had considerable experience as a commander of ships of the line. On 17 June 1813, when the *Bellerophon* was at sea off the coast of Newfoundland, he issued an order to his officers which specified the tasks to be carried out each day of the week 'when the weather and service will permit'.

On Sunday morning the men were to draw clean hammocks and sling them. After the lower deck and cockpit had been cleaned the crew were to dress smartly and muster for the church service. The afternoon was free, apart from 'seeing to the indispensible duties of the ship'. Monday was busier. In the morning the men were to wash their clothes, and hang them on the lines which had been rigged the evening before; they were then to exercise the great guns and small arms; in the afternoon they were to replace any deficiencies in the gun equipment and in the evening there were more gunnery exercises 'to make the men perfect in this duty'. On Tuesday morning the hammocks were to be scrubbed until 9.30. The marines were to exercise small arms. In the afternoon the bedding was to be aired. On Wednesday morning the men's bags, and also boat sails and covers, screens and blankets were to be scrubbed. The rest of the morning was to be devoted to exercises in reefing and furling the sails. In the afternoon one division of the great guns was to be exercised.

On Thursday the crew were mustered so that their clothes and bags could be inspected by the officers. During the muster the master-at-arms and corporals were to 'visit every part of the ship to pick up spare clothes, which are to be brought on the quarter-deck'. The afternoon was to be spent mending clothes. More washing of clothes took place on Friday morning, and another division of guns was to be exercised. Every other Saturday morning the ship's fire engine was to be used to wash the poop, and in dry weather the lower deck and cockpits were to be washed. The ship was to be pumped afterwards with the chain pumps.

The memoirs of various seamen of the period add colour and detail to this somewhat stark account of daily life at sea.[16] Depending on the captain and the time of year, the day began at 4 or 5 am when the cook and his mate got up and lit the galley fire, the men on overnight watch were relieved, and the men on the next watch were roused by the boatswain's mates in order to wash the decks – a job which involved scrubbing the decks with brushes, or blocks made of Portland stone (called holystones because they were the same shape and size as bibles). A seaman called Samuel Leech tells us: 'After the decks are well rubbed with these stones, they are wiped dry with swabs made of rope-yarns. By this means the utmost cleanliness is preserved in the ship.'[17]

The rest of the crew was woken at 7 am. Above and below deck the shrill, sharp whistles of the boatswain's calls were followed by the bellowed cry of 'All hands, ahoy!' Any seaman not responding rapidly enough was likely to receive a blow from a rattan cane or find his hammock cut down. As the men emerged from their slumbers, more shouts followed – 'Up all hammocks, ahoy!' – and with surprising speed the seamen dressed, lashed up their hammocks and carried them on deck where they were stowed in the hammock nettings along the sides of the upper deck. According to Samuel Leech, 'There is a system even in this arrangement; everything has its appropriate place. Below the beams are all marked; each hammock is marked with a corresponding number, and in the darkest night a sailor will go unhesitatingly to his own hammock. They are also kept exceedingly clean. Every man is provided with two, that while he is scrubbing and cleaning one, he may have another to use.'[18] Breakfast was at 8 and was usually gruel, a form of porridge made from oatmeal. The men were divided up into messes of between eight and twelve men and they ate together, each mess gathered around a table hung from the deck head and seated on benches, barrels or sea chests. One of their number fetched the food and drink from the galley. The rest of the morning followed along the lines described by Captain Hawker: washing clothes or hammocks, and exercising guns and small arms.

If any punishments were due, these took place at 11 am. Their frequency depended on the temperament of the captain, the discipline imposed by the officers, and the mood of the men under their command. The most common form of punishment was flogging and this was meted out for theft, fighting, drunkenness, disobedience, insolence to an officer, gambling, or neglect of duty. The crew were summoned by the ominous cry of 'All hands ahoy to witness punishment' and everyone assembled on deck. The officers stood by in full uniform, and the marines lined up with muskets and fixed bayonets. A heavy wooden grating from one of the hatches was set up vertically in the waist of the ship and the prisoner, who had been shackled in irons all night, was led out and lashed to the grating by his wrists and ankles. When the captain had read out the charge the prisoner's shirt was stripped off and the boatswain's mate removed the cat-of-nine-tails from the bag in which it had been hidden. At the order from the captain he laid on the first six or twelve lashes. If more lashes had been ordered another boatswain's mate laid on the second dozen. Young sailors watching a flogging for the first time were chilled by the sound of the lashes and horrified by the effect they produced. In the words of Samuel Leech, who had joined the navy at the age of thirteen and spent many years as an ordinary seaman, 'Now two dozen of these dreadful lashes have been inflicted; the lacerated back looks inhuman; it resembles roasted meat burnt nearly black before a scorching fire . . .'[19]

After witnessing the punishment the seamen returned to their duties, while the sea officers and the midshipmen fetched sextants and prepared to take the noon sight. By noting the angle of the sun at midday and consulting tables they were able to determine the latitude of the ship and by calculating the time difference with Greenwich the longitude, and these would be duly entered in the log-books they were each required to keep. Dinner followed, and an hour or an hour and a half was allowed for this, the main meal of the day. Depending on the cook and the day of the week, this might consist of boiled beef or boiled pork or dried peas and duff, or cheese and duff. It was accompanied by a pint of grog (rum diluted with water). The afternoon was spent on the tasks described by Captain Hawker. In addition to these there was a constant round of cleaning, polishing and repairing to be done: blacking the guns and rigging with a mixture of warm tar and seawater; polishing the brass with brick dust and rags; mending sails; and cleaning cutlasses, pikes, boarding axes, muskets and pistols with greasy rags. Any of these tasks, morning and afternoon, might be interrupted by sail changes, the firing of salutes, or general fleet exercises ordered by the commanding admiral.

Supper was at 4 or 5 pm and three-quarters of an hour was allowed for this meal which was usually whatever was saved from dinner, together with ship's biscuit and another pint of grog. Cocoa or tea were sometimes issued at meals, and, because the drinking water on board was so foul, the men were generally allowed to drink as much beer as they wanted. At 8 or 9 pm the order went out for the men to collect their hammocks, and they bundled them down below, slung them on their hooks and bedded down for the night. The cook extinguished the galley fire and the master-at-arms and his corporals went round the ship to make sure that no lights were left burning.

The daily regime when the ship was at sea did not allow much time for recreation but Sunday afternoons were usually free of duties and on many ships the men had an hour or so of free time in the evening. Some spent the time quietly: they would write letters home, or read; they would tie decorative knots, make ship models, or inscribe pictures on pieces of ivory or walrus tusks. Others would gather on the foredeck to tell each other stories, or sing traditional naval songs and ballads, or celebrate a recent victory with a new song set to an old tune. There was always someone on board who could play the flute or the violin and this provided an opportunity for some dancing which would be more or less energetic depending on the amount of beer which had been consumed. Gambling was forbidden by the Articles of War, but this did not stop many seamen playing with dice or cards for money, and many captains were prepared to turn a blind eye to this.

The music and dancing and singing lifted the men's spirits and for a while they could forget the physical hardships, the monotonous routine, the bad food, the constant cold and wet, and the fact that, until the war ended, they were virtual prisoners on one of His Majesty's ships. As Samuel Leech observed, 'A casual visitor to a man of war, beholding the song, the dance, the revelry of the crew, might judge them to be happy. But I know that these things are often resorted to because they feel miserable, just to drive away dull care.'[20]

FIFTEEN

Cruises in Northern Waters

1807–14

The destruction of the Combined Fleet of France and Spain at Trafalgar confirmed Britain's position as the world's dominant sea power, and for the next hundred years Britain ruled the waves. But for the people of Britain who were mourning the death of Nelson in the autumn of 1805 the future seemed far from secure. Napoleon still had at his disposal a considerable number of French warships and, as he extended his hold over the continent, these were augmented by the navies of Holland and Denmark. Collingwood, and those ships of the Mediterranean fleet which were not too severely damaged by the Battle of Trafalgar, continued to keep watch on Cadiz, Cartagena and Toulon, but the close blockade on Brest was relaxed on the orders of Lord Barham, the First Sea Lord. 'It is to little purpose now,' he wrote, 'to wear out our ships in a fruitless blockade during the winter.'[1]

The dangers of this relaxation soon became apparent. In December 1805 the French fleet at Brest put to sea and headed for the West Indies. The force of eleven ships of the line, four frigates and a corvette posed a serious threat to British merchant convoys until they were tracked down by Admiral Duckworth and defeated off St Domingo on 6 February 1806. This was the last fleet action by French warships in the war against Napoleonic France but there were other dangers to be countered. Privateers continued to operate with considerable success throughout the war. Privateering was a form of warfare at which the French excelled and they constantly harried merchantmen around the coasts of Europe as well as in the West Indies and the Indian Ocean. In February 1809 *Lloyds List* complained about 'the depredations of the numerous privateers, with which the Channel . . . is now infested,' and during the course of that year no fewer than 571 British merchant ships were lost to privateers.

Although the Battle of Trafalgar ended any realistic chance of a French invasion of England it was many years before Napoleon entirely abandoned his invasion plans. As late as November 1811 he was instructing Decrès, his Minister of the Marine, to keep 500 of the landing craft in good repair because he thought that the invasion threat would always be a powerful means of influencing Britain. He frequently spoke of the invasion of England during his voyage to Elba in 1814, and continued to dwell on the subject when he was exiled to St Helena. In one of his conversations on that remote island he said that he would have lured the British fleet away to the West Indies as originally planned but would have held command of the Channel with seventy ships of the line for two months rather than the two or three days he thought necessary when he was at Boulogne in 1805. He said he would have landed as near Chatham as possible, with twice as many men as the number he actually assembled at Boulogne, and would have reached London in four days. 'I should have proclaimed a republic, the abolition of the nobility and house of peers, the distribution of the property of such of the latter as opposed me amongst my partisans, liberty, equality and the sovereignty of the people. I should have allowed the House of Commons to remain; but should have introduced great reforms.' When the British fleet came back, 'they would have found their capital in the hands of an enemy, and their country overwhelmed by my armies.'[2]

More ominous than the invasion threat in the autumn of 1805 was the manner in which Napoleon swept aside all opposition on the continent. Two days before Trafalgar he had defeated an Austrian army under General Mack at Ulm. On 14 November he entered Vienna. At Austerlitz on 2 December a French army of 70,000 men routed an army of 86,000 Austrians and Russians. More than 18,000 Russian bodies were counted on the field after the battle. William Pitt, who had patiently assembled one coalition of allies after another to fight Napoleon's armies, saw his work in ruins. His famous remark, 'Roll up the map of Europe: it will not be wanted these ten years' proved to be all too true.

In July 1806 Napoleon became Protector of the newly created Confederation of the Rhine. In October he defeated the Prussians and Saxons at Jena and entered Berlin. He was now in a strong position to attack Britain by another means. On 21 November he issued the Berlin Decrees which inaugurated the Continental System. All the countries in the French Empire, including the subdued German states, were forbidden to trade with Britain. In January 1807 Britain retaliated with Orders in Council, which forbade neutral ships from trading between French ports. In view of Britain's command of the seas this was likely to do more harm to France than the Berlin Decrees were to do to Britain, but in June 1807 Napoleon's Grand Army crushed the Russians and Prussians at Friedland. The humiliated rulers, Alexander I of Russia and Frederick William II of Prussia, met Napoleon on a raft on the River Niemann to discuss terms. On 9 July France, Russia and Prussia signed the Treaty of Tilsit which extended the Continental System and meant that most of the ports of northern Europe, including those in the Baltic, were now closed to British ships. This was the most serious blow of all because it struck not only at Britain's rich trade with the continent, but also had the potential to cripple her navy.

Although the hull of the *Bellerophon* and those of most British warships built in the 1780s were entirely constructed of British oak and elm, their masts and spars came from the Baltic. Indeed for more than a century Britain had been dependent on foreign imports of masts and spars as well as other essential naval supplies such as hemp, sailcloth, tallow, turpentine, tar and pitch. Most of the timber came from the vast forests of Russia. The logs were hauled on sledges drawn by horses or oxen to the nearest river and were floated downstream to the ports in the form of huge rafts. The port of Riga had the reputation for shipping the best timber for masts but fine timber was also shipped from Memel, Danzig and elsewhere. The trade in mast timber and other naval stores was immense and Baltic convoys frequently consisted of anything between 600 and 1,000 merchant ships.

All the Baltic convoys had to pass through the Sound, the narrow entrance to the Baltic which was commanded by the guns of Copenhagen. So concerned was Britain by the threat to her navy that within weeks of the Treaty of Tilsit the British Admiralty despatched a massive fleet under Admiral Gambier to Denmark and laid siege to the Danish capital. Confronted by a force of 25 ships of the line, more than 40 frigates, sloops and bomb vessels, and 377 transport ships with 27,000 troops on board, the Danes had no chance. Once subjected to a bombardment which threatened to set the city on fire, the Danes surrendered their entire fleet and the dockyard at Copenhagen on 7 September 1807. The following spring Admiral Saumarez was sent to the Baltic with a powerful fleet to ensure the continued protection of the Baltic convoys. He remained there for much of the next four years, only returning home in the winter months when most of the Baltic ports were closed by ice. The *Bellerophon* joined the Baltic fleet during the summer of 1809 and her crew took part in two cutting-out expeditions. These were attacks made with boats on enemy shipping which, for sheer heroism in the face of enemy fire, might be straight from the pages of the Hornblower books or the novels of Patrick O'Brian.

On 8 June 1808 Captain Samuel Warren had taken over command of the *Bellerophon* from Captain Rotheram and the ship was ordered to join the North Sea fleet. The North Sea station extended from Selsey Bill to the Shetlands and the various squadrons of the fleet operated from the Downs, the Nore and Great Yarmouth. With most of northern Europe now dominated by France, and with Napoleon's brother Louis Bonaparte installed as King of Holland, a key role for the North Sea fleet was to blockade the ports of Holland and Belgium and prevent the Dutch Navy from putting to sea. Throughout the summer and autumn of 1808 the *Bellerophon* was stationed off the sand dunes of Holland between Camperdown and Texel Island. This was an area which had seen some famous naval actions in the past but it proved an uneventful time for the *Bellerophon*'s crew. They could see the masts of the Dutch fleet moored in the Texel anchorage and watch the distinctive Dutch fishing boats being launched off the beaches, and then it was back to the Yarmouth or the Downs to take on water and provisions.

The following year the *Bellerophon* sailed to the Baltic and joined the fleet commanded by Admiral Saumarez. In these waters Russia was now the enemy and, because Russia had invaded and annexed Finland in February 1808, this meant that any vessels encountered along the southern and eastern shores of the Baltic were likely to be hostile. During the evening of 19 June 1809 the *Bellerophon* was cruising off Hango on the coast of Finland, in company with the *Minotaur*, when three suspicious-looking luggers were spotted in an anchorage sheltered by offshore islands. The waters were too shallow for the two British warships and so they dropped anchor in 21 fathoms and a party of armed men was despatched in the ships' boats to attack the luggers. It was a calm night and they encountered no opposition until they had boarded and taken possession of the three vessels. They then discovered they were in a trap. Overlooking and protecting the anchorage was a Russian gun battery which began to bombard them with round and grape shot. There were other batteries on the more distant islands and a number of Russian gunboats anchored in the vicinity.

The British force was under the command of Robert Pilch, the first lieutenant of the *Bellerophon*, and he acted with a reckless bravery not unlike that shown by Nelson at Tenerife. He ordered the luggers to be set on fire, got his men back in the boats and led a spirited attack on the nearest Russian battery which was manned by more than a hundred soldiers. The ship's marines were armed with muskets and bayonets, the sailors with cutlasses and boarding axes and so furious was their attack that they drove the Russian sailors from the battery, spiked the 24-pounder guns and blew up the magazine. Now under fire from the more distant Russian batteries they scrambled back into the boats and rowed back to the two anchored warships. The *Bellerophon*'s log records that 'at 5 the boats returned on board, with 5 wounded men, Griffith Griffith, Peter Just, John Butterfield, Thomas McCarthy & Simon McLean.'³ The log also noted that in the raid they had lost three bayonets, four scabbards, three muskets, ten swords, four pole axes and one powder horn.

Two weeks later they were involved in a second cutting-out expedition, this time with similar heroism but with more productive results. The *Bellerophon* had joined a squadron under the command of Captain T. Byam Martin of the *Implacable*. On 17 July they were sailing off Percola Point in the Gulf of Narva when they sighted a Russian convoy of twelve vessels under the protection of eight gunboats anchored in a strong, defensive position in a small bay. The Russians had evidently been expecting them because they had mounted guns on the rocky cliffs on either side of the bay. In his report on the action Captain Martin wrote, 'The position taken by the Russian flotilla under Percola Point seemed so much like defiance, that I considered something was necessary to be done, in order to impress these people with that sense of respect and fear which His Majesty's other enemies are accustomed to show to the British flag.'

Martin decided to launch a night attack in boats. A force of 270 men under the command of Lieutenant Hawkey of the *Implacable* set off in the dusk at 9.30 pm. They were spotted by the waiting Russians and the quiet of the Baltic evening was shattered by a barrage of grapeshot. According to Captain Martin, the British boats 'advanced with perfect coolness and never fired a gun till actually touching the enemy, when they boarded sword in hand and carried all before them. I believe a more brilliant achievement does not grace the records of naval history; each officer was impatient to be the leader in the attack, and each man was zealous to emulate their noble example.'⁴

Lieutenant Hawkey was killed as they stormed the gunboats and Lieutenant Charles Allen of the *Bellerophon* took over command. The crews of the gunboats put up a fierce resistance and in the hand-to-hand fighting the British sustained heavy losses with 17 men killed and 37 wounded. One gunboat was sunk, one escaped but the rest were taken, together with the merchant vessels which proved to be carrying ammunition for the Russian army. At daylight the next day the men waiting on the anchored *Bellerophon* watched the British boats rowing back from the bay, 'having carried six of the enemy's gunboats and taken possession of all the shipping in the Road, viz. one ship, one brig, four galliots with cargoes, and four coasting luggers.'[5] They also had more than a hundred Russian prisoners who were later repatriated at Port Baltic under a flag of truce. Lieutenant Allen was rewarded for his conduct by being promoted to the rank of commander.

The *Bellerophon* continued to cruise the Baltic for the next three months. She was off the Aland Islands at the beginning of October, spent a week at anchor in the Swedish harbour of Karlscrona and then on 7 November she set sail with a convoy of 135 merchantmen, accompanied by the warships *Saturn*, *Erebus* and *Piercer*. Off Anholt Island they dropped anchor, put ashore a party of marines to join the British contingent on the island and then moored in Hawke Roads where they found the *Victory* and several other ships of the line. By 16 November, when they set sail for England, the convoy had grown to fifty vessels. They sighted the spire of Lowestoft Church five days later and on 21 November 1809, with the sun shining and a fresh breeze behind them, they stood in for Yarmouth Roads. That winter the *Bellerophon* lay anchored with the fleet at the Nore and did not return to the coast of Holland until the spring of 1810.

Meanwhile events were gathering pace on the continent. Napoleon continued to enlarge his empire and to bring more and more of Europe under his direct or indirect control. In June 1808 he installed his brother Joseph Bonaparte as King of Spain; in May 1809 he annexed the Papal States; and the following year he annexed Holland, then Westphalia and then North-West Germany. But now there was another general in the field who was to prove a more tenacious and formidable enemy than any of those he had brushed aside in the past. Wellington had not enjoyed the meteoric success of Napoleon. The two men were exactly the same age and had experienced a not dissimilar upbringing but, while Napoleon was winning his astonishing battles as a general commanding the Army of Italy, Wellington was an obscure colonel on his way to command an infantry regiment in India. When Napoleon was proclaimed First Consul in 1802 and became supreme ruler of France, Wellington was still fighting in India and had just been promoted to major-general. However Wellington had learnt his trade thoroughly and in the following year he completed a remarkably successful nine years in India with impressive victories at Assaye and Argaum. He received a knighthood and returned to England in 1805. As commanders, Wellington and Napoleon had much in common. They understood the importance of maps and topography and how to make best use of the terrain, they paid close attention to detail, and they made all the major decisions themselves. Above all, they both had a ruthless streak and a single-minded determination to win on the battlefield.

In April 1809 Wellington landed at Lisbon with a new British army to replace the troops who had been forced out of the country during the retreat under Sir John Moore at Corunna. Wellington defeated a French army under Marshal Soult at Oporto in May and within weeks he had entered Spain. In July he gained a spectacular victory over an army commanded by Marshal Jourdan and Joseph Bonaparte at Talavera. During the next four years he besieged and captured strongly fortified cities, defeated French armies in the field and steadily drove them out of Spain. His progress was an ominous warning which Napoleon ignored because he had more pressing concerns.

Tsar Alexander of Russia had proved a great disappointment to Napoleon, and when the Tsar failed to enforce the Continental System against Britain Bonaparte decided to take drastic action. In June 1812 he marched his Grand Army of 700,000 men across the River Niemen and invaded Russia. He defeated a Russian army at Borodino and on 14 September he entered Moscow. He found an empty, burning city. He remained there a week before withdrawing his army. But his disastrous retreat through the snow and ice of the Russian winter, under harrying attacks from Cossack horsemen, left 400,000 of his men dead or wounded and 100,000 Frenchmen taken prisoner. He was no longer invincible, and one by one the countries of Europe turned against him.

The *Bellerophon* returned to blockade duty off the coast of Holland in 1810 and spent all that year and the next two years cruising back and forth along the low, windswept coast from the Hook of Holland to Texel Island. Entry after entry in the ship's log-book is a variation on the same theme:

> 16 March 1811, Camperdown SE 3 or 4 leagues. Moderate and cloudy weather. 7 Wore ship. Men employed scrubbing hammocks. 9 Tacked. Observed in the Texel 2 sail of the line 1 sloop 3 brigs and 7 schooners. Shifted the courses. At 11 tacked ship. PM. Light airs and fine weather, Theseus, Defiance and Pilchard in company. Sounded in 15 fathoms . . .[6]

The only breaks in the monotonous watch on the Dutch coast were the occasional forays back to the Downs or Yarmouth Roads to load up with water and provisions and to carry out running repairs. And then in the spring of 1813 the *Bellerophon* received orders to sail to Newfoundland. She was to accompany a convoy of British merchant ships across the Atlantic and she was to convey Rear-Admiral Sir Richard Keats to St John's Harbour so that he could take up his appointment as Governor of Newfoundland. On 11 February 1813 Captain Edward Hawker took over command of the ship and was responsible for the preparations for the forthcoming voyage. On the afternoon of 22 April Sir Richard Keats was rowed out to the ship and came on board. They weighed anchor at 4 pm and headed down the Channel under easy sail accompanied by three other warships. Their convoy initially consisted of seventy-two merchantmen but by the time they reached the Lizard and were heading towards the Fastnet Rock the numbers of ships in the convoy had grown to 166. The chief danger now was not French privateers, most of whom had been captured or were blockaded in port. The new threat was from American warships and privateers. On 18 June 1812 America had declared war on Britain and her commerce raiders were proving extremely successful.

The War of 1812 between Britain and America was a relatively short, but bitterly fought struggle which did little credit to either side. For Britain it was always a sideshow compared to her life and death struggle with Napoleonic France, but it involved more than 10,000 British troops at a time when she could ill afford to have them on the other side of the Atlantic, and it resulted in some humiliating encounters between British frigates and a new generation of remarkably powerful American frigates. The popular view in America was that the war was fought for 'Free Trade and Sailors' Rights'. Congress had declared war on the basis of four grievances: the frequent raids made by British press gangs on American ports to press American seamen into the Royal Navy; the repeated violations of American territorial waters by British warships; the blockading of enemy coasts by Britain; and the British Orders in Council against neutral trade. These were the declared reasons for the war but many Americans also hoped that the war would provide them with an opportunity to conquer Canada, put an end to the Indian attacks on their western frontier, and open up more forest land for settlement by their land-hungry pioneers.

When the *Bellerophon* set sail across the Atlantic in the spring of 1813 she was once again sailing into hostile waters but this time she played no more than a peripheral role in the conflict. The outward voyage with a convoy of merchant men was slow but uneventful until they were nearing Newfoundland when they ran into thick fog. For nearly a week they groped their way through the damp, blinding mist, firing guns at half-hourly intervals to keep in touch. On 22 May strong gales swept the fog away as they approached Cape Ray but a few days later they faced another danger. No fewer than nineteen icebergs were sighted ahead of them. They had to alter course to avoid them and then they ran into fog again. It was an extremely hazardous situation but fortunately the fog cleared and they sighted land. Cautiously they worked their way northwards and on the morning of 31 May they sighted the entrance of St John's Harbour. The wind dropped and they had to warp the ship up the harbour. The next day Sir Richard Keats went ashore, accompanied by the captains of all the ships in the escorting squadron. As he left the ship, the crew manned the yards and fired a 17-gun salute in recognition of his status as Governor of the island.

On the same day that the guns of the *Bellerophon* were reverberating across St John's Harbour, the guns of another British warship were in action some 800 miles to the south. In the seas off Boston the 38-gun frigate *Shannon*, commanded by Captain Philip Broke, was locked in a fierce and bloody battle with the American frigate *Chesapeake*. The *Shannon* had been built at Frindsbury in the very same shipyard as the *Bellerophon*. She had been launched in 1806 (twenty years after the *Bellerophon*) and was one of a series of large frigates built around this time which were based on the lines of a captured French ship.[7] The *Chesapeake*, also of 38 guns, had an unlucky history and had been involved in an action which had nearly caused war between Britain and America back in 1807.[8] She was now under the command of Captain James Lawrence. The murderous duel which followed that afternoon resulted in the death of 34 British seamen, 69 American seamen and more than a hundred wounded in both ships. Lawrence was fatally shot by a British marine and his last words as he was carried below were 'Don't give up the ship.' Broke himself was badly injured in the battle but in the end won the day.

Having spent little more than a week in St John's Harbour, the *Bellerophon* set sail again, this time to escort a convoy of merchant ships which was heading south towards Bermuda. On the return journey she intercepted and boarded several American ships and captured an American privateer. She arrived back at St John's with her prize on 8 July. The rest of the year was spent patrolling the seas off Cape Race. She frequently encountered the sea fog which has always plagued this region and her crew must have been relieved to receive orders to return to Britain. They set sail with a convoy of thirty-three ships on 22 November and dropped anchor in Torbay just under a month later on 18 December. That winter and the following spring were spent at anchor in Spithead.

The next year, 1814, was an almost exact repeat of the previous year. The *Bellerophon* left Spithead with a convoy on 26 April, arrived in St John's on 4 June, patrolled the seas off Cape Race for six months and returned to Spithead at the end of December. She was still under the command of Captain Hawker but in March 1815 she sailed for the Nore and there, on 9 April, Captain Hawker left the ship and was superseded by Captain Frederick Maitland. The most famous chapter in the life of the veteran ship was about to begin.

SIXTEEN

Napoleon and the *Bellerophon*

1815

On 2 July 1815, two weeks after his defeat on the battlefield of Waterloo, Napoleon arrived at the port of Rochefort on the west coast of France. He had travelled in a carriage from Paris and for most of the journey he had avoided being recognised but when he arrived at Niort, the last stop before Rochefort, the news of his arrival rapidly spread around the town. The prefect insisted that he transfer from his lodgings in a local inn to the prefecture building, and the soldiers of the second regiment of hussars, who were billeted in the town, acclaimed him with cries of 'Vive l'Empereur.' A day of festivities followed, with a reception hosted by the prefect, bands playing martial music, and excited crowds gathering in the streets. Napoleon had wished to keep a low profile because he did not want to stir up civil war or to antagonise the provisional government in Paris. He had agreed to abdicate as emperor and had asked the provisional government to supply him with passports to the United States of America and the use of two frigates which were currently lying at anchor off Rochefort.[1]

To avoid any further celebrations, he and his retinue of faithful followers and servants left Niort at 4 o'clock the next morning. A troop of hussars with drawn swords provided a regal escort as their carriages rattled along the lovely valley of the Charente river. They drove through fields scattered with elms and tamarisk trees, passed through the gateway in the city walls of Rochefort and at 8 am they

drew up outside the imposing house of the maritime prefect, Captain
Casimir de Bonnefoux. The prefect was no friend of Napoleon. He
was a royalist, a Chevalier de St Louis (a title of the Ancien Régime),
and had not hesitated to hoist the white flag of the Bourbons over
the prefecture when Napoleon had been sent to Elba in 1814. He
also bore a grudge because Napoleon had refused to confirm his rank
as captain back in 1800 when he had asked to serve in the navy on
condition that he did not go to sea. However he greeted Napoleon
civilly enough and put the apartments of the prefecture at his disposal.

Having inspected the rooms, Napoleon called a meeting of his
aides, together with the maritime prefect, and a number of naval
officers who were stationed at Rochefort. He wanted their views
on his next move. The sailors were discouraging and supported the
opinion of Bonnefoux who had already warned Napoleon that the
British blockade of the coast made it impossible for French ships
to get away from Rochefort. Bonnefoux had sent a letter to
Napoleon at Niort the day before in which he said, 'The roadsteads
are almost entirely blocked by an English squadron. It seems to
me that it would be extremely dangerous for our frigates and those
on board to try and force a passage.'[2] This was unduly pessimistic.
The approaches to Rochefort were protected from the worst of the
Atlantic storms by two large islands and several smaller islands.
As a glance at a chart of the area clearly shows, the position of the
large islands – the Île de Ré and the Île d'Oléron – created three
entrances or channels to Basque Roads which was the anchorage
where the French frigates and other vessels were lying. It was
difficult, if not impossible, for one warship to keep an effective watch
on all three approaches, particularly at night. During the previous
month there had been three British ships in the vicinity but on the
day that Napoleon arrived in Rochefort, and for the next three days,
there was only one British warship on guard. This was the
Bellerophon which was currently patrolling the seaward entrance of
the middle channel.

The *Bellerophon* had set sail from Plymouth on 24 May with a
squadron under the command of Rear-Admiral Sir Henry Hotham.

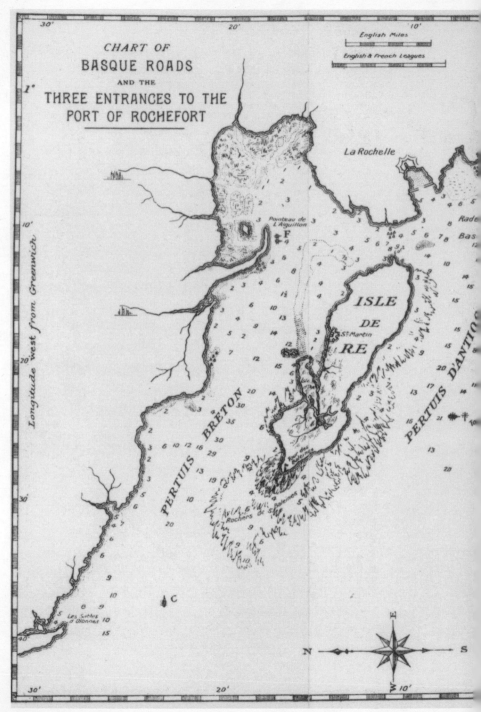

Chart of Basque Roads showing the position of the British and French ships in
July 1815. From Captain Maitland's *Narrative of the surrender of Buonaparte*, 1826.

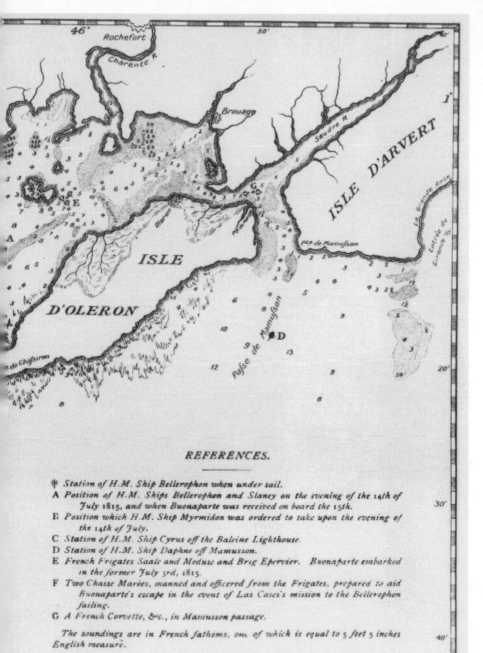

REFERENCES.

✳ *Station of H.M. Ship Bellerophon when under sail.*

A *Position of H.M. Ships Bellerophon and Slaney on the evening of the 14th of July 1815, and when Buonaparte was received on board the 15th.*

B *Position which H.M. Ship Myrmidon was ordered to take upon the evening of the 14th of July.*

C *Station of H.M. Ship Cyrus off the Baleine Lighthouse.*

D *Station of H.M. Ship Daphne off Mamusson.*

E *French Frigates Saale and Meduse and Brig Epervier. Buonaparte embarked in the former July 3rd, 1815.*

F *Two Chasse Marées, manned and officered from the Frigates, prepared to aid Buonaparte's escape in the event of Las Cases's mission to the Bellerophon failing.*

G *A French Corvette, &c., in Mamusson passage.*

The soundings are in French fathoms, one of which is equal to 5 feet 5 inches English measure.

When they arrived off the coast of Brittany the various ships in the squadron had separated. Hotham, in the *Superb*, had taken up a position off Quiberon Bay; the other ships had been despatched to watch the entrances of the River Loire and River Gironde; and the *Bellerophon*, together with the frigates *Myrmidon* and *Slaney*, had been despatched to Rochefort. The orders given to Captain Frederick Maitland were to report back to Hotham on the number and condition of the French ships of war lying at Rochefort, and to prevent a corvette putting to sea which it was believed was carrying proposals from Napoleon for the West Indian colonies to declare in his favour. The *Bellerophon* sailed into Basque Roads on 31 May and Captain Maitland noted that there were four ships of war at anchor in the lee of the Île d'Aix. There were two large frigates, the *Méduse* and the *Saale*; there was the corvette *Balladiére*; and a large brig, the *Épervier*. All were ready for sea.

For nearly a month the *Bellerophon* kept watch and occasionally intercepted coastal vessels. For the crew it was a return to the familiar routine of blockade duty: the location was not as hazardous as the rock-strewn coast of Brittany, and the summer weather was infinitely preferable to the cold, wet misery of patrolling off Ushant during the winter months, but it was nevertheless monotonous work. Nothing of any note happened until 28 June when Maitland learnt from one of the vessels he had captured that Napoleon had been defeated at Waterloo. Two days later a boat from Bordeaux came alongside and Maitland was handed a mysterious message. Written on thin paper and concealed inside a quill was a letter. It was not dated or signed and was evidently from a spy or an informer. The purpose of the letter was to warn the British that Napoleon was believed to have reached Bordeaux with the intention of fleeing the country, and 'to give the British Admiral advice of such intention, that he may instantly take the necessary steps in order to seize the man.'[3] The letter went on to provide details of the numbers of troops stationed at Bordeaux and to recommend that a sharp eye be kept on all American vessels.

The information about Napoleon's whereabouts was updated a week later when Maitland received further orders from Admiral

Hotham: 'Having this morning received information that it is believed Napoleon Bonaparte has taken his road from Paris for Rochefort, to embark from thence for the United States of America, I have to direct you will use your best endeavours to prevent him from making his escape in either of the frigates at Isle d'Aix . . .'[4] The letter was dated 6 July, and on 7 July Hotham despatched another letter to Maitland telling him that the British Government had received an application from the rulers of France for a passport and safe conduct for Napoleon to go to America but the request had been turned down.

Napoleon seems to have been overcome by an uncharacteristic weariness and lassitude after Waterloo. He listened to the conflicting advice of those around him but delayed making decisions. Five days were wasted in Rochefort while he reorganised his household, and waited for passports and for the arrival of the rest of his furniture and the books from his library. Every day the royalist forces were drawing closer and the white flag of the Bourbons was being raised in towns and villages across France. He eventually agreed to be rowed out to the Île d'Aix. 'I shall be close to the frigates there and in a position to embark whenever the winds are at all favourable to our getting away.'[5]

The winds were not favourable on 8 July when he and his retinue left the prefecture and drove to the beach at Fouras where a crowd had gathered to watch the departure of the former emperor. As the heavily laden boats left the shelter of Fouras Point they encountered the full force of a strong breeze from the north-west which whipped up short steep waves and soaked the oarsmen and passengers with salt spray. For an hour and a half they rowed towards the distant Île d'Aix but progress was so slow that Napoleon decided to head for the anchored frigates instead. At 7.30 pm he climbed up the side of the frigate *Saale*, followed by his aides. What he did not know was that he had already missed the best opportunity he would ever have of evading the British blockade and escaping to America. For three days (from 3 to 5 July) the *Bellerophon* had been the only British ship in the vicinity but on 6 July she had been joined by the frigates *Myrmidon* and *Slaney* and between them they were able to watch all the escape routes. Count Montholon later wrote, 'The reasons for our staying at Rochefort until the evening of July 8, when we embarked for the frigate *Saale*, were a mystery that I have never succeeded in fathoming, for I shall always refuse to believe that we remained five days at Rochefort merely to wait for packing cases and wagons . . .'6

The following day the wind eased and Napoleon decided to pay a visit to the Île d'Aix which he had last visited in 1808. Although barely a mile in length the island was a strongly fortified military settlement. Sheltered behind an encircling wall with ramparts and gun batteries was a small but attractive town with one main street dominated by the handsome façade of the commandant's house. The inhabitants of the island were fiercely patriotic and bitterly hated the British – with good reason. In 1809 a British fleet under Admiral Gambier had attacked a fleet of French warships anchored in Basque Roads by sending in fireships. Four of the French line of battle ships were destroyed and several other ships cut their cables and ran aground. By a curious accident of history Captain Maitland, then in command of a frigate, was present at the action as part of the advanced squadron led by Lord Cochrane.7 The humiliation of watching a French fleet destroyed before their eyes still rankled with the islanders. They associated Napoleon with past French triumphs and they gave him a warm welcome when he stepped ashore. He inspected the fortifications amidst the cheers of the inhabitants and the soldiers of the regiment stationed on the island. But when he returned to the frigate he found Captain Bonnefoux awaiting him with ominous letters from the provisional government in Paris.

'It is of the utmost importance that the Emperor leaves the soil of France as soon as possible,' one letter began. 'The interests of the State and the safety of his person make this absolutely necessary.'8 He was advised that he must leave within the next twenty-four hours, either on one of the frigates or on a smaller vessel, or if contrary winds prevented him sailing on either of these, he should consider going on board an English ship.

Napoleon could no longer delay a decision, but what were his options? If he and his party set sail on the frigates he risked a sea battle, the death or wounding of the men, women and children in his retinue, and ignominious capture by the British. If he remained in the vicinity of Rochefort he was likely to become a prisoner of the Bourbons or, worse still, the Prussians or the Austrians. Or he could surrender himself to the British and ask for political asylum in England. The latter choice seemed to him preferable. He therefore decided that General Savary and Count Las Cases must be despatched to the *Bellerophon* in order to find out from her captain how the British authorities were likely to respond to such a gesture.

At first light on the morning of 10 July the two envoys embarked on the schooner *Mouche*, flying a white flag of truce, and headed for the British warship which was sailing on her usual station off the seaward end of the Île d'Oléron. It was a fresh summer morning with a light breeze and a few scattered clouds in an otherwise clear sky. As the schooner drew closer, the *Bellerophon* hove to and lowered a boat. With a lieutenant in the stern giving directions the sailors rowed across the intervening water and intercepted the French vessel as she rounded up into the wind with her sails flapping. General Savary and Count Las Cases were helped down into the boat and just before 8 am they came alongside the massive, battle-scarred sides of the veteran ship. They were greeted at the companionway by Captain Maitland. The meeting of the three men marked the opening move in a political drama which would decide the fate of Napoleon and throw the spotlight of history on the *Bellerophon* and her captain.

Captain Maitland was in many ways ideally suited for the part he found himself having to play.[9] He came from the Scottish aristocracy and was a natural diplomat with a courteous and charming manner and a keen intelligence. He was also a highly experienced naval officer who had led an action-packed life. As the son of a distinguished naval captain who had served under Admiral Rodney and commanded the royal yacht, he entered the navy at an early age. He was present at the Battle of the Glorious First of June as a midshipman on the frigate *Southampton* and would have been in a good position to observe the heroic performance of the *Bellerophon* during the four-day action. As a junior lieutenant he had been court-martialled and honourably discharged for wrecking an 18-gun brig at the entrance of the River

Tagus. Chosen by the formidable Lord St Vincent to be his flag
lieutenant, he had been sent to investigate the Spanish fleet off
Gibraltar in a small, armed cutter. He had fought off one Spanish
warship, but been forced to surrender to another. The Spanish admiral
had been so impressed by his bravery that he returned him to the
British fleet without requesting an exchange of prisoners. In 1800
he commanded the armed launches during the landing of
Abercromby's army in Egypt and earned the praise of Sir Sydney
Smith for his conduct. Later, as commander of the frigate *Loire* and
then the frigate *Emerald*, he captured or destroyed no fewer than
seventeen enemy vessels on the southern coast of Spain. For his
daring raid on the vessels in Muros Harbour in 1805 he received the
thanks of the City of London, was presented with a sword by Lloyd's
Patriotic Fund and was given the freedom of the City of Cork.[10]

After two years in command of a 74-gun ship in the West Indies
and then in Halifax, Nova Scotia, he returned to Britain and was
preparing to take a convoy of transport ships across the Atlantic
when news reached England that Napoleon had escaped from Elba.
Maitland was recalled from convoy duty and appointed to command
the *Bellerophon* which was then lying in the Nore. On a fine spring
day in April 1815 he read his commission to the assembled crew and
a month later was on his way to the Bay of Biscay in the squadron
commanded by Sir Henry Hotham.[11] Maitland was now thirty-seven
years old, a tall, lean man with a slight stoop, a shock of unruly hair
and a distinctive Scottish accent. His pleasant, relaxed manner as a
commander was in contrast to his alarmingly efficient first lieutenant
Andrew Mott. This led Midshipman Home to speculate that Maitland
cleverly contrived to get a tartar appointed to this post, 'so that
between the captain's good nature and the lieutenant's severity, which
he occasionally checked and tempered when he thought the lieutenant
was likely to exceed bounds, the ship was kept in capital discipline.'[12]

When General Savary and Count Las Cases stepped on board the
Bellerophon on 10 July Captain Maitland took them to the great cabin
in the stern. This had been the seagoing home, office, war room and
retreat for no fewer than fourteen commanders of the ship over the
past twenty-nine years. It was furnished simply but elegantly with

fine mahogany furniture in the Regency style and every surface was
as clean and polished and scrubbed as the decks and gear throughout
the rest of the ship. The sweeping curve of the stern windows
provided a panoramic view across the glistening water towards the
green slopes of the nearer islands and the distant masts of the sailing
vessels anchored in the roadstead. After the preliminary courtesies
had been exchanged General Savary handed Maitland the following
letter which, although signed by General Bertrand, had been dictated
by Napoleon and was addressed to the admiral commanding the
British ships before the port of Rochefort:

Sir,

The Emperor Napoleon having abdicated the throne of France, and chosen
the United States of America as a retreat, is, with his suite, at present
embarked on board the two frigates which are in this port, for the purpose
of proceeding to his destination. He expects a passport from the British
Government, which has been promised to him, and which induces me to
send the present flag of truce, to demand of you, Sir, if you have any
knowledge of the above-mentioned passport, or if you think it is the
intention of the British Government to throw any impediment in the way
of our voyage to the United States. I shall feel much obliged by your
giving me any information you may possess on the subject.

    I have directed the bearers of the letter to present you my thanks,
and to apologise for any trouble it may cause.

    I have the honour to be,

        Your excellency's most obedient, etc, etc,

        Grand Marshall Count Bertrand.[13]

This was not an entirely honest letter because Napoleon had not
received a promise from anyone, let alone the British Government,
that the passports would be granted him. On the other hand Maitland
knew perfectly well that the request for passports had been refused
but at no time did he reveal that he was aware of this. Both sides
seem to have been playing a game of diplomatic poker, trying to find
out each other's intentions without giving too much away. At this
stage Maitland's orders were restricted to preventing Napoleon from

leaving France, but while he was still pondering his response to the letter a hail from the deck announced the arrival of another British ship. It was the *Falmouth*, a 20-gun sloop under the command of Captain Knight, with an urgent message from Admiral Hotham who was still on patrol off Quiberon Bay 120 miles to the north. The letter was dated 8 July and informed Maitland that the Admiralty now had definite news that Napoleon intended to escape to America with his family. Maitland was ordered to keep the most vigilant lookout for him, and 'if you should be so fortunate as to intercept him, you are to transfer him and his family to the ship you command, and there keeping him in careful custody, return to the nearest port in England (going into Torbay in preference to Plymouth) with all possible expedition.'[14] He was warned that the whole operation must be conducted with the strictest secrecy.

These new orders placed an increased responsibility on Maitland's shoulders. He was not only required to prevent Napoleon leaving France at all costs but must endeavour to get him on board the *Bellerophon*. He was aware that the future peace of Europe might depend on his actions. In the circumstances he decided not to reveal the British Government's intentions to Savary and Las Cases, a decision which has led some French commentators to accuse him of cynical double-dealing. Captain Knight was invited to sit in on the discussions which went on for nearly three hours. Savary and Las Cases kept plying Maitland with questions, and tried to persuade him that the peace of Europe would best be served if Napoleon were allowed to depart quietly from France. They said he wished only to retire and to spend his days in obscurity and tranquillity. When Maitland made it clear that he had strict orders to prevent the frigates leaving Rochefort they suggested that Napoleon be allowed to depart on a neutral, unarmed vessel, but again Maitland was discouraging. He set out his position in a letter which he gave them to take back with them. It was his formal answer to Bertrand's letter: 'In reply, I have to acquaint you, that I cannot say what the intentions of my Government may be; but the two countries being at present in a state of war, it is impossible for me to permit any ship of war to put to sea from the port of Rochefort.' With regard to the suggestion that the emperor proceed in a merchant vessel he was equally adamant. He could not allow a person of such consequence to pass in any vessel, under whatever flag, without the sanction of his commanding officer, Sir Henry Hotham.[15]

Around noon Savary and Las Cases returned to Napoleon on the frigate *Saale*. Two hours later Captain Knight departed in the *Falmouth* and headed back to Admiral Hotham, taking with him Bertrand's letter and a despatch from Maitland with his appraisal of the current situation. From the British point of view Maitland's conduct of the negotiations had been masterly. He had given nothing away, but he had learnt much from his discussions with the two envoys. In particular he had noted that the hardening attitude of the government in Paris and the approaching Allied armies were putting Napoleon under increasing pressure to escape from France. Maitland's problem was that he did not have a sufficiently strong force under his command to blockade the three approaches to Rochefort effectively. He later admitted that, from the moment he learnt that Napoleon and his party were on the frigates and intended to proceed to America, 'my duty became peculiarly harassing and anxious'. The *Bellerophon* was capable of stopping the two French frigates, but the *Myrmidon* and *Slaney*, which were only 20-gun sloops, were no match for them. Moreover it was impossible for the three ships to intercept every small vessel in the vicinity if Napoleon should decide to escape in a *chasse-marée* (a type of French coastal vessel notable for her speed under sail) as some of his followers were urging him to do.

A few hours after Savary and Las Cases had departed, Maitland sailed the *Bellerophon* up the channel towards the French frigates and dropped anchor in Basque Roads close to the Île d'Aix. He noted with some concern that the sterns of the frigates were loaded with vegetables, that small boats were constantly going to and fro between the ships and the shore, and that the position of the yards and sails of the frigates indicated that they were ready to put to sea at any moment. That evening Maitland took precautions to ensure that Napoleon did not give him the slip. He sent two boats to row near the frigates all night with orders to signal to him if the ships got under way. He ordered the *Bellerophon* and the *Myrmidon* to be anchored with slip buoys on their cables for immediate release; and he arranged for the topsail and topgallant yards to be hoisted and their sails held with thin yarn so they could be broken out and set at a moment's notice.

The next morning there was no sign of further activity on the frigates. Alarmed by reports that Napoleon was now planning to escape on a smaller vessel, Maitland decided he was not in the best place to keep watch on all the escape routes and gave orders for the *Bellerophon* to weigh anchor. With the *Myrmidon* and *Slaney* in company, they worked their way out to sea and resumed their patrol of the seaward approaches to Rochefort. On 12 July his flotilla was joined by welcome reinforcements: the *Daphne*, 22 guns, and the 20-gun sloop *Cyrus*. Maitland ordered the *Daphne* to take up a position at the entrance of the southernmost channel, the Passe de Mamusson, and the *Cyrus* to keep a watch on the northernmost channel, the Pertuis Breton. For the next two days the *Bellerophon* prowled restlessly back and forth, intercepting local craft and always keeping a wary eye on the frigates.

In the meantime Napoleon continued to hold discussions with his aides and delayed making any decision. When Savary and Las Cases returned to the frigate *Saale* after their visit to the *Bellerophon*, the rest of the day was spent discussing the implications of Maitland's letter and the possible options. Two of his followers thought Napoleon should return to the army but Bonaparte said that he did not want to be the cause of a single cannon shot. Most of his followers, notably Bertrand, Savary and Las Cases, were in favour of his surrendering to the British. One man, Captain Ponée, had an interesting alternative. Ponée was the commander of the *Méduse*, the other large frigate in the anchorage, and he proposed the following course of action:

I will go ahead of the *Saale* under cover of darkness, take the *Bellerophon* by surprise as she lies at anchor, grapple with her broadside on, and thus prevent her moving. The engagement might last two hours, and the *Méduse*, being a frigate of sixty guns while the *Bellerophon* has seventy-four, cannot fail to be sunk, but meanwhile the *Saale* could take advantage of the wind offshore that blows every evening, to get away, and the twenty-two gun corvette and advice-boat that made up the rest of the English flotilla would not be able to stop the *Saale*, a frigate of the first rank, carrying twenty-four guns in batteries and carronades of thirty-six on the bridge.[16]

It was a brave plan and preparations were put in hand. The decks of the frigates were cleared for action, and the topsails made ready for hoisting. But still Napoleon refused to act and all the time his situation became more perilous. The following day, 11 July, newspapers arrived from Paris which contained bad news. Paris had surrendered to the Allies and King Louis XVII had returned to the city to take up residence. This had grave implications for Napoleon's followers who were likely to be declared traitors and executed if caught. On 12 July the white flag of the Bourbons appeared for the first time in the immediate neighbourhood. The log of the *Bellerophon* records that at 5 pm a white flag was seen flying over La Rochelle, the ancient harbour town which overlooked the anchorage of Basque Roads. Maitland hoisted the British ensign and a white flag at the mainmast in acknowledgement, headed for the roadstead, dropped anchor and shattered the peace of the evening by firing a royal salute of 21 guns.

Captain Philibert, the commander of the *Saale*, who was a royalist at heart and had shown little enthusiasm at having to act as host to Napoleon, now declared that he could not agree to be part of Captain Ponée's audacious plan. Napoleon decided there was no future in using the frigates to escape, and later that day he disembarked from the *Saale* and went across to the Île d'Aix where he knew he could be sure of support from the loyal soldiers and the islanders. He took up residence in the commandant's house where he was given a room on the first floor, with a fine view over the anchorage. This was to be the last place on French soil that Napoleon stayed in.

On the morning of 13 July he received a surprise visit from his brother Joseph Bonaparte, the ex-King of Spain. Joseph had travelled from Bordeaux where he had chartered an American ship which was moored in the estuary of the Gironde. He was strongly against

Napoleon seeking political asylum in Britain and urged him to join him on the ship and sail to New York. Napoleon thanked him for his offer but turned it down and told him to return at once to Bordeaux and make good his escape. Six weeks later Joseph was in America.[17]

That evening Napoleon made his decision. He would surrender himself voluntarily to the British and put his trust in British justice and the country's long tradition of harbouring political refugees. Before going to bed he dictated the following letter to the Prince Regent, Britain's acting head of state during the illness of his father King George III:

> Your Royal Highness,
> A victim to the factions which distract my country, and to the enmity of the greatest powers of Europe, I have terminated my political career, and I come, like Themistocles, to throw myself upon the hospitality of the British people. I put myself under the protection of their laws; which I claim from your Royal Highness, as the most powerful, the most constant, and the most generous of my enemies.
> Rochefort 13 July 1815   Napoleon.[18]

The reference to Themistocles, the Athenian statesman of classical Greece who had surrendered to Artaxerxes, suggests that Napoleon saw his action as a grand gesture, an appeal from the vanquished leader to the conqueror. The letter brought tears to the eyes of General Gourgaud who was to be entrusted with delivering it to the Prince Regent. But first Napoleon wanted to be sure that there was no sign of the passports which would allow him passage to America. Early the next morning Las Cases and General Lallemand were despatched to the *Bellerophon* to see if there was any news of the passports, and, if not, to discuss the embarkation of Napoleon and his suite on the British ship. Once again the schooner *Mouche* headed across the water flying a flag of truce. Captain Maitland ordered breakfast for the two envoys and sent a signal to Captain Sartorius of the *Slaney* to join them on board. As on the previous occasion he wanted a witness to their discussions. When Sartorius arrived the four men settled down to detailed negotiations. Once again Las Cases put the case for allowing Napoleon to sail to America. He assured Maitland that, 'The emperor is so anxious to spare the further effusion of human blood that he will proceed to America in any way the British Government chooses to sanction, either in a French ship of war, a vessel armed *en flute*, or even in a British ship of war.'[19]

Maitland replied:

I have no authority to agree to any arrangement of that sort, nor do I believe my Government would consent to it; but I think I may venture to receive him into this ship and convey him to England. If, however, he adopts that plan, I cannot enter into any promise as to the reception he may meet with, as, even in the case I have mentioned, I shall be acting on my own responsibility and cannot be sure that it would meet the approbation of the British Government.[20]

Maitland was questioned on what sort of reception Napoleon might expect in England and, according to Las Cases, he assured him that 'Napoleon would find all the respect and good treatment he could wish for in England' and that 'in generosity of feeling and liberality of opinions the English people were superior to the throne itself.'[21] It is hard to believe that this was an accurate account of Maitland's conversation. Apart from the fact that he would have been well aware of the animosity and hatred of Napoleon in many quarters in England, he frequently repeated that he had no authority to grant terms of any sort and could take no responsibility for his reception there. They went on to discuss Napoleon's younger brother, Lucien Bonaparte, who had been captured by a British warship in 1810. He had been allowed to settle in a country house at Thorngrove near Worcester where he lived in some comfort under the supervision of a single police inspector. This may have been seen as an encouraging sign but it would have been naïve for the envoys to assume that the former conqueror of half Europe would be regarded in the same light.

As the French envoys were leaving, Las Cases assured Captain Maitland that he had little doubt that he would see the Emperor on board his ship. That evening a barge was rowed across from the French frigates and Las Cases, accompanied this time by General Gourgaud, arrived bearing a letter for Maitland which stated that Napoleon 'will proceed on board your ship with the ebb tide tomorrow morning, between four and five o'clock', and enclosing a list of the fifty members of Napoleon's suite who would be accompanying him. Maitland was also asked to arrange for General Gourgaud to be sent to England so that he could deliver Napoleon's letter to the Prince Regent.

Maitland agreed with all the requests. It seemed that he would be able to carry out the Admiralty's orders without a shot being fired. First he arranged for Captain Sartorious to sail on ahead in the *Slaney*, taking with him General Gourgaud, together with his own despatches to the Admiralty. Before midnight the *Slaney* weighed anchor and set off for England. He then discussed with Las Cases how best to accommodate Napoleon and his party. Maitland suggested that his own cabin, the great cabin at the stern of the ship, should be divided in two, one half for the use of Napoleon and the other half for the use of the ladies in his party. Las Cases inspected the space and said, 'If you allow me to give an opinion, the Emperor will be better pleased to have the whole of the after-cabin himself, as he is fond of walking about, and will by that means be able to take more exercise.'

Maitland replied, 'As it is my wish to treat him with every possible consideration while he is on board the ship I command, I shall make any arrangement you think will be most agreeable to him.'[22] Between them they worked out the accommodation for the rest of Napoleon's entourage. It was agreed that thirty-three of them would travel on the *Bellerophon*, and the remaining seventeen would be accommodated on the *Myrmidon*. They were still discussing these domestic arrangements late in the evening when a boat came alongside with a man bearing an urgent message. He reported that Napoleon had already put to sea in a *chasse-marée*, had sailed past La Rochelle and was intending to escape via the northern channel that night. Las Cases assured Maitland that the report could not possibly be correct. He left the ship soon afterwards.

Maitland stayed up till 1 o'clock in the morning supervising the arrangements for receiving his French guests. 'All was expectation and excitement,' wrote the midshipman George Home. 'The first lieutenant was engaged seeing all the belaying pins get an extra polish, and that every rope was coiled down with more than usual care.'23 At 3 am Maitland was woken by the officer of the watch who told him that another boat had come alongside and had confirmed the earlier report that a *chasse-marée* had been seen heading for the sea. Although this did nothing to allay Maitland's anxieties he felt that he had no choice but to trust Las Cases. As on previous nights when at anchor in Basque Roads he had arranged for two boats to keep guard in the vicinity of the frigates and these returned to the ship as the first glimmer of dawn lightened the sky over La Rochelle.

The morning of 15 July was grey and overcast with a freshening northerly breeze. The *Bellerophon* and the *Myrmidon* were anchored some 2 miles from the Île d'Aix, and by 5 am most of the sailors and marines were up on the decks staring expectantly at the island and the French warships moored nearby. Captain Maitland and his first lieutenant Andrew Mott took it in turns to stare at the distant anchorage through their telescopes, searching for any sign of movement. They were rewarded by the welcome sight of the topsails being hoisted on one of the smaller vessels, and then a white flag of truce being hoisted at her masthead. Soon she was under way, heeling over before the breeze, and they could see that she was the armed brig *Épervier*. She was having to beat into a headwind to get to the *Bellerophon* and by 5.30 she had only the last of the ebb tide to help her on her way. This would not have mattered if it had not been for the fact that the lookouts had seen a strange ship on the horizon. She was flying the flag of a rear-admiral so she must be the *Superb*, the flagship of Sir Henry Hotham. With the wind and tide in her favour she would be alongside them in a few hours. After the weeks of watching and waiting, and the hours of negotiations, Captain Maitland was naturally reluctant to relinquish to his superior officer the prize which was almost within his grasp. He therefore ordered Lieutenant Mott to take the *Bellerophon*'s barge, and bring Napoleon off the brig which was labouring slowly towards them. Within minutes the barge was pushing off from the warship and rowing smartly towards the *Épervier*.

Napoleon had spent his third and last night at the commandant's house on the Île d'Aix. It was, however, a short night because he and his party had to be down at the jetty by 2 am. His valet Louis-Joseph Marchand woke him in good time and helped him get dressed in the uniform which he had made famous and which was familiar to all those French soldiers who had seen him on the battlefield: the white waistcoat and breeches, military boots, and the green coat with scarlet cuffs and lapels of a colonel of the Chasseurs of the Imperial Guard. To keep out the chill of the early morning he put on his olive-coloured greatcoat and his black cocked hat with tricolour cockade. He was used to getting up in the early hours and inspecting his troops in the darkness before dawn but there were no troops around on this occasion. However there was a reminder of old times when he was rowed out from the jetty and his boat pulled alongside the brig *Épervier*. The crew shouted 'Vive l'Empereur' as he climbed aboard. The commander of the brig, Captain Jourdan de la Passadière, saluted him at the gangway and invited him to inspect the officers and marines drawn up on the deck. When the vessel got under way Napoleon asked for some coffee and he drank it while chatting to the captain. He was cheerful and full of questions. How many guns did the ship have? And how fast could she sail? He wondered what sort of hospitality he could expect from his enemies. Captain Jourdan thought he should have tried to break through the British blockade and believed he was wrong to trust Maitland.

'It is too late', Napoleon replied. 'They expect me; I am going.'

They were halfway between the Île d'Aix and the anchored British warships when the barge commanded by Lieutenant Mott was seen heading their way, four sets of oars rising and falling rhythmically, their progress helped by the brisk, following wind. The French brig hove to, the sailors in the barge brought her smartly alongside and the British lieutenant clambered up onto the deck. He spoke no French so Countess Bertrand, the wife of Napoleon's most senior adviser, acted as interpreter. Mott explained that he had come to collect Napoleon and had room for half a dozen others in the boat. Napoleon asked him how long it would take them to sail from Basque Roads to England. Mott reckoned it would take eight days. Napoleon pondered this for a moment and then turned to the ladies in his party. 'Well, mesdames, do you feel able to reach the English ship?'

The sailors helped Countess Bertrand and her three children and Countess Montholon and her child into the barge. General Bertrand and General Savary followed. Napoleon was the last to leave the French brig and step down into the British boat. It was a symbolic moment which was not lost on those present. The Emperor was surrendering to the enemy – the enemy which had opposed him and the armies of France for more than twenty years, ever since he had directed his guns at the British fleet during the siege of Toulon. Lieutenant Mott saw that many of the French soldiers and sailors lining the rail were in tears. Napoleon stood in the sternsheets of the barge, hunched in his greatcoat, and as he looked up at them they started cheering, and the cheering grew louder and more defiant as the British sailors bent to their oars and began pulling away. The cheering continued until the passengers in the barge were out of earshot and the sound was replaced by the regular thump and splash of the oars, and the cries of gulls soaring over the grey, windswept waters of the anchorage.

Back on the *Bellerophon* there was a general feeling of anticipation

Napoleon being rowed out to the *Bellerophon*
on the morning of 15 July 1815.

and excitement among the officers and men. The exception was Captain Maitland who was unable to conceal his anxiety and was observed trudging back and forth between the gangway and his cabin. Every now and again he would peer out of one of the quarterdeck ports to see if the barge was approaching. Earlier he had had to make a decision on a delicate matter of protocol. Should he receive Napoleon on board with the full ceremonial due to a head of state or should he treat him as an enemy officer who had come to surrender? He was conscious of the historic nature of the occasion and he was also acutely aware that he would be answerable to his commanding officer Admiral Hotham, and to his political masters in London, if he put a foot wrong during the next few hours.

He decided on what he hoped was a neat compromise. It was not customary on a British warship to engage in the ceremonial honours due to a person of high rank before 8 o'clock in the morning or after sunset. It was now 6 am. So it would be inappropriate at this hour to man the yards with sailors or fire a salute with the guns. Instead he ordered a guard of marines to be drawn up on the break of the poop deck. They were to come to attention when Napoleon came aboard but were not to present arms. The ship's officers were to wait on the quarterdeck, and the boatswain was to stand at the companionway ready to sound his whistle.

The boatswain was a 31-year-old Irishman from County Limerick called James Manning. He had been a blacksmith before joining the navy and was short and stout with a formidably bronzed face. While they were all waiting for Lieutenant Mott to return with the barge a young midshipman sauntered up to him and said, 'Manning, this is the proudest day of your life. You are this day to do the honours of the side to the greatest man the world has ever produced or ever will produce.'

The boatswain nodded and beamed with pride.

'And along with the great Napoleon, the name of Manning the boatswain of the *Bellerophon* will go down to posterity. And as a relic of that great man, permit me, my dear Manning, to preserve a lock of your hair.'[24] And with that the midshipman pulled out some of his whiskers and ran down below before anyone could stop him. The infuriated boatswain swore and hurled his hat after the midshipman which produced a half-suppressed burst of laughter from the crew on the deck.

At some time between 6 and 7 o'clock (the various accounts differ on this point) the *Bellerophon*'s barge returned from her trip to the French brig. As she came alongside, the sailor in the bows grabbed hold of the chains hanging beside the boarding ladder, and General Bertrand climbed up the sides of the warship and appeared on deck. He was Napoleon's most valued friend and supporter, a former engineer officer who had played a major part in the invasion of Egypt, and had been appointed Grand Marshal of the Palace. He approached Captain Maitland and told him that the Emperor was in the boat. There was a pause and then a man in a greatcoat buttoned to the chin and a black cocked hat appeared at the gangway. No one watching was in any doubt who this was. For years the British cartoonists had ridiculed the figure of Napoleon, accentuating his prominent belly, his round face and aquiline nose, and they were fond of depicting him with the angry scowl of a spoilt child. The reality was startlingly different. The man who now marched briskly across the deck had a commanding presence and an unmistakable air of authority. As the high-pitched shrill of Manning's whistle died away, Napoleon climbed the short stairway to the quarterdeck. There he pulled off his hat and addressed himself to Captain Maitland. Speaking in French, with a firm tone of voice, he said, 'I am come to throw myself on the protection of your Prince and your laws.'

Captain Maitland gave a deep bow, and led him into the great cabin. Napoleon looked around and remarked that it was a handsome room. Maitland replied, 'Such as it is, Sir, it is at your service while you remain on board the ship I command.'

Seeing a portrait hanging up on one of the walls, Napoleon asked, 'Who is that young lady?'

'My wife,' said Maitland.

'Ah! She is very young and very pretty.'

He went on to ask Maitland about his children and his naval service, and then said that he would like to be introduced to the ship's officers. Maitland sent for them and introduced them one by one. Napoleon wanted to know the age of each man, his rank, how long he had served in the navy and what actions he had been in. Before they left the cabin he had some flattering words for them.

'Well, gentlemen,' he said, 'you have the honour of belonging to the bravest and most fortunate nation in the world.'[25] He then turned to Maitland and said that he would like to look round the ship. Before taking him on a tour Maitland suggested that they conduct their conversations in English as he had heard that Napoleon understood the language while he, Maitland, had difficulty in expressing himself in French. That would be impossible, Napoleon told him, as he hardly understood a word of English. Maitland later wrote that the problem was that Napoleon spoke too fast for him to follow his meaning but after a few days he got used to this and was able to understand him perfectly. In the meantime they seem to have coped admirably, no doubt assisted by members of Napoleon's party who acted as interpreters.[26] They certainly managed to conduct a most interesting conversation as they toured the ship.

Napoleon had never been on a British man-of-war before and was fascinated by every aspect of the ship and her crew. He particularly wanted to find out why British ships were able to beat the French with such ease. He pointed out that the finest warships in the British Navy were French, and that French ships were bigger, had larger crews, and carried more guns, and guns of a larger calibre than their British equivalents.[27] Was it due to the quality of the British seamen who were so smartly turned out and were surely a different class of people from French seamen? Maitland said that he did not wish to take away from the merit of the British seamen but the key lay in the superior experience of the officers. British ships were constantly at sea and the officers were able to train up their crews in a way not possible for the French crews who were forced to spend most of their time in port. Napoleon had heard from some French sailors who had been detained on the *Bellerophon* for a few days, and then put ashore on the Île d'Aix, that Maitland frequently carried out gunnery practice and trained his men to fire at a mark.

'I did so because I considered it of the greatest importance,' said Maitland, and added that if the French frigates had attempted to put

to sea he would have had an opportunity to observe the effect of it.
Napoleon thought that two frigates with 24-pounders on their main
decks were surely a match for a 74-gun ship, and he asked whether
Maitland thought they would have been successful if they had
attempted to force a passage past the *Bellerophon*. Maitland thought
it unlikely because, as he explained in some detail:

> the fire of a two-deck ship was so much more compact, and carried such
> an immense weight of iron, in proportion to that of a frigate, and there
> was so much difficulty in bringing two or three ships to act with effect
> at the same time upon one, that I scarcely considered three frigates a
> match for one line-of-battle ship; that with respect to forcing a passage
> past the *Bellerophon*, it must have depended greatly on accident, but the
> chances were very much against it; as the frigates would have had to
> beat out against the wind for three or four leagues, through a narrow
> passage, exposed to the fire of a seventy-four gun ship, which, from
> being to windward, would have had the power of taking the position
> most advantageous to herself.[28]

At 9 o'clock they sat down for an English-style breakfast of tea,
coffee and cold meats. Napoleon ate very little and when Maitland
learnt that he was used to a hot meal in the morning he arranged
that, in future, Napoleon's cook should prepare his meals, 'and after
that we always lived in the French fashion, as far as I could effect
that object'. At 10.30 the *Superb* sailed into the roadstead and dropped
anchor nearby. Maitland immediately went across in a boat to report
to Sir Henry Hotham. He was greatly relieved to find that the Admiral
approved of his actions and thought it appropriate that the *Bellerophon*
should be the ship which carried Napoleon to England.

The afternoon was spent loading on board the former emperor's
baggage and at 5 o'clock the first of many grand dinners took place
in the stern of the ship. The meal was prepared by Napoleon's kitchen
staff and they ate off the imperial silver plate. Maitland noted that
Napoleon conducted himself in the manner of royalty: he led the
party into the dining-room, seated himself in the centre at one side
of the table, and placed Sir Henry Hotham on his right, Countess

Bertrand on his left and Captain Maitland opposite him. Cups of strong coffee were served when they had finished dinner, and Napoleon invited all those present to join him in the after-cabin. There he asked his valet Marchand to show them his camp-bed. This was an ingenious folding bed which he had used on many of his military campaigns. From two leather cases Marchand took out the steel bedstead, the mattress and green silk curtains and within three minutes he had erected a small but elegant bed. Before leaving the ship Hotham invited Napoleon, together with the ladies and his principal officers, to join him for breakfast the next day.

Captain Maitland was up early on 16 July and noted that all his instructions for the reception of his guests had been carried out. Nets had been stretched across the gunports to prevent the young children from falling overboard; an awning had been erected between the main and mizen masts to provide a sheltered space on deck for the ladies of the party; and two red-coated marines were standing guard outside the after-cabin. When Napoleon appeared on deck the officers in the vicinity removed their hats and when he prepared to embark for breakfast on the *Superb* he found a guard of marines drawn up alongside the companionway. Although there was a fresh breeze and an overcast sky the weather was mild enough for Napoleon to discard his greatcoat. Lieutenant Bowerbank noted in his journal that the great man was wearing his green uniform coat with the red collar and cuffs and two gold epaulettes; he had the star and cross of the Légion d'honneur and several other orders pinned on the left breast; and instead of his military boots he was wearing shoes with handsome gold buckles.

Admiral Hotham had decided to welcome Napoleon in style and, as the boat carrying the former emperor approached the *Superb*, the sailors swarmed up the shrouds and manned the yards, an honour normally reserved for a sovereign or head of state. Napoleon was piped aboard and found the ship's company assembled on the deck in divisions and a captain's guard of marines lined up on the quarterdeck. He was formally welcomed by Sir Henry who introduced him to the officers and took him on a tour of the ship. Much heartened by his regal reception, Napoleon delighted everyone by his lively conversation and his interest in the crew and in every detail of the ship from the guns and ammunition to victuals, clothing and methods of storage.

Around midday they returned to the *Bellerophon* and preparations were made for getting under way. The barge and the cutter were hoisted aboard and stowed amidships, the topsail yards were hoisted, and the crew manned the capstans and began heaving up the anchor. At around 2 pm they made sail and began working their way out of Basque Roads in company with the *Myrmidon*. Napoleon remained on deck throughout these manoeuvres, constantly asking Maitland what was happening. He noted that the British manner of getting under way was different from the French and was much impressed by the crew.

'What I admire most in your ship,' he said, 'is the extreme silence and orderly conduct of your men: on board a French ship everyone calls and gives orders, and they gabble like so many geese.'[29]

That evening General Bertrand invited the first lieutenant and the captain of the marines to join Napoleon and his party for dinner. It was a jovial affair and an onlooker would never have imagined that Napoleon was a defeated general in the midst of his victorious enemies. He was happy to speak at length about the Battles of the Nile and Trafalgar and mentioned the name of Nelson with approval. When the meal was finished he again went on deck and plied the officers with questions about the working of the sails and rigging. He remarked that the wind was not fair and asked what the distance was to England. At 7.45 pm he retired to his cabin for the night.

SEVENTEEN

Into Exile

1815

The morning of 17 July found the two ships out in the open sea with the French coastline no more than a distant blur on the horizon. They were having to beat into a light north-westerly breeze which meant that progress was slow, but the usually turbulent waters of the Bay of Biscay were relatively calm, allowing the French visitors to get acclimatised to the easy motion of the deck under their feet. Over the next few days a regular pattern was established. Napoleon rose between 8 and 9 o'clock, was served a hot breakfast and then spent the morning reading in his cabin or playing cards. He invited Maitland to join him in a game of *vingt-et-un* on one occasion, but Maitland excused himself on the grounds that he had left all his money at home with his wife and, in any case, he had his duties to attend to.

Napoleon frequently fell asleep on the sofa in his cabin during the course of the day and behaved with a lethargy which was uncharacteristic of a man famous for his energy and activity. The cheerfulness which he had shown during his first day on board deserted him and it was observed that for much of the time he seemed abstracted and deep in thought. He usually appeared on deck around 5 o'clock in the afternoon when he would question the ship's officers about the wind and weather, and the ship's progress. Dinner was served at 6 pm and, although this was a formal occasion with excellent dishes of meat and fish served in the French style, it rarely lasted longer than twenty or twenty-five minutes because Napoleon did not like to spend time over meals. Maitland noted that he ate a great deal but restricted his drinking to a glass or two of claret.

After dinner on the second day the midshipmen were persuaded to stage a play. They had occasionally produced plays to relieve the tedium of the weeks spent on blockade duty and when Napoleon heard of this he requested a performance. He and his party were treated to a comedy called *The Poor Gentlemen*. Midshipman Home reported that 'The stage was fitted up between decks, more, I am afraid, in ship-shape than theatrical style.'[1] According to another participant, 'It went off very well, our scenery was excellent.'[2] Madame Bertrand sat next to Napoleon and translated for him and he was apparently much amused by the efforts of some of the larger midshipmen to squeeze into women's clothing and impersonate ladies.

From the moment they stepped on board the *Bellerophon* the senior members of Napoleon's suite had established a regime which, on a much smaller scale, reflected the regal atmosphere they were accustomed to in the great palaces in Paris. When Napoleon appeared on deck the men removed their hats, and kept at a respectful distance unless invited to walk with him. No one was allowed to enter his cabin unless given permission to do so and then they would be formally announced and ushered into his presence. No one spoke to him unless he initiated the conversation. He decided who should be invited to dine with him and where they should be seated. The *Bellerophon*'s officers, taking their cue from Captain Maitland and Admiral Hotham, likewise treated Napoleon as if he were still emperor. They too removed their hats in his presence and called him 'Sire' but it was a different kind of deference from that shown by his followers. For the British sailors he was the most famous person they would ever come into contact with and they fully appreciated this. 'We are all so much overjoyed at our good luck that we hardly know if we stand on our heads or our heel,' wrote Lieutenant Henry Smith to his brother, 'while as for my own part the whole business seems to be a dream, no ship in the British Navy has so much as this ship to boast of . . .'[3] For Smith and his companions Napoleon was the object of intense scrutiny and several members of the crew kept journals in which they carefully noted his appearance, his moods and his daily regime.

'Napoleon Bonaparte is about five feet seven inches high' wrote Lieutenant Bowerbank:

> rather corpulent, remarkably well-made. His hair is very black, cut close, whiskers shaved off; large eyebrows, grey eyes, the most piercing I ever saw; rather full face, dark but peculiar complexion, his nose and mouth proportionate, broad shoulders, and apparently strongly built. Upon the whole he is a good-looking man, and when young must have been handsome. He appears forty-five or forty-six, his real age – greatly resembles the different prints I have seen of him in London.

Bowerbank noted that his walk more resembled a march and that when walking he generally kept his hands in his pockets or folded behind his back.

Another officer, Clement Shorter, observed that he never saw Napoleon with his arms folded across his breast in the manner he was usually portrayed. 'His more common posture was his right hand stuck in the breast of his waistcoat, or thrust into his breeches pocket . . .'[4] Like everybody else, Lieutenant Smith was impressed by Napoleon's keen and penetrating eye – 'his eye is like a hawke's he never sees anything once but he recollects it again' – but he was surprised by the former emperor's easy manner. 'He is very affable and pleasing in his manners, he speaks to anyone he comes athwart and is always in a good humour, he bears his misfortunes with a great deal of fortitude which to me is astonishing.'[5]

At dawn on 23 July, a week after they had set sail from Basque Roads, they sighted the lighthouse on the Isle of Ushant. This was the westernmost point of France and the last chance for the French men and women on board the *Bellerophon* to see their country before the ship headed up the English Channel and made for Torbay. Whether Napoleon was alerted by a shout from the crew on deck, or had given instructions to his valet to wake him, is not clear, but he surprised the sailors by emerging on deck at 4 am. Midshipman

Home had just arrived for the morning watch when he saw Napoleon preparing to ascend the ladder to the poop deck. The decks were slippery because the men had begun to wash them down and so Home immediately went across and offered Napoleon his arm to prevent him falling. Napoleon smiled and pointed upwards, saying in broken English 'the poop, the poop'. He climbed the ladder, leaning on the midshipman's arm. When they reached the poop deck, he thanked Home and pointing to the distant land he said, 'Ushant? Cape Ushant?'

'Yes, Sire,' Home replied. Napoleon took his pocket-glass from his pocket and stared fixedly at the island and the coast beyond.[6] He remained there for the rest of the morning. He was joined by several members of his suite but he spoke to none of them and remained oblivious to anything else around him, his eyes fixed on the slowly receding coast of France. Sixty years later the British artist Sir William Quiller Orchardson painted a memorable picture of the scene on the deck of the *Bellerophon* that morning. As the ship and all the people portrayed in the painting were long gone when he began work on the painting, Orchardson made use of the published journals of Captain Maitland and some of the other officers. He exhibited the picture at the Royal Academy in 1880 where it was much admired and it subsequently established itself in British history books as a popular and enduring image of Napoleon. It has never found favour in France, showing as it does a dejected and defeated emperor in the hands of his enemies.

They passed several other British warships as they crossed the Channel and, towards evening they sighted the coast of England. When Captain Maitland went along to the after-cabin to inform Napoleon he found him in a flannel dressing gown, preparing to go to bed. On hearing the news, he put on his army greatcoat and came up on deck. It was a fine summer evening but it was cool out at sea, a steady breeze from the north-west filling the worn and salt-stained sails of the *Bellerophon*. Ahead of them the sails of the *Myrmidon* gleamed in the dying sunlight. Beyond her, clearly visible on the horizon, was the high ground of Dartmoor. Napoleon stared at the distant hills through his pocket telescope. He asked Captain Maitland how far they were from Torbay and when they would arrive. They were making a good 8 or 9 knots and Maitland reckoned they would reach their destination at dawn the next day.

They were joined on the poop deck by other members of Napoleon's entourage. It was an emotional time. Madame Bertrand burst into tears when she caught sight of the English coast. With three young children to look after, she was increasingly anxious about the future. She was aware that they might never set foot in France again and, although she had spent many years living in England, she was less optimistic about the reception they might expect than Napoleon himself. During the seven-day voyage from Rochefort he had frequently talked of settling down and living the life of a country gentleman among his former enemies. His companions were not so optimistic. Although Captain Maitland had been a generous and charming host during the past week, they were aware that he was under orders from superior officers and could have little or no influence on the decisions which would be made in London.

At dawn the next day, 24 July, the two warships were sailing along the coast off Dartmouth. Napoleon looked out of the stern windows of the *Bellerophon* and pointed out to his valet the charming houses nestling among the wooded bays and rocky inlets. He said he would be pleased to live in one of them in solitude. He would take the name of Muiron or Duroc, two soldiers who had lost their lives during his campaigns: Muiron had saved his life by covering his body with his own during the siege of Toulon; Duroc had been killed at his side by a cannon ball.

Around 5 am Napoleon emerged from the captain's cabin and joined the small group of officers standing on the poop deck. He was delighted with the boldness of the coast and pointed out to Captain Maitland that England, with her numerous safe harbours, enjoyed a great advantage over France which was surrounded by rocks and dangers. As they passed close under the commanding heights of Berry Head and turned into the sweeping curve of Torbay, he could scarcely contain his delight at the beauty of the scenery. He frequently exclaimed in French, 'What a beautiful country!' and told Maitland that Torbay reminded him of the Bay of Ferrajo in the island of Elba.

The two warships headed towards Brixham Harbour at the southern end of the bay. Apart from some local fishing boats the only other vessels at anchor were an armed brig and the 20-gun ship *Slaney* which had sailed on ahead of them, carrying General Gourgaud with Napoleon's letter to the Prince Regent, and Maitland's despatches for Admiral Lord Keith, the commander of the Channel fleet. As the *Bellerophon* prepared to anchor, a boat pushed off from the *Slaney* and headed towards her. An officer in the stern of the boat had a letter from Lord Keith with instructions for Maitland to remain in Torbay until further notice. He was 'most positively ordered to prevent every person whatever from coming on board the ship you command, except the officers and men who compose her crew.'[7]

It was around 8 am when the men on the *Bellerophon* and the *Myrmidon* received the order to anchor. The sailors high up on the yard-arms hauled up the sails and the heavy anchors of the two ships splashed into the calm waters less than half a mile from the water-front of Brixham. As the ships swung round with the tide, a few rowing boats headed out towards them, their occupants hoping to sell fresh bread, fruit and farm produce to the sailors on board.

In one of the boats was a local baker called Michelmore, his young apprentice, and three schoolboys: John Smart, Charlie Puddicombe and his younger brother Dick. John Smart later recorded his experiences of that memorable day.[8] He recalled that he would normally have been at school but, in common with many English schoolboys that summer, he had been given an extra week's holiday to celebrate Wellington's victory over Napoleon at the Battle of Waterloo. Earlier in the month the coach from Exeter had brought a copy of the *Gazette* to Brixham with lists of the 15,000 men in Wellington's army who had been killed or wounded. John and his friends were too young to realise the extent of the grief which the news of the battle had brought to so many mothers and sisters. Their concern today was how to spend the two half-crowns which John had just been given for his birthday.

The boys were standing on the quay at Brixham when they saw the two warships sail round Berry Head and enter the bay. They heard the distant sound of the boatswain's whistle and watched the

sails being furled and the anchors let go. John told Dick to run up
to the baker's shop and tell Michelmore and his wife that two King's
ships had come in and would be wanting bread. Just then they saw
a large gig pull away from the larger warship and head for the shore.
There were eight sailors at the oars and three officers sitting in the
stern. The coxswain of the gig brought it expertly alongside the
jetty and two of the officers jumped ashore, one of them carrying a
portmanteau. One of them was Andrew Mott, the *Bellerophon*'s first
lieutenant. The other was a tall man of about thirty-five with a cloak
on his arm. This was Lieutenant Fletcher from the *Superb*, Admiral
Hotham's flagship. John and his friends had no idea who the two
officers were but they realised they must be on urgent business
because they saw them hurry along the quayside to the London Inn
to arrange for transport. Within ten minutes the horses had been
harnessed on to the old yellow postchaise, the postboy mounted, and
Lieutenant Fletcher was on his way to London. The younger officer
strode back to the pierhead and, before the boys could ask what it
all meant, he had jumped into the stern of the gig and was being
rowed back to the anchored ship.

'Bean't he in a hurry, then?' said the old baker. 'Come, boys, let's
be off to the ship.' The five of them climbed into a rowing boat,
and shoved off from the shore. Charlie and his brother handled one
oar, the baker's apprentice the other, John sat up in the bow, and
Michelmore sat in the stern and steered. The baker had brought
with him a large sack containing fresh loaves of bread in the
expectation that he would receive a lot more orders when they
reached the warships. As they drew near the 74-gun ship they saw
that the shore boats had gathered together some way short of the
massive wooden sides of the vessel. There was a furious argument
going on between someone on board the ship and a man who was
standing up in one of the boats. Michelmore steered alongside and
asked what was going on.

'They won't let us come alongside, and they say as how they don't
want no shore boats at all,' was the reply. Michelmore was sure the
sailors would want some fresh bread so he let his boat drift forward.
The tide took them right under the stern until they were looking

up at the elaborately carved stern galleries, the elegant windows of the stern cabins, the rakishly angled lanterns and the huge union flag flapping to and fro in the breeze. Immediately above them on the poop deck they could see a marine sentry in scarlet uniform with a musket. An officer beside him leant over the rail and shouted, 'Sheer off. No boats allowed here.'

Michelmore refused to be put off. He caught hold of the sill of one of the lower deck gunports with his boat hook and shouted back, 'But I've brought you some bread.'

'If we want bread,' the officer replied, 'we'll come ashore and fetch it, and if you don't let go I'll sink you.' John was alarmed to see the sentry put down his musket and pick up a cannon ball. He leant over and held it exactly above the boy's head. He called the baker an old fool and swore that, unless he let go, he would sink the lot of them. John was greatly relieved when Michelmore pushed them clear of the ship's stern and allowed them to drift out of harm's way.

As they moved clear, one of the warship's boats pulled alongside them filled with a dozen men armed with cutlasses. The officer in the stern warned them to keep out of trouble as he had orders to keep off all shore boats. They retreated to where the other shore boats were gathered. Michelmore was indignant. 'Man and boy have I sailed on these here waters,' he said, 'and never have I been so treated.' None of them could understand what was going on because usually when a ship returned from abroad the crew was eager to communicate with the shore and exchange news.

Discouraged by their reception, the other shore boats departed one by one. Michelmore was inclined to follow them but the boys persuaded him to stay. They were on holiday and were reluctant to cut short their outing. They decided to circle round the ship at a safe distance. They headed out into the bay until they were some way ahead of the anchored vessel but the tide was still running strongly and they found themselves being swept back towards her bows and then closer to her sides than they intended. While his companions heaved on the oars, John stared at the rows of open gunports moving steadily past them. He suddenly noticed that at one of the lower ports a sailor was trying to attract his attention. He was nodding his head violently but had his finger to his lips in a warning gesture. Unfortunately the tide continued to sweep them backwards past the anchored vessel and out of sight of the sailor. Greatly excited, John encouraged Michelmore to turn back. They once again circled the ship and when the guard boat was at a safe distance, they again approached the bows. The sailor was standing back in the shadows but his hand was clearly visible on the sill of the gunport. As they passed he let something fall from his fingers. Anxious not to attract attention, they waited until the object had drifted a hundred yards clear of the ship before rowing towards it. John had his hand dragging carelessly in the water until they were close enough for him to grab it.

The object proved to be a small black bottle. They were now acutely aware that any communication between the ship and the shore was strictly forbidden so John was too frightened at first to look at his prize in case they were being watched by someone on board with a telescope. However, they were too curious to wait until they reached the shore. Making sure that the baker's ample body hid him from sight, John examined the bottle more closely. 'It was a foreign-looking bottle, and as I drew the cork, its oiliness and perfume suggested that it had been used for some liqueur. I kept that bottle for a few years, but even now, without it, I can recall its shape and size and smell.'

Inside the bottle there was a small piece of paper rolled up. On the paper was written, 'We have got Bonaparte on board.' It is difficult for us today to realise what those words must have meant. Even before his escape from Elba and the events leading up to the Battle of Waterloo, Napoleon was, without doubt, the most famous person in the western world. To the boys in the boat on that bright summer day, hearing that Napoleon had arrived in Torbay was like hearing that a man had landed from the moon. Bursting with their news, they rowed full tilt back to the shore and within minutes the word had spread around Brixham. A crowd gathered on the waterfront and any boat that could be sailed or rowed was commandeered and pushed out into the harbour. Soon the *Bellerophon* was surrounded by vessels of all sizes and the cries of 'Bonaparte' warned those on board that the secret was out. The guard boat continued to prevent any vessel coming alongside but no attempt was made to hide the famous passenger and his companions. At first Napoleon was seen at the stern windows and then, around 3 pm, he came on deck where he viewed the crowds through his pocket-glass.

John Smart was surprised at how small the former emperor looked and thought he was rather fat. He noted that he wore a green uniform with red facings, gold epaulettes, white waistcoat and breeches and high military boots. 'He took off his hat which had a cockade on it and bowed to the people, who took off their hats and shouted "Hooray!" I recall a feeling of triumph mixed with a natural satisfaction at seeing a wonderful sight.'

Lieutenant Fletcher, the naval officer who had dashed off to London in the postchaise, only held his tongue until he got to Exeter, because that evening a number of carts and postchaises arrived from that city crammed with curious sightseers. During the course of the next day a great number of boats and yachts arrived from Torquay, Paignton, Dartmouth, and further afield. Every inn in Brixham was full and there was no room left for visitors or any stabling for horses. There was a gala atmosphere and an extraordinary sense of excitement in the town. A correspondent to *The Times* recorded his impressions:

> This day, July 25, proved a most gratifying one indeed to me; I have seen Buonaparte for nearly two hours. A few friends took a pilot boat and went into Torbay; we anchored near the Bellerophon, amidst thousands of boats, etc. Buonaparte repeatedly appeared at a cabin window, which was wide open; he appears rather stout, very full in the face, but very stern and thoughtful in his manner. The Captain of the ship was his only companion.

According to Lieutenant Bowerbank, Napoleon appeared pleased with the eagerness of the crowd to see him, and remarked, 'How very curious these English are.' He was also much taken by the beauty of the women among the onlookers. He kept repeating, 'What charming girls! What beautiful women!' and bowed to them as they

waved and smiled up at him.[9] Captain Maitland was besieged with
applications from people wishing to come on board. Among them
was a note from a lady which was accompanied by a basket of fruit.
She requested that a boat might be sent for her the next morning.
Maitland sent her a civil answer but informed her that his instructions would not allow him to comply with her request. He noted that
'no more fruit was sent from that quarter'.

At 3 am on 26 July, less than two days after their arrival in Torbay,
a boat rowed out to the *Bellerophon* with orders that she was to
proceed immediately to Plymouth. The politicians in London were
extremely concerned that Napoleon might escape while they were
debating what to do with him. Torbay was exposed to easterly winds
and although Plymouth had the disadvantage of being heavily
populated, and likely to attract even bigger crowds than Torbay, it
had a sheltered anchorage. Furthermore the presence of the naval
base, the flagship of Admiral Keith and many other warships made
it much easier to prevent any attempt to rescue Napoleon. It was
still dark when the *Bellerophon* weighed anchor and began working
her way out of the bay in company with the frigates *Myrmidon* and
Slaney. By 8 am they were off Bolt Head and heading due west. There
was a clear blue sky but a gusty, northerly breeze had stirred up a
choppy sea, sending clouds of white spray flying in the air as the
bows of the three ships dipped into the waves.

Napoleon remained on deck for most of the passage, silently
observing the rocky coastline of Devon. As they headed into
Plymouth Sound, Captain Maitland drew his attention to the
breakwater which was being constructed in the middle of the Sound.
Napoleon thought it a great national undertaking and was surprised
to learn that it was expected to be completed for less than a million
pounds.

'I have expended a large sum of money on the port of Cherbourg,'
he said, but he believed that this and similar projects would now be
neglected and allowed to go to ruin.

They dropped anchor around 4 pm and Maitland immediately set
off to report to Admiral Lord Keith, the commanding officer of the
Channel fleet. His flagship, the *Ville de Paris*, was anchored in

Hamoaze, the stretch of water in the inner harbour of Plymouth which runs past the naval dockyard. During the next two weeks Keith was the principal intermediary between the British Government and Napoleon. He was nearly seventy, a big man, with more than twenty years' experience as an admiral and an able administrator. He had made a fortune from prize money while commanding ships in the Far East and the Mediterranean, and between 1803 and 1814 he had held the key posts of commander-in-chief of the North Sea fleet and then of the Channel fleet. He congratulated Maitland on his successful blockade and on taking Napoleon onto his ship. He was keen to meet the former emperor but said that he could not do so until he had received instructions as to how he was to be treated. In the meanwhile he emphasised that nobody must be allowed to board the *Bellerophon* without his written permission. He told Maitland that he had just ordered the frigates *Liffey* and *Eurotas* to mount guard in the immediate vicinity. His detailed instructions to the captains of these vessels reflect the concern felt by the politicians in London that Napoleon must be closely guarded and isolated from any attempt to communicate with him:

The *Liffey* and *Eurotas* are to take up an anchorage on each side of the *Bellerophon* at a convenient distance, and observe the following directions, as well for the prevention of the escape of Bonaparte or any of his suite from that ship, as for restraining shore-boats and others from approaching too close to her, either from curiosity or from any other motive.

A constant watch of an officer, a quarter-watch, and double sentinels are to be kept by day, as well as a boat manned and armed alongside in constant readiness as a guard boat. The same precaution is to be observed all night, with the exception that one of the boats in charge of a lieutenant is to row guard and to be relieved every hour.

No shore boats, or others, are to be suffered either by night or by day to approach nearer the *Bellerophon* than one cable's length; and no boats are to be permitted to loiter about the ship even at that distance, either from curiosity or any other motive. Neither the captains of the *Liffey* nor *Eurotas*, nor any other officer belonging to those or any other ships, are to go on board the Bellerophon either to visit or on any pretence whatever without permission from me in writing.[10]

When Maitland returned to his ship he found that the frigates had already taken up their positions and the men in the guard boats were firing their muskets in an attempt to keep at bay the increasing numbers of boats crowded with sightseers. These measures greatly disturbed Napoleon and his followers and seemed to confirm the ominous reports they had seen in the British newspapers over the past few days. The courtesy and respect shown to them by Captain Maitland and Admiral Hotham had led them to believe that they would be given asylum in England. Napoleon had even talked of receiving the Order of the Garter from the Prince Regent. It was rapidly dawning on them that they were prisoners and not honoured guests. Worse still, it was being suggested in the newspapers that Napoleon would be sent to St Helena, a remote island in the South Atlantic.

Until now the French party on the *Bellerophon* had discounted some of the more savage newspaper reports. On 25 July, for instance, *The Times* had referred to 'the capture of that bloody miscreant who has so long tortured Europe' and had published a letter from a particularly hardline correspondent who signed himself 'Probus'. The writer, who undoubtedly represented the views of many British people, thought that Napoleon should be brought to trial and public execution, because, 'He has, for a long succession of years, deluged Europe in blood, to gratify his own mad vanity, his insatiable and furious ambition. It is calculated that every minute he has reigned has cost the life of a human being.' A softer line had been taken by the *Courier* which, in its issue of 21 July, had pointed out that Napoleon had voluntarily surrendered himself as a prisoner of war into the hands of the Prince Regent, and the law of nations prescribed that 'as soon as your enemy has laid down his arms and surrendered his person, you have no longer any right over his life.' However, the paper declared that now that he was in the safe custody of a British warship steps must be taken to ensure that 'he shall not be able to disturb again the repose and security of the world'.

A view of the town and harbour of Halifax, Nova Scotia, from *The Atlantic Neptune*, 1781, by J.Des Barres. The *Bellerophon* spent a month at this British naval base in September 1802.

British ships off the south coast of Jamaica in 1793, by George Tobin. The *Bellerophon* sailed into Port Royal, Jamaica, in April 1802 and spent two years patrolling the western Caribbean as part of the Jamaica Squadron.

Sketch for the Battle of Trafalgar, October 21, 1805, by Clarkson Stanfield. The action is shown at 2.30p.m. when the battle was at its height. Nelson's flagship, the *Victory*, is shown centre right with the sun illuminating her bows.

A photograph of 24-pounder guns on the middle gun deck of the *Victory*, a three-decker of 100 guns. The gun deck of the *Bellerophon* would have looked very similar to this when the ship was cleared for action.

The Fall of Nelson at the Battle of Trafalgar, by Denis Dighton. This shows the scene on the deck of the Victory around 1.15 p.m. with two red-coated marines going to the aid of Nelson who lies fatally wounded by a musket ball.

The Victory *Towed into Gibraltar*, by Clarkson Stanfield. A heavy sea is still running as the much damaged flagship is towed into Gibraltar Bay by the *Neptune* a week after the Battle of Trafalgar. The *Bellerophon* had arrived the previous day.

The wooden figure of a lieutenant in full dress uniform used as a shop sign outside a London shop selling charts and navigation instruments. The figure was familiar to Dickens who introduced him into his novel *Dombey and Sons*.

The Accommodation Ladder, by Thomas Rowlandson, c.1810. The Portsmouth lady has a ribbon in her hat with Nelson's famous signal 'England expects that every man will do his duty.' Around her waist she has a belt incribed 'Belly Rough One' and the officer climbing aboard has a sash inscribed 'Death or Victory', a reference to the words chalked on the *Bellerophon's* guns as she went into action at Trafalgar.

Portsmouth, by J.M.W. Turner, seen from the anchorage at Spithead. In the foreground an officer is being rowed ashore from a ship at anchor, and in the distance can be seen the narrow entrance of Portsmouth harbour guarded by forts on either side.

Napoleon on the Bellerophon, by Sir William Quiller Orchardson. Napoleon stares at the receding coast of France while his followers watch at a respectful distance. From left to right his followers are: Planat, Montholon, Maingaut, Las Cases (in civilian clothes), Savary, Lallemand and Bertrand. The boy leaning on the rail is the son of Las Cases.

The *Bellerophon* returning to Torbay from Plymouth to meet up with the *Northumberland* which will take Napoleon and his entourage to St Helena. A lively rendering of the scene by the distinguished marine artist Thomas Luny who lived locally.

The Bellerophon *in Plymouth Sound in August 1815*, by John James Chalon. The *Bellerophon* is in the centre background with the frigates *Liffey* and *Eurotas* anchored nearby. According to the artist, 'The time is six-thirty in the evening when Napoleon usually made his appearance.'

Sheerness as Seen from the Nore, 1808, by J.M.W. Turner. The dockyard and town of Sheerness can be seen in the distance on the right. The warship on the left is the Nore guardship and is probably the *Sandwich* of 90 guns.

The Fighting Temeraire *Tugged to Her Last Berth to Be Broken Up*, 1838, by J.M.W. Turner. The evidence suggests that the *Bellerophon* was also towed up the Thames to Rotherhithe to be broken up by the same firm that broke up the *Temeraire*.

The correspondent 'Probus' evidently had connections to someone in Whitehall because on 27 July *The Times* published another letter from him in which he wrote, 'It is said, this monster is to be sent to St Helena, and there to be guarded by an English regiment.' This was, of course, an accurate forecast but for several weeks the politicians had been undecided on the best course to take. The key players in deciding Napoleon's fate were Lord Liverpool, the Prime Minister; Lord Castlereagh, the Foreign Secretary; Lord Bathurst, the Secretary of State for War and the Colonies; Lord Melville, the First Lord of the Admiralty; and John Barrow, the civil servant who was the Permanent Secretary of the Board of Admiralty. The Duke of Wellington, who was in Paris during the course of the discussions, played no part in the final decision. He had strongly resisted the demands of the Prussians who wanted to execute Napoleon, and, according to Lady Shelley who met him at a party in Paris, he thought that 'Bonaparte ought to be shut up at Fort St George, as, by the laws, his life cannot be forfeited.'[11]

Lord Liverpool had originally been of the opinion that the best course would be to deliver Napoleon up to King Louis XVII of France but by 15 July he had decided that it was more appropriate that the British should take responsibility for him. In a letter to Castlereagh, who was in Paris, he wrote:

> we should be at liberty to fix the place of his confinement, either in Great Britain, or at Gibraltar, Malta, St Helena, the Cape of Good Hope, or any other colony we might think most secure. We incline at present strongly to the opinion that the best place of custody would be at a distance from Europe, and that the Cape of Good Hope or St Helena would be the most proper stations for the purpose.[12]

Other possible places mentioned in the newspapers were Dumbarton Castle in Scotland and the Tower of London. By 21 July, when news of Napoleon's surrender to Captain Maitland had reached London, Lord Liverpool had decided that it would be a mistake to confine Napoleon in Britain: embarrassing legal questions might arise; he would become an object of curiosity or even of compassion;

and his presence might stir up ferment in France. He sent another
letter to Castlereagh setting out the latest thinking:

> Since I wrote to you last, Lord Melville and myself have conversed with
> Mr Barrow on the subject, and he decidedly recommends St Helena as
> the place in the world the best calculated for the confinement of such a
> person . . . The situation is particularly healthy. There is only one place
> in the circuit of the island where ships can anchor, and we have the power
> of excluding neutral vessels altogether, if we should think it necessary.
> At such a distance and in such a place, all intrigue would be impossible;
> and, being withdrawn so far from the European world, he would very
> soon be forgotten.[13]

On 27 July, the day after the *Bellerophon*'s arrival in Plymouth, the
weather was hot and sunny with the lightest of breezes. It was a
perfect day for hiring a boat and by midday the waters of the Sound
were a colourful and jostling mass of yachts, local fishing vessels and
every rowing boat available. Lieutenant Bowerbank estimated there
were ten thousand people gathered around the ship, a number
confirmed by Maitland who reckoned there were at least a thousand
vessels, each carrying more than eight people. Most noticeable were
the large numbers of pretty young women and fashionable ladies
dressed in their Sunday best, but there were also many naval officers,
red-coated army officers, and smartly attired gentlemen who took off
their hats respectfully when Napoleon showed himself – as he did
before and after having his dinner at 6 pm. He seemed astonished by
the crowds and, as in Torbay, was impressed by the beauty of the
women. Among the sightseers was Captain Maitland's wife who came
alongside the *Bellerophon* in a boat with Sir Richard and Lady Strachan.
Napoleon went to the gangway, removed his hat, and asked her if she
would come up and visit him but she shook her head. Maitland told
him that his orders were so strict that he could not allow even her
on board.

'That is very hard,' Napoleon said. 'Milord Keith is a little too
severe, is he not, Madame?' and, turning to Maitland, he told him
that she was much prettier than the portrait he had seen of her.

When Maitland told him that Strachan was second in command of the Channel fleet he remarked that he seemed a very young man to hold so high a rank.

At 11 o'clock the next day Admiral Keith paid a visit to Napoleon but it was an unsatisfactory meeting. Keith had recently been informed that Napoleon must be treated as a general and not as a former head of state. He had also learnt that the politicians had finally decided on St Helena, but he was not yet at liberty to reveal this. Napoleon hoped for much from a meeting with such a high-ranking officer, especially as he had received a friendly letter from Keith thanking him for saving the life of his nephew who had been gravely wounded and taken prisoner in the skirmishes before the Battle of Waterloo. Napoleon had arranged for a surgeon to treat his wounds.[14] Keith later reported that they talked on many subjects – Toulon, Egypt and the East Indies – but he could give no satisfactory answers to Napoleon's questions. He could not allow him to walk on shore, even with officers attending him. He could not tell him what was to become of him or when his fate was to be determined.

That afternoon several transport ships entered Plymouth Sound and passed close to the *Bellerophon*. They were carrying French prisoners who had been taken at Waterloo, many of them wounded and bandaged. It was a depressing sight for the members of Napoleon's party who were on deck at the time and must have seemed a bad omen for what was soon to come.

On 31 July Admiral Keith returned to the *Bellerophon* bearing the news that they were dreading. He was accompanied by Major-General Sir Henry Bunbury who had arrived from London the previous day. Bunbury was Under-Secretary of State for War and he had with him a letter which set out the decision of the British Government. In the after-cabin of the ship Bunbury translated and read out the letter to Napoleon:

It would be inconsistent with our duty to this country, and to His Majesty's Allies, if we were to leave to General Bonaparte the means or opportunity of again disturbing the peace of Europe, and renewing the calamities of war: it is therefore unavoidable that he should be restrained

in his personal liberty to whatever extent may be necessary to secure
our first and paramount object.

The island of St Helena has been selected for his future residence. The
climate is healthy, and its local situation will admit of his being treated
with more indulgence than would be compatible with adequate security
elsewhere.[15]

The letter went on to say that Napoleon would be allowed to take
with him three officers, his surgeon, and twelve domestics or servants.
Rear-Admiral Sir George Cockburn would be conveying them to St
Helena and would be ready to embark within a few days. 'It is
therefore desirable that General Bonaparte should make without
delay the selection of the persons who are to accompany him.'

Napoleon listened carefully without interrupting and did not
appear surprised by the contents of the letter. When asked whether
he wished to have a written translation made he said there was no
need because he had understood perfectly what had been said. He
was handed the letter and laid it on the table. After a pause he
launched into a passionate and eloquent protest. The British
Government had no right to dispose of him in this manner, he said,
and he now appealed to the British people and the laws of the country
against its decision.

'I am come here voluntarily to throw myself on the hospitality of
your nation, and to claim the rights of hospitality. I am not a prisoner
of war. If I were a prisoner of war, you would be obliged to treat me
according to the law of nations. But I am come to this country a
passenger on board one of your ships of war, after a previous negoti-
ation with the commander.' It was a snare which had been set for him.
And as for the island of St Helena, it would be his death sentence.

'What am I to do on this little rock at the end of the world? The
climate is too hot for me. No, I will not go to St Helena; Botany Bay
is better than St Helena. If your Government wishes to put me to
death, they may kill me here.' He demanded to be received as an
English citizen. 'What danger could result from my living as a private
person in the heart of England under surveillance, and restricted in
any way the Government might imagine necessary?'[16] He reminded

them that he had been an emperor who had stood among the sovereigns of Europe and the British Government had no right to treat him as a mere general.

When Admiral Keith and Sir Henry Bunbury left the ship Napoleon sent for Captain Maitland. He showed him the letter which he had been given and angrily protested at the decision to send him to St Helena. 'To be placed for life on an island within the Tropics, at an immense distance from any land, cut off from all communication with the world, and every thing that I hold dear in it!' He would prefer to be delivered up to the Bourbons, or confined in the Tower of London. But within a few hours his anger had evaporated. He appeared on deck as usual that evening to show himself to the crowds, and astonished Maitland by his cheerfulness at dinner. However his companions were less able to contain their feelings.

The letter read out by Bunbury had specifically mentioned that General Lallemand and General Savary would not be allowed to accompany Napoleon to St Helena. This must mean that they would be returned to France where they would almost certainly be executed as traitors. They protested strongly to Captain Maitland. He had frequently assured them that their lives would be safe in British hands and Maitland now felt that his word and his honour were at stake. That evening he wrote a personal letter to Lord Melville on their behalf which concluded, 'I most earnestly beg your Lordship's influence may be exerted that two men may not be brought to the scaffold who claimed and obtained at my hands the protection of the British flag.'[17] Melville was not too pleased with the letter but in the end Savary and Lallemand were deported to Malta, then a British possession.

Other members of the French party were equally distressed but the most dramatic protest was made by Madame Bertrand. Like Napoleon she had fondly expected to be able to settle in England where she hoped to resume the place in society to which she was accustomed. It was evident that her husband, who was the highest-ranking and most devoted of all Napoleon's followers, would go with him to St Helena, a prospect which appalled her. Before Admiral Keith had left the *Bellerophon* she had accosted him with her fears:

'My husband is so weak as to be attached to that man, and he will go with him. I have three children. My health is bad; I shall never reach the island. We have no money. If I stay behind, I must starve. Besides, to leave my husband would kill me.'[18]

Around 9 pm that evening, after Napoleon had retired to his cabin, Lieutenant Bowerbank was on watch when he observed Madame Bertrand walking with her husband on deck and pleading with him not to accompany Napoleon into exile. When he refused her entreaties she suddenly broke away from him, and ran to Napoleon's cabin where she threw herself at his feet and said, 'Sire, do not go to St Helena. Do not take my husband!'

Napoleon, who had been listening to Las Cases translating the latest newspapers, regarded her in astonishment. 'But Madame, I am not forcing Bertrand to go with me,' he said. 'He is entirely free.'

Madame Bertrand then rushed into the ward room where the ship's officers and their French guests were gathered as usual for an evening drink of wine and hot punch.[19] Maitland invited her to sit down and join them but she refused and disappeared into the first lieutenant's cabin which she had been using during her stay on the ship. Montholon had noticed how distraught she was and followed her. He found her attempting to throw herself into the sea. She gave a loud shriek as she forced herself out of the quarter gallery window. Montholon caught hold of her legs and shouted for help. Someone shouted 'The Countess is overboard' and Maitland ran up on deck to alert the crew and lower a boat. He could see no sign of her in the water and, returning to the ward room, he found that she had been laid on her bed and was in a hysterical state. In his words she was 'abusing the English nation and its Government, in the most vehement and unmeasured terms; sometimes in French and sometimes in English.' In discussing her dramatic action later, most of the party, including Napoleon, seemed to think it was a protest gesture and not a genuine suicide attempt. But Montholon told Maitland that he had no doubt she would have fallen in the sea if he had not caught hold of her because he found her with most of her body outside the ship and only held by the protecting bar across the window.

The next week was a difficult one for all concerned. For much of the time Napoleon remained in his cabin and when he did appear he was pale, despondent, ill-looking and unshaven. He was heard pacing his cabin for much of each night and a rumour went around the ship that he was contemplating suicide. Madame Bertrand recovered but continued to besiege Maitland with protests about the British Government's decision, as did all the senior French officers except General Bertrand. Admiral Keith was having to field a succession of orders from London and was became increasingly concerned by the crowds which had descended on Plymouth Sound. 'The concourse of people to this place is beyond all imagination,' he wrote to Melville. 'The taverns are full and the sea covered with boats. Yesterday they pressed so much on the ship as to touch the side in defiance of the Guard Boats.' And he told his daughter, 'I am miserable with all the idle people in England coming to see this man.'[20] Even the crew of the *Bellerophon,* who had initially enjoyed being at the centre of such a great event, were losing patience. It was a long time since they had seen their families and they were beginning to feel they were as much prisoners as the French men and women because of the strict requirements that there must be no communication with the shore.

Meanwhile there were problems with the ship which was to take Napoleon to St Helena. The Admiralty had decided that the 29-year-old *Bellerophon* was not up to the 5,000-mile voyage to the South Atlantic and had selected the 74-gun ship *Northumberland* to take her place. The *Northumberland* had been built at Deptford and launched in 1798. By a curious irony of history she was not a British design but was based on the lines of one of the six French ships captured at the Battle of the Glorious First of June.[21] She had sailed round from the Medway to Spithead and was being loaded up with the stores for the voyage when some of her crew began objecting to being sent to St Helena. Twenty-four of them deserted the ship and her commander, Captain Ross, had to use the threat of armed troops and marines to avert a mutiny.

In London the authorities had their own concerns. They were worried about a legal challenge being mounted to their decision to exile Napoleon. (There was talk of a writ of Habeas Corpus being served.) They were worried about the crowds besieging the *Bellerophon*, and the possibility of Napoleon escaping. And they were worried by the massive publicity which Napoleon was attracting and the rabble-rousing tone of the articles in some of the newspapers.

On 3 August the Admiralty sent an order marked 'secret and confidential' to Admiral Keith. The *Bellerophon* and escorting frigates, together with the 80-gun ship *Tonnant*, must put to sea at once and take up a position off Start Point. They must remain there until the *Northumberland* arrived and the transfer of Napoleon and his suite could take place. If the weather proved unfavourable for a transfer off Start Point they must move to Torbay.

The *Bellerophon* weighed anchor at 9.30 am on 4 August. It was another fine, sunny day but the light, southerly breeze and incoming tide made it necessary for her to be towed from the anchorage by the guard boats. As they headed slowly out of Plymouth Sound, Maitland became suspicious of a rowing boat with a man in the stern which was intent on intercepting them. He ordered one of the guard boats to prevent the boat from approaching and he later learnt that there was a lawyer in the boat who had a subpoena for Napoleon. Once clear of the breakwater they set sail and beat slowly out to sea with the frigate *Eurotas* in company. Off Rame Head they joined the *Prometheus* which was waiting for them with Admiral Keith on board. He sent a boat across with a message for Maitland: 'I have been chased all day by a lawyer with a Habeas Corpus: he landed at Cawsand and may come off in a sailing-boat during the night; of course, keep all sorts of boats off, as I will do the like in whatever ship I may be in.'[22]

During the afternoon Keith transferred his flag to the *Tonnant* and that evening the flagship, accompanied by the *Bellerophon*, the *Eurotas*, the *Myrmidon* and the cutter *Nimble*, headed east along the coast to Start Point. Some of Napoleon's followers were encouraged by the unexpected move, thinking that the government might have had a change of heart about St Helena. Napoleon, however, became increasingly depressed. He no longer appeared on deck but remained shut in his cabin. His valet took his meals in to him and he spent most of his time with Bertrand and Las Cases. Madame Bertrand said that his legs had swelled up due to lack of exercise. Las Cases later reported that at one stage Napoleon talked about ending his life but was persuaded that he should accept his misfortunes in the spirit of the heroes of antiquity.

'But what can we do in that desolate place?' he asked Las Cases.

'We will live in the past, sire; there is plenty there to satisfy us. Do we not enjoy the lives of Caesar and Alexander? Better still, you will re-read your own writings, sire.'

'Very well, we will write our memoirs! Yes, one must work; work is Time's scythe. After all one must fulfil one's destiny; that is my chief doctrine.'[23]

For two days the ships waited in a loose formation off the coast between Start Point and Bolt Head. The fine weather gave way to misty, overcast conditions with occasional showers of rain. The grey sea under the louring, grey sky seemed to reflect the air of gloom which had settled over the passengers on the *Bellerophon*. At last, at 9 am on Sunday 6 August, the *Northumberland* appeared on the eastern horizon, accompanied by the troopships *Bucephalus* and *Ceylon*. The wind had been increasing since dawn and Keith decided that they must seek a more sheltered position for the rendezvous, so he ordered the flotilla under his command to sail to Torbay where they anchored to the westward of Berry Head. The *Northumberland* anchored nearby. As yet Napoleon had refused to make a decision on who should accompany him to St Helena but he now produced a list which was handed to Sir George Cockburn when he came aboard. The list included General Bertrand, his wife, and their three children; General Montholon, his wife and one child; Count Las Cases and his son; General Gourgaud; Napoleon's valet Marchand; a cook, a butler and eleven servants. That evening Napoleon had a meeting with Captain Maitland and once again made a formal protest against his treatment by the British Government which was very different from what he had hoped for and expected.

'My only wish,' he said, 'was to purchase a small property in England, and end my life there in peace and tranquillity. As for you, Capitaine, I have no cause for complaint; your conduct to me has been that of a man of honour; but I cannot help feeling the severity of my fate, in having to pass the remainder of my life on a desert island.'[24]

The atmosphere at breakfast on 7 August was subdued and tense. Maitland and Bertrand were preoccupied with all the arrangements for the transfer of people and luggage to the *Northumberland*. Madame Bertrand again pleaded with her husband not to accompany Napoleon and when he remained silent she launched into an attack on the British which provoked an uncharacteristically sharp response from Maitland.

'Madame, you talk like a very foolish woman; and if you cannot speak more to the purpose or with more respect of the Government I have the honour to serve, I request you will not address yourself to me.'[25]

After breakfast Maitland was called in to see Napoleon. It was the last conversation they were to have alone. Napoleon thanked him once again for his kindness, and asked his opinion of the *Bellerophon*'s surgeon Barry O'Meara who had volunteered to go to St Helena in place of his French surgeon. Maitland warmly recommended O'Meara who had served with him for many years.[26] Later in the morning Montholon came to see Maitland to tell him that Napoleon particularly regretted not having been permitted an interview with the Prince Regent because he had intended to ask him as a favour to promote Maitland to the rank of Rear-Admiral.

By mid-morning the children and the servants who were to go to St Helena had been taken across to the *Northumberland*, together with several boatloads of luggage and personal effects. The entire ship's company of the *Bellerophon* had assembled on deck. Admiral Keith and Sir George Cockburn had been piped aboard and were waiting outside the cabin where Napoleon had been closeted with Bertrand since breakfast. Cockburn became impatient and wanted to remind Napoleon that they were all waiting but Keith restrained him. 'Much greater men than either you or I have waited longer for him before now. Let him take his time; let him take his time.'

There were emotional scenes when Napoleon came to say goodbye to those of his followers who were staying behind. Tears were shed as they embraced but Napoleon himself remained calm and dry-eyed.

'Be happy, friends,' he told them. 'We shall never see each other again, but my thoughts will never leave you nor any of those who have served me. Tell France that I pray for her.'[27]

Napoleon being transferred from the *Bellerophon*, which can be seen
in the background, to the *Northumberland*, the 74-gun ship
which conveyed him and his followers to St Helena

When Napoleon eventually left the after-cabin and stepped out on
deck, he was greeted by total silence. He had not been seen by most
of the crew for four days and they were shocked by the change in
his appearance. He was unshaven, his face was pale and drawn, and
his clothes appeared ill-fitting. Bowerbank thought he looked
confused. As he crossed the quarterdeck the marines presented arms
to the accompaniment of three drum rolls, the salute due to a general.
He raised his hat in acknowledgement, went up to Maitland and
again thanked him. Turning to the ship's officers he said, 'Gentlemen,
I have requested your captain to express my gratitude to you for
your attention to me and to those who have followed my fortunes.'

He walked to the gangway, paused and turned to face the dense
crowd of sailors gathered on the deck. He took off his hat again, and
solemnly bowed two or three times before climbing down into the
waiting barge. He was followed by the French men and women who
would be going with him to St Helena. As the barge headed towards
the *Northumberland* the entire crew of the *Bellerophon* lined the rails

to watch. Napoleon had been on the ship for twenty-four days and had made an indelible impression on all of them. Maitland was impressed by the mood of the men and asked his servant what the sailors thought of Napoleon.

'Why, sir,' he said, 'I heard several of them conversing together about him this morning; when one of them observed, "Well, they may abuse that man as much as they please; but if the people of England knew him as well as we do, they would not hurt a hair of his head" in which the others agreed.'[28] It was a sentiment Maitland understood perfectly. When he came to write his own account of Napoleon's surrender and the subsequent events he noted that the man possessed, to a wonderful degree, the facility for making a favourable impression upon those with whom he entered into conversation. Admiral Keith had been equally impressed and thought he would have charmed the Prince Regent.

'Damn the fellow,' he said, 'if he had obtained an interview with his Royal Highness, in half an hour they would have been the best of friends in England.'[29]

That evening the *Bellerophon* and the *Tonnant* got under way and headed back to Plymouth. An hour later the *Northumberland* weighed anchor and three days later she set sail down the Channel at the head of a convoy which included the frigate *Havannah*, two troopships filled with soldiers and seven armed brigs loaded with stores.

Three weeks after Napoleon vanished into exile over the horizon, the *Bellerophon* received orders which were to consign her to an exile as humiliating for a great ship as St Helena was for the former emperor. Her exile was to take place, not in a remote island, but on the river where she had been built and launched, and had spent the early years of her life. On Friday 1 September she anchored at the mouth of the River Medway and the next day she moored alongside the dockyard at Sheerness. Over the next two weeks the crew stripped her of everything that had made her a warship. The guns were removed; and the stores of the bosun, the cook, the carpenter, the gunner, and the sailmaker were taken out. The rigging was dismantled, and the masts and bowsprit lifted out by the sheer hulk. Out too came the the barrels of food and water, the coal for the galley, and several tons of shingle ballast. The last job of the crew was to scrub the hammocks and wash down the decks.

Wednesday 13 September was a bright and sunny autumn day with scarcely a breath of wind. At 11 o'clock the Pay Captain from the dockyard came aboard and paid the sailors of the ship's company. The marines had already been discharged to the barracks in Chatham. Midshipman Home provides a vivid picture of the departure of the ship's company in an atmosphere reminiscent of the last day of school. It was, he says, a glorious scene of confusion as the men collected their pay and left the ship, some blessing and some cursing their officers as they went. People were shaking hands and saying goodbye to their messmates, and wishing them a safe passage home. Midshipman Home wanted to tell Captain Maitland how kind he had been to him but when he got to the quarterdeck his words of thanks stuck in his throat and all he was able to say was, 'Fare you well, Captain Maitland!'

'Fare you well,' the Captain responded cheerfully. 'I cannot offer you a ship just now, but should I get a command again, which I am afraid will not be soon, you have only to show your face, and you shall have what vacancy I can give you. I wish you well.'[30]

Home wasted no more time on board the ship. He took up the chest which held all his belongings and climbed down to a vessel which was waiting alongside ready to take people upstream to Limehouse and Wapping. There were some sixty men from the lower deck in the vessel but he was not worried about receiving any insults because he knew he had never treated any of them severely. He observed that the *Bellerophon*, stripped of her masts, rigging, guns and ballast, had become 'a mere hull, with an empty bottle hung at her figurehead, to show that the grog was out'.

The only sign that the ship was still a naval vessel was the long commissioning pennant which normally flew at the mainmast but which now hung limply from the flagpole at the stern. That evening Captain Maitland made a final entry in the ship's log-book. He concluded with the words: 'Sunset, haul down the pendant.' And underneath he signed his name 'Fred. L. Maitland, Captain.' The *Bellerophon* had ended her life as a ship of the line.

EIGHTEEN

A Hulk on the Medway

1815–36

During the first two weeks of January 1817 the southern counties of England were deluged by rain. In Kent the marshes surrounding the cathedral city of Canterbury were constantly flooded, and so high was the water level on the tributaries of the River Stour that the water-mills were prevented from working. The River Medway overflowed its banks at Maidstone and Yalding and the lower reaches of the river took on the appearance of the sea. Sheerness, perched at one end of the Isle of Sheppey, seemed more isolated than ever. The forts, the dockyard, and the houses huddled behind them, were almost marooned. On three sides were the swirling grey waters of the Thames and the Medway, and much of the marshland to the east of the town was under water.

A line of warships was anchored in this desolate, watery landscape, and beyond them, swinging from massive chains anchored to the riverbed, were two misshapen hulks. From a distance they seemed like vast and crudely built houseboats. Their massive hulls floated too high in the water. Their upper decks were hidden beneath overhanging wooden sheds with low pitched roofs and smoking chimneys. A naval man would have seen, from their size and the number of their gunports, that they had once been 74-gun ships, but they had little else in common with the ships which Nelson had led into battle. Instead of towering masts and taut lines of rigging, the hulks had two stumpy poles from which were hung clotheslines filled with flapping shirts. The curving sides of the hulks were disfigured by heavy wooden battens, nailed on to give protection against barges and other vessels bumping alongside. The gunports no longer revealed gleaming black gun barrels waiting to be run out, but were barred by iron grilles. Behind the bars in each ship were more than 400 convicts, condemned to several years' hard labour before being transported to Australia. One of these hulks was the *Bellerophon*.

Within a month of Napoleon and his suite leaving the ship, the *Bellerophon* had sailed back to the River Medway. But, instead of returning to the friendly noise and bustle of Chatham, Rochester and Frindsbury, she was stationed off Sheerness dockyard at the mouth of the Medway. Her crew was paid off and the Navy Board agreed to her being converted into a prison hulk. The shipwrights and carpenters in the dockyard tore her apart and fitted long lines of cages below deck. During the summer of 1817 she was anchored near the hulk *Retribution* and received her first batch of convicts.

The forbidding appearance of the prison hulks, and the melancholy atmosphere of the surrounding marshes, are vividly depicted in the early chapters of *Great Expectations*, first published in 1860–61. For these descriptions, Charles Dickens drew on his childhood memories of the Cooling Marshes which border the estuaries of the Thames and Medway, and his later explorations of the area when he was living at his house in Gad's Hill.[1] On the second page of the novel Dickens introduces us to Magwitch, a convict who has escaped from a prison hulk, 'a fearful man, all in coarse grey, with a great iron on his leg.' He grabs hold of young Pip who has been looking at the graves of his father, his mother and his brothers in a deserted and overgrown churchyard. The convict is smothered in mud and ravenously hungry. When he learns that Pip lives nearby with his sister who is married to a blacksmith, he demands that Pip bring him some food as well as a file from the blacksmith's workshop. Pip hurries off in the gathering dusk. 'The marshes were just a long black horizontal line then, as I stopped to look after him; and the river was just another horizontal line, not nearly so broad nor yet so black; and the sky was just a row of long angry red lines and dense black lines intermixed.' On the

edge of the river Pip can just make out the only two vertical features
in the landscape: a beacon used as a mark by the sailors; and a gibbet
with chains hanging from it which had once held a pirate. 'The man
was limping towards the latter, as if he were the pirate come to life,
and come down, and going back to hook himself up again.'

Pip returns at dawn the next day with a meat pie and a file for
the convict. Later that day he finds himself joining a group of soldiers
who are hunting for Magwitch and another convict. They find both
men together in a ditch. The soldiers handcuff the convicts and lead
them back to the river where there is a boat waiting to collect them
and return them to their floating prison. 'By the light of the torches,
we saw the black hulk lying out a little way from the mud of the
shore, like a wicked Noah's ark. Cribbed and barred and moored by
massive rusty chains, the prison-ship seemed in my young eyes to
be ironed like the prisoners.'

The bleak reports in the newspapers of the early nineteenth
century give the impression that most ships ended their days dramatically: lost with all hands during a gale; driven ashore and smashed
to pieces on the rocks; or wrecked on the hidden hazards of the
Goodwin Sands or the constantly shifting shoals of the East Coast
and the Thames Estuary. In the days before radar and reliable engines
there were all too many merchant ships and fishing boats lost around
the shores of Britain every year, but this was rarely the fate of the
wooden warships. Remarkably few men-of-war of Nelson's era were
wrecked or lost at sea and none were sunk in action. Of the 126 74-
and 64-gun ships built in British yards between 1755 and 1783 (the
period dominated by the designs of Sir Thomas Slade) only seventeen were wrecked, four were burnt and three were captured by the
enemy. The remaining 122 ships died slow, lingering deaths as their
seams opened up and wet rot and dry rot gradually softened and
crumbled their oak timbers to the point where they had to be sent
to the breaker's yard to be destroyed. The average lifespan of a
warship of the Slade era was twenty-seven years. Some lasted for
forty-five years or more, but the later years of most warships were
spent not on active service but in retirement.

The fate of the majority of Nelson's ships was to be hulked. That is to say they were decommissioned, their crews were paid off, their masts and guns were removed, and they were put to use in the various royal dockyards as hulks. Many were converted into receiving ships: these were used as floating barracks for sailors between commissions or for the accommodation of volunteers and pressed men before they were assigned to a warship. Some of the hulks became store ships for coal or gunpowder. Some were converted into floating hospital ships or convalescent ships or were used as quarantine ships (called lazarettos) for men suspected of having infectious diseases. A few became sheer hulks or floating cranes, and several were even used as breakwaters. During the Napoleonic wars many old warships were converted into prison ships for the thousands of French prisoners of war captured during the various battles of the period. They can be seen in several contemporary paintings, moored two deep in a long line down the centre of Portsmouth Harbour, their mutilated hulls bearing little resemblance to the warships they once were. In each ship were crammed anything from 500 to 1,000 prisoners. They were given no work, they got no exercise, and they barely survived on the rations provided by dishonest contractors who supplied them with bad fish,

An engraving by E. W. Cooke of a prison ship
in Portsmouth harbour, 1828.

inadequate amounts of beef and potatoes, and inedible bread so that they looked like 'a generation of dead men rising for a moment from their tombs, hollow-eyed, wan and earthy of complexion, bent-backed, shaggy bearded, and of a terrifying emaciation.'[2]

In addition to the ships for prisoners of war there were the convict ships. These came into existence in the 1770s when the American War of Independence put an end to the long-standing system of transporting convicted criminals to the American colonies. English judges continued to sentence people to transportation but, with the gaols already overcrowded, some other solution was urgently needed and it was decided, as a temporary expedient, to house the convicts in floating hulks. A law was enacted in July 1779 which decreed that any man convicted of grand larceny or similar offence normally punishable by transportation could henceforth be punished by being confined on board ships or vessels properly converted for that purpose and that they should be 'employed in hard labour in the raising sand, soil, and gravel from, and cleansing the River Thames, or any other river navigable for ships of burthen . . .' The temporary expedient lasted for eighty years. In addition to heaving sand and gravel from the Thames, the convicts were set to work on many other tasks, mostly in and around the dockyards. The work was either mindlessly repetitive, like picking oakum or chipping the rust off roundshot, or involved heavy manual labour: unloading iron and shingle ballast from ships, removing and stacking timber in the dockyards, unloading coal, breaking stones, and cleaning out sawmills, tanks and drains.

The offences for which the convicts were punished varied from the serious to the trivial. At Maidstone Assizes in March 1782, for instance, ten men were sentenced to hard labour on the Thames. James Robinson and Jonathan Bassett got three years for breaking into a house at Deptford and stealing two pairs of shoe buckles, five silver seals and a pair of silver salt spoons. John Watts was sentenced to two years for stealing three chickens from an outhouse at Eynesford belonging to Sir John Dyke. Samuel Mackew got two years for entering a dwelling house at Milton and stealing a silver pint mug and two silver milk pots. And Stephen Woolley got one year for breaking into a store in Sheerness dockyard and stealing 'sundry pieces of new and old iron, part of His Majesty's naval stores'.[3] These men got off relatively lightly. The majority of the men on the convict ships were not only sentenced to hard labour in the dockyards but were later transported to Australia which proved a convenient alternative to the former American colonies.

Initially there were just two convict ships, the *Justitia*, an old Indiaman, and the *Censor*, a former frigate, which were moored in the Thames near Woolwich so that the convicts could be put to work in the dockyard and the Royal Arsenal. By the end of the Napoleonic war in 1815 there were five convict ships. The *Justitia* was still moored at Woolwich. In addition there was the *Retribution* at Sheerness, the *Portland* moored in the bleak expanse of Langstone Harbour near Portsmouth; and in Portsmouth Harbour itself were two convict hulks, the *Captivity* and the *Laurel*.

In July 1815 Mr John Henry Capper, a 41-year-old civil servant who had been a clerk in the Home Office, was appointed to take charge of the prison hulks. His official title was 'Superintendent of the several ships and vessels for the confinement of offenders under sentence of transportation', and he was to remain in this post for the next thirty-two years. It is a pity that we have no idea what he looked like and have only his twice-yearly reports to the Home Office to go on. He comes across as a Dickensian character, a senior functionary in the Circumlocution Office perhaps, not so grand as Mr Tite Barnacle but considerably more conscientious than Mr Wobbler. He is at pains to assure his masters that everything is always under control. He does not entirely ignore problems but does his best to make them appear as local difficulties of little consequence. The opening paragraph of his report of 24 July 1823 is entirely typical: 'Sir, I have the honour of reporting to you, that the Prisoners on board the respective Convict Ships have since my last Report, continued to behave in a very orderly manner (with the exception of a few Convicts at Woolwich, who attempted to escape) and that they have fulfilled their tasks of labour when on shore, to the satisfaction of the persons under whom they have been employed.' He goes on to stress how much the prisoners have earned by comparison with the overall expense of the hulks, and reveals that 'the health

of the Prisoners has been generally very good, and although an indi-
cation of scurvy had manifested itself in one of the ships in a rather
formidable shape, that disease, has, by timely attention, been subdued
without the loss of one prisoner.'

Capper was particularly zealous in carrying out his duties during
his first few years as Superintendent and was evidently keen to make
a good impression on Lord Sidmouth, the Home Secretary. Sidmouth,
who was the former Henry Addington, was a man of considerable
influence. Educated at Winchester and Oxford, he had been an MP,
Speaker of the House of Commons, first Lord of the Treasury,
Chancellor of the Exchequer and President of the Council. He had
been created Viscount Sidmouth in 1805 and had been Home
Secretary since 1812. Capper had received from Sidmouth a detailed
list of instructions which set out his responsibilities, and those of his
staff.[4] The instructions laid down how the convicts were to be treated,
how many hours they were to work, how they were to be clothed,
and their daily allowance of food. There was a strong emphasis on
good discipline and cleanliness. Hammocks were to be taken down
each morning and aired, the decks to be washed twice a week and
swept every morning and afternoon. The surgeons appointed to the
convict ships must 'inquire into the mental state as well as the bodily
state of every sick person' and render the necessary assistance. The
chaplains assigned to each ship must read prayers and preach a
sermon every Sunday and visit every prisoner who requested spiri-
tual aid.

The instructions to Capper emphasised that all healthy convicts
must be sent on shore every day to labour. Following an inspection
of his new domain, Capper despatched a report to Lord Sidmouth on
16 October 1815 in which he noted that there was no useful
employment for those convicts imprisoned in the *Portland Hulk* in
Langstone Harbour. Moreover the hulk was so rotten that it was not
worth carrying out any alterations to its accommodation. He pointed
out that there was at least four years' worth of work to be carried
out in the dockyard at Sheerness and he therefore recommended that
the 450 convicts on the *Portland Hulk* should be transferred to another
ship at Sheerness. He suggested that the Lords of the Admiralty be

requested to supply a suitable ship and he went on to make a specific recommendation: 'The class of ship, which I take the liberty of observing as most suitable for this service, would be a seventy-four, of about the same dimensions as the Bellerophon in the river Medway, being of easy draft of water and lofty between decks.'[5]

These words were to decide the fate of the *Bellerophon*. She was now twenty-nine years old. She had seen more than her fair share of action but she was capable of many more years of active service. The report on her sailing qualities completed by her captain in 1812 had found her to be a strong and well-built ship with no unusual symptoms of weakness. She had performed 'very well' or 'uncommonly well' on all points of sailing and her rate of sailing compared with other ships was 'in general superior'. But she was surplus to requirements. With Napoleon safely incarcerated on a remote island in the South Atlantic and with every prospect of a lasting peace coming out of the negotiations in Paris, Britain no longer needed a wartime navy.

At the time of Trafalgar in 1805 the navy had 241 ships of 20 guns or more (first to sixth rates), 310 smaller vessels in sea service, and some 90,000 seamen and 30,000 marines. By the summer of 1815 the numbers of men had dropped to 70,000 seamen and 20,000 marines but there were still 182 ships of more than 20 guns and 233 smaller vessels on the books. The Admiralty could no longer justify the expense of paying and victualling this number of sailors, nor could it justify maintaining the wartime level of warships. Of the twenty-eight ships which had taken part in the Battle of Trafalgar, ten had already been hulked or broken up, including the *Temeraire*, which had become a receiving hulk at Sheerness in 1813.

The Admiralty and the Navy Board had never been sentimental about old ships, however illustrious, and so Mr Capper got his way. The ship which had once been called 'the Flying Bellerophon' was condemned to spend the next ten years of her life as a convict hulk. But first she had to be converted from a warship into a floating prison. In his report Mr Capper had particularly requested that he be allowed to supervise the fitting out of the ship and asked that she be brought into dock at Sheerness for that purpose. In December

1815 the *Bellerophon* was towed into the dock and work began on preparing her for her new role.

It took the shipwrights, carpenters and blacksmiths of the dockyard nine months to carry out the necessary alterations. Iron grilles were fitted in all the gunports on the upper deck and the gun deck, and small additional ports were created on the orlop or lower deck which were likewise fitted with grilles. In a 74-gun ship loaded with guns and ballast, the orlop deck was below the water-line and was used as a storage area, but on a convict hulk floating high in the water it provided an additional deck for the accommo-dation of prisoners. Being immediately above the bilges it was a foul-smelling and airless place and was allotted to the worst of the prisoners. In place of the precarious steps used by the sailors to enter and leave the ship a permanent gangway was constructed down one side of the ship. This led down to a landing stage at water level. Two wooden huts were built on the foredeck, one of them for the storage of hammocks and the other to be used as a laundry. Beside them was erected a large crane to facilitate the loading of water, provisions and stores. A platform was built above and behind the figurehead and on this was constructed a shed which formed a wash house and toilet for the prisoners.

While the alterations above deck entirely altered the outward appearance and character of the ship, the alterations below deck were even more drastic. In the first generation of convict ships the pris-oners were simply locked down below decks at night. There was no adequate supervision and no attempt to separate young boys from grown men, which inevitably resulted in the physical and sexual abuse of those unable to defend themselves from the more violent and predatory prisoners. By the time that the *Bellerophon* went into dock for fitting out, it had been agreed that the interior layout of convict ships should allow for visual supervision of the prisoners by the warders at night, and that the prisoners should be locked into cells holding no more than eight men in each cell. In effect this meant creating two lines of iron cages down the side of each deck with a corridor down the middle. The result was similar to that of the lion house or monkey house in a traditional zoo, a resemblance that was

Engravings from *The Criminal Prisons of London* by
Henry Mayhew and John Binney showing the chapel
and prison ward on the convict hulk *Defence*.

remarked upon by visitors to the convict hulk *Defence* at Woolwich in the 1840s:

> On reaching the top deck we found it divided by strong iron rails (very like those in the zoological gardens, which protect visitors from the fury of the wild beasts) from one end to the other, into two long cages as it were, with a passage between them. In this passage a warder was pacing to and fro, commanding a view of the men, who were slung up in hammocks, fastened in two rows, in each cage or compartment of the ship.[6]

There were eighteen cells or cages for prisoners on the orlop deck, twelve on the lower deck and twelve on the upper deck. The supervising staff had their quarters in the stern where the *Bellerophon*'s officers had recently been accommodated. There were separate cabins for the first mate, the second mate, the third mate, and the steward. There was a cabin set aside as a surgery and a room for the chaplain. The warders shared a ward room below. The captain of the hulk, who acted as prison governor, was allotted the great cabin recently occupied by Captain Maitland and lent to Napoleon during his three-week stay on the ship. There is no record of the appearance of the cabin at this period but the visitors to the convict hulk *Defence* were particularly struck by the contrast between the governor's quarters and the rest of the ship. According to one account, 'We next adjourned to the governor's comfortable breakfast-room, with its pretty stern-windows, and its light blue and white walls. The military salute of the convict-servant who entered from time to time, with his white apron about his loins, was the only reminiscence of the hulk as we sat at the morning meal.'[7]

A major alteration to the interior of the *Bellerophon*, as with the other convict ships, was the construction of a large chapel which doubled as a schoolroom. A section was cut out of the gun deck to increase the height of the chapel. This created an upper gallery for visitors who wished to attend the church services, and provided a cavernous space in which all the inmates could be assembled for church services. The chapel was dominated by a majestic two-tier pulpit for the chaplain and a reader. The size of the chapel, and its fine panelling and supporting columns, emphasised the importance placed by the authorities on reforming the characters of the convicts. The total cost of fitting out the ship as a convict hulk was £12,081,[8] which was a relatively small sum compared with the cost of building a new prison on dry land but was surprisingly expensive when it is recalled that the original cost of building the *Bellerophon* and fitting her with masts, yards and rigging was £38,000.[9]

In his report to the Home Office of 10 July 1816 John Capper noted that 'The ship Bellerophon, fitting at Sheerness, as a convict hulk, will (I have every reason to expect) be ready by the end of this month, for the reception of the Portland's establishment.' The work was completed by Sheerness dockyard in September 1816 and in January 1817 Capper was able to report that the prisoners from the *Portland* in Langston Harbour had been transferred to the *Bellerophon* 'and have been constantly employed upon the public works carrying on under the directions of the Navy Board'.

From the reports of John Capper and his chaplains, the Home Office instructions of 1815, and the observations of visitors to the *Defence* in the 1840s, it is possible to build up a detailed picture of the daily regime on the hulks. A typical day on board the convict hulk *Bellerophon* began around 4 am when the convict cook climbed out of his hammock. He made his way to the galley in the foc's'sle and got the fire going in the great stove which had once provided meals for the sailors of the *Bellerophon*. He raked the coals, and began heating up several gallons of cocoa in a giant copper pot. The rest of the convicts were still asleep in hammocks strung across the upper part of their caged cells and hung within a few inches of each other. At 5.30 the ship's bell sounded three bells. The warders began shouting at the men to get up and turn out. Within a few minutes all the men were up, dressed, and had their hammocks rolled up neatly. They then filed out of their cages onto the upper deck and stowed their hammocks in numbered lockers in the hammock houses. They clinked and clanked as they walked because every convict had to wear iron fetters on his legs.[10] After a visit to the heads to relieve themselves, they returned to their cells, washed themselves in buckets, brushed their boots, scrubbed the plain deal tables, and waited for breakfast. At this point a roll call took place and the warders checked each cell to make sure everyone was present.

Each cell of eight or ten men formed a mess in naval fashion, and one man was detailed to be messman for the day and fetch the breakfast from the galley. This consisted of loaves of coarse bread which were brought along in a basket, and a large can of cocoa. The men ate and drank out of tin plates and mugs which they were expected to keep highly polished. Breakfast was eaten in a silence broken only by the sound of 400 jaws munching the dry bread. When they had finished, the convicts washed their mugs and plates and arranged them neatly on the tables.

At 7 o'clock the big brass bell on the upper deck sounded nine bells. All the duty warders assembled on deck to be inspected by their senior officers to ensure they were smart and sober. Two longboats, manned by convicts in seamen's glazed hats and jerseys, pulled alongside the gangway, raised their oars smartly in the air, and made fast. Under the eye of several armed warders the convicts filed up from below deck, and tramped down the gangway and into the longboats. The visitors to the prison hulk *Defence* were much impressed by the military precision of the embarkation of the convicts, and thought it exciting 'to see the never-ending line of convicts stream across the deck, and down the gangway, the steps rattling, as they descend one after another into the capacious boat, amid the cries of the officer at the ship's side – "Come, look sharp there, men! Look sharp!"'[11]

Each boat took about a hundred men and, as soon as the first boat was filled, the oarsmen lowered their oars, pushed off and headed for the shore. By 7.30 the convicts were assembled in gangs in the dockyard and were ready for work. Before setting off, each man was searched by a warder to ensure that he was not concealing civilian clothing to enable him to pass himself off as a free dockyard employee and escape. Having satisfied themselves that all was well, the warders marched the men off to their workplaces. For the next four and a half hours the convicts were engaged in the various types of hard labour currently required by the dockyard officers: unloading ships, shifting and stacking timber, cleaning docks and drains, and filling with rubble and hard core the marshy area called Mayor's Marsh. At noon the men stopped work for lunch. They were rowed back to the *Bellerophon* for a meal of meat and potatoes. By 1 pm they were back in the dockyard and worked for another four and a half hours in the summer months, three hours in the winter.

At 5.30 pm (4 o'clock in winter) the men returned to the prison hulk. Supper was at 6 o'clock. The basic ration for each man was 6 ounces of bread and 1 pint of gruel (a thin porridge made from oatmeal) and this was augmented on certain days of the week by a pint of soup, and a few ounces of meat and potatoes. Having washed their tin plates and mugs and scrubbed clean their tables, the men had half an hour or so of relaxation which they spent reading or chatting among themselves until they assembled for evening prayers in the chapel. This was not compulsory but, according to the *Bellerophon*'s chaplain, about 350 men out of the total of 435 usually attended.[12] At 8 o'clock the tables and benches in each cell were cleared to one side, and the men slung their hammocks which had been brought down in the afternoon by some of the men left behind on the ship. They were allowed to talk and read until 9 o'clock when all talking stopped, the men climbed into their hammocks and the lights were extinguished. The warders locked each cell and at 10 o'clock the hatches were padlocked as added security.

This was the daily routine for the majority of the convicts who were fit and able to carry out manual labour in the dockyards. On an average day about 300 men went ashore from the *Bellerophon*, leaving a hundred or more on board. Some of these carried out domestic duties such as scrubbing the decks, mending hammocks, making shoes, and washing the convicts' clothes and hanging them out to dry. Fifty or so men remained on board each day to attend school. The convicts took it in turns to do this and each man would attend school for one day in every nine or ten. The lessons were taken by the chaplain and a clerk or schoolmaster, and were heavily religious. There was some attempt to teach reading, writing and arithmetic but much of the time was spent learning or reciting verses from the Bible. The visitors commented:

It is a melancholy sight. Some of the scholars are old bald-headed men, evidently agricultural labourers. There, amidst sharp-featured men, are dogged-looking youths, whom it is pitiful to behold so far astray, and so young. And now the clerk who read the prayers may be seen teaching the men; but it is evidently hard work, and few, it is to be feared, care for the school, further than for the physical repose it secures them.[13]

The chaplain on the *Bellerophon* was a man called Edward Edwards. He had been chaplain of the *Portland* hulk in Langstone Harbour and had been transferred to the *Bellerophon* at the same time as the convicts. He remained the ship's chaplain for the next nine years. His twice-yearly reports to John Capper have a ponderous and self-satisfied air about them but he seems to have been exceedingly zealous in his determination to improve the minds and morals of his flock. Much of his time was spent in the composition of his Sunday sermons. Aware that many of the men were 'very ignorant as well as obdurate', he would address them in plain and strong language, making sure that his diction was clear and correct. He made himself available in the afternoons for any prisoner who wanted his advice. He attended the daily evening chapel and afterwards he would sometimes visit the prisoners below deck 'and if I see or hear any thing amiss or tending to immoralise, I instantly administer reproof, and report the offender or offenders to the Commanding Officer, whom I always find ready and active to co-operate in the promotion of virtue and in checking vice.'[14]

If his reports are to be believed Mr Edwards made remarkably good progress in reforming and educating the prisoners. In his second report as chaplain of the *Bellerophon* he noted that four-fifths of the convicts on the ship conducted themselves in a very becoming manner, 'yea, I may say, very many of them in an exemplary manner . . . I feel exquisite satisfaction in stating my conviction that many of them are sincere and reclaimed.' He noted that 230 men and boys attended the school on board and the boys in particular were improved beyond expectation. Twenty were able to repeat the Thirty-nine Articles from memory and many were able to read the proper lessons, epistle and gospel on Sunday services. The chaplain was particularly pleased with the observations of a local clergyman who took the service one Sunday and said, 'Well, I am astonished! I do not think that there is in all England a congregation who conduct themselves during Divine Worship so orderly, and apparently so devout as yours do.'

This rosy picture is echoed in the reports of Mr Capper. He confirmed that the schools were attended with much zeal, the state of the prisoners' health was very good, and that 800 prisoners from the two hulks at Sheerness had been employed daily in the dockyard 'in a very advantageous manner'. There is no doubt that the governors of each convict hulk maintained a highly disciplined regime and provided a useful supply of manual labourers for work in the dockyards. Indeed Capper's reports go out of their way to show how the earnings of the convicts helped to offset the expenses of running the hulk establishment. But other commentators were damning in their observations on the whole system of incarcerating convicts in prison ships.

Peter Bossy, who was the surgeon of the *Warrior* hulk moored off Woolwich, produced a devastating report in which he showed that, of the 638 convicts on board the hulk in 1841, no fewer than 400 had to be admitted to the hospital and 38 men died. He noted that most of the men who died were housed on the lower deck or the middle deck, both of which were permanently damp, poorly ventilated and evil-smelling. Men with scurvy, scrofula, ulcers and infectious diseases were cooped up together in the worst possible conditions. When cholera broke out on board one of the hulks the chaplain refused to bury the dead in person but ordered the coffins to be transported to the marshes for burial and read the burial service at a mile distant from the graves. Patients admitted to the convict hospital ships faced conditions which were often worse than the prison ships themselves. In the *Unite* hospital ship the majority of patients were infested with vermin and had no regular supply of clean bed linen. No towels or combs were provided for prisoners and 'the unwholesome odour from the imperfect and neglected state of the water-closets was almost insupportable'.

W. Hepworth Dixon, who published a book on London prisons in

1850, observed that the hulk system debased and corrupted the prisoners, was condemned by every impartial person who was competent to give an opinion on the matter, and was only maintained because the labour of the convicts on public works was useful and valuable to the government. A report by the Directors of Prisons on the management of the hulk establishment particularly condemned the rotten and dilapidated condition of the ships and strongly urged the government to replace them with properly built shore-based prisons with decent sleeping cells for all the prisoners.[15]

One of the most scandalous aspects of the hulk establishment was that for many years it was the usual practice to imprison boys in the same ships and the same cells as adult males. Many of the boys were aged between ten and fifteen and a few were even younger. It has already been noted that the situation was at its worst in the early days of the convict hulks when the prisoners were simply locked below at night without any supervision. Of this period, the Victorian philanthropist Henry Mayhew wrote, 'The state of morality under such circumstances may be easily conceived – crimes impossible to be mentioned being commonly perpetrated.'[16] When the second generation of convict ships, which included the *Bellerophon*, were divided into separate cells below decks, with a corridor running down the centre to allow a warder to patrol below decks at night, the situation was marginally improved but there were still eight or ten convicts in each cell and the men were still locked up with the boys.

In 1823 the system was belatedly changed. Mr Capper was ordered to separate the boys from the men and to provide separate accommodation for them. All the boys in the various convict hulks were moved to the *Bellerophon* and the adult prisoners on the ship were transferred to other ships in the convict fleet. In his report of 22 January 1824 Capper was able to record that 320 boys, most of whom were under fourteen years old, were now confined on board the *Bellerophon*, and that for the past eight months they had been employed in making clothing and other articles for the convict establishment. Capper had a low opinion of most of the boy convicts and was agreeably surprised by their behaviour under the new regime. Mr Edwards, the chaplain, thought that they generally conducted themselves in a becoming manner but found that all too many of them were illiterate, and had no ability to learn, 'and others are so depraved that they will not apply themselves.' He soon had them committing large chunks of the Bible to memory and within six months of their arrival on the *Bellerophon* was able to report that some of the boys had memorised 421 chapters of Holy Writ, with an average of twenty verses per chapter, and 131 boys were able to repeat the Church Catechism once a week.

For two and a half years the *Bellerophon* was a boys' prison. As if to hide this dark period in her life she was given another name. From 5 October 1824 she was officially called the *Captivity* hulk, though out of habit, or perhaps to avoid confusion, Mr Capper still referred to her as the *Bellerophon* in his reports. The daily regime was as rigid as it had always been but with the important difference that the boys were not taken ashore each day to do hard labour in the dockyard but spent all their time imprisoned on board the ship. Their days were a dreary round of prayers in chapel; inspections and punishments; washing down the ship; meals of gruel, bread and cheese (with the addition of boiled beef three or four times a week); and long hours spent in makeshift workshops. In spite of the oppressive conditions the boys seem to have been remarkably productive. In one year Mr Capper reported that they had made for the convict service more than 6,000 pairs of shoes, 15,500 garments, 'and various articles of cooperage and bedding'.

Neither Capper nor his chaplain give us any idea of the atmosphere and working conditions on the ship but Charles Dickens provides us with some insight into what it must have been like. The period when the *Bellerophon* was a convict ship for boys exactly coincided with the time that Dickens's father was sent to the Marshalsea Prison and Dickens's schooling was interrupted by his unhappy employment in a blacking warehouse. We therefore need look no further than the pages of *Little Dorrit, David Copperfield* or *Nicholas Nickleby* to get some idea of the conditions on board the *Bellerophon*. A visitor entering the chapel of the ship on a winter's morning would have been confronted with a scene similar to that which faced Nicholas Nickleby when he entered the schoolroom of Dotheboys Hall:

Pale and haggard faces, lank and bony figures, children with the countenances of old men, deformities with irons upon their limbs, boys of stunted growth, and others whose long meagre legs would hardly bear their stooping bodies, all crowded on the view together; there were the bleared eye, the hare-lip, the crooked foot, and every ugliness or distortion that told of unnatural aversion conceived by parents for their offspring, or of young lives which, from the earliest dawn of infancy, had been one horrible endurance of cruelty and neglect . . . there were vicious-faced boys, brooding, with leaden eyes, like malefactors in a jail; and there were young creatures on whom the sins of their frail parents had descended, weeping even for the mercenary nurses they had known, and lonesome even in their loneliness.

And in the riverside warehouse of Murdstone and Grinby, where the ten-year-old David Copperfield was sent to work, sticking labels on bottles, we catch a glimpse of a building not unlike the decayed hulk of a convict ship rising and falling with the tide:

It was a crazy old house with a wharf of its own, abutting on the water when the tide was in, and on the mud when the tide was out, and literally overrun with rats. Its panelled rooms, discoloured with the dirt and smoke of a hundred years, I dare say; its decaying floors and staircase; the squeaking and scuffling of the old grey rats down in the cellars; and the dirt and rottenness of the place . . .

During the winter of 1825–6 the authorities came to the conclusion that the *Bellerophon* was no longer suitable for the confinement of boys, apparently because her internal layout did not allow sufficient space for workshops. In January 1826 Mr Capper noted that 'The Convict Boys, consisting of 350, under 16 years of age, have recently been transferred from the Bellerophon to the Euryalus at Chatham, the ship specially fitted for them.' The *Euryalus* was the former 36-gun frigate commanded by Captain Henry Blackwood which had kept watch on the enemy fleet at Cadiz in the weeks preceding the Battle of Trafalgar. At the end of the action Collingwood had shifted his flag from the dismasted *Royal Sovereign* to the *Euryalus* and in the great storm following the battle the frigate had taken the damaged flagship in tow. The *Euryalus* was now converted into a boys' prison with proper workshops but, being much smaller than the *Bellerophon*, the accommodation for the boys was extremely cramped. A year later Capper was having to admit that the boys confined on board 'have, upon two or three occasions been refractory, and committed outrages on the persons of the Officers. The Ship in which they are confined is found too small . . .'[17]

The prison authorities decided that the *Bellerophon* would be more useful at Plymouth than moored at the mouth of the Medway. On 26 April 1826 she was taken into one of the docks at Sheerness, the old copper plates were taken off her bottom and she was re-coppered and prepared for the trip to Plymouth, a coastal voyage of some 300 miles.[18] She sailed from Sheerness on 4 June, called in at Portsmouth en route to pick up a batch of convicts, and arrived at Plymouth on 8 June. Her progress was reported in the *Plymouth Herald*:

CONVICTS. On Wednesday last, the Captivity Hulk (late the Bellerophon, 74, having been fitted up for the reception of convicts) arrived here from Portsmouth, having on board 80 convicts, who are to be employed in the Dock Yard, in a similar manner as individuals of the same description at Portsmouth. The Hulk the following day came up the harbour. It is reported that the convicts of the four Western Counties are to be in future regularly sent here.[19]

This is confirmed by Capper's report of 26 July 1826 which noted that the *Captivity*, now stationed at Devonport (the dockyard area of Plymouth) had 80 convicts on board. By the following January the number of convicts on board had been increased to 149 and the ship had acquired a chaplain, by the name of William Prowse. He was much impressed by the behaviour of the convicts which was 'far beyond what I had expected from persons of their former habits. Both during Divine Service and at the School they behave in a serious and becoming manner.'[20]

For the next eight years the ship remained moored in the river at Plymouth, a melancholy sight among the sails of the ships and small craft moving to and fro and the smoke and activity of the nearby dockyard. By 1833 she had 445 convicts on board, ten more than she had accommodated in the days when Edward Edwards, the chaplain, was preaching his sermons and encouraging the men to learn the Thirty-nine Articles. However, the ship's days were drawing to a close. Capper had received instructions from Lord Melbourne, the Home Secretary, to reduce the number of convict ships and he solved the problem by drastically increasing the number of men transported to the colonies. In 1834 he reported that 4,216 convicts had been sent to the settlements in Australia and 400 had been sent to Bermuda. He was therefore able to abolish the convict hulks at Plymouth and Sheerness. In July 1834 Capper informed the Home Secretary that the hulks on these stations had been handed over to the Naval Department.[21] In the ledger which had followed the progress of the *Bellerophon* in and out of the royal dockyards and had noted the cost of every repair carried out to her hull, masts and rigging there is a final entry which simply states, 'Sold 21st Jany 1836 for £4030.'[22]

The navy would have sold the hulk to a firm of shipbreakers and the evidence suggests that the *Bellerophon* was broken up by John Beatson's yard in London.[23] Beatsons was a well-established family firm situated on the south bank of the Thames at Rotherhithe. The yard was experienced in breaking up East Indiamen as well as warships and in previous years had broken up several third-rate ships. The largest ship to be broken up by Beatsons was another Trafalgar veteran, the 98-gun *Temeraire*. Like the *Bellerophon*, she had spent several years as a prison ship at Plymouth before being moved to Sheerness to become a receiving hulk. Her last journey to the breaker's yard in September 1838 was commemorated by Turner in his famous painting *The Fighting Temeraire*, a haunting image of a great ship being towed upstream by a steam tug. As steam-powered paddle tugs were increasingly being used around the coasts of Britain, it seems likely that the *Bellerophon* made her last journey in a similar manner. The writer William Thackeray wrote a lengthy review of Turner's painting. He described the tugboat as 'a little, spiteful, diabolical steamer' belching out a volume of malignant smoke, but his words for the *Temeraire* might equally well have been applied to the *Bellerophon*. Behind the furiously paddling tugboat, 'slow, sad, and majestic, follows the brave old ship, with death, as it were, written on her . . .'[24]

EPILOGUE

For sailors who had spent months at sea, the island of St Helena was a pleasant oasis in the vastness of the South Atlantic. The trade winds tempered the equatorial heat, and a variety of plants and trees thrived in the mild, damp climate. For Napoleon, who bitterly resented the fact that he had not been allowed to retire to a country house in England, St Helena was a prison – an open prison without walls but a prison from which all escape was impossible. Two British warships constantly circled the seas around the sheer cliffs of the island and intercepted any approaching vessels; sentries from the garrison of 2,000 British soldiers kept a constant watch on his movements; and the climate only seemed to add to the monotony of everyday life. Major Gorrequer remarked that 'it blows continually in the same direction and is always raining; the shores of the island are frightful precipices without any beach. Bonaparte calls it the Island of Desolation.'[1]

The *Northumberland*, carrying Napoleon and his retinue, had dropped anchor off Jamestown on 17 October 1815 after a voyage of seventy days. For the first three months Napoleon stayed as a guest of the Balcombe family while a residence was being prepared for him. Mr Balcombe was a representative of the East India Company and had gathered his family at the entrance of his house to receive the former emperor. His fourteen-year-old daughter Betsy vividly recalled Napoleon's arrival: 'He was deathly pale, and I thought his features, though cold and immovable, and somewhat stern, were exceedingly beautiful . . . When once he began to speak, his fascinating smile and kind manner removed every vestige of the fear with which I had hitherto regarded him.'[2] The smile, which had made such an impression on so many people in the past, was to be seen rarely when Napoleon was moved to Longwood, his permanent quarters on a windswept plateau on the upper reaches of the island. Longwood had been built sixty years earlier by the Lieutenant Governor of St Helena as a barn to store grain. It was later used as a stable until the Governor converted it into a summer residence. Additional rooms were hurriedly built to house Napoleon's followers and servants. These created more space but did not improve the overall atmosphere of the residence which was damp and gloomy. Mildew flourished on the walls and furniture and there were so many rats that the servants sometimes caught as many as twenty in one day.

A British warship off the island of St Helena.

A watercolour by William Innes Pocock,

the naval son of the marine artist Nicholas Pocock.

Napoleon survived for five and a half years on St Helena. During the first year he established a regime which helped to pass the time. He was woken at 6 am by his valet, drank a cup of tea or coffee, and then shaved and washed in a silver basin. If the weather was favourable he would go for a ride on horseback until 10 when it was time for an early lunch. Hot soup was followed by a main course of grilled or roast meat and vegetables, followed by cheese and coffee. After lunch he spent three hours dictating his memoirs. In the afternoon he took a bath and would frequently remain in the bath for an hour and a half while reading or talking to Count Las Cases or one of his generals. At 4 o'clock he received visitors and then he might go for a drive in a carriage. Dinner in the evening was a formal affair. Madame Bertrand and Madame de Montholon joined their husbands, Las Cases, General Gourgaud and Napoleon himself for a five-course meal served by servants dressed in the imperial livery. After coffee Napoleon would read aloud to the company. He had brought a library of 1,500 books with him and the choice in the evening was usually from the works of Molière or Racine. At 11 pm he went to bed and Las Cases or Montholon would read to him until he dozed off.

As the months and years passed, Napoleon became increasingly depressed by the the sheer boredom of life at Longwood. According to Las Cases, 'He spent most of his day alone in his room, leafing through a few books or, more often than not, doing nothing . . . It was easy to see that he no longer had any preoccupation with the future, did not reflect on the past nor care for the present.'[3] It is now known that he suffered for many years from a chronic ulcer and this became malignant and developed into cancer of the stomach.[4] His father and sister had suffered from the same condition and he himself expected to die from the same disease. By January 1821 it was evident that he was seriously ill: he was frequently vomiting, had a pain in his right side 'like jabs from a penknife' and was losing weight. His mind remained active and inquisitive but he knew the end was not far away. 'I'm not afraid of dying,' he told Bertrand, 'the only thing I'm afraid of is that the English will keep my body and put it in Westminster Abbey.'[5] In fact Hudson Lowe, the Governor of St Helena, had orders that his body was not to be removed from the island.

Napoleon died as the sun was setting on 5 May 1821. He was buried with full military honours in a shady valley near Longwood at a spot which he had once admired. Twenty years later his body was taken back to France and buried beneath a magnificent tomb in Les Invalides. The state funeral in Paris was a lavish and patriotic event on a scale similar to those, in London, of his two greatest enemies, Nelson and the Duke of Wellington.

Captain Maitland also died thousands of miles from home. For the first three years after leaving the *Bellerophon* he lived the life of a country gentleman with his wife Catherine on the family estate in Scotland. In 1818 he was recalled to active duty and appointed to command the *Vengeur*, a 74-gun ship named after the French ship which had sunk at the Battle of the Glorious First of June. He sailed to South America, but within a year was back in Europe and was ordered to Naples where he received King Ferdinand on board and conveyed him to Leghorn to attend the European Congress. In 1830 he was promoted to Rear-Admiral and made a Knight Commander of the Order of the Bath. For five years he was Admiral Superintendent of the dockyard at Portsmouth and then in 1837 he was appointed commander-in-chief of the East Indies and China station. He sailed for Bombay in the *Wellesley*, a 74-gun ship, and early in 1839 he provided naval support for the landing of troops at Karachi. He died on 30 November 1839 on board his flagship off Bombay. He was sixty-two. He was buried in St Thomas's Cathedral, Bombay, and a handsome monument of white marble was erected to his memory by the officers of the Indian Navy 'to mark their sense of the kind and considerate conduct uniformly shown to their corps during his command . . .'[6]

Of the *Bellerophon*'s other commanders, five of them reached flag rank. Her first commander, Sir Thomas Pasley, was already a Rear-Admiral when he fought at the Glorious First of June and by the time of his death in 1808 he had attained the rank of Admiral of the White. His flag captain at the battle, William Johnstone Hope, became a Rear-Admiral in 1812, was knighted in 1815, and for a while served as a Lord of the Admiralty. Captain Darby, who had commanded the *Bellerophon* at the Battle of the Nile, ended his career with a knighthood and the rank of Admiral of the Blue. Lord Garlies, who commanded the ship for less than eight months in 1801, went on to become a Vice-Admiral, and Edward Hawker, who made the two voyages to Newfoundland, became an Admiral. On his retirement he became a correspondent for *The Times*, writing under the by-line 'A Flag Officer'.

Lieutenant Cumby, who had taken command of the *Bellerophon* at Trafalgar when his captain was killed, never rose to the exalted rank of admiral but played an active role as a naval captain during the remainder of the war against France. He spent several years in the West Indies and was then given command of the *Hyperion*, a 32-gun frigate.[7] When Napoleon surrendered to Captain Maitland off La Rochelle, Cumby was keeping watch on the French coast off Lorient, less than 150 miles away. On the declaration of peace in 1815 Cumby went on half pay on the grounds of ill-health and returned to the family home in the village of Heighington, County Durham. Like so many sailors he had seen very little of his wife and children while serving at sea, and tragically his wife died a few months before peace was declared. For a while the three children were looked after by their grandparents and their nurse, but in October 1815 Cumby joined them with his black servant John Peters and his dog. With his prize money he was able to buy a farm with 116 acres to add to the family estate. He married again, became a local magistrate and played a leading part in the life of the community.

On Trafalgar Day every year he organised a festival in the village with a bonfire and entertainment for the local children. It was an opportunity for a reunion with his former shipmates. On 21 October 1829, for instance, his guests included three of the midshipmen who had served on the *Bellerophon* at Trafalgar – the cousins Robert and Hugh Patton (both now naval captains) and the explorer John Franklin who had just returned from an expedition to north-west Canada. Also present was Alexander Scott, the former chaplain of the *Victory* who had been at Nelson's side during the last hours of his life. Scott, a nervous, scholarly man who had worshipped Nelson, had been deeply affected by his death and in recalling him later he admitted, 'I become stupid with grief for what I have lost.' In 1816

Scott became vicar of Catterick which was only a few miles from Heighington and so he was a regular guest at Cumby's reunions.

Portraits and personal relics of several of the *Bellerophon*'s captains remain in the hands of their descendants or have found their way to various museums. They include the sword, dirk and pistol of Captain John Cooke, the huge silver-gilt trophy presented to Admiral Pasley by Lloyds of London, the couch from Captain Maitland's cabin and the skull of the goat which supplied the milk for Napoleon's breakfast. These are tangible reminders of events which took place some 200 years ago, but it is the log-books which provide the truest picture of the life of the *Bellerophon*. Every day for the twenty-five years that the ship was on active service, the entries record her position, the days and nights of fresh breezes and cloudy weather, the sudden squalls with lightning and rain, the exercising of the guns, the floggings, the occasional drownings, the weeks spent at anchor in foreign ports, the sightings of strange ships, the signals exchanged with other British warships, and then, after months away from England, the beating up the Channel towards a home port.

As for the *Bellerophon* herself, only a few fragments survive. Captain Maitland bought part of her figurehead and some of her stern ornaments from the ship-breakers and deposited them in the naval collections at Portsmouth. The helmeted head can be seen today in the Royal Naval Museum at Portsmouth. It is all that remains of the full figure of the heroic warrior which once confronted and survived the bombardment of enemy guns in the Atlantic on that distant first of June, in the darkness of the Egyptian night off the mouth of the Nile, and in the glare of the midday sun off the shoals of Cape Trafalgar.

APPENDIX 1: PROGRESS BOOKS FOR H.M. SHIPS

Rate Guns 3d 74 *Bellerophon*				
At What Port	*Arrived*	*Docked*	*Sheathed*	*Graved*
Frindsbury Edwd Greaves	Began	May 1783		
Chatham	7 Octr 1786	7 March 1787	Coppered	March 1787
do	----------	----------	Coppered August 1790	----------
Sheerness	21 Nov 1790	Taken in hand Mar & Completed		
Chatham	31 Aug 1791	28 Mar 1793	Copper rep'd	Mar 1793
Plymouth	21 July 1793			
Portsmouth	12 Octr 1795	27 Octr 1795	Copper rep'd	
do	16 Aprl 1800	5 Sep 1800	Copper taken off Reccopp'd June 1801	

The *Bellerophon*'s progress in and out of the royal dockyards from 1786 to 1801 with the costs in pounds, shillings and pence. From 'Progress Books for H.M. Ships' (PRO:ADM.180/6)

Launched	Sailed	Built or nature of the repairs	Charge of the Hull, Masts & Yards	Rigging & Stores	Total
7th Octr 1786	7th Octr 1786	Built	30,232:14:3	Hull only	
20th March 1787	Coppd & fitted	for ordy	3,389:8:7	4,987:6:7	8,376:15:2
----------	15 Augt 1790	Fitted	735:13:7	3,804:14:9	4,620:8:4
April 1791	20 April 1791	Fitted	95	1,733	1,828
29 Mar 1793	26 April 1793	Fitted	2,128	2036	4,164
	8 Aug 1793	Made good Deptford	1,725	2,289	4,014
13 Novr 1795	16 Novr 1795	do	3,266	4,837	8,103
27 June 1801	9 Aug 1801	Midd & rep Fitted	21,099	10,909	32,608

67	Rate Guns			Launch'd			
	3d 74		***Bellerophon***				
At what Port	Arrived	Dock'd	Copper'd	Launch'd Or Undock'd	Sail'd	Built or Nature of the Repair
Portsmouth	24 Aug 1804	5 Sep 1804	Copper taken off Recopperd Oct 1804	8 Oct 1804	1 Nov 1804	Refit
Plymouth	14 Dec 1805	24 Dec 1805	Copp repd & dress'd	20 Jan 1806	26 Feb 1806	Defects
do	19 Oct 1807	2 Nov 1807	Copper taken off & Recoppered Nov 1807	5 Nov 1807	23 Jan 1808	do
Sheerness	3 Jan 1810		Copper repaired		18 Feb 1810	do
Portsmouth	6 Nov 1810	15 Nov 1810	Copper taken off & repaired Nov 1810	30 Nov 1810	13 Dec 1810	Reftd
do	19 Dec 1812	22 Jan 1813	Repaird copper and Doubling	17 Feb 1813	26 Mar 1813	Defects
do	26 Jan 1814	7 Feb 1814	Copper taken off & recoppered	24 Feb 1814	30 Mar 1814	do
Sheerness	2 Sept 1815	Taken in hand Decr. 1815 & completed Sept 1816				Fitted for a Conv't Hulk
		27 April 1826	Copper taken off felted,& recoppered & fixed Protectors	24 May 1826	4 June 1826	Fitted to be navigated
Plymouth	8 June 1826					to Plymouth
		Sold 21st Jany 1836 for £4030				

from No3 F108 named Captivity – A.O. 5 Octr 1824

Hull			Masts and Yards			Rigging and Stores			Grand Total
...erials	Workmans'p	Total	Materials	Workmans'p					
49	992	4341	2,352	108	2,460	5,015	98	5,113	11,914
6	2049	5695	2856	41	2897	9460	30	9490	18,082
9	1293	2882	1693	36	1729	3254	161	3415	8026
8	395	1493	188	22	210	1603	7	1610	3313
5	775	2300	938	11	949	2966	45	3011	6260
3	1807	7110	2034	47	2081	5528	137	5665	14,856
6	1002	3838	888	32	920	8121	163	8284	13,042
	114	114		1	1	674	1	675	790
	395	1233							1233

APPENDIX 2: 'BONEY WAS A WARRIOR'

Boney was a warrior,
Way-aye-yah!
A warrior, a terrier,
Johnny Franswor!

Boney beat the Prussians,
The Osstrians and the Rooshians.

He beat the Prussians squarely,
He whacked the English nearly.

We licked him in Trafalgar's bay,
Carried his main topm'st away,

'Twas on the plains of Waterloo,
He met the boy who put him through,

He met the Duke of Wellington,
That day his downfall had begun.

Boney went a–cruisin'
Aboard the Billy Ruffian.

Boney went to Saint Helen',
An' he never came back agen.

They sent him into exile,
He died on Saint Helena's isle.

Boney broke his heart an' died,
In Corsica he wisht he styed.

He wuz a rorty general,
A rorty, snorty general.

Anonymous

APPENDIX 3: THE SAILS OF A SQUARE-RIGGED SHIP

1 Flying jib
2 Jib
3 Fore topmast staysail
4 Fore staysail
5 Foresail, or course
6 Fore topsail

7 Fore topgallant
8 Mainstaysail
9 Maintopmast staysail
10 Middle staysail
11 Main topgallant
   staysail

Engraving by J. T. Serres showing the sails of a
square-rigged ship hung out to dry in a calm.

12 Mainsail, or course   16 Mizzen topmast   19 Spanker
13 Maintopsail   staysail   20 Mizzen topsail
14 Main topgallant   17 Mizzen topgallant   21 Mizzen topgallant
    staysail   staysail
15 Mizzen staysail   18 Mizzen sail

GLOSSARY

aft, after Situated at the back or stern part of a ship or vessel.

barge A large ten- or twelve-oared boat carried by a warship and used by admirals and senior captains. Also refers to a certain type of cargo-carrying merchant vessel (such as a Thames barge).

block A pulley containing one, two or more sheaves, used to increase the power applied to ropes.

block and tackle An arrangement of pulleys and ropes used to raise heavy loads, and to increase the purchase on ropes used for the running rigging.

boatswain/bosun The warrant officer in charge of sails, rigging, anchors and associated gear.

bowsprit A heavy spar pointing forward from the stem or front of the vessel.

brace A rope used to control the horizontal movement of a square-sailed yard.

brig A two-masted vessel, fully square-rigged on both masts, with a fore-and-aft sail on the lower part of the mainmast.

brigantine A two-masted vessel having a fully square-rigged foremast and a fore-and-aft rigged mainmast with square sails on the main topmast.

broadside The simultaneous firing of all the guns on one side of a ship.

bulkhead A vertical partition inside a ship.

bumboat A small boat used to bring out and sell fruit, vegetables and other produce to the sailors on ships anchored some distance from the shore.

cable A measure of distance, in Britain equal to 100 fathoms (200 yards). Also refers to any large rope such as the rope used for anchoring a ship.

caulk To seal the gaps between the planks with oakum and pitch.

clipper The very fast, square-rigged sailing ships which were used to transport tea, wool and other bulk cargoes in the second half of the nineteenth century.

colours The flags worn by a vessel to show her nationality.

companionway The staircase or ladder down to a cabin or the lower deck; or up to the quarterdeck.

cutter A small one-masted vessel rigged with a fore-and-aft mainsail, foresail and jib. In the eighteenth century a cutter usually had a square topsail as well. Also a ten-oared ship's boat used for carrying light stores and passengers.

deadeye A round wooden block with three holes for extending the shrouds.

duff A boiled pudding made from flour, fat, sugar and water. Currants and raisins, when available, were added to make plum duff.

ensign The national flag usually flown by ships at or near the stern of the vessel.

fathom A measure of about 2 metres (6 feet), used to describe the depth of water.

East Indiaman A large ship engaged in trade with the East Indies.

flagship A ship commanded by an admiral and flying the admiral's distinguishing flag.

flag captain The captain of a ship carrying an admiral and flying his flag. (Captain Hardy was Nelson's flag captain on board HMS. *Victory* at the Battle of Trafalgar.)

fore Situated in front; the front part of a vessel at the bow.

fore-and-aft At bow and stern; backwards and forwards or along the length of the ship.

fore-and-aft rig Having mainly fore-and-aft sails, i.e. sails set lengthwise (and not at right-angles to the ship's hull, as is the case with square-rigged sails).

forecastle/fo'c's'le The short deck built over the fore part of the main deck.

foremast The mast at the front of the vessel.

foretop A platform at the head of the lower foremast serving to spread the topmast rigging and provide a place for sailors working aloft.

frigate A fast cruising warship, less heavily armed than a ship of the line. Most frigates were fifth- and sixth-rates with between 44 and 20 guns.

galley The ship's kitchen.

gig A light, clinker-built boat carried by a warship and often favoured by captains for their own use.

grog A drink of rum diluted with water.

gunwale The upper planking along the sides of the vessel.

guardship A ship kept in reserve but, unlike a ship in ordinary, she was fully rigged and partly armed and manned, and could be ready for action in a few days. Most guardships were 74s or 64s but in a major port such as

Plymouth or Portsmouth a three-decker often served as the flagship of the port admiral.

halyard A rope for raising and lowering a sail or yard.

hatch boat A type of fishing boat used in the Thames Estuary.

hawser A large rope or a small cable.

heave to (*past tense*: **hove to**) To check the course of a vessel and bring her to a standstill by heading her into the wind and backing some of the sails.

helm The tiller or wheel which controls the rudder and enables a vessel to be steered.

hulk An old ship taken out of service and moored in a harbour. Hulks were used as prison ships, convict ships, hospitals, floating barracks and receiving ships for pressed men.

jury rig A makeshift arrangement of masts, yards and sails used to replace those damaged by storm or enemy action.

larboard An old word for *port* (the left side of a vessel facing forward) which was preferred for helm orders. It was abandoned in 1844.

league A measure of distance: 5 km (3 miles).

lee The side or direction away from the wind, or downwind.

lee shore The shore onto which the wind is blowing; a hazardous shore for a sailing vessel particularly in strong or gale-force winds.

log, log-book A journal or diary which recorded the ship's position, speed and course, with notes on the wind direction, weather, sail changes, flag signals, and other vessels met en route. The official log-book in a British warship was kept by the ship's master (navigator) but the captain and lieutenants also kept log-books and so did the midshipmen.

longboat The largest and heaviest boat carried by a warship, used for laying out anchors, and carrying water casks and other heavy loads.

lugger A vessel rigged with one or more fore-and-aft lugsails. Each sail is set on a yard, of which about one-third is on the fore side of the mast.

mainmast 1. The mast at the centre of the ship or vessel, always the largest in square-rigged ships. **2.** The name of the first and lowest section of the mainmast in a square-rigged ship; the others are the maintopmast, maintopgallant mast, and main royalmast.

mainsheet The rope at the lower corner of the mainsail for regulating its position.

man-of-war An armed ship belonging to the navy of a country.

mizenmast The mast at the stern or back of a vessel.

(in) ordinary Ships laid up in reserve with their masts, rigging and guns removed.

pendant (pronounced 'pennant') This term can be used for any long tapering flag. The commissioning pendant of a naval ship was a very long flag like a streamer flown from the main masthead and it distinguished a warship in commission from a merchant ship.

pennant *See* **pendant**

pink 1. A merchant vessel with a relatively shallow draught and a narrow stern, variously rigged as a brig, a sloop, or a ship. **2.** The term also applied to a type of Dutch fishing boat which was launched off the beaches near Scheveningen.

poop deck The aftermost and highest deck of a ship.

port The left side of a vessel facing forward.

press gang A group of men led by an officer, employed to round up men for service in the Royal Navy.

prize A ship or vessel captured from the enemy in time of war.

quarter The side of a ship towards the stern.

quarterdeck A deck above the main deck which stretched from the stern to about halfway along the length of the ship. It was from this deck that the captain and officers controlled the ship.

quarter gallery A covered gallery with windows which projected from each side of the ship at the stern, used as a lavatory or toilet by the captain and officers.

rate (as in first-rate, second-rate, etc) Warships were grouped into six different categories according to the number of guns they carried. In the eighteenth century a first-rate ship had 100 guns, a second-rate ship had 90 guns, a third-rate had 80, 74, or 64 guns, a fourth-rate had between 64 and 50 guns, a fifth-rate had between 44 and 32 guns, and a sixth-rate had between 28 and 20 guns.

reef To reduce the area of a sail by rolling it up or bundling part of it and securing that part with short lines called reef-points.

running rigging Ropes which run through blocks or are moved in any way to operate the sails and gear of a vessel, as distinct from **standing rigging**.

schooner A two-masted vessel, fore-and-aft rigged on both masts. Some vessels had square topsails on the foremast or on both topmasts.

scuppers Holes in a ship's side through which water could drain off from the deck.

sextant An instrument with a graduated arc of 60 degrees, used for navigation.

sheet A rope made fast to the lower corner or corners of a sail to control its position.

sheer hulk A vessel, usually an old ship, fitted with a pair of sheer legs (two large spars forming an 'A frame') to hoist masts in and out of vessels; a floating crane.

ship 1. A vessel with three or more masts and fully square-rigged throughout. **2.** The term is also used to describe any large sea-going vessel.

ship of the line A warship large enough to take her place in the line of battle. In the late eighteenth century this usually ranged from third-rate ships of between 64 and 80 guns up to first-rate ships of 100 guns or more.

shrouds The set of ropes forming part of the standing rigging and supporting the mast or topmast.

sloop 1. A vessel having one fore-and-aft rigged mast with mainsail and a single foresail. **2.** In the Royal Navy any ship or vessel commanded by an officer with the rank of master and commander, usually rigged as a ship or brig with 16 to 28 guns.

slop seller A supplier of clothes for sailors.

spar A stout wooden pole used for the mast or yard of a sailing vessel.

square-rigged The principal sails set at right-angles to the length of the ship and extended by horizontal yards slung to the mast (as opposed to fore-and-aft rigged).

standing rigging That part of the rigging which supports the masts and spars and which is not moved when operating the vessel, as distinct from **running rigging**.

starboard The right side of a vessel facing forward.

supernumerary A person borne on the ship's books in addition to the established complement.

tack To change the direction of a sailing vessel's course by turning her bows into the wind until the wind blows on her other side.

tender A vessel attending a larger vessel and used to supply stores or convey passengers.

three-decker The largest class of warship with upwards of 90 guns on three gundecks.

top (as in foretop, maintop, mizentop) A platform built at the head of the lower mast serving to spread the topmast rigging and provide a place for sailors working aloft.

topmen The sailors who went aloft to raise or lower the sails.

topsail A sail set on the topmast.

van The foremost or leading ships of a fleet.

warp (noun) A rope used in towing or warping.

warp (verb) In calms or contrary winds it was often necessary to warp a vessel in and out of harbour or along a river. This was done by taking a rope or ropes from the ship to a fixed point ashore, or to a heavy post or pile driven into the river bed alongside the channel, and then heaving in the rope to haul the ship along.

warrant officers These ranked below the commissioned officers (the captain and lieutenants) and included the master, purser, surgeon, gunner, boatswain, carpenter and cook.

wear (as in 'to wear ship') To change the direction of a sailing vessel's course by turning her bows away from the wind until the wind blows on her other side (the opposite manoeuvre from tacking, when the bows are turned into the wind).

weather (adjective) The side facing the wind. The weather column of a fleet is the column to windward or nearest the direction from which the wind is blowing.

weigh anchor To pull up the anchor.

yard A long spar suspended from the mast of a vessel to extend the sails.

yard-arm Either end of a yard.

BIBLIOGRAPHY

Albion, Robert, *Forests and Sea Power* (Annapolis, Maryland, 1926)

Banbury, Philip, *Shipbuilders of the Thames and Medway* (Newton Abbot, 1972)

Barnard, Derek, *Merrily to Frindsbury: a history of the parish of Frindsbury* (Rochester, 1996)

Barrett, Charlotte, editor, *Diary and Letters of Madame D'Arblay* (London, 1891)

Bateson, Charles, *The Convict Ships: 1787–1868* (Glasgow, 1959)

Berry, Captain Edward, *An authentic narrative of the proceedings of His Majesty's Squadron from its sailing from Gibraltar to the conclusion of the glorious Battle of the Nile* (London, 1798)

Blackburn, Julia, *The Emperor's Last Island: a journey to St Helena* (London, 1992)

Blake, Nicholas, and Lawrence, Richard, *The Illustrated Companion to Nelson's Navy* (London, 1999)

Boudriot, Jean, *The Seventy-four Gun Ship*, vol. 1 (first published Paris, 1973; English edition, 1986)

Campbell, Charles, *The Intolerable Hulks: British shipboard confinement 1776–1857* (Maryland, USA, 1994)

Chandler, David, *Waterloo, the hundred days* (London, 1980)

Coad, Jonathan, *Historic Architecture of the Royal Navy* (London, 1983)

Coleman, Terry, *Nelson, the man and the legend* (London, 2001)

Collingwood, G.L. Newnham, *A selection from the public and private correspondence of Vice-Admiral Lord Collingwood* (London, 1829)

Cordingly, David, *Nicholas Pocock, 1740–1821* (London, 1986)

Cronin, Vincent, *Napoleon* (London, 1971; edition cited, 1994)

Deane, Anthony, *Nelson's Favourite: HMS. Agamemnon at War 1781–1809* (London, 1996)

Duffy, Michael, *Soldiers, Sugar and Seapower: the British expeditions to the West Indies and the war against Revolutionary France* (Oxford, 1987)

Duffy, Michael, and Morriss, Roger, *The Glorious First of June: a naval battle and its aftermath* (Exeter, 2001)

Fraser, Edward,

Bellerophon: the Bravest of the Brave (London, 1909)

The Enemy at Trafalgar (London, 1906)

Fresselicque, Reverend John, *A sermon of praise and thanksgiving & preached on board His Majesty's Ship Bellerophon at sea, on Sunday 8th of June, 1794* (Gosport, 1794)

Gardiner, Robert, editor,

Fleet Battle and Blockade: the French Revolutionary War 1793–1797 (London, 1996)

Nelson against Napoleon: From the Nile to Copenhagen, 1798–1801 (London, 1997)

The Campaign of Trafalgar, 1803–1805 (London, 1997)

The Line of Battle: the Sailing Warship 1650–1840 (London, 1992)

Grant, Gordon, *The Life and Adventures of John Nicol, mariner* (London, 1822)

Hay, M.D., editor, *Landsman Hay: the memoirs of Robert Hay 1789–1847* (London, 1953)

Holmes, Richard,

Coleridge: Darker Reflections (London, 1998)

Coleridge: Selected Poems (London, 1996)

Home, George, *Memoirs of an Aristocrat and Reminiscences of the Emperor Napoleon by a midshipman of the Bellerophon* (London, 1838)

Howarth, David, *Trafalgar: the Nelson Touch* (London, 1969; edition cited, 1972)

Jackson, Hilary W., *A County Durham man at Trafalgar: Cumby of the Bellerophon* (Durham County Local History Society, 1997)

Johnson, W. Branch, *The English Prison Hulks* (London and Chichester, 1957)

Jones, A.G.E., 'Sir Thomas Slade, 1703/4–1771' (*Mariners Mirror*, London, 1977), vol. 63, pp. 224–226

Kauffmann, Jean-Paul, *The Dark Room at Longwood* (1997; edition cited, 1999)

Keegan, John, *The Price of Admiralty* (London, 1988)

Knight, R.J.B.,

'New England Forests and British seapower: Albion revised' (*American Neptune*, XLVI, 1986)

'Sandwich, Middleton, and Dockyard appointments' (*Mariners Mirror*, London, 1971), vol. LVII, pp. 175–192

'The introduction of copper sheathing into the Royal Navy 1779–1786' (*Mariners Mirror*, London, 1973), vol. LIX, pp. 299–309

Laughton, Sir John Knox, *Letters and Papers of Charles, Lord Barham, 1758–1813* (Navy Records Society, London, 1906–1910), vols. 32, 38 and 39

Lavery, Brian,

Nelson's Navy: the Ships, Men and Organisation, 1793–1815 (London, 1989; edition cited, 2000)

The Arming and Fitting of English Ships of War 1600–1815 (London, 1987)

The Ship of the Line: the development of the battle fleet 1650–1850 (London 1983), vol. I

Building the Wooden Walls: the design and construction of the 74-gun ship Valiant (London, 1991)

Nelson and the Nile: the Naval War against Bonaparte 1798 (London, 1998)

Lavery, Brian, editor, *Shipboard life and organisation, 1731–1815* (Navy Records Society, London, 1998)

Leech, Samuel, *Thirty years from home, or a voice from the main deck* (London, 1843)

Lyon, David, *The Sailing Navy List: All the ships of the Royal Navy 1688–1860* (London, 1993)

Maitland, Sir Frederick Lewis, *The Surrender of Napoleon, being the Narrative of the surrender of Buonaparte, and of his residence on board HMS. Bellerophon* (London, 1826; edition cited, 1904)

Marchand, Louis-Joseph, *In Napoleon's Shadow*, English language edition of the memoirs of Napoleon's valet, edited by Proctor Jones (San Francisco, California 1998)

Marshall, John, *Royal Navy Biography*, 4 vols., (London, 1823–1835)

Marshall, P.J., editor, *The Oxford History of the British Empire*, vol. II, *The Eighteenth Century* (Oxford, 1998)

Martineau, Gilbert, *Napoleon Surrenders* (English language edition, London, 1971)

Mayhew, Henry and Binny, John, *The Criminal Prisons of London and Scenes of Prison Life* (London, 1862)

Morriss, Roger, editor, *The Channel Fleet and the Blockade of Brest 1793–1801* (Navy Records Society, London, 2001)

Naish, George, editor, *Nelson's letters to his wife and other documents, 1785–1831* (London, 1958)

Nicolas, Sir Nicholas Harris, *The Dispatches and Letters of Vice-Admiral Lord Viscount Nelson*, 7 vols. (London, 1844–1846)

O'Meara, Barry Edward, *Napoleon in Exile: or, a voice from St Helena: the opinions and reflections of Napoleon on the most important events of his life and government, in his own words*, 2 vols. (London, 1822)

Pasley, Rodney, M.S., editor, *Private Sea Journals 1778–1782, kept by Admiral Sir Thomas Pasley* (London, 1931)

Pengelly, Colin, *The First Bellerophon* (London, 1966)

Pocock, Tom, *Horatio Nelson* (London, 1987; edition cited, 1988)

Pope, Dudley, *Life in Nelson's Navy* (London, 1981)

Richardson, William, *A Mariner of England: An account of the career of William Richardson from cabin boy in the Merchant Service to Warrant Officer in the Royal Navy as told by himself* (London, 1908)

Roberts, Andrew, *Napoleon and Wellington* (London, 2001)

Rodger, N.A.M.,

The Insatiable Earl: a life of John Montagu, Fourth Earl of Sandwich (London, 1993)

The Admiralty (Lavenham, Suffolk, 1979)

Shorter, Clement, *Napoleon and his fellow travellers* (London, 1908)

Smetham, Henry, *Charles Roach Smith and his friends* (London, 1929)

Thompson, J.M., *Napoleon Bonaparte* (London, 1952)

Thornton, Michael J., *Napoleon after Waterloo: England and the St Helena decision* (Stanford, California, 1968)

Tucker, J.D., *Memoirs of the Right Hon. the Earl of St Vincent* (London, 1844)

Warner, Oliver,

The Battle of the Nile (London, 1960)

The Glorious First of June (London, 1961)

Watson, J. Steven, *The Reign of George III, 1760–1815* (Oxford, 1960)

White, Colin, *The Nelson Encyclopedia* (London, 2002)

Willyams, Reverend Cooper, *A voyage up the Mediterranean in His Majesty's Ship Swiftsure & with a description of the Battle of the Nile* (London, 1802)

Woodman, Richard, *The Victory of Seapower. winning the Napoleonic War 1806–1814* (London, 1998)

Woods, Joanna, *The Commissioner's Daughter: the story of Elizabeth Proby and Admiral Chichagov* (Witney, Oxfordshire, 2000)

NOTES

List of Abbreviations

PRO Public Record Office, Kew, London
NMM National Maritime Museum, Greenwich, London
ADM Admiralty documents in the Public Record Office
DNB Dictionary of National Biography

Introduction

1 John Capper's Report of 24 July 1823: PRO, House of Commons Parliamentary Papers, 1824, vol. XIX, p. 183.
2 Letter from Ephraim Graebke, assistant-surgeon, to his mother, included as an additional appendix in Sir Frederick Lewis Maitland, *The Surrender of Napoleon, being the Narrative of the surrender of Buonaparte, and of his residence on board HMS. Bellerophon* (first published London, 1826; edition cited, 1904), p. 242.
3 Preface to Maitland's *The Surrender of Napoleon*, p. vii.
4 NMM: LBK/38.
5 Maitland, p. 97.

Chapter 1

1 Letter from Sir J. Henslow to Lord St Vincent, 9 November 1899. NMM manuscript: AGC/J/6/1.
2 See article by A.G.E. Jones, 'Sir Thomas Slade 1703/4–1771' in *Mariners Mirror*, vol. 63, 1977, pp. 224–6.
3 The text on the gravestone is quoted in *The Gentleman's Magazine*, 1810, p. 629.
4 Letter from the Admiralty, 12 August 1755. PRO: ADM7/340, f504.
5 PRO: ADM.95/12,20/4/1750. Quoted by B. Lavery in *The Ship of the Line* (London, 1983), p. 94.

6 The British naval architect M. Stalkaart in his *Marine Architecture*, pp. 135–6.

7 *The Gentleman's Magazine*, 1810, p. 629.

8 The ships built by Greaves at Limehouse include the *Resistance*, 44, launched in July 1782; the *Romulus*, 36; the sloop *Calypso*; and a transport ship. See Greaves's letters to the Navy Board, ADM.106/1271; ADM.106/1212; and Minutes of the Surveyors' Office, ADM.106/2791 and ADM.106/2792.

9 *Kentish Gazette*, 24 August 1790.

10 Greaves's letters to the Navy Board are in PRO: ADM.106/1271, and ADM.106/1212.

11 Navy Board minutes, 14 December 1781, PRO: ADM.106/2606.

12 Navy Board to Admiralty, 9 January 1782: 'Mr Edward Greaves having made us an offer to build a 74 & 32 gun ship at Frinsbury near Rochester, for His Majesty's Service and removed the objections we had to building so near Chatham Yard by entering into an Engagement (under a Penalty) not to employ any Artificers from the Kings Yard, We desire you will please to let us know the pleasure of the Rt Honble the Lords Commisr of the Admiralty whether we are to accept the offer . . .', PRO: ADM.106/2209.

13 On the verso of Greaves's letter are the following notes (by the secretary or a clerk): 'Contracts to be prepared accordingly / The payments for the 36 [sic] must be the same as to other persons / Acq the Admiralty we have agreed for the 74 & 32 agreeable to their order of 11 instant / River Price for 74: 17.17.6 / Ditto for 32 : £11.15.0 / Mr Greaves will build a 74 & 32 Gun ship at Frinsbury', PRO: ADM.106/1271.

14 The *Bellerophon*'s contract is in the collections of the National Maritime Museum, Greenwich. NMM: ADM.168/170, item 114.

15 The first mention of the name appears in the minutes of the Surveyors' Office which on 3 April contain a list with the names of thirty new ships which are to be built. PRO: ADM.106/2791.

16 'Why she and the Bellyruffron seem to have pretty well shared and shared alike.' Captain Marryat, *Poor Jack* (London, 1840), ch. XIII.

17 The Navy Board ordered the officers at Chatham to inspect the timber and report whether there was enough elm for the keel as well as other timber to proceed, and on 28 June the Chatham officers were ordered 'to take a survey of the 74-gun ship building by him at Finsbury and give him a certificate for his first bill . . .', PRO: ADM.106/2608.

18 The information about oaks for shipbuilding is taken from: B. Lavery, *Building the Wooden Walls* (London, 1991); Robert Albion, *Forests and Sea Power* (Annapolis, Maryland, 1926); Jean Boudriot, *The Seventy-four Gun Ship*, vol. 1 (first published Paris, 1973; English edition, 1986).

19 *Progress of Works* book for Portsmouth Dockyard, quoted by Lavery in *Building the Wooden Walls*, p. 128.

20 See N. Rodger, *The Insatiable Earl* (London, 1993), p. 149.

21 *The Gentleman's Magazine*, October 1786, p. 895.

Chapter 2

1 Out-letters from Resident Commissioner to the Admiralty: NMM: CHA/X/2.

2 *The Kentish Gazette*, issue of September 29 to October 3, 1786.

3 *The Times*, 6 October 1786.

4 *Nelson's letters to his wife and other documents, 1785–1831*, edited by George Naish (London, 1958), pp. 21–22.

5 Quoted by Vincent Cronin in *Napoleon* (London, 1971; edition cited, 1994), p. 102.

6 *Diary and Letters of Madame D'Arblay*, edited by Charlotte Barrett (London, 1891), vol. IV, p. 169.

7 For a more detailed account of the workings of the Admiralty and Navy Board, see: N. Rodger, *The Admiralty* (Lavenham, Suffolk, 1979); Brian Lavery, *Nelson's Navy* (London, 1989; edition cited, 2000), pp. 21–25; N. Rodger, *The Insatiable Earl* (London, 1993); Sir John Knox Laughton, *Letters and Papers of Charles, Lord Barham, 1758–1813* (Navy Records Society, London, 1906–1910), vol. 38; J.M. Collinge, *Navy Board Officials, 1660–1832* (London Institute of Historical Research, 1978, no. VII); R.J.B. Knight, 'Sandwich, Middleton, and Dockyard appointments' (*Mariners Mirror*, London) LVII (1971), pp. 175–192.

8 Charles Middleton (1726–1813) was the son of a Scots customs officer. He joined the navy and was a captain when appointed Controller of Navy in 1778. He was created a baronet in 1781, became a Lord of the Admiralty in 1794, and was First Lord of the Admiralty in 1805, the same year that he was created first Baron Barham.

9 Quoted by N. Rodger in *The Admiralty* p. 79.

10 Laughton, *Letters and Papers of Charles, Lord Barham* (NRS, 1906–1910), vol. 38, p. 236.

11 Ibid, p. 236.

Chapter 3

1 For ships in sea pay in October 1786 see PRO: ADM.8/62. For ships in ordinary see PRO: ADM.42/77; ADM.42/743; ADM.42/1123; KDM.42/1539.

2 PRO. ADM 42/77.

3 For a detailed discussion of the advantages, and problems, of copper sheathing, see: B. Lavery, *The Arming and Fitting of English Ships of War 1600–1815* (London, 1987), pp. 62–65; and N. Rodger, *The Insatiable Earl* (London, 1993), pp. 294–298.

4 The *Bedford*, 74 guns, was coppered at Plymouth Yard in 1779 and required 1,329 thin copper sheets and 1,412 thick copper sheets. See B. Lavery, *The Ship of the Line* (London, 1983), vol. 1, p. 207.

5 For further information on Chatham dockyard, see Brian Lavery, *Building the Wooden Walls* (London, 1991) and Jonathan Coad, *Historic Architecture of the Royal Navy* (London, 1983).

6 Letter from Chatham, 11 October, in *The Kentish Gazette*, 10 October to 13 October 1786.

7 The minutes of the Surveyors' Office for 8 August 1786 include a list of overseers of ships under construction by private contractors. The overseers are ordered to 'let the Board know when the respective ships building under their inspection will be completed.' Henry Peake is listed as overseer for the *Bellerophon*. PRO: ADM 106/2796.

8 The information about Commissioner Proby is taken from his letters to the Admiralty and the Navy Board, and from Joanna Woods, *The Commissioner's Daughter: the story of Elizabeth Proby and Admiral Chichagov* (Witney, Oxfordshire, 2000).

9 Letter from Proby to Philip Stephens, Secretary to the Admiralty, 30 July 1783. NMM: CHA/X/2.

10 Whether Britain ever had a coherent naval strategy in the eighteenth century is arguable. For an excellent discussion of this and the thinking behind Britain's naval policy in the eighteenth century, see Nicholas Rodger, 'Sea Power and Empire' in the *Oxford History of the British Empire*, vol. II, *The Eighteenth Century*, ed. P.J. Marshall (Oxford, 1998) pp. 169–183.

11 Thomas Pasley (1734–1808) was born in the village of Craig near Kirkcudbright. He was the fifth son of James Pasley and of Magdalen, daughter of Robert Elliot, elder brother of Sir Gilbert Elliot, the first baronet. See DNB; *The Gentleman's Magazine*, December 1808, p. 1131; *Naval Chronicle*, December 1800; and Rodney M.S. Pasley, ed., *Private Sea Journals 1778–1782, kept by Admiral Sir Thomas Pasley* (London, 1931).

12 Lavery, *Nelson's Navy*, p. 119.

13 Ibid, p. 118.

Chapter 4

1 *Diary and Letters of Madame D'Arblay*, edited by Charlotte Barrett (London, 1891), vol. III, p. 477.
2 Message from the King to the House of Commons, as reported in *The Times*, 29 January 1793.
3 For the operations of the press gangs in the spring of 1793, see reports in *The Times* on 14 and 23 February and 5, 9 and 27 March.
4 This is Admiral Samuel Hood (1724–1816), first Viscount Hood, who had made his name with Admiral Rodney at the Battle of the Saints and other actions in the West Indies against the French in the 1780s. Not to be confused with his brother Admiral Sir Alexander Hood (1727–1814), later Lord Bridport, who was a flag officer in Lord Howe's Channel fleet and took part in the Battle of the Glorious First of June.
5 Log entry for 30 September 1793, PRO: ADM 51/99.
6 PRO: ADM 95/39, folio 36.
7 PRO: ADM 95/45, folio 11.
8 William Johnstone Hope was born in Finchley in 1766, the youngest son of a London merchant and part-time writer. He went to sea with his uncle Captain Hope who was later Commissioner of Chatham dockyard. He married Lady Anne, eldest daughter of Lord Hopetoun, and had seven children.
9 Letter from *Bellerophon*, Spithead, 16 February 1794. PRO: ADM 1/2311.
10 Letter from Pasley to the Admiralty, 29 January 1794, PRO: ADM 1/2311.
11 Ibid.

Chapter 5

1 The French squadron under Nielly did not join up with the Brest fleet under Villaret-Joyeuse until 30 May.
2 The account in this chapter of the four-day action which culminated in the battle of the Glorious First of June is drawn from the following sources: the captain's log of the *Bellerophon*, PRO: ADM.51/1162, part 6; Nicholas Pocock's First of June notebook, NMM: JOD/12; Oliver Warner, *The Glorious First of June*, (London, 1961); *The Glorious First of June: a naval battle and its aftermath*, edited by Michael Duffy and Roger Morriss (Exeter, 2001); *Fleet Battle and Blockade: the French Revolutionary War 1793–1797*, edited by Robert Gardiner (London, 1996); Matthew Flinders, *A Journal kept on board His Majesty's ship Bellerophon*, NMM: FLI/8b.
3 Quoted by Duffy and Morriss, p. 85. The original letter is in the National

Maritime Museum, PAR/193.

4 For the full text of the journal and a biography of the artist, see David Cordingly, *Nicholas Pocock, 1740–1821* (London, 1986).

5 Duffy and Morriss, p. 85.

6 Quoted by Edward Fraser in *Bellerophon* (London 1906).

7 Ibid.

8 NMM: JOD/12.

9 From a letter by Jonathan Wilkinson of the *Queen*. Duffy and Morriss, p. 80.

10 Warner, op. cit., p. 51.

11 Ibid, p. 53.

12 NMM: FLI/8b.

13 Fraser, *Bellerophon*, p. 82.

14 The highly eccentric spelling of Wilkinson's letter has been altered here but the full text of the original letter is reproduced in Duffy and Morriss, p. 80.

15 Warner, p. 79.

16 Ibid, p. 76.

17 Duffy and Morriss, p. 94.

18 Warner, p. 126.

19 Ibid, p. 37.

Chapter 6

1 Although the French had developed a series of shutter telegraph stations in 1792 to connect the French dockyards with Paris, the British did not set up a similar system until 1796 when two chains of telegraph stations were set up, one of them linking London with Dover, the other linking London with Portsmouth and Plymouth.

2 PRO: ADM 1/100; Howe's despatch of June 2, and his supplementary letter providing more detail of the action, are printed in full as an appendix in Oliver Warner, *The Glorious First of June* (London, 1961).

3 *The Times*, London 11 June 1794.

4 John Fresselicque, *A sermon . . . preached on board . . . the Bellerophon* (published 1794). There is a copy in the British Library.

5 *The Times*, 16 June 1794.

6 Thomas Pasley became a full admiral and died at Winchester on 29 November 1808 at the age of seventy-five. See *The Gentleman's Magazine*, December 1808, p. 1131; entry in DNB; and Rodney Pasley, *Private Sea Journals 1778–1782, kept by Admiral Sir Thomas Pasley* (London, 1931).

7 Warner, *The Glorious First of June*, p. 143.

8 The French ships captured at the First of June were: *Sans Pareil*, 80 guns; *Le Juste*, 80; *L'America*, 74; *L'Achille*, 74; *Le Northumberland*, 74; and *L'Impétueux*, 74.

9 The sitting of 16 June of the National Convention, Paris, reported in *The Times*, London, 24 June 1794.

Chapter 7

1 Lord Cranstoun to the Admiralty, from *Bellerophon*, Spithead, 3 December 1794. PRO: ADM.1/1619.

2 Captain's log, PRO: ADM.51/1142 (part 11).

3 Letter from the marines, *Bellerophon*, Spithead, April 16 1795. Included with the records of the Court Martial on 29 September 1795. PRO: ADM.1/5333.

4 Lord Cranstoun to the Admiralty, from *Bellerophon*, 23 May 1795. PRO: ADM.1/1620.

5 Despatch from Vice-Admiral Cornwallis to the Admiralty, from *The Royal Sovereign* at sea, 19 June 1795. Quoted in full in *The Times*, Monday, 29 June 1795.

6 Captain's log, 17 June 1795. PRO: ADM.51/1142 (part 11).

7 Cornwallis's despatch, *The Times*, Monday, 29 June 1795.

8 Ibid.

9 Log of *Phaeton*: 'Fresh breezes and clear answered the private signal to the supposed fleet 5 min past 3 made the Signal No 14 to the Admiral with 1 gun 25 min past 4 made the Signal No 36 with 1 gun. our signal No 6 & shewed our signal more distinctly (5) repeated General Signal No 9 to the supposed Fleet at 5 [illeg] Royals Studding Sails & Staysails at 6 Royal Sovn. NE 9 miles General Signal 140 Enemys Fleet caesed firing General Signal No 9 Wore . . .' PRO: ADM.51/1147.

10 Ibid.

Chapter 8

1 Tom Pocock, *Horatio Nelson* (1987; edition cited, 1988), p. 131.

2 Ibid, p. 132.

3 Ibid, p. 135.

4 PRO: ADM.1/5339.

5 J.D. Tucker, *Memoirs of the Right Hon. the Earl of St Vincent* (London, 1844), vol. 1, p. 326.

6 PRO: ADM.1/5340.

7 Tucker, vol. 1, p. 326.

8 Ibid, vol. 1, p. 327.

Chapter 9

1 *Diary and Letters of Madame D'Arblay*, edited by Charlotte Barrett (London, 1891), vol. IV, p. 168.

2 *The Times*, Saturday, 10 February 1798.

3 Richard Holmes, *Coleridge: Selected Poems* (London, 1996), p. 50.

4 Quoted by Brian Lavery in *Nelson and the Nile* (London 1998), p. 9.

5 Tom Pocock, *Horatio Nelson* (London, 1987; edition cited, 1988), p. 153.

6 Ibid, p. 145.

7 Ibid, p. 146.

8 *The Private Papers of George, second Earl Spencer*, edited by Julian S. Corbett (Navy Records Society, London, 1913–14), vol. 2, p. 441.

9 PRO. ADM.51/1262.

10 Lavery, *Nelson and the Nile*, p. 124.

11 Ibid, p. 129.

12 J.M. Thompson, *Napoleon Bonaparte* (London, 1952; edition cited, 1988), p 109

13 Lavery, *Nelson and the Nile*, p. 138.

14 PRO: ADM.51/1262.

Chapter 10

1 For further reading, see Brian Lavery, *Nelson and the Nile* (London 1998), a meticulously researched and beautifully written account of the battle and the events leading up to it. See also Oliver Warner, *The Battle of the Nile* (London, 1960); Rev. Cooper Willyams, *A Voyage up the Mediterranean in His Majesty's Ship Swiftsure . . . with a description of the Battle of the Nile* (London, 1802).

2 Quoted by Lavery, p. 170.

3 George Bellamy (1773–1863) was born in Plymouth and came from a naval family. He had joined the navy in 1793 as surgeon's mate on the *Myrmidon*, and had been acting surgeon on the cutter *Ranger* at the First of June. After the Nile he continued as a surgeon on board various ships. He married, had eight children and later became Mayor of Plymouth. I am grateful to Peter Langford, a descendant, for sending me Bellamy's obituary which appeared in a Plymouth newspaper dated 17 October 1863.

4 *List of men wounded in the Action of 1ˢᵗ August 1798 and List of Officers &* *others who died of their wounds in Cockpit during the Fight.* Hand-written notes by George Bellamy, Surgeon, 5 August 1798. Private collection, England.

5 ADM.51/1262.

6 See Clement de la Jonquière, *L'Expedition d'Egypte, 1798–1801,* vol. 2, p. 417.

7 *The Times,* 5 October 1798.

8 Sir Nicholas Harris Nicolas, *The Dispatches and Letters of Vice-Admiral Lord Viscount Nelson,* (London, 1844–1845), vol. VII, Additional Notes, p. CLV.

9 See Nelson's despatch to Admiral Lord St Vincent, 3 August 1798, in Nicolas, vol. III, p. 59; and La Jonquière, vol. 2, p. 419.

Chapter 11

1 *Nelson against Napoleon,* edited by Robert Gardiner (London, 1997), p. 42.

2 Brian Lavery, *Nelson and the Nile: the Naval War against Bonaparte 1798* (London, 1998), p. 247.

3 Ibid, p. 247.

4 Tom Pocock, *Horatio Nelson* (London, 1987; edition cited, 1998), p. 171.

5 Ibid, p. 181.

6 Ibid, p. 182.

7 Lavery, *Nelson and the Nile* p. 252.

8 Ibid, p. 256.

9 From The Vernon Papers, quoted in Michael Pawson and David Buisseret, *Port Royal, Jamaica* (Oxford, 1975), p. 132.

10 J.P. Thompson, *Napoleon Bonaparte* (London, 1952), p. 218.

11 Ibid, p. 221.

Chapter 12

1 Entry for 20 August 1778, *Private Sea Journals 1778–1782, kept by Admiral Sir Thomas Pasley,* edited by Rodney M.S. Pasley (London, 1931).

2 Robert Gardiner, 'The Convoy System', in *The Campaign of Trafalgar, 1803–1805* (London, 1997), p. 51.

3 ADM. 180/6; PRO.

4 J.M. Thompson, *Napoleon Bonaparte* (London, 1988; edition cited, 2002), p. 229.

5 For an excellent description of the invasion flotilla and illustrated plans of the various types of invasion craft, see Robert Gardiner, *The Campaign of Trafalgar, 1803–1805,* pp. 57–68.

6 Fernand Nicolay, *Napoleon at the Boulogne Camp* (London, MCMVII), p. 348.

7 Ibid, p. 349.

8 Ibid, p. 351.

9 Thompson, p. 230.

10 Letter from Soult to the Minister of War, 22 July 1804, quoted in full by Fernand Nicolay, p. 179.

11 Letter to Villeneuve, 13 August 1805, quoted by Nicolay, p. 389.

12 Letter to Ganteaume, 22 August 1805, quoted by Nicolay, p. 390.

13 For illustrations of the army engineer's drawings of the tower at Mortella, and details of the attack on the tower, see *Fleet Battle and Blockade*, edited by Robert Gardiner (London, 1996), pp. 100–101, 108.

14 Nicholas Blake and Richard Lawrence, *The Illustrated Companion to Nelson's Navy* (London, 1999), p. 183.

15 *The Times*, Friday, 2 August 1805.

16 *The Times*, Monday, 26 August 1805.

17 Captain John Cooke (1763–1805) was the second son of Francis Cooke, Cashier of the Navy. He served under Howe in the *Eagle* as a midshipman and distinguished himself at the attack on Rhode Island. At the Battle of the Saints he was first lieutenant of the 90-gun *Duke*. Nicholas Pocock's painting of the frigate action off Brest was exhibited at the Royal Academy in 1798 with the title, 'Capture of the Resistance and Constance, French frigates, close in with Brest, March 9, 1797, by his Majesty's frigates St Fiorenzo, Capt. Sir H.B. Neale, Bart., and the Nymph, Captain Cook.'

18 William Pryce Cumby (1771–1837) came from a naval family and had joined the navy at the age of eight. He received high praise for his conduct at Trafalgar and was rewarded after the battle by being promoted to commander and post-captain in quick succession. For a useful life of Cumby, see: Hilary W. Jackson, *A County Durham man at Trafalgar: Cumby of the Bellerophon* (Durham County Local History Society, 1997).

19 The original of Cumby's letter is in the National Maritime Museum, together with several of his notebooks containing copies of orders and memoranda and some of his letters. NMM manuscripts: JON/7 (44.MS.9850).

20 Tom Pocock, *Horatio Nelson* (London, 1987; edition cited, 1988) p. 314.

Chapter 13

1 Quoted by Edward Fraser in *The Enemy at Trafalgar* (London, 1906), p. 308. From a letter dated 'Bellerophon off the Start, Dec.2, 1805' which appeared in a Portsmouth newspaper and was written by an officer who was one of the prize crew sent to take possession of the *Monarca*.

2 NMM: JON/7.

3 Ibid.

4 Ibid.

5 PRO: ADM.51/4417 (part 7).

6 Letter from Villeneuve to Decrès, 21 August 1805. Quoted by John Keegan, *The Price of Admiralty* (London, 1988), p. 33.

7 Minutes of Council of War held on *Bucentaur* on 8 October 1805. Quoted in David Howarth, *Trafalgar: the Nelson Touch* (London, 1969; edition cited, 1972), p. 95.

8 Keegan, p. 58.

9 Howarth, p. 70.

10 NMM: JON/7.

11 Edward Fraser, *Bellerophon: the Bravest of the Brave* (London, 190), pp. 230–231.

12 She was usually referred to as the French *Swiftsure* after her capture, because in 1804 another *Swiftsure* was launched at Bucklers Hard. The replacement *Swiftsure*, a 74, also fought at Trafalgar and was in the lee column led by Collingwood.

13 Ibid, p. 245.

14 Quoted by Fraser in *The Enemy at Trafalgar*, pp. 207–8.

15 NMM: JON/7.

16 Ibid, p. 206.

17 Quoted in *The Campaign of Trafalgar, 1803–1805*, edited by Robert Gardiner (London, 1997), p. 159.

18 According to Cumby's letter 'the Achille 74 took fire and blew up at half past five took possession of the Spanish 74 Bahama . . .', NMM: JON/7.

19 Howarth, p. 221.

20 Keegan, p. 90.

Chapter 14

1 Letter from Collingwood to William Marsden, quoted in *The Campaign of Trafalgar, 1803–1805*, edited by Robert Gardiner (London, 1997), p. 166.

2 David Howarth, *Trafalgar: the Nelson Touch* (London, 1969; edition cited, 1972), p. 229.

3 Quoted by Richard Holmes in *Coleridge: Darker Reflections* (London, 1998). Coleridge sailed from Spithead on 9 April 1804. He was a passenger on the merchant brig *Speedwell*, which was part of a convoy of thirty-five merchantmen carrying guns and supplies to British and allied ports in the Mediterranean.

4 Quoted by Colin Pengelly in *The First Bellerophon* (London, 1966), p. 209.

5 Cumby was promoted to commander as from 24 December 1805 and post-captain from 1 January 1806.

6 The survey is contained in a large manuscript volume, *The Letters of Captain Edward Rotheram 1799–1830*, in the collections of the National Maritime Museum, London. NMM: LBK/38.

7 The official complement of the *Bellerophon* was 590. In 1807 the ship mustered 401 officers and seamen, 25 boys and volunteers, and 109 marines, giving a total of 535. (See the *Bellerophon*'s Muster Book for 1 May 1807, PRO: ADM.37/516.) Subtracting the officers, warrant officers, marines and boys from this number produces a figure of 387 which is the number of seamen for whom Rotheram provides details.

8 Nils Ingemarsson Linnaeus (1707–1778) was the father of taxonomy. His system for naming, ranking and classifying organisms is still in wide use today.

9 Although there was 7 foot between the planks of the gun deck and the underside of the upperdeck planks above, the deck was supported at close intervals by massive deck beams and the height from the gun deck to the underside of these beams was only 5 ft. 8 in. See the *Bellerophon*'s contract, NMM: ADM.168/170, item 114.

10 See Colin White, *The Nelson Encyclopedia* (London, 2002), p.150. Colin White's book includes the latest research on Nelson and explodes many of the commonly held myths about his life, his health, his appearance and his naval actions.

11 Order issued by Captain Edward Hawker, 9 April 1814. NMM: HAW/8.

12 William Richardson, *A Mariner of England* (London, 1908), p. 119.

13 Rotheram's survey does not indicate whether the men were pressed or volunteers, and neither do the *Bellerophon*'s muster rolls for this period.

14 The *Bellerophon*'s schoolmaster and chaplain were not included in Rotheram's survey.

15 Captain Hawker's Order Book of HMS. *Bellerophon* is in the NMM: HAW/8.

16 For descriptions of shipboard routine, see *Landsman Hay*, edited by M.D. Hay (London, 1953); Samuel Leech, *Thirty years from home, or a voice from the main deck* (London, 1843); Dudley Pope, *Life in Nelson's Navy* (London, 1981); Brian Lavery, *Nelson's Navy* (London, 1989); Nicholas Blake and Richard Lawrence, *The Illustrated guide to Nelson's Navy* (London, 1999).

17 Samuel Leech, p. 47.

18 Ibid, p. 25.

19 Ibid, p. 29.

20 Ibid, p. 42.

Chapter 15

1 Quoted by Richard Woodman in *The Victory of Seapower* (London, 1998), p. 17.

2 O'Meara, *Napoleon in Exile* (London, 1822), vol. I, p. 349.

3 PRO: ADM.51/1925, part 5.

4 Quoted by Fraser in *Bellerophon, the Bravest of the Brave* (London 1909), p. 262.

5 PRO: ADM.51/2024, part 1.

6 PRO: ADM.51/2024, part 2.

7 Messrs Joseph and Thomas Brindley of Strood took over the shipyard at Frindsbury around 1800. Between that date and 1814 they built three 74-gun ships, two frigates, and several armed sloops and brigs. The *Shannon* was based on the lines of the French ship *Hebe* which had been taken in 1782.

8 In June 1807 off Chesapeake Bay the British ship *Leopard* came alongside the USS. *Chesapeake* and demanded the right to search her crew for British deserters. When the American captain refused, the *Leopard* fired three broadsides, boarded the *Chesapeake* and impressed four men from her crew.

Chapter 16

1 The details in this and the following chapter on Napoleon's surrender are taken from: Sir Frederick Lewis Maitland, *The Surrender of Napoleon, being the Narrative of the surrender of Buonaparte, and of his residence on board HMS. Bellerophon* (first published London, 1826; edition cited London, 1904); Michael J. Thornton, *Napoleon after Waterloo: England and the St Helena decision* (Stanford, California, 1968); Gilbert Martineau, *Napoleon Surrenders* (English language edition, London, 1971); Clement Shorter, *Napoleon and his fellow travellers* (London, 1908), includes journal of Lieutenant Bowerbank; Louis-Joseph Marchand, *In Napoleon's Shadow* (English language edition of the memoirs of Napoleon's valet, edited by Proctor Jones, San Francisco, California, 1998); George Home, *Memoirs of an Aristocrat and Reminiscences of the Emperor Napoleon by a midshipman of the Bellerophon* (London, 1838); J.M. Thompson, *Napoleon Bonaparte* (London, 1988; revised edition, 2001); *The Times*. Details of the Bellerophon's movements, the weather, etc, are taken from the captain's log-book, ADM.51/2024 (part 8).

2 Quoted by Gilbert Martineau, *Napoleon Surrenders*, p. 73.

3 Maitland, p. 5.

4 Quoted by Maitland, p. 14.

5 From Montholon, *Récits de la Captivité*, quoted by Martineau, p. 85.

6 Ibid, p. 81.

7 The action of Basque and Aix Roads took place between 11 and 16 April 1809. Maitland was then in command of the frigate *Emerald*, 36 guns.

8 Letter from Admiral Denis Decrès, Minister for the Marine, quoted by Martineau, p. 89.

9 Frederick Lewis Maitland was born at Rankeillor near Perth on 7 September 1777. His grandfather was the Earl of Lauderdale, his father was Captain the Hon. Frederick Maitland, RN, and his mother was Margaret Deck, heiress of the Makgills, an old Scottish family. Maitland was the third son and followed his father into the navy. Following the surrender of Napoleon in 1815 he was made a Companion of the Bath. He was knighted in 1831 and by the time of his death on 30 November 1839 he had attained the rank of Rear-Admiral. There is a detailed account of his naval career in Marshall's *Royal Naval Biography*, II (I), p. 381.

10 Maitland was in command of the *Loire*, 40 guns, at Muros and captured the 490-ton *Confiance* and the brig *Bélier*.

11 Captain Maitland took command of the *Bellerophon* at the Nore on 9 April 1815. See captain's log, ADM.51/2024 (part 8).

12 George Home, p. 209.

13 Quoted by Thornton, p. 17.

14 Martineau, p. 105.

15 Maitland, p. 30.

16 Martineau, p. 109.

17 Joseph Bonaparte chartered the American brig *Commerce* under the name of Bouchard and landed in New York on 28 August 1815.

18 Thornton, p. 28.

19 Maitland, p. 42.

20 Ibid, p. 42.

21 Quoted by Martineau, p. 17.

22 Maitland, p. 50. The ante-room to the great cabin became a dining room as well as a waiting room for those attending on Napoleon. On each side of the ante-room were two small cabins, one to serve as Napoleon's dressing room, and the other for the use of his valet. Maitland moved his cot to the officers' quarters alongside the ward room on the deck below.

23 George Home, p. 215.

24 Ibid, p. 218.

25 Maitland, pp. 69–72.

26 Countess Bertrand, Savary and several other members of Napoleon's suite had spent time in England and spoke fluent English.

27 Captured French ships were frequently taken onto the strength of the British

Navy, and usually retained their French names. There were three French ships in the British fleet at Trafalgar: the *Belleisle*, 74; the *Spartiate*, 74; and the *Tonnant*, 80. The *Temeraire*, although named after a French prize, was built at Chatham dockyard.

28 Maitland, pp. 75–77.

29 Ibid, p. 95.

Chapter 17

1 George Home, *Memoirs of an Aristocrat and Reminiscences of the Emperor Napoleon by a midshipman of the Bellerophon* (London, 1838), p. 238.

2 Letter from Ephraim Graebke, assistant-surgeon, to his mother, 30 July 1815. Reproduced as an additional appendix in Maitland's *The Surrender of Napoleon*, p. 244.

3 Letter from Lieutenant Smith to his brother Richard, date 19 July 1815, and quoted by Henry Smetham in *Charles Roach Smith and his friends* (London, 1929), p. 136.

4 Clement Shorter, *Napoleon and his fellow travellers* (London, 1908), p. 305.

5 Smetham, p. 135.

6 George Home, *Memoirs of an Aristocrat*, quoted in Gilbert Martineau, *Napoleon Surrenders* (London, 1971) p. 139.

7 Letter from Admiral Keith to Captain Maitland, 23 July 1815 Gilbert Martineau, *Napoleon Surrenders* (London, 1971). quoted in Maitland, p. 109.

8 Shorter, p. 295.

9 Ibid, p. 312.

10 Orders from Admiral Keith, 26 July 1815. See Michael J. Thornton, *Napoleon after Waterloo: England and the St Helena decision* (Stanford, California, 1968), p. 89.

11 Quoted by Andrew Roberts, *Napoleon and Wellington*, (London, 2001), p. 196.

12 Thornton, p. 59.

13 Ibid, p. 62.

14 Keith's nephew James Elphinston was a captain in the 7th Hussars. He was taken prisoner by the French during the fighting at Belle Alliance on 7 June 1815.

15 Thornton, pp. 125–126.

16 Ibid, p. 127.

17 Following the departure of the *Northumberland*, Savary and Lallemand were sent on board the *Eurotas* which took them to Malta, a British possession, where they were detained until their release in 1816. The letter from Maitland, dated 31 July 1815, is reproduced by Thornton, p. 136.

18 Thornton, p. 131.

19 For those readers interested in these things they were drinking a punch known as bishop, described by Maitland as 'a mixture consisting of Port, Madeira, nutmeg, and other ingredients, well known to sailors and much relished by our foreign guests.' It would also have included red wine and water.

20 Thornton, p. 144.

21 The *Northumberland* was built by Barnards of Deptford and launched in 1798. Her lines were taken from the French ship *Impétueux*, 74 guns.

22 Thornton, pp. 157, 175. The man in the boat did not have a writ for Habeas Corpus. His name was Anthony Mackenrot and he wanted Napoleon to act as a witness on his behalf in a libel case.

23 Las Cases, *Mémorial de Sainte-Helene*, quoted by Martineau, p. 173.

24 Maitland, p. 185.

25 Ibid, p. 193.

26 Ibid, pp. 194–5. Barry O'Meara remained on the island of St Helena until July 1818 and later wrote a book about his experiences.

27 Thornton, p. 214.

28 Maitland, p. 220.

29 Ibid, p. 208.

30 Home, p. 260.

Chapter 18

1 According to Jerome Meckier in 'Dating the action in *Great Expectations*', *Dickens Studies Annual* 21 (1992), pp. 157–194, the action in the early chapters takes place in December 1812. Dickens and his family lived at Chatham between 1817 and 1822 when he was aged between five and ten. In 1857, when he had achieved success as a writer, Dickens took a house at Gad's Hill, some 5 miles from the Cooling Marshes.

2 *The Times*, 1807, quoted by W. Branch Johnson in *The English Prison Hulks* (London and Chichester, 1957) p. 61.

3 Report of the Lent Assizes at Maidstone in *The Kentish Gazette*, 16 to 20 March 1782.

4 Instructions to John Henry Capper from Lord Sidmouth, 23 August 1815. PRO: House of Commons Parliamentary Papers, 1816, vol. XVIII, pp. 288–385.

5 John Capper's Report of 16 October 1815.

6 Henry Mayhew, and John Binny, *The Criminal Prisons of London and Scenes of Prison Life* (London 1862), p. 208.

7 Ibid, p. 218.

8 John Capper's Report of 24 August 1818 includes 'An Account shewing the Expense of the Hulk Establishment, from the 1st of January to 1st July 1818'. This notes that the expense of the Navy Account for fitting *Bellerophon* as a Convict Hulk in the year 1816 was £12,081.14s.10d.

9 The cost of building the Pentonville Penitentiary in 1842 was £85,000, see Charles Campbell, *The Intolerable Hulks* (Maryland, USA, 1994), p. 122. The cost of building the hull of the *Bellerophon* was £30,232.14s.3d. The masts, yards, rigging and stores cost an additional £8,376.15s.2d. (PRO: Progress Books for H.M.Ships, ADM.180/6.)

10 Instructions to John Capper, issued by the Home Secretary on 23 August 1815, stated that 'No convict is to be allowed to go about the hulk without an iron upon one or both of his legs.'

11 Mayhew and Binny, p. 216.

12 Report of the Chaplain of the *Bellerophon* Hulk at Sheerness to J.H. Capper, 1 January 1817; PRO: House of Commons Parliamentary Papers, 1817, vol. XVI, p. 141 (accompanies Capper's Report of 16 January 1817 which has a table of expenses and notes that the average number of convicts on board the *Bellerophon* from 1 January to 1 July 1817 was 435.)

13 Mayhew and Binny, p. 219.

14 Report of the Chaplain, 1 January 1817. PRO: House of Commons Parliamentary Papers, 1817, vol. XVI, p. 141.

15 'Report of the Directors of the Convict Prisons on the Discipline and Management of the Hulk Establishment,' 1854, quoted by Mayhew and Binny, pp. 200–203.

16 Ibid, p. 199.

17 John Capper's report of 27 January 1827. PRO: Parliamentary Papers, 1827, vol. XIX, p. 137.

18 See the relevant entries in Progress Books for H.M.Ships. PRO: ADM. 180/10, folio 67.

19 *Plymouth Herald*, Saturday 10 June 1826. I am most grateful to Ian Criddle of the Local Studies and Naval History Library at Plymouth for bringing this to my attention.

20 Report of the chaplain of the *Captivity* in Capper's report of 27 January 1827. Parliamentary Papers, 1827, vol. XIX, p. 137.

21 The last appearance of the *Bellerophon* in Capper's reports to the Home Office occurs in his report of 10 July 1834 when she is listed (under the name of *Captivity*) as having 218 convicts on board. Parliamentary Papers, 1835, vol. XLV.

22 Progress Books for H.M.Ships. PRO: ADM. 180/10, folio 67.

23 In his *Memorials to serve for a history of the Parish of St Mary, Rotherhithe* (Cambridge, 1907), p. 170, Edward Beck includes the following under his entry for John Beatson: 'He broke up most of the old East India Company's ships, among others the *Sesostris* and the *Thames*. Of Government vessels the best known were the *Temeraire*, the *Bellerophon* and the *Justitia* . . .' This is confirmed by Stuart Rankin in *Shipbuilding in Rotherhithe*, part 1 (Rotherhithe Local History Paper no.4a, London, 2000), p. 7. The daybook and ledger of Beatsons for 1835–1858 are held by the Southwark Local History Library but unfortunately there is no mention of the *Bellerophon* or the *Captivity* in either volume.

24 Judy Egerton, *Turner, The Fighting Temeraire*, catalogue of the exhibition held at the National Gallery (London, 1995), p. 88.

Epilogue

1 J.M. Thompson, *Napoleon Bonaparte* (London, 1952) p. 389.

2 Jean-Paul Kauffmann, *The Dark Room at Longwood* (1997; edition cited, 1999), p. 21.

3 Ibid, p. xviii.

4 Thompson, p. 400.

5 Vincent Cronin, *Napoleon* (London, 1971), p. 433.

6 From an article on 'The Captain of the Bellerophon' in the Clan Maitland Society Journal, no. 7, July 1964. I am grateful to Alan Maitland for supplying me with a copy of this article which contains personal information not found in the detailed entry on Maitland's naval service in Marshall's *Royal Naval Biography*, II (I), pp. 381–401.

7 For a full account of the life of Captain William Pryce Cumby, see Hilary W. Jackson, *A County Durham man at Trafalgar: Cumby of the Bellerophon* (Durham County Local History Society, 1997).

INDEX

Page numbers in *italic* refer to text illustrations

A NOTE ON THE AUTHOR

David Cordingly was Keeper of Pictures and Head of Exhibitions at the National Maritime Museum for twelve years, where he organised such exhibitions as 'Captain James Cook, Navigator', 'The Mutiny on the Bounty', and 'Pirates: Fact and Fiction'. His other books include *Life Among the Pirates* (*Under the Black Flag* in the US) and *Heroines and Harlots* (*Women Pirates and Pirates' Women* in the US).

A NOTE ON THE TYPE

The text of this book is set in Bell. Originally cut for John Bell in 1788, this type was used in Bell's newspaper, *The Oracle*. It was regarded as the first English Modern typeface. This version was designed by Monotype in 1931.